ENTREPRENEURSHIP, GROWTH, AND PUBLIC POLICY

While the public policy community has turned to entrepreneurship to maintain, restore, or generate economic prosperity, the economics profession has been remarkably taciturn in providing guidance for public policy for understanding the links between entrepreneurship and economic growth as well as for framing and weighing policy issues and decisions. The purpose of this volume is to provide a lens through which public policy decisions involving entrepreneurship can be guided and analyzed. In particular, this volume provides insights from leading research concerning the links between entrepreneurship, innovation, and economic growth that shed light on implications for public policy. The book makes clear both how and why small firms and entrepreneurship have emerged as crucial to economic growth, employment, and competitiveness as well as the mandate for public policy in the entrepreneurial society.

Zoltan J. Acs is University Professor at the School of Public Policy and Director of the Center for Entrepreneurship and Public Policy, George Mason University, Virginia. He is also a Research Scholar at the Max Planck Institute for Economics in Jena, Germany, and Scholar-in-Residence at the Ewing Marion Kauffman Foundation, Kansas City, Missouri. In addition, he is a member of the Industry Studies Committee of the Alfred P. Sloan Foundation, Research Professor at Durham University, and a Visiting Professor at the University of Pécs in Hungary, where he received an honorary doctorate. Previously, he held the position of Doris and Robert McCurdy Distinguished Professor of Entrepreneurship and Innovation in the Robert G. Merrick School of Business, University of Baltimore. He is co-founder and co-editor of *Small Business Economics: An Entrepreneurship Journal*. Dr. Acs is a leading advocate of the importance of entrepreneurship for economic development. He received the 2001 International Award for Entrepreneurship and Small Business Research on behalf of the Swedish National Board for Industrial and Technical Development. He has published more than 100 articles and 25 books.

David B. Audretsch is the Director of the Max Planck Institute of Economics in Jena, Germany. He also serves as a Scholar-in-Residence at the Ewing Marion Kauffman Foundation. In addition, he is an Honorary Professor at the Friedrich Schiller University of Jena, Research Professor at Durham University, a Distinguished Professor and the Ameritech Chair of Economic Development and Director of the Institute for Development Strategies at Indiana University, an External Director of Research at the Kiel Institute for the World Economy, and a Research Fellow of the Centre for Economic Policy Research (London). Dr. Audretsch's research focuses on the links among entrepreneurship, government policy, innovation, economic development, and global competitiveness. Dr. Audretsch is ranked as the twenty-first most-cited scholar in economics and business, 1996–2006. He is co-founder and co-editor of *Small Business Economics: An Entrepreneurship Journal*. He was awarded the 2001 International Award for Entrepreneurship and Small Business Research by the Swedish Foundation for Small Business Research.

Robert J. Strom is Director of Research and Policy at the Ewing Marion Kauffman Foundation in Kansas City. His responsibilities include support for academic and policy-oriented research in the field of entrepreneurship. Prior to joining the Foundation in June 1994, Dr. Strom was a visiting professor at the Bloch School of Business at the University of Missouri–Kansas City and vice president of the National Council on Economic Education. Dr. Strom was assistant vice president for public affairs at the Federal Reserve Bank of Kansas City from 1986 to 1991. He was president of the Missouri Council on Economic Education and a Professor of Economics at the University of Missouri–Columbia from 1976 to 1986. Dr. Strom has also been a member of the economics department at Miami University in Oxford, Ohio.

Entrepreneurship, Growth, and Public Policy

Edited by

Zoltan J. Acs

George Mason University

David B. Audretsch

Max Planck Institute of Economics

Robert J. Strom

Ewing Marion Kauffman Foundation

CAMBRIDGE
UNIVERSITY PRESS

CAMBRIDGE UNIVERSITY PRESS
Cambridge, New York, Melbourne, Madrid, Cape Town, Singapore, São Paulo, Delhi

Cambridge University Press
32 Avenue of the Americas, New York, NY 10013-2473, USA

www.cambridge.org
Information on this title: www.cambridge.org/9780521894920

First published 2009

Printed in the United States of America

A catalog record for this publication is available from the British Library.

Library of Congress Cataloging in Publication Data

Kauffman–Max Planck Summit on Entrepreneurship Research and Policy (1st : 2006 : Munich,
Germany)
Entrepreneurship, growth, and public policy / edited by Zoltan Acs, David Audretsch, Robert Strom.
p. cm.
This volume contains selected papers presented at the Kauffman–Max Planck First Annual
Summit on Entrepreneurship Research and Policy, held in Munich in May 2006.
Includes bibliographical references and index.
ISBN 978-0-521-89492-0 (hardback)
1. Entrepreneurship – Congresses. 2. Economic development – Congresses. 3. Industrial policy –
Congresses. 4. Technological innovations – Economic aspects – Congresses. I. Ács, Zoltán J.
II. Audretsch, David B. III. Strom, Robert, 1946– IV. Title.
HB615.K38 2006
338′.04–dc22   2008045474

ISBN 978-0-521-89492-0 hardback

Contents

Contributors

Zoltan J. Acs University Professor, School of Public Policy, George Mason University; Max Planck Institute of Economics, Jena; and The Kauffman Foundation

Taylor Aldridge Chief of Staff and Research Fellow, Entrepreneurship, Growth and Public Policy Group, Max Planck Institute of Economics; and doctoral student, University of Augsburg

David B. Audretsch Director, Entrepreneurship, Growth and Public Policy Group Max Planck Institute of Economics; Distinguished Professor, Director of Institute of Development Strategies, Ameritech Chair of Economic Development, Indiana University; and Ewing Marion Kauffman Foundation Scholar-in-Residence

William J. Baumol Harold Price Professor of Entrepreneurship and Academic Director, Berkley Center for Entrepreneurial Studies, Stern School of Business, New York University; and Senior Economist and Joseph Douglas Green, 1895, Professor Emeritus, Princeton University

Heike Grimm Director, Erfurt School of Public Policy, and Associate Professor for Public Policy, University of Erfurt, Germany

John Haltiwanger University of Maryland, NBER, IZA, and Bureau of the Census, Research Associate of the Center for Economic Studies; and Senior Research Fellow with the LEHD program at Census

Max Keilbach Max Planck Institute of Economics, Jena

Steven Klepper Carnegie Mellon University, Pittsburgh, Pennsylvania

Robert Litan Vice President, Research and Policy, Ewing Marion Kauffman Foundation; and Senior Fellow, The Brookings Institution

David C. Mowery William A. & Betty H. Hasler Professor of New Enterprise Development, Haas School of Business, University of California, Berkeley

Alexander Oettl Research Fellow of the Entrepreneurship, Growth and Public Policy Division, Max Planck Institute of Economics; and doctoral student, Rotman School of Management at the University of Toronto

Edmund S. Phelps Department of Economics, Columbia University, New York

Nathan Rosenberg Professor of Economics (Emeritus), Stanford University

Paul A. Samuelson Professor of Economics, Massachusetts Institute of Technology, Cambridge, Massachusetts

Carl Schramm President and Chief Executive Officer, Ewing Marion Kauffman Foundation; and Batten Fellow, Darden School of Business, University of Virginia

Robert J. Strom Director, Ewing Marion Kauffman Foundation

Roy Thurik Centre for Advanced Small Business Economics (CASBEC) at Erasmus University Rotterdam; EIM Business and Policy Research (a Panteia company), Zoetermeer; Max Planck Institute of Economics, Jena; and Free University Amsterdam

Mirjam van Praag University of Amsterdam; Amsterdam Center for Entrepreneurship; Max Planck Institute of Economics, Jena; Tinbergen Institute; IZA Institute for the Study of Labour

Acknowledgments

This volume contains edited versions of selected papers presented at the Kauffman–Max Planck First Annual Summit on Entrepreneurship Research and Policy, which was held at Schloß Ringberg in Tegern See in the Alps outside Munich in May 2006. The editors would like to express their appreciation and gratitude to a number of people who contributed to this volume. Both the Max Planck Society, under the leadership of President Peter Gruß, and the Ewing Marion Kauffman Foundation, under the CEO and President Carl Schramm, provided generous financial support. Bob Litan of the Kauffman Foundation provided great organizational leadership in the early stages of planning the Summit as well as guiding us in publishing this volume. Madeleine Schmidt and Kerstin Schuck of the Max Planck Institute of Economics provided expert assistance with both the Summit and the editing and organization of this volume. Betty Fiscus of the Institute of Development Strategies at Indiana University provided excellent support in preparing the various drafts of the manuscript. Adam Lederer contributed his usual editorial excellence in helping the editors move from the first draft of the manuscript to its final published version. Finally, we would like to thank Scott Parris of Cambridge University Press for his support and encouragement, as well as his advice, in helping us move this project from an idea to this book.

ENTREPRENEURSHIP, GROWTH, AND PUBLIC POLICY

Introduction

Why Entrepreneurship Matters

Zoltan J. Acs, David B. Audretsch, and Robert Strom

1.1. Introduction

When the three editors of this volume studied and prepared for their doctoral degrees in three different American Ph.D. programs during the late 1970s, not one of them heard a word about entrepreneurship and small business. All three of them had a specialization in the field of industrial organization within economics, the field most closely related to issues concerning firm size and organization. In all three Ph.D. programs, as was no doubt true across the entire landscape of American graduate schools, the focus was exclusively on large corporations and their impact on the economy. The large corporation was widely accepted as the source of jobs – good-paying ones – and security. No wonder that when the Chairman of General Motors, Charlie "Engine" Wilson, exclaimed, "What's good for General Motors is good for America,"[1] the country believed. There certainly was no room for the study and analysis of something as peripheral and tangential as small business and entrepreneurship in the nation's top graduate programs in economics. Nor was there any room or interest within the entire economics profession. The 1990 edition of *Palgrave's Encyclopedia of Economics*, consisting of over a dozen volumes and spanning thousands of pages covering virtually every topic imaginable on economics, barely touched on the issues of small business and entrepreneurship, a gap unfilled until 2008 The most influential economics book in the modern history of the profession, *Principles of Economics*, by

---

[1] David Halberstam, in *The Fifties* (New York: Villard Books, 1993), p. 118, corrects this conventional wisdom. What Wilson actually said was, "We at General Motors have always felt that was good for the country was good for General Motors as well."

Paul Samuelson, barely contains reference to small business and entrepreneurship. Until 2007, the classifications of topics and fields in economics organized by the *Journal of Economic Literature*, the guiding light of the profession, contained only a scant mention of entrepreneurship, included in a sub-category of a sub-category under "business studies."

Given this apparent conviction by the economics profession of the irrelevance of small business and entrepreneurship for economics issues, it must have been startling when the public policy community started looking to entrepreneurship as an engine of economic growth, employment, and a high standard of living. For example, the European Council of Lisbon, along with then President of the European Union, Romano Prodi (2002, p. 1), in an effort to revive economic growth and employment prospects committed Europe to becoming not just the world's knowledge leader but also the leader in entrepreneurship: "Our lacunae in the field of entrepreneurship needs to be taken seriously because there is mounting evidence that the key to economic growth and productivity improvements lies in the entrepreneurial capacity of an economy."

It is not just the European Union that has turned to entrepreneurship to generate growth, employment, and competitiveness in a global economy. The National Governors Association in the United States named innovation and entrepreneurship as the overriding theme for state strategy in 2007. Communities, cities, regions, and nations throughout the world have been turning to entrepreneurship as an engine of growth, jobs, and competitiveness.

While the public policy community has turned to entrepreneurship to maintain, restore, or generate economic prosperity, the economics profession has been remarkably taciturn in providing guidance for public policy to understand the links between entrepreneurship and economic growth as well as an analytical lens through which policy issues and decisions can be framed and weighed. Both the Ewing Marion Kauffman Foundation in the United States and the Max Planck Institute of Economics in Germany are committed to providing such an economic framework and lens through which public policy decisions involving entrepreneurship can be guided and analyzed. Thus, the Kauffman-Max Planck Annual Summit on Entrepreneurship Research and Policy was created through a joint venture by both institutions to foster the economic analysis of entrepreneurship with a particular emphasis on generating a framework to guide the public policy community. The first Summit was held in May 2006 at the Schloß Ringberg in Tegern See, in the Alps outside Munich, assembling the leading scholars in the world on entrepreneurship. The purpose of this volume is to provide insights from leading research concerning the links among entrepreneurship, innovation, and economic growth and to shed light on implications for public policy.

In the following section, the shift from physical capital to knowledge is explained. How and why large firms discouraged innovation and growth based on that knowledge is explained in the third section. The mandate for public policy in the entrepreneurial economy is the focus of the fourth section. A summary of definitions is presented in the fifth section. Finally, how the individual contributions contained in this volume fit together in a coherent manner to help us begin to make sense of the links among entrepreneurship, growth, and public policy is presented in the concluding section.

1.2. Was Entrepreneurship Really so Unimportant?

There is a reason why entrepreneurship and small business were absent from the literature and focus not just in economics, but throughout the social sciences during the postwar era. Robert Solow was awarded the Nobel Prize for identifying what mattered for economic growth in his famous 1956 and 1957 papers. What Solow found, or at least formalized, is that essentially two factors, physical capital and labor, were the driving forces of economic growth. It should be emphasized that in the formal growth accounting of the Solow model, the unexplained residual was attributed to technical change, which was interpreted as falling like manna from heaven. According to Nelson (1981, p. 1030), "Robert Solow's 1956 theoretical article was largely addressed to the pessimism about full employment growth built into the Harrod-Domar model.... In that model he admitted the possibility of technological advance."

Solow's articulation and formalization of physical capital as the key factor shaping economic performance corresponded to, if not triggered, a central focus in both the scholarly and policy communities on physical capital. The famous "Cambridge Capital Controversy" involved a bitter dispute between scholars located at universities in the two Cambridges separated by a common ocean. Whether and how physical capital could be measured and then subsequently linked to economic growth within the framework of the Solow growth accounting model was sharply contested by scholars such as Joan Robinson and other colleagues at Cambridge University in the United Kingdom.

The emphasis on physical capital as the crucial factor driving economic welfare had a corresponding influence on scholarly thinking about how resources should best be organized and deployed at the levels of both the firm and industry. Leading scholars of firm organization and strategy, such as Alfred Chandler (1977, 1990), meticulously showed how firm efficiency and strategy revolved around size, in terms of both scale as well as scope. Similarly, scholars such as F. M. Scherer (1970) painstakingly documented a growing body of empirical evidence suggesting that the most efficient organization of an industry typically involved a high degree of concentration of resources within just a handful of large corporations.

The primacy of capital as the driving force of efficiency and competitiveness subsequent to the Second World War focused the entire field of industrial organization on analyzing and understanding the efficiencies and implications associated with firm size and industry concentration. The field galvanized around the task of identifying the perceived trade-off between economic efficiency resulting from size and concentration, on the one hand and political and economic decentralization, on the other, which could be used to frame policy-making decisions. Scherer (1970) amassed a vast literature addressing three main issues: (1) What are the efficiencies rendered from large-scale production? (2) Does the concentration of economic assets and decision making have consequences for economic welfare? and (3) What are the trade-offs confronting public policy?

Thus, compelling theoretical models and empirical evidence supported the conclusion of Joseph A. Schumpeter's (1942, p. 106) conclusion, "What we have got to accept is that the large-scale establishment or unit of control has come to be the most powerful engine of progress and in particular of the long-run expansion of output." John Kenneth Galbraith (1956, p. 86) echoed Schumpeter's conclusion: "There is no more pleasant fiction than that technological change is the product of the matchless ingenuity of the small man forced by competition to employ his wits to better his neighbor."

The ensuing policy debate revolved around how best to live with the perceived trade-off between size and efficiency versus decentralization and, presumably, greater democratic participation. The policy response throughout Organisation for Economic Co-operation and Development (OECD) countries was generally to constrain the freedom of firms to contract, using the three main policy instruments of regulation, public ownership, and antitrust, or what the rest of the world outside the United States refers to as competition policy. Sweden and France had a greater emphasis on state ownership of firms, the United Kingdom and Germany on regulation, and the United States was the most interventionist in terms of antitrust policy. While at the time a heated debate emerged concerning which approach was superior, in retrospect the debate actually involved which instrument was the most effective approach to solving the policy trade-off inherent in a capital-based economy. As Audretsch and Thurik (2001) and Audretsch (2007b) concluded, each country found its own unique approach to living with this inherent policy trade-off in the managed economy.

There seemed to be little role for small business and entrepreneurship in the capital-driven managed economy of the postwar era. Organizing and deploying physical capital at a small scale seemingly contradicted the fundamental findings, insights, and policy prescriptions that emerged from the pervasive and compelling economics and management literature. The marginalization, if not outright abandonment, of small business and entrepreneurship implicit in the analyses and subsequent conclusions of the scholarly literature was reflected in the public policy community. Even advocates of small business conceded that small firms were no match for the breathtaking efficiencies generated by large-scale manufacturing pouring out of the large corporation. What such advocates of small business were willing to sacrifice, however, was a modicum of efficiency, in order to attain other non-economic goals, such as social and political contributions made by small business. Thus, public policy toward small business was essentially "preservationist," with the goal of preserving a type of business and industry organization that might otherwise have become extinct due to its inherent inefficiency. For example, with passage of the Small Business Act of July 10, 1953, the U.S. Congress created the Small Business Administration, with an explicit mandate to "aid, counsel, assist and protect ... the interests of small business concerns."[2]

By the mid-1970s, in the United States the comparative advantage in physical capital–based manufacturing began to erode. Imported autos and steel poured into the United States from more efficient competitors in Germany and Japan. Previously, "the U.S. was virtually unchallenged as industrial leader. Americans could make anything, and because their products were the best, they could sell whatever they made, both at home and abroad. But somewhere around 1973," *Business Week* lamented, "the gravy train was derailed – and it has never really gotten back on track. U.S. producers met fierce competition from foreign industries that churned out high-quality goods made by low-wage workers."[3]

Nevertheless, as the capital-intensive industrial heartland of the American Midwest – which became known as the rustbelt – suffered waves of job layoffs and plant closings due to international competition, some firms, industries and regions were thriving in the new global environment.

---

[2] http://www.sba.gov/aboutsba/sbahistory.html
[3] "Can America Compete?" *Business Week*, April 27, 1987, pp. 45–69.

Scholars were quick to point to the common denominator for success: a shift away from the factor of physical capital toward knowledge capital, which generally consisted of science, technology, creativity, and ideas.

Knowledge and the shift from physical capital was formally introduced into macroeconomic growth models by Romer (1986) and Lucas (1993). Not only was knowledge explicitly recognized as a key factor of production, but it also had a particularly potent impact on economic growth as a result of its propensity to spill over for commercialization by third-party firms.

While the fundamental factors driving economic growth, employment, and competitiveness shifted dramatically from physical capital to knowledge capital, the role that small business and entrepreneurship could play seemingly remained the same: marginal at best. As scholars turned their analyses to the study of innovation and technological change, from both the management and economics perspectives, the large corporation seemed to have a competitive advantage over its smaller counterparts.

For example, Zvi Griliches (1979) formalized the thinking about innovation prevalent in the economics literature by introducing the model of the knowledge production function. According to this view, the firm is exogenous, and by investing in the creation of knowledge capabilities, innovative output is endogenous. The framework of focusing on innovation as a decision by exogenous firms to endogenously generate innovative output corresponded to a growing literature in management strategy, with its roots dating back to Edith Penrose (1958) and its more modern rendition of the resource-based theory of the firm (Barney and Clark, 2007). The emphasis not only on a firm's investments in research and development (R&D) as a strategy for generating knowledge but also its capacity to absorb external knowledge (Cohen and Levinthal, 1989, 1990) seemingly corresponded to a mounting body of empirical evidence pointing to scale economies in R&D rendering the competitive advantage in knowledge investments, again, to the large corporations. While the policy instruments prescribed in the new endogenous growth theories, such as university research, patents, human capital, R&D, and creativity, were strikingly different from those of the capital-based managed economy, small business and entrepreneurship remained an afterthought.

1.3. Entrepreneurship as a Conduit of Knowledge Spillovers

Nevertheless, the public policy and scholarly communities have discovered that, despite the enormous contribution by the endogenous growth theory in highlighting the central role of investments in new knowledge, there remains a missing link to economic growth, employment creation, and international competitiveness. For example, as measured by the most common benchmarks of knowledge investments, such as R&D, university research, patents, human capital, education, creativity and culture, Sweden has ranked consistently among the world's leaders. However, following more than a decade of stagnant growth and rising unemployment, concerned policymakers in Sweden started to worry about what they termed "the Swedish Paradox." Romano Prodi, then President of the European Union, along with the Commission of the European Union were so impressed by this articulation of persistent stagnant economic growth despite high levels of knowledge investments that they adapted it for the European context, by highlighting "the European Paradox."

In fact, had the Europeans looked across to the other side of the Atlantic, they would have discovered the Americans also suffering from an inability to harvest innovation and economic growth from costly knowledge investments. As Senator Birch Bayh pointed out in 1978, "A wealth of scientific talent at American colleges and universities – talent responsible for the development of numerous innovative scientific breakthroughs each year – is going to waste as a result of bureaucratic red tape and illogical government regulations."[4]

Acs et al. (2004) and Audretsch et al. (2006) identified what they termed as the *knowledge filter* as impeding the spillover of knowledge for commercialization, innovation, and ultimately economic growth. The knowledge filter is an artifact of the conditions characterizing knowledge and differentiating it from the more traditional factors of production, such as physical capital and labor. The value of any new idea is inherently uncertain and asymmetric. Different people with different backgrounds will not only assign a different expected value to any given new idea, but the costs of transacting the perspectives emanating across different experiences and sets of backgrounds are typically prohibitively high to make anything approaching a consensus about the value of a new idea almost impossible. Thus, a large and compelling literature has documented decision after decision reached at large corporations not to pursue new ideas that ultimately led to valuable innovations and in some cases triggered entire new industries. Examples include the copy machine, the fax machine, the personal computer, and the flat screen.

---

[4] Introductory statement of Birch Bayh, September 13, 1978, cited from the Association of University Technology Managers Report (AUTM) (2004, p. 5).

All of these ideas were caught in the knowledge filter of an incumbent large corporation (Audretsch, 2007a).

As Audretsch (1995), Acs et al. (2004, 2006), Acs and Armington (2006), and Audretsch et al. (2006) suggest, entrepreneurship provides a unique and valuable contribution to economic growth by serving as a conduit for the spillover and commercialization of knowledge and ideas that might otherwise have been abandoned or remained dormant in the corporations and organizations creating those ideas in the first place. Many of the most visible and successful companies of today were created by people who tenaciously stuck with ideas rejected by the decision-making bureaucracy of large corporations and choose to pursue and commercialize those ideas by becoming entrepreneurs. Examples include Apple Computer, SAP, Xerox, Microsoft (IBM turned down Bill Gates's offer to buy the company), and Intel. Other companies, such as Google and Genetech, are the result of entrepreneurs taking ideas and knowledge developed at universities and facilitating their spillover and commercialization by starting a new firm. According to the knowledge spillover theory of entrepreneurship (Acs et al., 2004, 2007; Audretsch et al., 2006), as the knowledge context increases, entrepreneurship becomes more important because it provides a missing link for economic growth by commercializing investments in knowledge and ideas that might otherwise have remained uncommercialized.

1.4. Public Policy for the Entrepreneurial Economy

The entrepreneurial economy refers to an economy where entrepreneurship capital, as well as physical capital, human capital, and knowledge capital, is an important source of economic growth. In neither the Solow (1956) model nor the endogenous growth models of Romer (1986) and Lucas (1993) did entrepreneurship capital seem to matter at all or make any contribution to economic growth. However, by including a measure of entrepreneurship capital within the context of an endogenous growth model, Audretsch et al. (2006) find compelling evidence that in Germany, those regions with a greater endowment of entrepreneurship capital exhibit a higher level of economic growth. Entrepreneurship capital reflects the capacity of a spatial unit of analysis, such as a community, city, region, state, or country, to generate entrepreneurial activity in the form of new-firm start-ups. While they did not include an explicit measure of entrepreneurship capital that was linked to economic growth, empirical evidence linking entrepreneurship to economic growth for the United

States was provided by Acs and Armington (2006) and for OECD countries by Acs et al. (2004).

It is one thing to provide an econometric link between entrepreneurship capital and economic growth, but another to suggest how entrepreneurship capital can be increased. Still, a massive effort is being made at virtually every level of government and community to try to create and augment entrepreneurship capital in an effort to generate growth, employment, and competitiveness. The mandate for public policy in the entrepreneurial economy spans a broad spectrum of institutions, policy agencies, and instruments, ranging from education to immigration and health care. In addition, it also involves all levels of policy, from the most local to the broadest, such as the European Union. However, the goal is singular: how to increase entrepreneurship capital.

1.5. Distilling and Defining Terms

In this volume a number of common conceptual terms are used and repeated throughout. Although entrepreneurship is important for the economy, it is still a relatively new academic field, and, consequently, consistent and specific definitions for terms that have broad general meanings are still lacking. To help set the stage, the basic definitions are provided here.

Because entrepreneurs and their actions is the dominate theme of this volume, it is important to define entrepreneur. Joseph A. Schumpeter provides an excellent starting point, going back to 1911, when in his classic treatise, *Theorie der wirtschaftlichen Entwicklung*, he proposed a theory of creative destruction, where he was unambiguous about the organizational structure most conducive to entrepreneurs: new firms infused with entrepreneurial spirit would displace the tired old incumbents, ultimately leading to vigorous innovative activity, which in turn would generate a higher degree of economic growth. Thus what made entrepreneurs different from other agents in the economy was their willingness to pursue innovative activity, "The function of entrepreneurs is to reform or revolutionize the pattern of production by exploiting an invention, or more generally, an untried technological possibility for producing a new commodity or producing an old one in a new way.... To undertake such new things is difficult and constitutes a distinct economic function, first because they lie outside of the routine tasks which everybody understands, and secondly, because the environment resists in many ways" (Schumpeter, 1942, p. 13). As Scherer (1992, p. 1417) points out, "In his 1911 book,

Schumpeter insisted that innovations typically originated in new, characteristically small, firms commencing operation outside the 'circular flow' of existing production activities. To be sure, the small innovating firms that succeeded would grow large, and their leaders would amass great fortunes. They started, however, as outsiders." In this volume the perspective of the earlier Schumpeter is adapted to the entrepreneur as the person involved in starting a new firm. This corresponds with the definition by Gartner and Carter (2003): "Entrepreneurial behavior involves the activities of individuals who are associated with creating new organizations rather than the activities of individuals who are involved with maintaining or changing the operations of on-going established organizations."

Stepping back, entrepreneurship generally refers to the process by which new opportunities are discovered and implemented. Casson (2003) suggests that an entrepreneurial opportunity exists when "new goods, services, raw material and organizing methods can be introduced and sold at greater than their costs of production."[5]

Several concepts used throughout this book may sound similar but have slightly different and nuanced connotations. For example, human capital generally refers to the stock of productive skills and capabilities embodied in labor, while knowledge capital is a broader, more inclusive concept that includes dimensions such as creativity and ideas. Regions or entire economies possess not just stocks of physical capital and knowledge capital, but also entrepreneurship capital, which is defined as the capacity of a region or economy to generate entrepreneurship (Audretsch, 2007b).

The managed economy, a term introduced by Audretsch and Thurik (2001, p. 206), was the set of public policies and institutional approaches used after World War II. During this era, large corporations were the driving force of economic growth and employment creation. The result is that "What may have been perceived as a disparate set of policies at the time appears in retrospect to comprise a remarkably singular policy approach – a managed economy." Audretsch (2007a) suggests that, regarding the managed economy, "the right institutions and policies to create a workforce and external conditions that could make an economy centered around the large corporation work the best." By contrast, the entrepreneurial economy is defined as an economy where entrepreneurship is a driving force of economic growth and employment (Audretsch and Thurik, 2001; Audretsch et al., 2006; Acs and Stough, 2008). A more detailed exploration of the managed economy, the

---

[5] Cited from Shane and Venkataraman (2000, p. 220).

entrepreneurial economy, and the differences between the two is provided in Chapter 10.

1.6. Conclusions

The chapters that follow address the most fundamental and important links among entrepreneurship, innovation, and economic growth, and identify the most salient implications for public policy in the entrepreneurial economy. The first section of the volume focuses on the link between entrepreneurship and innovation, the second section on the link between entrepreneurship and economic growth, and the final section on the role of public policy in the entrepreneurial economy.

Part I of this book examines the link between entrepreneurship and innovation. In Chapter 2, William J. Baumol, Robert Litan, and Carl Schramm explain why the entrepreneurial economy, or what they term "entrepreneurial capitalism," is more conducive to economic growth than is the managed economy, which they characterize as big-firm capitalism.

In the third chapter, Edmund S. Phelps explains how innovative activity is shaped by the underlying institutions of society. He combines both a theoretical perspective from a long scholarly tradition with the contemporary context. Phelps highlights how European institutions have constituted a barrier to entrepreneurship. Paul Samuelson considers "Advance of Total Factor Productivity from Entrepreneurial Innovations" in Chapter 4. In particular, Samuelson shows how innovation contributes to total factor productivity and ultimately to the real standard of living.

In Chapter 5, Steven Klepper provides a compelling case study supporting the knowledge spillover theory of entrepreneurship. In particular, Klepper explains why entrepreneurship was needed for knowledge to spill over in the form of spinoffs from the investments made by highly successful firms in both the automobile industry and the semiconductor industry that ultimately generated the innovative clusters of Detroit decades ago and the more contemporary Silicon Valley. Klepper's meticulous research shows that innovation does not fall like manna from heaven, as the Solow model suggested, nor does it passively blow over from the neighbors, as the Romer model suggested. Rather, as the knowledge spillover theory of entrepreneurship posits, a conduit for facilitating the spillover of knowledge is required – the entrepreneur who takes knowledge that might otherwise have remained uncommercialized in the successful high-performing incumbent firm and uses those ideas to launch a new start-up.

Part II of the book is devoted to the link between entrepreneurship and economic growth.

Chapter 6, by John Haltiwanger, provides an empirical link between entrepreneurship and growth. In particular, Haltiwanger uses the Longitudinal Data Base of the U.S. Census Bureau to identify how entrepreneurship impacts employment growth. Most strikingly, Haltiwanger shows that it is young, entrepreneurial firms that are the engine of employment growth, at least in the context of the United States.

In Chapter 7, Nathan Rosenberg examines how the universities have played a crucial role in entrepreneurship. In Chapter 8, David B. Audretsch, Taylor Aldridge, and Alexander Oettl provide an analysis of university scientists who become entrepreneurs, thus serving as a conduit for knowledge spillovers and ultimately economic growth. The exact role of entrepreneurs as a conduit for knowledge spillover entrepreneurship and the theoretical and empirical links between entrepreneurship and economic growth is explained by Max Keilbach in Chapter 9.

Implications for public policy emerging from the shift from the managed economy to the entrepreneurial economy are provided in Part III. In Chapter 10, Roy Thurik introduces the model of the "Entrepreneurial Economy," which provides a basis for an "Entrepreneurship Policy Framework," which offers a lens through which public policy can be formulated and evaluated. David C. Mowery explains in Chapter 11 how federal legislation enacted by the U.S. Congress triggered a new role for universities in the economy. In Chapter 12 Mirjiam van Praag explains why public policy in the European context needs to place a special emphasis on entrepreneurial education in schools. In Chapter 13, Heike Grimm explains the European public policy approach to shifting from the managed economy to creating an entrepreneurial Europe. In Chapter 14, Zoltan Acs provides a path-breaking analysis of the role of philanthropy in reinvesting wealth accruing from one generation of entrepreneurs into knowledge to create opportunities to create new wealth for the next generation of entrepreneurs.

Taken together, these chapters provide an integrated view of the crucial links among entrepreneurship, innovation, and economic growth, and how public policy can best promote these linkages. While the field of entrepreneurship scholarship may only be in its incipiency, the research presented in this volume will go a long way in meeting the demand from the public policy community for an integrated framework for analyzing and understanding the entrepreneurial economy and for providing a lens through which to formulate public policy for the entrepreneurial economy.

References

Acs, Zoltan J., and Catherine Armington. 2006. *Entrepreneurship, Geography and American Economic Growth*. Cambridge: Cambridge University Press.

Acs, Zoltan J., and David B. Audretsch. 1990. *Innovation and Small Firms*. Cambridge: MIT Press.

Acs, Zoltan J., and David B. Audretsch. 1988. "Innovation in Large and Small Firms: An Empirical Analysis." *American Economic Review*, 78(4), 678–690.

Acs, Zoltan J., David B. Audretsch, Pontus Braunerhjelm, and Bo Carlsson. 2005. "The Knowledge Spillover Theory of Entrepreneurship." *CEPR Discussion Papers*, 5326.

Acs, Zoltan J., David B. Audretsch, Pontus Braunerhjelm, and Bo Carlsson. 2004. "The Missing Link: The Knowledge Filter and Entrepreneurship in Economic Growth." *CEPR Working Paper*, 4783.

Acs, Zoltan, and Roger Stough, eds. 2008. *Public Policy in an Entrepreneurial Economy: Creating the Conditions for Business Growth*, Springer.

Anselin, Luc, Attila Varga, and Zoltan J. Acs. 1997. "Local Geographic Spillovers between University Research and High Technology Innovations." *Journal of Urban Economics*, 42(3), 422–448.

Audretsch, David B. 1995. *Innovation and Industry Evolution*. Cambridge: MIT Press.

Audretsch, David B. 2007a. *The Entrepreneurial Society*. New York: Oxford University Press.

Audretsch, David B. 2007b. "Entrepreneurship Capital and Economic Growth." *Oxford Review of Economic Policy*, 23(1), 63–78.

Audretsch, D., and A. Roy Thurik. 2001. "What's New about the New Economy? Sources of Growth in the Managed and Entrepreneurial Economies." *Industrial and Corporate Change*, 10(1), 267–315.

Audretsch, David B., Max Keilbach, and Erik Lehmann. 2006. *Entrepreneurship and Economic Growth*. New York: Oxford University Press.

Barney, Jay B., and Delwyn N. Clark. 2007. *Resource-Based Theory: Creating and Sustaining Competitive Advantage*. New York: Oxford University Press.

Baumol, William. 2002. *Free Market Innovation Machine: Analyzing the Growth Miracle of Capitalism*. Princeton: Princeton University Press.

Baumol, William, Robert Littan, and Carl Schramm. 2007. *Good Capitalism, Bad Capitalism, and the Economics of Growth and Prosperity*. New Haven: Yale University Press.

Casson, Mark. 2003. *The Entrepreneur – An Economic Theory*. Cheltenham: Edward Elgar.

Chandler, Alfred D. 1977. *The Visible Hand: The Managerial Revolution in American Business*. Cambridge: Belknap Press.

Chandler, Alfred D. 1990. *Scale and Scope: The Dynamics of Industrial Capitalism*. Cambridge: Harvard University Press.

Cohen, Wesley M., and Daniel A. Levinthal. 1989. "Innovation and Learning: The Two Faces of R&D." *The Economic Journal*, 99(397), 569–596.

Cohen, Wesley M., and Daniel A. Levinthal. 1990. "Absorptive Capacity: A New Perspective on Learning and Innovation." *Administrative Science Quarterly*, 35, 128–152.

Galbraith, John Kenneth. 1956. *American Capitalism*. Boston: Houghton Mifflin.

Gartner, William, and Nancy Carter. 2003. "Entrepreneurial Behaviour and Firm Organizing Processes." In Z. Acs and D. Audretsch (eds.), *International Handbook of Entrepreneurship* (New York: Springer).

Griliches, Zvi. 1979. "Issues in Assessing the Contribution of R&D to Productivity Growth." *Bell Journal of Economics*, 10(1), 92–116.

Lucas, Robert E. 1988. "On the Mechanics of Economic Development." *Journal of Monetary Economics*, 22(1), 3–42.

Lucas, Robert E. 1993. "Making a Miracle." *Econometrica*, 61, 251–272.

Nelson, Richard. 1981. "Research on Productivity Growth and Differences: Dead Ends and New Departures." *Journal of Economic Literature*, 19(3), 1029–1064.

Penrose, Edith. 1958. *The Theory of the Growth of the Firm*. New York: Oxford University Press.

Prodi, R. 2002. *For a New European Entrepreneurship*. Public Speech. Instituto de Empresa in Madrid.

Romer, Paul M. 1986. "Increasing Returns and Long-Run Growth." *Journal of Political Economy*, 94(5), 1002–1037.

Scherer, Frederic M. 1970. *Industrial Market Structure and Economic Performance*. Chicago: Rand McNally.

Schramm, Carl. 2006. *The Entrepreneurial Imperative: How America's Economic Miracle Will Reshape the World (and Change Your Life)*. New York: Harper Collins.

Schumpeter, Joseph A. 1911. *Theorie der wirtschaftlichen Entwicklung. Eine Untersuchung über Unternehmergewinn, Kapital, Kredit, Zins und dem Konjunkturzyklus.* Berlin: Dunker und Humblot. (English translation, 1934, The Theory of Economic Development, trans. Redvers Opie, Cambridge: Harvard University Press.)

Schumpeter, Joseph A. 1942. *Capitalism, Socialism and Democracy*. New York: Harper and Brothers.

Schumpeter, Joseph A. 1952. *Theorie der wirtschaftlichen Entwicklung. Eine Untersuchung über Unternehmergewinn, Kapital, Kredit, Zins und den Konjunkturzyklus.* Reprint 1997, 9th ed., Berlin: Duncker & Humblot.

Shane, Scott, and S. Venkataraman. 2000. "The Promise of Entrepreneurship as a Field of Research." *Academy of Management Review*, 25(1), 217–226.

Solow, R. 1956. "A Contribution to Theory of Economic Growth." *Quarterly Journal of Economics*, 70, 65–94.

PART I

THE ROLE OF ENTREPRENEURSHIP IN INNOVATION

2

Capitalism

Growth Miracle Maker, Growth Saboteur

William J. Baumol, Robert Litan and Carl Schramm

For the general welfare, growth is arguably the most pressing of all economic issues. It is the one process that can raise living standards without letup and promise substantial reduction of the world's widespread poverty, which George Bernard Shaw rightly described as humanity's greatest crime. The pressing issue, then, is what can be done to stimulate economic growth substantially or at least to preclude its decline?

Just a few years ago many of us thought that we had the answer, and that the answer was obvious. When the Soviet empire collapsed it seemed clear that the magic formula was contained in one word: "capitalism." After all, no small role in the collapse was played by the poverty of the Soviet economy, and its resulting inability to keep up with the West. This, along with envy of the economic miracles that so many capitalist nations had been able to produce, were all obviously attributable to rejection of the capitalist system by the communist regimes, or so it seemed. However, this conclusion is only partly true, and even when true, the story requires some nuance (Schramm 2004). The decade of disappointing economic performance in Russia and the repeated economic crises in Latin America and other such phenomena clearly must give us pause. In our book, *Good Capitalism, Bad Capitalism*, we offer what we believe to be the explanation. Capitalism is not a homogeneous animal. The term represents a number of species. And, as the saying goes, while they are all equally capitalistic, some are more equal than others.

This chapter is a partial précis by William J. Baumol, Robert E. Litan, and Carl J. Schramm, *Good Capitalism, Bad Capitalism* (New Haven: Yale University Press, 2007).

2.1. Capitalism and Its Subspecies

We find it convenient to define capitalism as the form of economic organization in which the preponderance of instruments of production, that is, of plant and equipment, is privately owned and privately operated. This is evidently consistent with common usage and focuses on such a system's most critical attribute. But once we agree to proceed on the basis of this connotation, it should be clear that the overall class of capitalist economies can encompass a substantial variety of governance mechanisms. For example, the instruments of production in Great Britain and South Korea are both largely private property, but the resulting systems of economic governance and the locus of primary power are, or at least until recently were, very different. Certainly, several decades ago, the government played a far greater micro-managerial role in South Korea than in the United Kingdom. This invites classification of these economies into two different subcategories, because we have good analytical reasons and substantial empirical evidence that lead us to conclude that market control of an economy can elicit behavior and performance very different from those that can emerge under governmental direction.

As usual, a classification process does not automatically impose a unique set of subcategories. In our analysis, we found it useful to designate four types of capitalism, which we call "state-guided," "oligarchic," "big firm," and "entrepreneurial."

The meaning of the first of these seems self-evident. The second category, oligarchic capitalism, refers to a state of affairs in which the bulk of the wealth and the instruments of production are in the hands of a few individuals or a few families, clearly powerful and typically surrounded by an impoverished population. Africa and Latin America provide obvious examples.

The third category, big-firm, sometimes called oligopolistic capitalism, refers to the case in which a few gigantic firms account for a disproportionate share of output and a correspondingly great share of ownership of the means of production. Since, as we know, oligopoly has its very distinctive forms of operation and performance, we can expect that capitalisms in this third category will also have their distinct consequences.

Finally, we use the term "entrepreneurial capitalism" to describe economies in which new firm creation is easy and frequent, in which the resulting small and competitive enterprises play a significant role in the production process, and in which the competitive market mechanism is ultimately the main governing power. This definition is consistent with the one provided by Acs, Audretsch, and Strom in the first chapter.

We conclude that the disparity of performance of the capitalist economies of reality is to a substantial degree attributable to the form of capitalism that prevails in a society. Some forms of capitalism are inherently resistant to innovation and growth, while others can be expected to stimulate and promote them. Some appear to be effective in the takeoff process, helping powerfully to push a stagnant economy on to the expansion path. But with the passage of time, those same governance mechanisms can become a handicap to further growth and an instrument for sclerosis.

Specifically, we conclude that it is oligarchic capitalism from which we can expect the worst growth performance; oligarchs are happy with the status quo, fearing that change will throw a spanner into the works and upset their comfortable positions. The state-guided capitalisms have included some in which takeoff was indeed a successful and impressive process. But we argue that this form of economic organization generally requires modification if stultification is not eventually to overwhelm the growth process.

Our main conclusion is that it is neither a regime of pure oligopoly nor pure entrepreneurship that is the most promising form of capitalism, but rather a combination of the two, for reasons that will become clear later in this discussion.

2.2. On the Growth Miracle of Capitalism

It is easy to understand why capitalism in general and without qualification seemed so obviously to be the miracle cure for stagnation. Even Karl Marx and Friedrich Engels, hardly the most enthusiastic of proponents of capitalism, were deeply impressed by its growth accomplishments:

The bourgeoisie [i.e., capitalism], during its rule of scarce one hundred years has created more massive and more colossal productive forces than have all preceding generations together .... It has accomplished wonders far surpassing Egyptian pyramids, Roman aqueducts and Gothic cathedrals .... Subjugation of nature's forces to man, machinery, application of chemistry to industry and agriculture, ... clearing of whole continents for cultivation ... what earlier generation had even a presentiment that such productive forces slumbered? (Marx and Engels, *The Communist Manifesto*, 1847, ordering slightly modified)

Similarly, Alan Greenspan, the now retired Chairman of the U.S. Federal Reserve Board and certainly a man not inclined to exaggeration, is reported to have estimated that in the past century the United States was able to achieve a thirty-fold increase in material wealth. If we compare this with the average growth rate – zero – in the more than 15 centuries following the fall of the Roman Empire, we see what an incredible record the capitalist period of history has been able to achieve.

The capitalist growth miracle, indeed, is beyond comprehension by an inhabitant of one of today's industrialized countries. Yet it is illuminating to note that in Europe until the eighteenth century, famines, about every ten years on the average, were the normal state of affairs; and during famines it was common to see the corpses of the starved on the streets. This even occurred as recently as the mid-nineteenth century in countries as prosperous as Belgium. It is now completely unimaginable today in North America, Western Europe, or the successful countries of the Far East, all of them with capitalist economies.

Equally difficult to grasp is the explosion of invention that the capitalist economies have brought with them. As a rather parochial example, we may recall that in the working lifetime of one of the authors of this article, faculty members normally would write out their papers in pen and ink, having carried out their computations on a calculating machine powered by a hand crank that required at least one day for a simple statistical regression. The paper, given to the secretary, would need to be typed up, and if an error was found after the typical six carbon copies were made, each of the copies would need to be hand-corrected. Quoting a journal not owned by the library of the author's institution required an inter-library loan, entailing considerable paperwork and a delay of perhaps a month and a half. And in little more than a generation, this has become ancient history.

Thus, capitalism can, indeed, produce miracles, and the conclusion that it is the magic elixir that produces unbelievable growth is not to be ascribed to pure naivete. There can be no doubt, in light of the powerful evidence of which only a minuscule sample has been offered here, that capitalism is *at least sometimes* capable of producing miracles that would have been entirely beyond the comprehension of our ancestors. But the fact that it *can* do so does not mean that it always will. And there is abundant evidence that it sometimes will not.

We need only recall our proposed criterion that we use to determine whether it is appropriate to classify an economy as "capitalist," and the requisite counterexamples are easily provided. In most of Latin America the bulk of the instruments of production are in private hands. This is also true in much of Africa, and is certainly the hallmark of the post-Soviet economy of Russia. Yet it is obvious that the performance of most of these economies has been far from stellar. The famines that plague the African states are widely publicized, as they should be. These countries have managed to perform the difficult task of carrying out a *reduction* of per capita income. For example, between 1990 and 2001, per capita income in the former communist countries of Europe fell by a quarter. Latin America and the Caribbean experienced a decade of falling per capita income in the 1980s. And worst of all, in Africa (with nearly 13 percent of world population, but only 3 percent of world GDP), per capita income in 2001 was below its 1980 peak (Maddison 2003). This, indeed, is a difficult task in a world where an outpouring of productivity-enhancing inventions can and do rapidly cross national boundaries with surprising ease, so that, in the economies in question, if nothing had changed but the introduction of some of these innovations, output per inhabitant should have risen rather than decline.

Much publicized, too, is the case of Russia, where for many years after the fall of the Berlin Wall there was a substantial decline in living standards even below the pitiful levels under the Soviet regime. All this is proof positive that the mere adoption of a capitalist structure for the economy is no guarantee of even modest success. It must follow that not all capitalisms are equal, and that if there are some forms of this institution that can be relied on to stimulate growth and innovation effectively, there are others that fail to satisfy that criterion. Thus, it surely behooves us to distinguish among the forms of capitalism that do and do not offer hope, if we are seeking a promising prescription for reduction of poverty in the drastically wretched portions of the globe, and at the same for maintenance of the growth performance in the successful economies.

That, then, is the task undertaken by the authors of this chapter and our book on which it is based. Let us, therefore, return to our four forms of capitalism, discussing each in turn to provide an evaluation of its qualities as an engine of growth. We discuss them in order of growth-enhancement capacity, beginning with the least promising of the four.

2.3. Oligarchic Capitalist Regimes

Theoretically, oligarchies are capitalist countries, though they are either dominated by a few large family-owned enterprises, as in much of Latin America, or by autocrats, as in parts of Africa, or some mixture of the two, as in the Middle East. This form of capitalism is startlingly common, encompassing perhaps one billion or more of the world's population. In oligarchic capitalistic economies, incomes and wealth are generally distributed extremely unequally. Thus, the Gini coefficients – as standard measures of inequality – for the member countries of the Organization for Economic Cooperation and Development (OECD) fall in the 25–40 range, while the coefficients for Latin America are much greater, roughly near 50 to 60, indicating that incomes in the latter are distributed far more unequally. Countries in which this form of capitalism prevails have a number of common attributes that constitute significant impediments to growth.

2.3.1. Underground Economic Activity

Oligarchic economies are plagued by the high share, in their true GDP, of "informal" (illegal) activity, constituting extensive underground operations. To be sure, informality often entails economic activities that are inherently constructive – house building, selling of goods and services, and so on – but in ways that lack the requisite official approvals, licenses, or land titles. Thus, informal activity can be constructive and contribute to growth, but economies in which it is widespread nonetheless could grow faster if informal businesses were allowed to surface from the underground and do business in the open, where they have access to formal credit and networks that facilitate more rapid expansion. A widespread underground economy also deprives the government of resources, as a result of systematic tax evasion. The critical consequence is, typically, inadequate and rapidly decaying infrastructure, bad roads, poor telecommunications, inadequate schools, shortage of health care facilities, and the like – these, in combination, constitute a serious impediment to growth.

In oligarchic capitalism informality tends to be widespread and persistent because the ruling families do not consider the extension of formal rights throughout the population to serve their narrow economic interests. These families do not want the competition that new, formal entrants into the economy can provide. The problem of informality is prevalent in Africa, Asia, India, and China. Even Russian President Vladimir Putin has acknowledged the difficulty in Russia, where the influence of the oligarchs is substantial.

2.3.2. Corruption

Oligarchic economies typically are plagued by corruption, even more than under other forms of capitalism. Governments that make it difficult for citizens to obtain licenses or approvals for competitive activities – the preconditions that lead to informality – also create opportunities for lesser officials to take bribes. Although the few firms and families that dominate oligarchic countries are the powers behind the throne, they too may suffer from the corruption. Government officials still have the means to make life easy or hard for all of those who engage in economic activity or seek permission to do so. This, evidently, opens the way to demands for bribes from everyone by the leaders in charge.

Corruption stunts growth in a number of ways. It diverts entrepreneurial energy away from productive activities like the development and adoption of innovations and directs them toward socially wasteful endeavors. In addition, by increasing the cost of doing business, corruption discourages investment, both at home and from abroad.

2.3.3. Growth Disincentives

Oligarchies tend to be characterized by little economic growth, with the autocrats characteristically taking measures to prevent the establishment of competitors to the enterprises that are the sources of their incomes. As part of this effort, they seek to exclude foreign investment, the most promising instrument of economic expansion in their countries. Still, in these societies the government and the ruling elites may seek to promote some modest growth as a peripheral objective to keep the natives from rebelling and overthrowing the regime.

2.4. State-Guided Capitalism

This second form of capitalism, entailing much government intervention in the economy, is found most frequently in developing countries whose governments target certain industries where low cost, but highly productive labor, coupled with somewhat advanced technology, can generate considerable employment. The main goals of state guidance are to ensure widespread national employment, to raise wages, and to stimulate exports. Examples are provided by many of the countries in Southeast Asia, where governments have used one or more of the instruments of guidance available to them to favor certain sectors, primarily for the stimulation of exports. State guidance has in a number of cases worked in achieving growth, but primarily in economies that are far behind and have available to them the experience of successful economies, from which they are in a position to copy improved technology and widely demanded products. For economies at the frontier of productivity and prosperity, in contrast, there is no evidence that the state can do better than the marketplace in facilitating the emergence and survival of winner activities.

As the label suggests, state-guided capitalism exists where it is the government, not private investors, that decides which industries and even which individual firms should be given the means to grow. Government economic policy is then geared to carry out those decisions, using various policy instruments to help out the chosen "winners." The overall economic system nonetheless remains capitalist because, with some exceptions, the state recognizes and enforces the rights of property and contract; markets guide the prices of the goods and services produced and the wages of workers employed; and at least some small-scale activities remain in private hands.

Under state-guided capitalism, governments nonetheless typically take the position that growth can best be stimulated if the government directs all of this activity. Governments have a number of means at their disposal to guide growth, perhaps the most important of which is explicit or implicit ownership of banks, which are the principal conduits in virtually all countries for transferring the finances of those who save to those who invest the savings. In developing economies, such as India and China, and in even some developed ones, such as Germany, the government still owns a significant share of the banking sector. Even without direct ownership, governments can direct or "persuade" banks to do their bidding. The governments guide their economies in other ways as well, for example, by favoring certain companies or sectors with tax advantages, exclusive licenses (legalized monopolies), or government contracts. Favored companies thus can become "national champions," whose success is assured by government policy. Governments can also support industries through protective measures such as tariffs, insulating domestic companies from foreign competition. In addition, governments can guide the activities of foreign investors or partners, allowing them only in certain sectors and under certain conditions (commonly, that the foreign partner share and eventually transfer its technology and know-how to the local partner).

State-driven capitalism should not be confused with central planning. In centrally planned economies, the state not only picks winners, but it also *owns the means of production, sets all prices and wages, often cares little about what consumers may want, and thus provides essentially no incentive for innovation that benefits the individual.* Central planning, by its nature, is not conducive to the adoption of breakthrough nonmilitary technology and has generated little in the way of pervasive long-run economic benefits.

2.4.1. Accomplishments of State-Guided Capitalism

As the remarkable growth of the state-guided economies of Asia attests, this form of capitalism can be highly successful and occur over long periods. This success is most easily achieved by economies that lag well behind those at the technological frontier and that can find some way to gain access to cutting-edge foreign technology, or something reasonably close to it, and then combine it with lower-cost labor to turn out products that sell well in international markets. Foreign technology can be imported through foreign direct investment, by sending nationals abroad to foreign universities, or even by encouraging emigration of domestic residents to technological-leader countries such as the United States, hoping that they will either return to the home countries or facilitate from abroad the startup and growth of new homegrown enterprises. Ironically, the successive multilateral liberalizations of tariffs and other at-the-border restrictions, or the effort to make the global economy more market-driven, has also made it possible for those countries that have used state guidance to carry out a strategy of "export-led growth" to succeed – so far.

2.4.2. Pitfalls of State-Guided Capitalism

However, despite its impressive successes, state-guided capitalism has its perils that seem to be most threatening as these successfully state-guided capitalist economies approach the per capita income levels of richer, less state-regulated economies. It can be tempting to conclude that indefinite continuation of the same approach will yield growth benefits. But recent events have begun to raise doubts about such a view. This path is beset by a number of dangers.

One potential pitfall is *excessive investment*. South Korea and Japan provide dramatic examples of the tendency of government intervention to lead to this result. Long accustomed to directing its banks to provide loans to the economy's larger conglomerates, the government is easily induced to lead too many of them to invest excessively in the expansion of production capacity in particular industries. When a financial crisis arises, the country's banks and the companies that had borrowed to expand can be so over-extended that the economy is driven close to collapse. The problem is that the banks have applied not commercial but rather government-directed, criteria to the country's lending.

Excess investment is not the only peril of enduring state-guided capitalism. As such countries approach the technological frontier, it becomes much more difficult *to pick the winners from the losers* – and, specifically, to identify and help sectors or industries whose futures will prove to be as successful as the state may believe them to be. Governments in state-guided economies are not comfortable with the seemingly chaotic, unplanned, rough-and-tumble process that is the hallmark of capitalism unconstrained by bureaucracy. Instead, having seen first-hand their initial success at picking sectors for their export prospects (with sales in the domestic economy to follow), these governments are apt to believe that the same process of guidance can continue to produce the winners of the future. But once economies are at the frontier where success is not so easy to generate – because there are no clear leaders to copy or follow – mistakes are easy to make. There are many well-recognized examples of the resulting misdirection of investment resources.

There is a closely related problem that is apt to plague such economies. Once having committed the resources and prestige of the state to partic-ular ventures or sectors, it can be hard to "pull the plug" on them when it becomes clear that they need major restructuring or even that they must give way to competitors in other countries. Either governments do not want to lose face or, more commonly, politically powerful interests impede the ability of even well-intentioned governments to abandon their inter-ventions. The most pervasive examples of this problem are agricultural subsidies extended by virtually all rich-country governments, despite the falling and now relatively small share of employment engaged in agricul-ture.

As in oligarchies, state-guided economies are susceptible to corruption. After all, in economies where a business firm's success depends on whether it receives favors from government, there is always the danger that willing buyers and sellers of government largesse will find ways to transact "busi-ness." In China corruption is a well-known feature of the system.

In sum, states can often guide their economies successfully when they have well-defined targets to aim for. But as economies begin to approach the technological frontier, the easy targets will have been mastered. At this point, or perhaps well before it, the drawbacks of state-guided capitalism become more evident: Excessive investment, an inability to come up with radical innovation, the reluctance to channel resources from low-yielding activities toward potentially more rewarding ventures, and susceptibility to corruption become the norm.

2.5. Big-Firm Capitalism

Big-firm, or oligopolistic, capitalism is the state of affairs in which economic systems are dominated by large companies. Ownership of such enterprises is widely dispersed among many shareholders, often including some large "institutional" investors (such as insurance companies, pension funds, universities, and foundations). Professional managers are the "agents" of these "principals," giving rise to the well-known "principal-agent" problem – that of ensuring that the managers continually act in the best interests of the owners of the firms they manage.[1] Japan is a prime example of this phenomenon.

2.5.1. Advantages of Big-Firm, Oligopolistic Capitalism

Oligopolies can have their advantages, however. If the cost structure or network effects in a market support only a few firms, then oligopoly will tend to be the most efficient outcome for consumers, even with some markup for higher profits. Indeed, because of their supra-normal profits, firms in oligopolies have the cash flow to finance the development of the incremental improvements in technology that are the hallmark of large firms. Two Japanese giants, Honda and Toyota, exemplify the best of big-firm enterprises, firms that not only have continuously improved their automobiles, but have been radical innovators as well. A few large Korean manufacturers – Hyundai and Samsung – also have displayed innovative zeal in recent years. And Western European economies, as well, are host to a number of successful and innovative large firms, which are strong in the automobile, capital goods, and consumer appliance industries, among others.

Indeed, large firms are essential to the functioning of *any* economy if for no other reason than that the entrepreneurial founders of vibrant, new companies – the entrepreneurs – eventually must pass the reins of power to nonfounding managers. If the initial firm was a radical innovator, it is unlikely that it will repeat that success in its second and third generations of management, however. Larger, second-generation companies typically have flatter, more lock-step compensation systems that cannot reward individuals or groups within the firm for breakthrough inventions to the same degree that the market rewards lone inventors or entrepreneurs. In addition, breakthrough technologies can quickly make existing products and services obsolete and for that reason may be fiercely resisted within large organizations.

These factors help explain some interesting facts: why, for instance, only a small portion of research and development expenditures by big

---

[1] This problem was recognized in the 1930s by Adolf Berle and Gardiner Means as inherent when ownership is separate from control (see Berle and Means, 1932). Economists in recent decades have relabeled it the "principal-agent problem."

companies are directed toward radical innovation, and why, at the same time, small-firm innovation is twice as likely to be linked to scientific research and patents filed by small firms and are at least twice as likely to be "high impact" patents as those filed by bigger firms. Or why large U.S. firms like Procter & Gamble, Intel, and large pharmaceutical companies, among other large enterprises, increasingly seem to be "outsourcing" much of their research and development to smaller firms, which come up with new products and then sell themselves to those larger companies. Or why Sony of Japan – which originated the transistor radio, the Walkman, and the Trinitron television and was once one of the most successful innovative large firms – seems to have lost its way.

But big firms nonetheless can grow and prosper by constantly refining existing products and services, and occasionally developing new ones, typically after considerable market research about what consumers will and will not buy. The innovation process becomes routine and predictable, rather than seeking the breakaway product. Such constant, albeit routine, refinement is necessary in any economy.

Indeed, big firms are also essential to mass-produce and gradually improve some of the innovations that radical entrepreneurs are unable by themselves to manufacture in a cost-effective way. Examples are legion: Ford with the mass production of the automobile, which had seen a long line of inventors before;[2] Boeing, Lockheed, McDonnell-Douglas, and Airbus with the airplane that was invented by the Wright brothers; IBM with the mainframe computer that was designed at the University of Pennsylvania; Dell with the personal computer that had been developed by Apple; Microsoft with the PC operating system that was created by Gary Kildall; and large pharmaceutical companies, which have the resources to conduct the expensive and time-consuming clinical trials on breakthrough therapies invented in universities and in small companies.

In these and many other cases (including the radical innovations we discuss below), the early innovations were usually in a primitive state, limited in capacity, and often subject to frequent breakdown. It eventually took the bigger firms, with their permanent and well-trained research staffs, to refine them and to turn the innovations into products that consumers wanted and could afford.

[2] Henry Ford did invent a self-powered vehicle, but so did others before him (Carl Benz, Charles Edgar, J. Frank Duryea, Elwood Haynes, Hiram Percy Maxim, Charles Brady King, George Selden, among many others); Ford's genius was in applying assembly line manufacturing to the mass production of affordable automobiles.

Understandably, in such environments, the research arms of these firms give priority to product improvements that enhance capacity, reliability, and user-friendliness rather than to imaginative breakthroughs. Nonetheless, these incremental refinements are essential. Without such "routinized" R&D activities of big corporations, economies in developed (and developing) countries would be far less productive, and the reliability, practicality, and user-friendliness of many innovative products would be far more circumscribed.

2.5.2. Disadvantages of Big-Firm, Oligopolistic Capitalism

Often, but not always, big-firm capitalism is *oligopolistic*. That is, it is characterized by large firms operating in markets that, because of their limited size, are capable of supporting only a few competitors who may be able to take advantage of any significant economies of scale provided by the current technology. Or these markets may contain only one or a few firms because of "network effects," where the value of a good or service depends on how many others use it, as is the case for communications networks, stock markets, and various high-technology products, notably computer software. Such markets tend to be highly concentrated, even to be characterized by substantial monopoly power – the power to raise and maintain prices well above competitive levels – because the firms that succeed in building a substantial body of customers can thereby outcompete would-be entrants.

One great danger of oligopolies is that they can become lazy, living off their cash flow without innovating, while leveraging their power in one market into other markets, thereby stunting the growth of new technology and handicapping the entrepreneurs who could commercialize it. Oligopolistic firms sometimes seek to distort government policy, seeking protection by the courts or regulatory agencies from more efficient domestic and foreign competitors. The U.S. automobile and steel industries are prime examples of large firms in oligopolistic markets that lost their competitive zeal, and then sought and obtained trade protection to blunt – but not totally thwart – more-efficient competitors from abroad. The domestic counterpart of trade protection here is antitrust litigation aimed at benefiting particular big-firm competitors rather than the entire economy. The typical approach here is for a firm that falls behind a rival in efficiency to accuse that rival of "predatory behavior," with such litigation mounted by increasingly enterprising plaintiffs' lawyers, state attorneys-general, and occasionally federal antitrust authorities (Baumol 2002).

But the critical Achilles heel of big-firm capitalism lies in its tendency toward sclerosis, especially if the large firms that dominate it are successful in thwarting competition. In that event, the drive for continued improvement may wane. The quest for job security can become the highest priority. It is not an accident that in the leading exemplars of big-firm capitalism – continental Europe and Japan – labor markets are rigid, employment security is taken for granted, and firing is rare. The irony, of course, is that in their quest for security, these big-firm economies have failed to provide it. After outperforming the United States with lower unemployment rates through the 1950s, 1960s and 1970s, Western European economies over the last decades have suffered structural unemployment rates that substantially exceed those in America. Restrictive labor rules that make it difficult for firms to fire or lay off redundant employees also discourage them from hiring new ones. Moreover, the fear of being stuck with a labor force that they cannot later modify deters entrepreneurs from getting started in the first place or, if they do manage to begin, from hiring beyond any threshold that triggers the job protection requirements. Yet both Europe and Japan now find themselves aching to create an entrepreneurial culture to help generate the new jobs that their existing big firms cannot.

In short, big-firm, or oligopolistic, capitalism, at its best, has the incentive and generates sufficient cash flows to finance internally the continuing, incremental improvements in products and services that are staples of any modern economy. At its worst, however, big-firm capitalism can be sclerotic, reluctant to innovate and resistant to change.

2.6. Entrepreneurial Capitalism

Finally, we come to our fourth category: entrepreneurial capitalism, the capitalist system in which large numbers of the individual actors within the economy, or the small firms they create, not only have an unceasing drive and incentive to innovate, but also undertake and *commercialize* radical or breakthrough innovations. These innovations are bolder than the incremental innovations that characterize big-firm capitalism. Together, the original breakthrough innovations and the incremental improvements have improved living standards beyond anything our ancestors could have believed. Examples include the automobile and the airplane; the telegraph, which led to the telephone and eventually the Internet; the generation of electricity, which has transformed the way we work and live; and the air conditioner, which has permitted massive migrations of peoples from colder climates to warmer climates, not just in the United States but around the world, and has increased worker productivity by no small amount along the way.

This is just a small sample of the radical innovations that have transformed our lives and have spawned entire industries around them. They either become "platforms" on which products or technologies are built (e.g., electricity and computer operating systems), or "hubs" that help create and support many "spokes" (automobiles and their supplier industries). The industries spawned by these radical innovations in turn enhance productivity, and thereby contribute to economic growth.

2.6.1. New Firms and Breakthrough Innovations

In fact, a major share of the radical breakthroughs that introduced living standards undreamed of in earlier centuries were initially created and introduced by a *single individual* or *new firm* – our *entrepreneurs*. These individuals were often (although not necessarily) inventors, but they also were all able to recognize an *opportunity* to sell some thing or service that had not been there before, and then act on it. As David Audretsch and Max Keilbach (2005) have written, "Entrepreneurship becomes central to generating economic [growth] by serving as a conduit for [new] knowledge." Or as J. B. Say noted at the beginning of the nineteenth century: "[Without the entrepreneur, scientific] knowledge might possibly have lain dormant in the memory of one or two persons, or in the pages of literature" (*Traité d'économie politique*, 1832 (originally published in 1807), p. 81).

With rare exceptions, truly innovative entrepreneurs can only be found in capitalist economies, where the risk of doing something new – and spending time and money to make it happen – can be handsomely rewarded and the rewards safely retained by the innovator. These are key preconditions for entrepreneurial capitalism. Given the importance of innovation, the virtue of a free-market, opportunity-maximizing economy is that it taps the talents of the many. Such an economy is open to continual experimentation and interchange of ideas by self-directed individuals, who are more likely to come up with and carry out good ideas than any group of planners or experts. Thus, the very "un-plannedness" of a free-market economy, which may seem to be a great weakness, turns out to be an enormous strength. No one could have planned the myriad developments exemplified by the progression from the first successful airplane of the Wright brothers to the Boeing 777 and beyond. No one even foresaw them. Yet they led to entirely new industries employing millions and benefiting many millions more.

Other countries have witnessed these remarkable developments and are learning from them. Israel, Ireland, and the United Kingdom all have or are in the process of shedding the guiding role of the state in their economies and turning to the entrepreneurs, all with growing and even remarkable success. India, a long-time practitioner of state-guided capitalism, has embraced entrepreneurship, more by accident than design, in a small but growing corner of its economy: call-in centers and software design.

2.6.2. Large Firms and the Contagion of Innovation

For much of its history, the United States has been the leading exemplar of entrepreneurial capitalism. It is no accident that so large a share of the world's radical innovations originated in the United States, where entrepreneurship has been celebrated and encouraged.

Of course, even in the United States, entrepreneurs have not had a monopoly on all radical innovation, and large second-generation firms are essential to ensure that radical innovations are made effectively usable and attractive to the market. Our brief discussion of the different types of capitalism may suggest the conclusion that only the first form of capitalism – the "entrepreneurial capitalism" that has powered the U.S. economy toward a higher growth rate since the 1990s and that seems to be taking hold in other parts of the world – is the unique form of "good capitalism." But the evidence suggests a more complex conclusion: that it takes a mix of innovative firms *and* established larger enterprises to make an economy grow rapidly and to continue to do so. A small set of entrepreneurs may come up with "the next big things," but few if any of them would be brought to market unless the new products, services, or methods of production were refined to the point at which they could be sold in the marketplace at prices such that large numbers of people or firms could buy them (Baumol 1993). It is this insight that leads us to the conclusion that the *best* form of "good capitalism" is a blend of "entrepreneurial" and "big-firm" capitalism, although the precise mix will vary from country to country, depending on a combination of cultural and historical characteristics that we hope others will help clarify in the years ahead.

To summarize, entrepreneurial capitalism is the system we believe is most conducive to radical innovation. But no advanced economy can survive only with entrepreneurs. Big firms remain essential to refine and mass-produce the radical innovations that entrepreneurs have a greater propensity to develop or introduce.

2.7. How Do We Get There?

Our discussion has brought out what we believe to be the most effective institutional instrument for the elicitation and continuation of growth. But the obvious and most critical question that remains is: What means can be used to introduce this instrument? How can the inhabitants of an impoverished nation, held in a state of stagnation by its oligarchic capitalist regime, move to the blend of entrepreneurial and big-firm capitalism that seems the most promising avenue for amelioration of their condition? The answer, clearly, is beyond economics, and may entail measures such as the offering of incentives by foreign countries or international agencies, more direct forms of intervention, or even political revolution. Perhaps we can appropriately be criticized with the help of the old joke about the consultant who advises a population suffering from drought-created famine to grow more food. When asked how they can do so under the circumstances, the consultant replies: "But I've solved your problem. Surely you can work out the details."

But there is at least one point we can make here, with conviction. Because radical change is so disruptive, transition to an entrepreneurial economy may well raise justified fears among the population that stands to gain eventually, that the process will involve a protracted and painful period of adjustment. Those in the populaton who are particularly vulnerable will have reason to resist such change, even if it quickly benefits the population as a whole. This provides a crucial role for properly constructed safety nets that can shield at least the most vulnerable victims of change from its harshest consequences. Well-designed safety nets that catch the fallen without destroying their incentive to get back up can be even more important in high-income, entrepreneurial economies than in economies with lower average standards of living. This is because the potential losers from change in high-income countries have more to lose and thus greater incentive to try to stop it or slow it down. Moreover, when innovation provides benefits to the society as a whole that substantially exceed in market value the losses of those who bear the resulting damage, it is surely indefensible for the winners to refuse to part with a portion of their gains sufficient to provide compensation to the victims (see Kletzer and Litan 2001).

But the basic point here is not an attempt to preach the requirements of social virtue, but to point out that an adequate safety net can serve to reduce resistance to change and thereby can constitute one step toward the wider adoption of a form of capitalism that promises to enhance living standards and reduce or even eliminate poverty, in place of another regime, a variant of capitalism that impedes attainment of these goals.

References

Audretsch, David B., and Max Keilbach. 2005. *Entrepreneurship Capital – Determinants and Impact. CEPR Discussion Paper,* 4905, London: Centre for Economic Policy Research (February).

Baumol, William J. 1993. *Entrepreneurship, Management and the Structure of Payoffs.* Cambridge, MA: MIT Press.

Baumol, William J. 2002. *The Free-Market Innovation Machine: Analyzing the Growth Miracle of Capitalism.* Princeton: Princeton University Press.

Berle, Adolf A., and Gardiner C. Means. 1932. *The Modern Corporation and Private Property.* New Brunswick, NJ: Transaction Publishers (1991 ed.).

Kletzer, Lori, and Robert E. Litan. 2001. "A Prescription to Relieve Worker Anxiety." *Brookings Policy Brief No. 73.* Washington, D.C.: The Brookings Institution (March).

Maddison, Angus. 2003. "The West and the Rest in the International Economic Order." *OECD Observer.* Paris: Organization for Economic Cooperation and Development (May). Available at http://oecdobserver.org.

Marx, Karl, and Friedrich Engels. 1847. *The Communist Manifesto.* London: Penguin Classics (2002 ed.).

Schramm, Carl J. 2004. "Building Entrepreneurial Economies." *Foreign Affairs,* 83 (No. 4, July/August).

Shaw, George Bernard. 1930 (1907). *Plays XI: John Bull's Other Island, How He Lied to Her Husband, Major Barbara.* New York: W. H. Wise & Company.

Toward a Model of Innovation and Performance Along the Lines of Knight, Keynes, Hayek, and M. Polanyí

Edmund S. Phelps

3.1. The Beginnings of Capitalism Theory

A student relying on secondary sources might surmise that the theory of capitalism's dynamism originates in the classical case for competitive markets – a case first made by Adam Smith two centuries ago. This classical thesis was that the presence of many buyers and sellers competing with one another in the marketplace caused wasteful resource allocations to be weeded out "as if by an invisible hand." Under equilibrium conditions, efficiency in production prevailed. (One person's choice could be expanded only at the expense of another's.) This valuable feature of unimpeded markets, even if not fully realized, could not be matched by a government bureau: there were just too many goods and factors for a central planner to cope with. The point was made against communism by both "market socialism" theorists and capitalism theorists in the interwar years of the twentieth century.[1]

Going farther, Ludwig von Mises, another of the early moderns (and also a champion of capitalism), argued in the early 1920s that market socialism, a new system then beginning to be envisioned, would also fail to match the efficiency of market economies under private ownership. If managers did not receive the profit and bear the risks of their decisions, the resource allocations of socialist competition would be

---

This section expands and revises material I wrote with contributions and suggestions from Roman Frydman and Andrzej Rapaczynski in 2001 for the Web site of the Center on Capitalism and Society.

[1] Oskar Lange famously attributed the proposition to Mises. So had Hayek a little earlier. Mises, thinking of his book as a more original and profound criticism of market socialism, did not welcome the credit.

highly inefficient – an argument that effectively founded property-rights theory.[2]

However, Mises's theoretical argument that competition with private ownership delivered greater economic efficiency than state-run competition did not imply that the former competition also delivered greater dynamism – or indeed any dynamism. It was left open whether competition among firms suffices to generate dynamism without private owners, and whether private ownership suffices for dynamism without competition.

It might be thought that the theory of capitalism's dynamism originates in the pioneering work on economic advances by the German school led by Arthur Spiethoff and Gustav Cassel in the first decade of the twentieth century. Thanks to them, economic advances became a leading object of research for decades to come. Their work linked innovations to forces taken to be exogenous to the market economy, such as technological breakthroughs and the opening up of overseas markets and materials.[3] A new discovery created new outlets for investment. The investments made "express the zeal of employers to profit by meeting the increased demand of the community for fixed capital."[4] This provided a useful view of some historically important innovations – those sparked by technological shocks outside markets.[5]

Their work was not fundamentally about capitalism, however. Although their analysis ran in terms of a competitive economy with unfettered firms, they did not imply that economic systems of the capitalist kind were better at seizing the investment opportunities presented. Indeed, they may not have believed that the selection of economic institutions – among capitalist ones or among a broader set with socialist or corporatist ones – was important for the response of economies to new exogenous opportunities. Furthermore, their model did not provide an economics of innovations in normal times, when new commercial ideas are not sparked by the latest technological development but simply draw upon a vast stock of technologies inherited over centuries.

---

[2] Mises, 1936. In the same theoretical vein, Joseph Stiglitz in our time has laid the failure of the market-socialist experiment (and of communism) to the inefficiencies resulting from its failure to institute suitable incentive mechanisms. See Stiglitz, 1994.

[3] Spiethoff, 1903. Alvin Hansen marvelously surveys this chapter of economic thought (1951, chap. 16). He explains that in introducing knowledge shocks Spiethoff was not repeating but was paralleling Michel Tugan-Baranowski's work on financial shocks to investment.

[4] Cassel, 1924, quotation p. 622.

[5] Phelps and Zoega (2001) build on Cassel.

Comparative evidence on dynamism. Empirically, the kind of economic system in place does appear to make a difference for dynamism. A few central European economies twice became laboratories in recent decades for testing competition without private ownership. From the late 1960s to the late 1980s they allowed each state-owned firm to set its own prices, outputs, wages, and workforce in competition with the others. Whether or not efficiency improved, it was clear that economic dynamism did not ensue. It was said in defense of these state firms that their managers' plans for them were often blocked by the state and the managers knew they would not be fired for not innovating nor rewarded for innovating, so they did not need to. In the 1990s, the state firms were put on their own. This time, with their backs to the wall, they began innovating like mad, hoping that with luck it would be their ticket to survival. But these state firms were not able to innovate profitably.[6] Competition, it appears, is not sufficient for economic dynamism. Private ownership is necessary (and maybe more than just private ownership is needed).

Recent evidence on corporatist systems, where ownership is private but capital is not very free (entrepreneurs are fettered, financing is distorted, the state is freely interventionist, and more), is also quite negative. The corporatist economies of continental western Europe, which by copying new methods and products overseas posted outsize productivity growth from the mid-1950s even to the early 1990s, thus largely catching up to U.S. productivity in the process, remained impassive when visions of the Internet revolution caused entrepreneurs and financiers in the United States, United Kingdom, and Canada – but nowhere in continental Europe – to bolt out the starting gate in the last half of the 1990s.[7] The corporatist economies of east Asia, which achieved wonders as long as there was a wide gap between them and the West, ran into trouble in 1997 when state intervention in their corporate sector through permissions, subsidies, and guarantees led to mass over-investment and insolvency.[8] On this thesis, private ownership is not sufficient for dynamism, either: Capitalism, in which capital is free to go in new directions without a green light from the state, the community, and power blocs, becomes necessary at some point in a country's economic development if dynamism is to emerge.

---

[6] Frydman et al., 2000.
[7] See Phelps, 2000. See also Phelps and Zoega, 2001, secs. 1 and 5.
[8] This is the hypothesis in Phelps, 1999.

3.1.1. Schumpeter's Extensions of the Classical Model

As noted in Chapter 1, Joseph A. Schumpeter, in his groundbreaking 1911 book, sketched a model of economic change through innovations internal to the markets of capitalist economies:[9] An innovation was a new commercial development, a "new combination of productive means," and not to be confused with past inventions and discoveries by scientists and engineers, which were economically barren until subsequent innovations made application of them. Implementation of an innovative project might or might not require hiring scientists or engineers.[10] These innovations typically arose from perceptions of unexploited business opportunities on the part of business people drawing on their observations of commercial and industrial practice. This view was all the more natural because Schumpeter's innovations included not only new production methods but also new steps on which recent scientific advances might have little to contribute – new goods for consumers, new markets, and new business organizations.

In Schumpeter's system, implementation and development for the market of such an innovation required an "entrepreneur" with the "will" to undertake the venture[11] – generally in "new firms." The impression given is that an innovation may have to wait for an entrepreneur who is in the right place with the right stuff and the needed time. If the stock of innovations made possible by science is advancing without bound, "best practice" methods might forever lag behind the best possible methods.[12] A decline of entrepreneurs or of their entrepreneurship would slow the rate at which innovations were proposed or deemed suitable for backing with new capital. In this system, bankers

[9] Schumpeter, 1934, quotation p. 66. By Schumpeter's "model" I mean the stylized relationships and behavior he emphasizes and not the occasional concessions to reality that he makes.

[10] "[A]lthough entrepreneurs *may* be inventors just as they may be capitalists, they are inventors not by nature of their function but by coincidence and vice versa. . . . [Thus] the innovations which it is the function of entrepreneurs to carry out need not necessarily be any inventions at all" (p. 89).

[11] "The individuals whose function it is to carry out [new combinations] we call 'entrepreneurs'" (p. 74). The French term *entrepreneur*, meaning undertaker of a project, was first used in economics by Richard Cantillon and was made familiar by Jean Baptiste Say. John Stuart Mill imported it into English and Marshall broadened it to include managers. Schumpeter followed Say. The reference to "new firms" is on p. 66.

[12] Schumpeter notes the implication that "the 'best method' of producing . . . is to be conceived as the 'most advantageous among the methods which have been empirically tested and become familiar.' But it is not the 'best' of the methods *possible* at the time" (p. 83, emphasis added).

selected the investment projects to back. Finally, the successful start-ups stimulated other entrepreneurs to imitate and together they caused "creative destruction" of some existing products and jobs in the process of creating new ones.

This Darwinesque model of chance mutation and extinction was widely taught, and Schumpeter became justly renowned for it. Though many went on viewing entrepreneurship as the earlier Germans did – as merely the unfailing market reactions to new exogenous inventions – Schumpeter had directed a powerful spotlight on the distinct role of entrepreneurs' innovations and the challenge of their peculiar task:

[The] economic leadership [of innovators] must ... be distinguished from "invention." As long as they are not carried into practice, inventions are economically irrelevant. And to carry any improvement into effect is a task entirely different from the inventing of it, and a task, moreover, requiring entirely different kinds of aptitudes.[13]

[E]very step outside the boundary of routine has difficulties and has a new element .... [O]utside accustomed channels, the individual is without those data for his decisions and those rules of conduct which are usually very accurately known to him .... [The entrepreneur] must really to some extent do what tradition does for him in everyday life, viz., consciously plan his conduct in every particular.[14]

Schumpeter thus created new concepts: a gap between "best practice" and perceptions of the "best possible," innovations, the successful ones of which chip away at closing that gap, and the Schumpeterian entrepreneur, who in deciding on an innovation to undertake plays a role in determining the path of productivity and its industrial directions.

Yet the mechanisms with which he closed his model – how he modeled the emergence of entrepreneurs, the nature of their projected enterprises, and the award of funds to submitted projects – are strikingly premodern. He supposed that bankers can discern the worth of the projects submitted, just as they would do in the transparency of the classical economy. Implicitly, the ones getting funding are bankable propositions and those unfunded are not.

It has been denied that such knowledge is possible. The reply is that all banks that answer have knowledge and act on it. The giant banking concerns of England have their organs or subsidiaries that enable them to carry on that old tradition: The necessity of looking after customers and

[13] Pp. 88–89.
[14] Pp. 84–85.

constantly feeling their pulse is one of the reasons for the division of labor between the big banks and the discount houses in the London money market. However, this is not only highly skilled work, proficiency in which cannot be acquired in any school except that of experience, but also work that requires intellectual and moral qualities not present in all people who take to the banking profession.[15]

Thus the Schumpeterian banker, although exposed to irreducible random influences that may affect an individual project, is safe from the unanticipated consequences that would tend to occur if there was an appreciable degree of "unmeasurable uncertainty" even about whole classes of projects. In this respect, Schumpeter's mechanism is not consonant with subsequent understanding that the finance decision with regard to highly novel kinds of projects is problematic and with the perception that financial institutions may undersupply such projects in favor of some others offering greater "visibility."

Schumpeter's very concept of an innovation is different from that of the theorists in the interwar period. He acknowledges that the entrepreneur's plan "is open . . . to other kinds of errors than those occurring in customary action," presumably errors regarding the costs of design and launch, production cost, and user demand.[16] Yet there is no suggestion that entrepreneurs might be misguided as a group. (Some interpreters of Schumpeter's system even liken his entrepreneurs to people who stumble on five dollar bills on the street.) Moreover, though Schumpeter introduced "innovations" and linked them to people in business, the Schumpeterian entrepreneur seems to be a vessel for acting on information about unexploited opportunities detected and talked about by members of the business community, not generally by the entrepreneur himself.

It is no part of the [entrepreneur's] function to "find" or to "create" new possibilities. They are always present, abundantly accumulated by all sorts of people. Often they are generally known and being discussed by scientific or literary writers. In other cases, there is nothing to discover about them because they are quite obvious. . . . It is, therefore, more by will than by intellect that the leaders fulfill

---

[15] Schumpeter, 1939. Quotation from the abridged 1964 ed., pp. 90–91. I cannot find any passage on loan decisions in the 1934 English translation of the 1926 edition. And if Schumpeter during the writing had already viewed bankers as an independent factor, that role would surely have been made explicit in the 1911 book. So it appears that Schumpeter tied up the loose end of finance only decades later.

[16] P. 85.

their function, more by "authority," "personal weight," and so forth than by original ideas.[17]

The early moderns emerging a decade later differed radically on the essential nature of innovations – and blurred the sharp distinction Schumpeter had drawn between innovation and invention.

3.1.2. The Early Moderns' Understanding of Capitalism and Its Dynamism

Conceiving the nature of entrepreneurs' activity was the grand project of Frank Knight and, later, Friedrich Hayek. As is well known, it was Knight who in his 1921 book elaborated the distinction between two kinds of risk: there is measurable risk, which is insurable by purchasing an insurance contract from a diversified insurer, and there is what he called uncertainty, which he refers to as "indeterminate, unmeasurable." The latter, usually called Knightian uncertainty, insurers will not touch, since, absent an intensive investigation such as a financier might make, they have no way of typing and calibrating it, so the risk is unknown. The occurrence of a pure profit or pure loss is attributed to Knightian uncertainty, which lies behind the difference between "actual competition and perfect competition."[18] Without that, all income of an enterprise, net of depreciation, and any charge for managerial services by the owners, would be essentially interest income. Mere "change" is neither necessary nor sufficient for (pure) profit or loss.[19]

Knight's principal thesis was that, at least in capitalist economies (which are the object of his discussion), the prospects lying ahead for

[17] P. 88. Elaborating on why entrepreneurship is scarce, Schumpeter says that "nobody may be in a position to *do* it.... [I]t is this 'doing the thing,' without which possibilities are dead, of which the leader's function consists.... [Even in] a casual emergency, most or all people may see it, yet they want someone [else] to speak out, to lead and to organize" (p. 88). "The *entrepreneurial* kind of leadership... is colored by the conditions peculiar to it. It has none of that glamour which characterizes other kinds of leadership, it appeals [only in rare cases] to the imagination of the public... its success [depends on] a certain narrowness which seizes the immediate chance and *nothing else*... [and] full appreciation of the service rendered takes a specialist's knowledge of the case. Add to this the precariousness of the position... and the fact that when his economic success raises him socially he has no cultural tradition or attitude to fall back on but moves about in society as an upstart, whose ways are readily laughed at" (pp. 89–90). (Later he explains that the interest rate test serves to constrain the rate of innovation to the supply of available savings or what is left after rival sorts of investment have claimed their share.)

[18] Knight, 1921, see pp. 19–20. Nowadays "risk" is apt to designate the first kind of "uncertainty," which is opposite to Knight's terminology.

[19] Ibid., 35–38.

every business decision, including decisions to produce more or less of existing goods, involve elements in the calculation of demand and cost that are not known, not even statistically. Since entrepreneurs starting up a new project must consider far-future projects, they especially face Knightian uncertainty.

The universal form of conscious behavior is thus action designed to change a future situation inferred from a present one. It involves perception and a two-fold inference. We must infer what the future situation would have been without our interference, and what change will be wrought by our action. Fortunately or unfortunately, none of these processes is infallible, or indeed ever accurate and complete. We do not perceive the present as it is and in its totality, nor do we infer the future from the present with any high degree of dependability, nor yet do we accurately know the consequences of our own actions.[20]

At the bottom of the uncertainty problem in economics is the forward-looking character of the economic process itself. Goods are produced to satisfy wants; the production of goods requires time, and two elements of uncertainty are introduced.... First, the end of productive operations must be estimated from the beginning. It is notoriously impossible to tell accurately when entering upon productive activity what will be its results in physical terms, what quantities and qualities of goods will result from the expenditure of given resources. Second, the wants which the goods are to satisfy are also, of course, in the future to the same extent, and their prediction involves uncertainty in the same way.[21]

The general cause of the uncertainty – the reason why past experience is not sufficient to estimate at all closely the probabilities of the possible future returns on the project – is the endless heterogeneity of past data.

The liability of opinion or estimate to error must be radically distinguished from probability or chance ... for there is no possibility of forming in any way groups of instances of sufficient homogeneity to make possible a quantitative determination of true probability. Business situations, for example, deal with situations which are far too unique, generally speaking, for any sort of statistical tabulation to have any value for guidance. The conception of an objectively measurable probability or chance is simply inapplicable.[22]

Knight in an insightful discussion argues that the "producer" rather than the consumer bears the uncertainty.

[T]he consumer does not even contract for his goods in advance, generally speaking. A part of the reason might be the consumer's uncertainty as to his ability to pay at the end of the period ... [but] the main reason is that he does not know what he will want, and how much, and how badly; consequently he leaves it to

[20] Ibid., 201–202.
[21] Ibid., 237–238.
[22] Ibid., 231.

producers to create goods and hold them ready for his decision when the time comes.... [A]n outsider [such as a producer] can foresee the wants of a multitude with more ease than and accuracy than an individual can attain with respect to his own. This phenomenon gives us the most fundamental feature of the economic system, production for a market.[23]

Some people are better at making entrepreneurial judgments or have more confidence in their judgments or positively like to work on "original" projects and seem "to prefer rather than shun uncertainty" (p. 242). These people typically bear the uncertainty.

In [a handicraft] system every individual would be an independent producer.... [But it] passes over into a system of "free enterprise" which we find dominant today. The difference between free enterprise and mere production for a market [is]... specialization of uncertainty-bearing. [The anticipation of wants and control of production with reference to the future], already removed from the consumer himself, is further taken out of the hands of the great mass of producers as well and placed in charge of a limited class of "entrepreneurs" or "business men." [24]

Finally, investors and lenders helping to finance a new project have the possibility of spreading the uncertainty by diversifying their investments and loans over several or many producers.

The minute divisibility of ownership and ease of transfer of shares enables an investor to distribute his holdings over a large number of enterprises.... [T]he losses and gains in different corporations must tend to cancel out in large measure and provide a higher degree of regularity and predictability in his total returns. And... the chance of loss of a small fraction of his total resources is of less moment even proportionally than a chance of losing a larger part.[25]

Today, it might be commented, "structured," or "layered," contracts carve out pieces of the project – both equity and debt instruments – that specialized financial entities such as hedge funds and pension funds find well suited to their needs. Moreover, the start-up entrepreneur stands to lose his equity stake and his control of the enterprise if targets set by the investors and lenders are not met. So, as in Knight's day, entrepreneurs must bear plenty of uncertainty.

Thus Knight's risk gives a deep analysis of the radical uncertainty that is a distinctive, pervasive, and central feature of capitalist economies. But although his portrait of capitalism may be logically complete, it leaves out

[23] Ibid., 241.
[24] Ibid., 244.
[25] Ibid., 254.

something too big to be a telling likeness of capitalism. Innovation – therefore creativity in business, the novelty possessed by many new proposals, the asymmetry of information about them, and the expansion of knowledge that may result – never comes to have a central place in Knight's model of capitalist economies. In a passage late in the book he takes up – generally from the view of its relation to uncertainty – the presence of (new) knowledge, "or what may be designated by the term 'invention' in the broad sense" (p. 339). He acknowledges that there is "discovery" and there is "creation" (p. 340) – the latter a "result of deliberate thought, investigation and experiment" (p. 341). But this fleeting allusion to knowledge formation was too thin and too late to have an impact on thinking about innovation.[26]

John Maynard Keynes entered the stage about the same time as Knight, and some of his enduring insights complemented those of Knight. Keynes's book on probability theory was aimed at understanding decisions under unmeasurable uncertainty.[27] His contribution was to show that a rational response to such uncertainty was to behave as if the probabilities of the explicit possibilities summed to a number less than one, thus leaving room for the sense that there were contingencies not identified or not fully appreciated. His recognition of the uncertainty that faces entrepreneurial projects was to carry over to the macroeconomics of capitalist economies that he started in the mid-1930s.[28] His famous allusion to "animal spirits," a term of Plato's, behind businessmen's investment decision making served to underline his view that the volume and directions of entrepreneurial projects and of investment projects in general depended heavily on the entrepreneur's instinctive feeling about what the future would hold for the project, not just on financial and engineering data. Finally, it was Keynes who first emphasized that, in an entrepreneurial economy at any rate, the uncertainty of the future inevitably leads to diversity of opinion about where prices might go and where profits might lie; yet rules of thumb may prevail in some markets, making prices there quite sluggish until one or more

---

[26] Where Knight says that "some individuals want to be sure . . . while others like to work on *original hypotheses*" (p. 242) he means for all we know that some business people prefer to manage, say, an existing power company, with all the uncertainties it may hold in store, while others would prefer the uncertainties of starting up a new power company. The "original" project may mean nothing more than trying the ith project that some concept suggests would find a profitable market after the previous $i - 1$ projects based on the same project have succeeded.

[27] Keynes, 1921.

[28] Keynes, 1936.

developments make some things clearer – and, possibly, a new rule of thumb begins to form.[29]

Incidentally, though it is a long story, it is fair to say that, in the 1920s, when Lenin was constructing a communist economy in Russia and Mussolini a corporatist one in Italy, Keynes stayed on the side of capitalism.[30] He opposed laissez-faire (i.e., the "free market"), believing that the state has useful functions to play, had a low regard for wealth accumulation, and a distaste for money grubbing. But for him these were not essentials of capitalism. Certainly, he saw the depression that struck Britain and the United States in the interwar period as signaling a serious lapse in capitalism's performance. He thought that capitalism remained valuable as an engine for generating commercial innovation and thus raising productivity. Capitalism will survive in a country as long as people's ideas of a good economy allow it. "The world," he said in answer to Marx, "is ruled by ideas and little else."[31]

Hayek comes in where Knight and Keynes leave off. Hayek, beginning in the second half of the 1930s, emphasized the untried and thus the speculative nature of what the entrepreneur with a new project is attempting. He introduced in the mid-1930s a distinction between two kinds of knowledge.[32] In the classical view, knowledge is unambiguous and complete, so its implications are fully determinable. There is no sense of knowing there are things we do not know, things we may come to know eventually and things we will never know. In the modern view adopted by Hayek, actors in the world have to make judgments that are not fully implied by their formal models. As Keynes wrote, "It is necessary finally to act." And that requires them to draw upon their tacit, or personal, knowledge: "We know more than we can say," in the aphorism of Michael Polanyí. In the growth-of-knowledge theory of Hayek and Polanyí, formal knowledge advances in the sciences as scientists combine their current tacit knowledge with existing formal knowledge in conceiving and selecting hypotheses to test and experiments to make.[33] That is how formal knowledge advances.

Hayek then applied this growth-in-knowledge theory to the activities of innovation and discovery in capitalist economies. The entrepreneurs come

[29] Keynes, 1937.

[30] To digress more, in the late 1930s he objected to the expense of Beveridge's plan for a welfare state and in the 1940s he teased Hayek for extolling individualism while proposing state healthcare and other activities.

[31] Keynes, 1936.

[32] Hayek, 1935a, 1948.

[33] Three classic references are Hayek, 1945 and 1978; and Polanyí, 1962.

to their distinctive judgments through their distinctive personal experiences and resulting personal knowledge, or "know-how" in his terminology. Similarly, the technical work in engineering and marketing new products or methods involves personal knowledge. "[M]uch of the knowledge that is actually utilized is by no means 'in existence' in [a] ready-made form. Most of it consists in a technique of thought which enables the individual to find new solutions."[34] Thus capitalist economies generally draw on a diversity of tacit knowledge that in the aggregate is vastly more than any one banker or shareowner or central planner could possibly possess or even conceive of. (Hayek held that since innovations entail creative leaps and invariably these leaps involve tacit knowledge, which is outside recognized knowledge and hence goes beyond what can be communicated in explicit terms, a state investment bank would not be well suited to select among entrepreneurs' projects: Being accountable to the central government for its mistakes, it would avoid all the very innovative proposals because of the ambiguity of the evidence for them and the consequent impossibility of communicating their appeal to higher authorities or to the public.)

It follows that the many lenders and investors selecting among entrepreneurs' projects in a capitalist economy are also, like the entrepreneurs, not immediately able to grasp the worth of every entrepreneurial project offered for financing. Thus financiers must also depend in part on their intuition, deciding to take or not to take an initial and limited chance on an applicant in spite of the ambiguity of the evidence. If the typical innovative project is in part inherently not capable of being articulated, how successful the bankers and venture capitalists prove to be in selecting among them hinges not only on the partial and tentative understanding they initially acquire about the entrepreneurial projects submitted to them but ultimately also on the willingness of the entrepreneur to enter into a provisional relationship with the entrepreneur that provides the entrepreneur with some leeway to experiment and prove himself and thus the financier to acquire more knowledge about the project. This is a far cry from Schumpeter's "bankable propositions."

It further follows that the success of an innovation remains a matter of considerable uncertainty until it is determined by the reception it finds among potential users in the marketplace. As Hayek commented, the strength of the demand for the novels of C. P. Snow could not be known

---

[34] Hayek, 1935, reprinted in Hayek, 1948, p. 155.

beforehand, not even by the author himself, until they were produced and offered to the book-buying public.[35] Every innovation is like a scientific experiment in which, characteristically, the probabilities of the various results are not determinable beforehand – nor fully determinable afterwards either.

The potential users themselves may have little idea how much they will like the new product or method unless and until they try it. (Users cannot plausibly be assumed to know that a priori if, as Hayek supposed, the entrepreneur, who is an expert and himself a consumer, does not know he has anticipated all the things that might deny him success.) Thus households and firms deciding on a new product or method have the same knowledge problem as do the entrepreneur and financier behind the product or method. Economies of dynamism are shot through with Hayekian knowledge formation.

There is one other point. If the individual upstart entrepreneur is central to innovation, how can we resolve the puzzle that would have troubled Mises? Large firms are bureaucratic and, especially in the United States, typically owned by passive shareowners so they do not usually have a principal lender or core investor who could choose in-house "intrapreneurs" to back and advise on their innovative projects. Yet the large firms account for the lion's share of the industrial research and seemingly of innovation as well. The resolution may be that the new and successful ideas of the start-up entrepreneurs owe most of their further development and possible extensions to high-capital-cost projects at the large firms – including the large firms that the start-up firms sometimes grow to be and the large firms that buy up successful start-up firms. If the germinal material for innovation by large firms is the underdeveloped innovations of recent start-ups, models of large-firm innovation based on the "defensive innovation" of Schumpeter in 1942 "work" only thanks to the stimulus of the 1911 Schumpeterian start-ups. The interplay between the small-firm sector and the large-firm sector perhaps overcomes the bureaucratic organization of the large corporations, especially public companies.

Knight's recognition of the uncertainty surrounding business decisions and Hayek's bottom-up theory of discovery and growth of knowledge have ramifications for a wide range of subjects and influenced many economists and political scientists, including Jane Jacobs, Milton Friedman, Michael

---

[35] Hayek, 1961, reprinted in Phelps, ed., *Private Wants and Public Needs* (New York: W. W. Norton, 1962).

Oakeshot, and James C. Scott.[36] Yet the conceptual advances of Hayek, Knight, and Keynes on innovation and dynamism are little imbedded into formal models and thus into orthodox theory. No doubt further effort is needed.

This survey virtually stops here not on any perception that no further core developments in the subject occurred in the second half of the twentieth century (other than Hayek's last writings) but because an adequate review would involve a much larger cast of contributors – and much less radical contributions – than are found in the interwar period. Yet I can refer readers to the seminal contributions that stand out in my mind among an undoubtedly larger number that would deserve equal mention. There is the contribution by Schumpeter in the wartime and early postwar years in which he argued that oligopolists are motivated to engage in defensive innovation in order to avoid losing the profits they already have from their market share, a thesis recently taken up by William Baumol.[37] Another is the work by Richard Nelson and Thomas Marschak arguing that financiers can largely meet the problem of having far from complete knowledge about one or more key parts of an entrepreneurial project by entering into an agreement that metes out the finance sequentially upon the entrepreneur's meeting successive benchmarks.[38] The Nelson-Phelps model has reverberated in recent years not only for its much-tested implications about the role of education but also because it implies that entrepreneurs will be reluctant to develop and market an innovation in a market where few potential adopters are highly educated.[39] Another salient contribution is the work by Amar Bhidé in which it is argued that small firms have a distinctive role in innovation owing to their advantage in coping with Knightian uncertainty and large firms have a distinctive role in innovation owing to their advantage in managing and financing projects with high capital costs.[40] A significant portion of the analyses we have to date about evolving economies is

---

[36] Jacobs, 1961; Friedman, 1962; Oakeshot, 1962; and Scott, 1998. Referring to medical practice, Friedman wrote, "[A] faith healer may be just a quack who is imposing himself on credulous patients, but maybe one in a thousand or in many thousands will produce an important improvement in medicine. The effect of restricting the practice of what is called medicine . . . is certain to reduce the amount of experimentation that goes on and hence to reduce the rate of growth of knowledge in the area" (p. 157).

[37] Schumpeter, 1942; 2nd enlarged ed., 1947. See also Baumol, 2002.

[38] Nelson and Marschak, 1962. Of course, the financiers may nevertheless have to choose their entrepreneurs in the dark to start with, and that may deter a large quantity of finance.

[39] Nelson and Phelps, 1966.

[40] Bhidé, 2000.

presented in the book by Nelson and Winter.[41] There is also the work of recent years by Roman Frydman and Michael Goldberg developing an economics applicable to an economy where there is inherently imperfect knowledge about its current structure and how it unfolds over time.[42] Finally, my recent work argues that economics has failed to take into account the benefits of economic dynamism in modeling and evaluating capitalism: The philosophy called "vitalism" implies that the processes of problem-solving and discovery are an end, or reward, in themselves, not just a means; high productivity derives much of its social utility by enabling more people to afford taking jobs that are rewarding in those nonpecuniary ways.[43]

3.2. A Rudimentary Framework for Theoretical Study of Innovation

I want to sketch here the core element of a model capturing the essential aspects of a capitalist economy in the sense of an economy driven by proposals of private business participants to private financiers for backing of innovative projects. The first objective is to construct in broad outline a micro-founded model of the mechanism governing what we might call the "flow supply" of new ideas to the innovation market coming from entrepreneurs and the "flow demand" from financiers. The subsequent objective is to consider, albeit somewhat informally in the present chapter, how certain market forces that would otherwise not be present – such as the circumstances and expectations of entrepreneurs and those of financiers – affect the outcome of their interaction. It will be a source of satisfaction to have market models of the supply of entrepreneurial ideas to the market and their selection, or demand, by financiers, since innovative ideas are central to business life in a capitalist economy. Furthermore, having such a component in our larger model of the economy may help us organize hypotheses about how an economy's performance is impacted by the institutions and about other conditions impacting on some of the central figures generating (or failing to generate) dynamism – the entrepreneurs and the financiers. We have to study the entrepreneur as a micro-actor and to study the entrepreneurial economy as an interactive system involving entrepreneurs and financiers. (This first pass, though, avoids the richness of institutions found in real capitalist economies.)

---

[41] Nelson and Winter, 1982.
[42] Frydman and Goldberg, 2007.
[43] Phelps, 2007.

3.2.1. The Construct of an "Innovation Fair"

The classic supply-and-demand apparatus does not apply to the core market of capitalist economies: the capital market, particularly the market for capital going to entrepreneurs' innovative projects. The least of the complications is that every entrepreneurial project is a different good, just as every new house placed on the market differs from the others. That each entrepreneur's idea is idiosyncratic, hence unique, does not by itself preclude a manageable model of equilibrium.

Let me in the interest of simplicity introduce a construction that reflects the fact that an economy is spread out over space, so the economy's actors are not ordinarily in contact with large numbers of others, yet they can convene with others intermittently for purposes of important transactions. I will suppose that periodically – once every five years, for example – all the entrepreneurs who in the previous period have hit upon a new idea they regard as worth the trip travel to a sort of fair to seek financing. A comparable number of financiers, each with a large pool of liquid capital, attend the fair to seek entrepreneurial projects to invest in or make loans to. They are the abstract counterparts of today's hedge funds and venture-capital funds.[44] (I was delighted to learn about a year ago that such fairs actually take place! The entrepreneurs reportedly remain stationary while a procession of the financiers circulates around them.) Once they contract to finance a project they will act as partners of the entrepreneur, drawing on their generally different experience to solve problems in the development and launch of the new product or method. With the project's completion the financiers will sell their shares in an IPO on the stock exchange and their bonds on debt markets.

It might be thought that the capital-market model devised by Irving Fisher and James Tobin, originally applied to many heterogeneous investment projects, could be a satisfactory tool to analyze this innovations market.[45] Whether applied to investment projects or to innovation projects, that model implicitly supposed that there is no ambiguity about the promise of each such project. As a result there is agreement among the financiers about the value of each project: it is the present value of the agreed expectations of the stream of future gross earnings it would

---

[44] A hedge fund marks to market its assets, so its investors have an idea of the price they could expect for their shares if they decide to leave the fund. Investors in a venture-capital fund are more nearly locked in.

[45] I. Fisher (1898), "Precedents for Defining Capital," *Quarterly Journal of Economics*, 18, 386–408, and J. Tobin (1965), "Money and Economic Growth," *Econometrica*, 33(4), 671–684.

generate. The investment cost of each project is also a given. It then followed, as Tobin showed, that the capital market would rank highest for financing the project(s) with the highest calculated value per dollar of investment cost, would rank second-highest the project(s) with the next highest ratio of value to cost, and so forth until there were no more projects with a positive rent – with a value-to-cost ratio (Tobin's Q ratio) greater than one. An inframarginal entrepreneur collects from his financier(s) a rent that, added to the above investment cost, leaves the financier with the same zero expected profit on that investment as would be expected on the marginal project.

I would comment that such a Fisher-Tobin equilibrium may exist even if the profitability of each project is subject to exogenous sources of uncertainty (i.e., Knightian uncertainty in which no one knows the probabilities of all the various conceived outcomes or even knows all of the possible outcomes there are). An unambiguous ranking of projects would still exist if some war of unknown probability would be expected by all, should it occur, to reduce the value of all projects in equal proportion; in that case the ranking would not even be affected (though fewer projects might make the cut). More generally, a ranking would still exist if it is understood that exogenous shocks of unknown probability would impact unequally on the values of the various projects, provided the financiers are alike in their judgment of those impacts and the weight they give to the shock and their judgment of those impacts and the weight they give to the shock.

But complications set in once we recognize, following Hayek and Polanyí, that the entrepreneur's idea presents some ambiguity: The entrepreneurs are to some extent like fighter pilots: unable to explain the thinking behind their decisions.[46] So, in any brief initial interview, the financiers can see only dimly what each idea is, what would be involved to implement it, and what the selling points and the snags might be if it were marketed. Moreover, since financiers weighing projects have to use their own limited experience and specialized knowledge, and these differ from financier to financier, the financiers do not all make the same valuations. Hence, even if each financier falls into a group of like-minded financiers, each of whom views the entrepreneurs' proposals the same way, one such group might rank the projects differently from another. So if we are to build a usable model of the intersection of the entrepreneurs' projects and the financiers' capital it is necessary to see whether disagreements in financiers' rankings are apt to be a barrier to the conclusions we might hope to reach.

---

[46] The post-Polanyí literature includes Dreyfus (1979), and Klein (1998).

To narrow down possibilities I propose to give the model more structure by supposing that each financier prefers to back the idea of an entrepreneur whose "model" is most resonant with his own – his thinking with
regard to which industry is the best bet, swinging for the fences or not,
and so forth.[47] So the "capital market" is a sort of matching process that
matches a financier to an entrepreneur whom the former sees as having a
model compatible with his own model. Thus capitalism is a system producing a profusion of ideas representable as competing models of the
economy (or a piece of it) and when an entrepreneur and financier sense
they have roughly the same model they band together in a bet on its ability
to prove itself. In this way the financiers are matched to the entrepreneurial
projects to which their collaboration can contribute the most in view of
their nearly identical outlook.

After the entrepreneurs have had their initial interviews, some of them
will generally enter into a further discussion and that may lead to a letter of
intent, called in the trade a terms sheet, from a financier (and his or her
possible partners). The penalty for withdrawing from such a commitment
makes it quite unlikely that the financier will fail to sign the indicated
contract and choose instead to send a new letter of intent to another
entrepreneur. Entrepreneurs who do not receive or do not accept such
letters leave the game, their project having failed to gain finance.

3.2.2. Equilibrium and Disequilibrium in
the Innovation Market

To discuss forces acting on equilibrium and departures from equilibrium
we need to define it. As I customarily do, I will use the expectational
definition of market equilibrium, which was originated by Marshall and
Myrdal. I use a macro version of this equilibrium, referring to representative agents. And I put intertemporal considerations aside, leaving intertemporal equilibrium as a separate concept.

Such an equilibrium in the innovations market requires that the entrepreneurs as a whole are not overestimating the average value per investment dollar being placed on the projects of the other entrepreneurs, so the
entrepreneurs are not being misled by such an expectational error into

---

[47] The Bradley brothers, two celebrated entrepreneurs in Minneapolis some decades ago,
remarked on precisely this core aspect of entrepreneurship (without benefit of reading
Hayek, so far as I know). "The entrepreneur," they wrote, "invents a new model of the
world from which he derives his new business project." (Quoted by memory from
documents ca. 1998.)

holding out for higher terms than they would otherwise do; similarly, the entrepreneurs as a whole are not underestimating the average value per investment dollar. This equilibrium also requires that the financiers as a whole are not overestimating the average value per investment dollar that the other financiers are offering, so the financiers are not being misled by such an expectational error into offering higher terms on the projects they want than they would otherwise do; similarly, the financiers are not generally underestimating the average value per investment dollar.[48] Obviously the case of equilibrium does not rule out that *some* entrepreneurs have been misled by his or her expectations about the outcomes on the market; it only specifies that the errors have roughly canceled out – that the representative entrepreneur has not overestimated the demand for his project by financiers.

This expectational equilibrium does not imply market clearing. Indeed it is reasonable to suppose that, even if their market expectations (just discussed) were correct, some of those entrepreneurs were overly bullish about the appeal of their own project and some subset of these entrepreneurs finally found themselves having no more offers to agree to. Although they may have made successive inferences leading to successive reductions of their "acceptance price," not all of them necessarily reduced their acceptance terms fast enough to avert the result that their projects are not under contract by the time all the financiers have committed all or nearly all their funds on other projects. (There is no "recontracting" here. The discussion after the initial interview that may lead to letters of intent may have high opportunity costs, so that penalties are provided for withdrawing from a commitment.) A rather different point is that an entrepreneur may be willing to gamble on holding out for a price above his reservation price, knowing that he is not facing perfectly elastic demand. (In reality, entrepreneurs can also wait for the next fair, which some do.) So our equilibrium is of the non-market-clearing kind, which is familiar in labor-market models.

Another observation is that even if the innovation market finds equilibrium, it does not follow that this equilibrium is completely independent of which transactions happen to be made early as one project after another is adopted by financiers: path dependence is conceivable and no doubt possible. Owing to Hayek's point that much of the entrepreneur's understanding of his proposed innovation is personal knowledge, a financier will have far from complete knowledge about it and will have little idea

---

[48] The above requirements for equilibrium in the innovation market capture the spirit of the concept, even if it should be found that some further requirements are appropriate to add.

of what any other person's knowledge about it is. Thus there may be learning in this regard over the course of the market's allocations of projects and the information on the terms at which they are sold. Further there may be some chance factors influencing whether or not some subset of projects are bought up early. So the future of the bidding may depend to some extent on which projects happen by chance to be sold early in the process. So the equilibrium in the market for these Hayekian objects may not be uniquely determined. However, the possibility that there is some indeterminacy around the equilibrium and maybe not pure white noise should not deter us from investigating the effects of forces acting on equilibrium and the effects of disequilibrium as long as the answers to the questions asked are not sensitive to the particulars of the equilibrium that is or would have been reached.

3.2.3. What Drives Financiers to Back Any Innovation at All?

It is perfectly natural to wonder whether an equilibrium in this innovation market is necessarily one in which a positive number of projects win financing. Maybe it is only because entrepreneurs can finance themselves or they are friends or relatives of a financier that they can get their projects going. On this issue, I would argue that even in the case of perfect ignorance on the part of the financiers – so that financiers were unable to distinguish one entrepreneur's project from another (and one entrepreneur's character and talent from another's) – financiers would generally supply some financing and some innovation will go ahead. My argument is this: If all the new projects offered looked the same to financiers, applications of pseudo-entrepreneurs would explode if Tobin's Q ratio exceeded one or even equaled one, since a great many people would prefer being an entrepreneur to being a salaried employee – especially an entrepreneur paid an entrepreneur's wage. So the expected Q ratio in every period would have to lie in a range below one. And if the entrepreneurs valued projects only for the positive rent they received from it – the rent consisting of the excess financiers' pay over the investment cost (figured at market wage rates) – then none of the innovative projects would be undertaken. But if there are some entrepreneurs who estimate highly enough the nonpecuniary satisfactions that would accrue from doing their project (the thrill of it, the learning experience) and if these entrepreneurs would accordingly subsidize the project with a reduced salary in order to fill the gap between the investment cost (figured at normal salaries) and the deficient valuation put on their project by financiers, then they will be able start their projects. If the promise of entrepreneurs to work at subsidized wage rates out of professed love of their work looks to be incentive-incompatible (maybe the entrepreneur will restore his wage, causing the financier's returns to suffer), the entrepreneur may be able to signal his love of the project by investing resources of his own or of family members in spite of the less-than-normal rate of return that is expected. (For what it is worth, James Tobin told me at Yale that Schumpeter believed that entrepreneurial projects earned a below-normal rate of return. I have not found that in print, though.)

A more general point here is that in any case – the case of financiers' perfect ignorance and the case of financiers' initially imperfect knowledge – some portion of the entrepreneurial activity taking place is the result of the large concessions (in returns or leisure sacrificed) that some of them, whether or not all, make through their own labor or on their own capital investment in order to save the project and thus have its nonpecuniary satisfactions.[49] If that is so, the supply side of entrepreneurial projects is more important than it is perhaps generally understood to be. The higher those expectations, the lower will be the supply price (or reservation price in other terminology) at which the entrepreneur will supply the attention and concentration necessary for conceiving of the entrepreneurial idea. Moreover, once the project has been conceived, the acceptance price that the entrepreneur requires to let it go to the prospective financier (rather than hold off for a better offer) will also be lower, the higher his expectations of the project's nonpecuniary reward to him. The latter is in contrast to the "textbook" model: In the Fisher-Tobin model of investment, which can be applied in principle to investing in new products and methods, an entrepreneur with his already conceived project is activated, or deployed, by the financial sector if and only if its expectations of the value of the entrepreneur's project exceeds the opportunity cost of the project; the entrepreneur's expectations do not figure in. (That is, existing projects are supplied perfectly inelastically.)

3.2.4. Comparative Statics: Expected Reward, Wealth, Economic Culture, Institutions

The perspective of the market model I have been using here suggests to me four exercises that may be useful to get a sense of how the "model" works.

---

[49] Their overly enthusiastic forecasts of the rate of return on investments in the project will also tip them toward accepting worse terms from financiers to get the project over the top.

First, as implied in the just previous discussion, entrepreneurs' expectations of the nonpecuniary rewards from entrepreneurial labor and their expectations of the pecuniary rewards from their own capital investment in the project matter for the volume of entrepreneurial activity – that is, the volume of projects started – not just financiers' expectations. My own macro models would then lead to the corollary that that the expectations of both actors matter for the determination of total business activity, as measured by total employment. To be definite, improved expectations of entrepreneurial job satisfaction would operate to increase the number of entrepreneurs supplied to the market (i.e., the fair). And the acceptance wage would presumably shift down. The "incidence" would include a reduced pecuniary wage and an increased volume of entrepreneuring. (Note that an optimal contract between entrepreneur and financier will reflect any difference of optimism between entrepreneur and financier. Standard contract theory implicitly posits that the parties to a contract share the identical "rational expectations," since they have the identical model of the world. Work in that vein does not fit in a theory of capitalist economies, in which views are never homogeneous and may be wildly diverse.)

An increase in the expected pecuniary reward, which is the expected entrepreneur's wage after any concessions made to obtain financing, is not exactly analogous to an increase in the nonpecuniary reward. But an increase in pecuniary reward net of the concessions, meaning a decrease of the necessary concessions, is analogous. If the market for innovations becomes stronger, so that entrepreneurs need to offer a smaller concession to draw financing, that would increase the number of entrepreneurs supplied.

Second, the wealth of entrepreneurs and that of financiers also matter for the level of entrepreneurial activity and as a consequence for total business activity. If the size of the concessions that some or all entrepreneurs would be willing to make upon sensing that their project was turning out to be marginal are a "normal good," so that a given entrepreneur would have a lower supply price (or reservation reward) the wealthier he is, an increase of his wealth operates to shift outward (and downward) the supply curve of entrepreneurs willing to develop projects at any given price or reward; on this account, taken alone, the increased wealth would expand the number of projects offered to the market and thus the number started up. On the other hand, greater wealth could have the opposite effect of reducing the zeal of the potential entrepreneur to gamble on coming up with a project bringing big nonpecuniary or pecuniary reward.

Moreover, the same increase in wealth could shift up the acceptance price, since the wealthier entrepreneur can better afford to wait, which operates to reduce the number of projects started up in our equilibrium model. So the end result of higher wealth among entrepreneurs is in doubt on two counts. But what is noteworthy is the implication that increased wealth could deter innovation by making potential entrepreneurs less keen and make those who do develop projects more choosy about the deal.

An increase in the wealth of financiers or of the depositors who invest in the venture-capital and hedge funds run by the financiers may boost the demand for entrepreneurial projects, that is, boost the supply of finance. My long-time collaborator Hian Teck Hoon points out that if the economy is coming off an innovation-based boom in which a generation of entrepreneurs have made a great deal of money, that may boost the supply of finance to the next generation of entrepreneurs.

The modeling and the statistical investigation by Aghion, Howitt, and associates proposes a somewhat similar yet distinct hypothesis: The credit worthiness, or credit line, that an entrepreneur has may be roughly proportional to the entrepreneur's wealth. That mechanism leads the authors to the theoretical implication that increased wealth is positive for entrepreneurial development activity and the resulting rate of innovation.[50] The statistical findings in recent papers support their hypothesis. But it remains to be seen whether increased wealth in the wealthy economies promotes innovation. (But see discussion below involving incentive-type contracts.) In any case, the framework here by itself poses a potential conflict between wealth's effect on the supply of projects, which is potentially negative, and its effects on the demand, which is presumably positive. Provisionally, I incline to see wealth in relation to wage rates as, on balance, a drag on entrepreneurial projects, especially start-up projects, in part because such a drag may be one of the few mechanisms governing a country's rate of innovation. A plausible hypothesis, for example, is that activity rates of all kinds, including rates of entrepreneurial activity, wane as wealth climbs relative to wage rates. Whether the U.S. record in the past half-dozen years is an important outlier for that hypothesis remains to be determined.

Third, there is the implication that a country's economic culture may play a part in the determination of the volume and quality of entrepreneurial activity. The inclination of would-be entrepreneurs to avoid non-entrepreneurial jobs in the production of already existing consumer goods in favor of entrepreneurial jobs in the development of new goods causes a

---

[50] See, e.g., Aghion et al., 2005.

contraction of the supply of consumer goods and an expansion of the supply of entrepreneurial projects (with corresponding effects on interest rates and wealth accumulation). Hence, it is not obviously bad economics to admit the possibility that some economies, for example those in western continental Europe, suffer low entrepreneurial activity not solely because of costly impediments to entry and so on or poor financial institutions but because they have a low level of "entrepreneurial spirit." (The possibility this is so does not mean it is so, of course.) Furthermore, there is the possibility of variability through time in the strength of this spirit, even wide mood swings.[51]

The "spirit" of financiers also comes in as an influence on the valuation that a financier puts on a potential entrepreneurial project. Here, of course, the financiers' willingness to endure Knightian uncertainty is important. That does not mean, though, that low share prices, for example, are a sure sign of high aversion to uncertainty. The question is the demand price at some reference level of the innovation volume, possibly measured in persons engaged in innovational activity. One has to estimate and compare across countries the demand schedules for innovation. A low demand in the schedule sense may be the result of a culture hostile to innovation. Or it may instead be evidence of economic institutions adverse to innovation.

Last, the framework is compatible with influences from existing economic institutions. Obviously, hindrances to entrepreneurs will translate into lower forecasts of the profitability of available entrepreneurial projects and thus curtail the number of projects receiving finance. Institutional inefficiencies and deficiencies clearly also have an impact on the demand curve for innovations.

3.2.5. The Structuring of Innovation Finance

I want to touch on another aspect of the interaction of partially ignorant financiers with entrepreneurs bearing new projects – the sort of contract between entrepreneur and financier that would create suitable incentives for the entrepreneur in the present context where the financier faces the ambiguity of what the entrepreneur is able and willing to explain. Would a suitable contract entail bond financing by the venture capitalist or other financier? Or, say, convertible preferred stock? Or what? Relatedly, do contracts that provide a suitable "incentive reward" have the effect that "incentive wages" have in the labor market – namely, to lead to better

---

[51] Two examples are Wiener, 1982, and Olson, 1982.

incentives though at the cost of creating an equilibrium at non-market-clearing terms? This is part of the work that Max Amarante and I are currently doing.

Tentatively, it appears that complete reliance neither on convertible preferred stock nor on debt finance nor on a combination of the two can perfectly align the interests of the entrepreneur and the financier. An optimal contract is not knowable in an exact way. But maybe the features possessed by an optimal contract, in very simple settings at any rate, could be deduced.

It is also beginning to appear that, from the point of view of incentive theory, the lead financier can be expected to offer the entrepreneur incentive arrangements not offset by a compensated decrease of the entrepreneur's salary. Can it be formally argued that financiers drive up the terms of the standard contract in an attempt to give the entrepreneur something to lose if his estimated efforts or acumen are found deficient, which makes financing more expensive than is portrayed in a neoclassical (Fisher-Tobin-type) theory, so that there will be fewer entrepreneurs financed per financier and in toto? The answer would seem to be yes, generally speaking, insofar as the incentive arrangements are a second-best deterrent to the entrepreneur's self-dealing in ways that are difficult or impossible to "monitor" or detect.[52] (But I would add that the presence of performance-related bonuses does not necessarily lead to a failure of the market for entrepreneurs to "clear," just as the practice of paying according to output ("piecework") does not lead to involuntary unemployment.)

Regarding incentive-compatible contracts, it should be remarked that they create a channel through which the entrepreneur's wealth works in the opposite way to what was suggested earlier: The wealthier the entrepreneur, the harder it is for financiers to motivate him to make a highly stressful level of effort and to incentivize him not to engage in self-dealing. This incentive consideration, taken alone, operates to make entrepreneurial activity decrease with increased wealth in the hands of entrepreneurs. A similar effect from an adverse economic culture could result.

3.3. Economic Performance: The Role of Innovative Activity

Two propositions appear to be implicit in most recent commentary. First, a sort of triad of features – an abundance of new entrepreneurial ideas,

---

[52] There is an argument to that effect in Phelps (1985). See also theoretical modeling to this end in work by Joseph Stiglitz.

entrepreneurs capable (often in partnership with financiers) of providing suitable development of their ideas, and a pluralism of financiers with a background sufficient to make a good selection of ideas and entrepreneurs for backing – is central to innovation and thus to high economic perform- ance. Second, shortcomings or barriers in some or all of these respects lie at the heart of the unsatisfactory performance characteristics that the western Continent's economies are widely inferred to have. I subscribe to both propositions. Yet we need to be clearer about what we mean by economic performance and why a country's economy must be structured for inno- vative activity – particularly innovation by indigenous innovators – to be a high-performance economy.

The extent of an economy's performance capabilities and the satisfactory use of its capabilities are two quite separate concepts. A high-performance car may be used just to go down the street for groceries. Analogously, a high- performance economy may be largely devoted to – some might say wasted on – the provision of social insurance and social assistance; an economy may be a very poor performer yet an exemplar of free-market principles, includ- ing the austerity of its entitlement programs, if any. The distinction is between choosing a bad point on the frontier and having a bad frontier of points to choose among.

The valuable capabilities that an economy may possess to one degree or another – the capabilities described by the economy's frontier – are several, of course. In advanced economies, a good prospect of surviving long enough to have a meaningful life is obtainable at such a small cost that we can skip over that and go to the capabilities that are more costly – capabilities without which survival might not be valued much. Of huge importance, I believe, is the economy's capability of providing people prospects of careers generating mental stimulation, intellectual challenge, problem solving, and maybe the exercise of creativity, thus prospects of personal development (self-realization) and various attainments (independence, recognition, and pride in earning one's way). This philosophy of life, by the way, is sometimes called vitalism, which runs from Aristotle to Cervantes to William James and Henri Bergson.[53] There are other capabilities, of course. The productivity that labor and capital support is also an important capability even in an advanced economy. High productivity is to be preferred to lower productivity in part because increases in income have valuable uses but also because increases in the wage rate across the economy help workers to afford to opt for the more

[53] Phelps, 2007.

engaging and rewarding jobs. Another capability is the freedom and the means to find and take preferred employment opportunities, which translates into rights to enter, to be free of licenses and fees, to be permitted to hold property and to accumulate wealth. Yet another capability is the degree of security from destitution, which involves the provision of private or social insurance arrangements. An increase in one capability would generally permit nationals through substitution to "take out" the gain in the form of enjoying more of every capability. But a capability might require some factor of production specific to that capability, so that the abundance of the other capabilities will not help in providing that capability.

A thesis of mine is that if an economy's capability in providing rewarding work is to go from some barely adequate level to a level out of which can come substantial personal development and attainment, the economy needs the dynamism to generate a sufficient flow of innovations. Further, a well-functioning capitalist system possesses the dynamism to generate adequate innovation: Capitalism's dynamism – the abundance of the entrepreneurial ideas it stimulates, the diligence with which entrepreneurs are motivated to develop their ideas, and the acumen of a pluralism of financiers in selecting the ideas for backing – generates successive entrepreneurial ideas that serve to provide mental stimulation in the workplace, to pose new problems to be solved, and thus to open the way to self-realization and gratification. (Of course, not every job can be exciting and fascinating, but virtually all jobs are more engaging and challenging in relatively capitalist economies than in the others – from the Continent's corporatism to the earlier socialism of Eastern Europe.)

The vitalist quality of the workplace in a country and even the innovativeness of the economy creating it, if they are present, cannot be easily observed and measured. But various statistics can be interpreted as signs of the quality of business life: the labor force participation rates of men and of women, the quit rate of employees and the unemployment rate, the length of the work week and number of vacation days, and the level of hourly productivity (adjusted where needed for low-skilled persons excluded from employment). Some other indicators may constitute circumstantial evidence of engaging and rewarding work or the dearth of it: a high saving rate, a low retirement age, and a relationship between employees and employers that seldom breaks out into open conflict. In short, ample vitalist rewards and challenges in the workplace and thus the dynamism that fuels them leave markers that add up to a visible sense of prosperity or flourishing.[54]

---

[54] This was the main theme in Phelps, 2006.

So my thesis leads me to interpret the data in western continental Europe – preponderantly high unemployment rates, low labor force participation rates, short work weeks, and somewhat low productivity relative to the United States (and some other comparators, including Ireland, Australia, the United Kingdom, and Canada) – as evidence of relatively poor economic performance in a fundamental dimension: an insufficiency of stimulation, engagement, and intellectual challenge in the workplace. And, in my thesis, this deficiency can in turn be laid to an insufficiency of innovation. The latter also affects performance in another dimension: relative productivity. This interpretation of the Continent's apparently unsatisfactory state requires defense, however.

Proponents of the supply-side interpretation argue that it is the "excess burdens" of the welfare system on the Continent that largely accounts for its relatively low employment and the dearth of enterprising spirit among potential innovators. They blame the Continent's increased unemployment and its failure fully to catch up on the ill-effects of the Continent's social model, which expanded enormously in the 1970s and 1980s, rather than on the economic model – the economic system (institutions and culture) in the terminology here. By the late 1980s Richard Layard and Stephen Nickell were contending that the increased unemployment rates were simply the result of huge replacement ratios that had come to be built into unemployment compensation programs. I myself showed in my 1994 book *Structural Slumps* that increases in the tax rate on labor, thus cuts in the after-tax real wage rate, had distributed-lag effects on the unemployment rate and in a 1997 paper found some evidence in U.S. time series for believing that the level of the welfare state might make a difference.[55] But I subsequently noticed that some evidence brought up by Robert Mundell, in the form of a cross-section scatter diagram of the OECD economies, was pretty thin. A look at such data in 1998 and a further analysis in 2004 made me skeptical that the welfare state was the main culprit in the low employment on the Continent.[56] So for some years I have attributed the Continent's poorly performing system far less to its social model than to its economic model.[57] The near-stagnation striking several continental economies,

[55] Phelps and Zoega, 1997.
[56] Phelps and Zoega, 1998, 1994.
[57] This thesis was first stated and developed to some extent in Phelps, 2002, and broadened somewhat to include economic culture in a keynote speech, "The Continent's High Unemployment: Possible Institutional Causes and Some Evidence," Conference on Unemployment in Europe, CESifo, Munich, December 2002.

one after the other, over the past ten years has only strengthened my conviction.

Some opposing the dynamism thesis say that the Continent's economic performance is not inferior to that in the United States whether or not the Continent's dynamism is less. They deny that a wide comparison of economic performance would favor the United States and they suggest that if dynamism should be found relatively deficient on the Continent, that would only show that dynamism is not very important for high performance. They point to particular uses of the economy to which they are partial, such as extensive provisions for protection of the environment and for the economic security of the poor and the aged. They also point to high levels of saving and wealth. But the perceptions, such as mine, of relatively poor economic performance on the Continent are focused on nonpecuniary rewards from jobs, employment, wages, and productivity. And there cannot be much doubt that the Continent as a whole is inferior on that score to the fifty states of the Union as a whole.[58]

Some other opponents of the dynamism thesis say that the Continent's dynamism is not inferior to that in the United States whether or not the Continent's economic performance is poorer. They deny that the evidence over the sweep of history points to a deficiency of dynamism on the Continent. They point to the era previous to the Continent's slump – the "glorious years" from the mid-1950s to the mid-1970s – when West Germany and France, later Italy and some of the smaller economies, experienced a great spurt in productivity and an accompanying surge of employment, dubbed the "economic miracle." But does that prove that the Continent's economic system is dynamic now – no less than the U.S. system? Or dynamic then?

In an opinion concurring with the dynamism thesis on its main point yet different from my formulation, the late Mancur Olson argued that the Continent was fairly dynamic then, thanks to the war, which wrested the

---

[58] Those with long memories might observe that over the century as a whole continental unemployment was not worse than in the United States. It is a fact that in the 1930s, when depression tendencies were worldwide, the Continent did a better job at combating unemployment than the United States did. But the poorer record of the United States in that respect was almost certainly not inherent in the nature of the contrasts between the Continental and the U.S. economic systems. The United States could have greatly moderated the rise of unemployment through a monetary policy that avoided a deep deflation early in the decade and refrained from industrial policies that must have had a chilling effect on entrepreneurs' spirits in the second half of the decade. Similarly, the Continent's better record on unemployment appears also to have owed much to its more vigorous public works rather than any immunity of its economic system to double-digit unemployment rates.

economy from the paralyzing grip of entrenched monopolies and old wealth, and to such liberal reformers as Ludwig Erhard and Luigi Einaudi, who were favored over the postwar socialists and communists. In Olson's view, though, the Continent gradually lost its dynamism in ensuing decades as powerful unions and monopolies retook power.[59] I have to pass over his argument here.

I take the simpler position, of which Herbert Giersch was perhaps the leading forerunner. In my view, the Continental economies have never been dynamic – not since sometime in the 1920s. How then to reconcile the Continent's rapid productivity growth with a dearth of dynamism? I argue that in the Continent's glorious years the spurt of productivity and wages was fueled by the abundant stock of new methods and products overseas – mostly innovations made in the United States; once the war was over and the rails and bricks were put back together, the Continental economies with at least some amount of financial resources and some spread of university education could copy or adapt at little or no cost the U.S. goods and methods. Yet as more and more of the low-hanging fruit was picked, the growth rate of continental productivity was bound to slow more and more until it had sunk back to the growth rate in the United States. Moreover, the stock of private wealth, which had not kept up with wages when they were rising rapidly, grew to a normal level relative to wages once wages were again rising slowly, with the result that employees became more demanding and employer costs increased. Also, investing in training, marketing, and plants had to be cut, with the result that many jobs were lost. Unemployment rates were forced up, leveling off only in the mid-1980s. Thus the continental economies stood revealed as seriously lacking in dynamism after all. (They eked out some more productivity gains vis-à-vis the United States until the early 1990s, but the impression of a dearth of dynamism was largely confirmed.)

This explanation does not persuade all economists. Many remember the glorious years as full of continental innovation – endogenous, thus Schumpeterian, and indigenous, not borrowed innovation from overseas. Some recall the innovators who grew famous in Italy and France in the 1950s and 1960s, such as Dior, Gucci, de Laurentis, Pinin Farina, and a few others. It seems to these observers that the Continental system must have been "dynamic," otherwise these innovators would not have

---

[59] Mancur Olson, *The Rise and Decline of Nations* (New Haven: Yale University Press, 1983). I do not recall seeing any suggestion in his later writing that there was or might have been a rebirth of dynamism later on.

been on the stage; and if the institutions are much the same now, it is surely the case that the Continent still possesses dynamism: the premature halt to the productivity catch-up and the stubborn elevation of unemployment can only be the result of something else, such as a deterioration of economic prospects – demographic or technological. Yet this conventional impression is ripe for re-examination. First, it is striking that the great entrepreneurial figures just mentioned were nearly all confined to a handful of industries in what was a large and diversified economy, mainly design and cinema. And the successful innovations in the other industries during that period, such as Chanel and Dassault, started up in the 1930s, so they do not bespeak of an Olsonian postwar dynamism.[60]

Another reply I would make refers again to wealth levels. The wavelet of innovation peculiar to the glorious years was the result of a dearth of wealth in the 1950s and the 1960s relative to wages, which spurred many entrepreneurs to venture on new ways that might succeed in rebuilding their wealth, which a few managed to find. By the 1980s, when ample wealth-wage ratios were again widespread among Italians, Germans, and the French, there were few entrepreneurial types hungry enough to want to battle the system for a place to try out their new ideas; or they had come up with no ideas, knowing how fruitless it would be to have a new commercial idea. In this argument of mine, more wealth meant fewer would-be entrepreneurs; that argument does not contradict the earlier hypothesis that more wealth also made each given entrepreneur more able to afford to make a concession to financiers in order to do the project he or she had set sights on. Vastly more wealth across the population by the 1970s and 1980s meant that more young people entering the university or the labor force aimed to be "entrepreneurs" in the political world, high society, and the arts, where they would spend part of their wealth, not add appreciably to it by going into business. (In Thomas Mann's *Buddenbrooks*, if I remember correctly, those inheriting a fortune from their father did not have the same drive nor the same gifts for business that their father had and went into other pursuits; and the grandchildren went still farther afield.) Although the managerial positions were undiminished and had to be filled somehow, often by reaching down to a lower economic or social status, the number of entrepreneurial positions simply shrank. Perhaps the influx into the United States of immigrants who, with wealth levels generally far below the national average, were eager to

---

[60] See Jestaz, 2005.

replenish the stock of entrepreneurs has given this country a huge advantage over the continental nations, whose borders have been almost closed until relatively recently.

Let me sum up my interpretation of the bearing of the continental experience on the connection of performance, particularly the more vitalist elements of performance, to economic dynamism: The slowdown that developed on the Continent in the late 1970s was widely thought to be the initial descent toward a soft landing onto some path that be might be equivalent or superior to the path on which the more capitalist economies were following. But it was beginning to be apparent by the late 1980s that the Continent's future was to run a steady second place behind the innovative pace setter – its workplace duller than the American, hence its labor force participation lower and unemployment higher, and its productivity level a respectful distance behind the U.S. level. As it turned out, the Continent's catch-up with the United States in productivity terms came to an abrupt halt in the early 1990s, when U.S. productivity growth picked up – leaving hourly productivity noticeably lower than in the United States. In the mid-1990s, unemployment rates were also generally higher on the Continent and labor force participation rates generally lower than in the United States and the United Kingdom.

It should not have been puzzling that this performance was lackluster. The relative performance of France, Germany, and Italy in the previous normal period – the 1920s – was worse. Even in the abnormal period of the 1930s, the growth rate productivity in the United States continued its record-setting pace, which the continental economies were unable to match. Evidently the "high years" of continental innovations that stretched into the first decade of the twentieth century could not survive the changes to the economic system that came into place in the interwar period and were largely retained and further articulated after World War II. Between one century and the next there was a system shift.

Since the mid-1990s, an economic decline of sorts has set in as growth rates of hourly productivity dropped far below the U.S. rates: first the Netherlands in 1996, then Germany in 1998, next Spain in 1999, and then France and Italy in 2001. Unemployment rates, which had fallen for a time in the 1990s, were generally up again (Italy and Spain excepted) in 2005 and higher than in 1995, while in the United States the reverse has happened. The premature end of the catch-up turned into a serious falling-back, which has still not come to a halt.

The question is, then, what are the main sources of the poor performance characteristics and thus the relatively poor dynamism found in most if not all the Continental economies – compared with the United States and possibly other comparators?

What I have come to in the past couple of years is a speculative hypothesis that, while still speculative, is a more refined view than I held until a few years ago:[61] It is very difficult to find a unique "smoking gun" in the form of some particularly deadly economic institution or subset of economic institutions – in corporate governance, in finance, in regulation, and so forth – that could account for the relative dearth of dynamism on the Continent. Research aimed at weighing the total influence of those institutions must go on and I will be active in contributing to that. Yet we must widen our net.

It is necessary, I believe, to give more weight to economic culture than I was prepared to do in previous years as recently as 2002 and 2003. The explanation modified thesis is that the Continent (and to some extent the United Kingdom too) is in the grip of a culture hostile to enterprise and innovation. But I will leave the development of these thoughts for another occasion.

3.4. Concluding Remarks

The ongoing research I have discussed is aimed at modeling capitalism along the modern (or modernist) lines proposed at various times by Knight, Keynes, Hayek, and M. Polanyí – and inevitably Schumpeter, though many of his concepts remained unnaturally classical. In the modern theory, business participants hit upon new commercial ideas inspired in large part by their specialized knowledge and idiosyncratic experience. Those interested in becoming entrepreneurs implementing their idea must first invest the time required to prepare a case for presentation to potential financiers. At the innovation market, or "fair," the entrepreneurs supplied to the market compete for an experienced financier to provide financing and advice on their project, and the financiers try to match up with a likeminded entrepreneur through interviews and the offer of a contract. A match between entrepreneur and financier permits them to develop the entrepreneur's new idea. If that development is successful, the innovation is launched and marketed in an attempt to win early acceptance and rapid spread of the new product or service or organization among potential users, either producers or consumers. An unsuccessful innovation is one that is shelved owing to insufficient prospects for demand, although the

---

[61] I focused on economic institutions in the previous decade. See Phelps, 2002.

idea and its development will perhaps be retained for a time by some in the economy. A successful innovation is one that finds a demand among users sufficient to warrant putting the innovation into regular production. Through time, understanding of the attractions of the innovation may diffuse through the market, causing the demand to widen. Such an innovation may ultimately earn a pure profit, also known as an economic profit, or instead a pure loss, or economic loss.

Thus capitalism is seen as a system for producing and using new ideas, and these ideas could in principle be represented as new models of the economy (or a piece of it). Some new models succeed in establishing themselves at least for a time, while others fail. The innovation process thus produces an accumulation of models, which we could imagine reaching some steady-state level, though the current extant models have the property that they have driven out previous models. One of the obstacles to a "model" of the capitalist system has been the difficulty of conceiving how financiers are able and willing to back entrepreneurial projects when, as is generally the case, these financiers can have little idea of what the true prospects of profitability are. In Section 3.2 of this chapter I provided a sketch of a model that offers a way out of that problem – whether or not it is the only way or the best way.

There is the strong possibility that the current assortment of models being applied in the production sector is preferable to the previous assortment, given existing tastes and scientific knowledge. However, for active-age people in economically advanced countries it is the process – the stimulation, problem solving, and personal development that comes out of the creation, development, marketing, pioneering use, and learning experienced by those who are engaged in the production and use of the innovation – that may provide the greater part of the benefit to the economy's participants. So the dynamism generated by the innovation process does not have to produce faster growth than produced by all fundamentally different systems for the innovations of a capitalist, thus an entrepreneurial economy, to be essential for rewarding careers.

References

Aghion, Philippe, Peter Howitt, and David Mayer-Foulkes. 2005. "The Effect of Financial Development on Convergence [of the Productivity Growth Rate]: Theory and Evidence." *Quarterly Journal of Economics*, 120, 173–223.

Baumol, William J. 2002. *The Free-Market Innovation Machine: Analyzing the Growth Miracle of Capitalism.* Princeton: Princeton University Press.

Bhidé, Amar V. 2000. *The Origin and Evolution of New Businesses*. Oxford: Oxford University Press.

Cassel, Gustav. 1924. *Theory of the Social Economy*. New York: Harcourt, Brace and World, 622.

Dreyfus, Hubert, L. 1979. *What Computers Still Can't Do: A Critique of Artificial Reason*. Cambridge, Mass.: MIT Press.

Friedman, Milton. 1962. *Capitalism and Freedom*. Chicago: University of Chicago Press.

Frydman, Roman, and Michael Goldberg. 2007. *Imperfect Knowledge Economics: Exchange Rates and Risk*. Princeton: Princeton University Press.

Frydman, Roman, Marek Hessel, and Andrzej Rapaczynski. 2000. "Why Ownership Matters: Entrepreneurship and the Restructuring of Enterprises in Central Europe."*C.V. Starr Center for Applied Economics*. New York University, Working Paper 00–03.

Hansen, Alvin. 1951. *Business Cycles and National Income*. New York: W.W. Norton.

Hayek, Friedrich A. 1935a. *Collectivist Economic Planning: Critical Studies on the Possibilities of Socialism*. London: George Routledge.

Hayek, Friedrich A. 1935b. "Socialist Calculation II: The State of the Debate." In *Collectivist Economic Planning*. London: George Routledge.

Hayek, Friedrich A. 1945. "The Use of Knowledge in Society." *American Economic Review*, 35(4), 519–530.

Hayek, Friedrich A. 1948. *Individualism and Economic Order*. Chicago: University of Chicago Press.

Hayek, Friedrich A. 1961. "The Non Sequitur of the Dependence Effect." *Southern Economic Journal*, 27.

Hayek, Friedrich A. 1978. "Competition as a Discovery Procedure." In *New Studies in Philosophy, Politics, Economics and the History of Ideas*. Chicago: University of Chicago Press, 179–190.

Jacobs, Jane. 1961. *The Death and Life of Great American Cities*. New York: Vintage Books.

Jestaz, David. 2005. "Reflexions sur le modele francais." Manuscript, Alliance Program, Columbia University, July.

Keynes, John M. 1921. *A Treatise on Probability*. London: Macmillan.

Keynes, John M. 1936. *The General Theory of Employment, Interest and Money*. London: Macmillan.

Keynes, John M. 1937. "The General Theory of Employment."*Quarterly Journal of Economics*, 51(2).

Klein, Gary. 1998., *Sources of Power: How People Make Decisions*. Cambridge, Mass.: MIT Press.

Knight, Frank H. 1921. *Risk, Uncertainty and Profit*. New York: Houghton Mifflin, 19–20.

Mises, Ludwig Edler von. 1936. *Socialism: An Economic and Sociological Analysis*. London: Jonathan Cape.

Nelson, Richard R., and Thomas Marschak. 1962. "Flexibility, Uncertainty and Economic Theory." *Metroeconomica*, 14, 42–58.

Nelson, Richard R., and Edmund S. Phelps. 1966. "Investment in Humans, Technological Diffusion and Economic Growth." *American Economic Review*, 56(1–2) 69–75.

Nelson, Richard R., and Sidney Winter. 1982. *An Evolutionary Theory of Economic Change*. Cambridge, Mass.: Harvard University Press.

Oakeshott, Michael. 1962. *Rationalism in Politics*. New York: Basic Books.

Olson, Mancur. 1982. *The Rise and Decline of Nations*. Yale University Press.

Phelps, Edmund S. 1985. *Political Economy: An Introductory Text*. Norton.

Phelps, Edmund S. 1999. "Lessons from the Corporatist Crisis in Some Asian Nations." *Journal of Policy Modeling*, 21(3), 331–339.

Phelps, Edmund S. 2000. "Europe's Stony Grounds for the Seeds of Growth." *Financial Times*, August 9, 2000.

Phelps, Edmund S. 2002. *Enterprise and Inclusion in Italy*. Dordrecht: Kluwer.

Phelps, Edmund S. 2006. "The Continent's High Unemployment: Possible Institutional Causes and Some Evidence," Keynote Lecture, Conference on Unemployment in Europe, CESifo. In Martin Werding (ed.), *Structural Unemployment in Western Europe: Reasons and Remedies*. Cambridge, Mass.: MIT Press, 53–74.

Phelps, Edmund S. 2007. "The Economic Performance of Nations: Prosperity Depends on Dynamism, Dynamism on Institutions." Conference on Entrepreneurship, Innovation and the Growth Mechanism of the Free-Market Economies, November 2003. In Eytan Sheshinski, ed., *The Growth Mechanism of Free Enterprise Economies*. Princeton: Princeton University Press.

Phelps, Edmund S., and Gylfie Zoega. 1994. "Searching for Routes to Better Economic Performance." *Forum*, CESifo.

Phelps, Edmund S., and Gylfie Zoega. 1997. "The Rise and Downward Trend of the Unemployment Rate in the U.S." *American Economic Review*, 87(2), 283–289.

Phelps, Edmund S., and Gylfie Zoega. 1998. "Natural-Rate Theory and OECD Unemployment." *The Economic Journal*, 108(448), 782–801.

Phelps, Edmund S., and Gylfie Zoega. 2001. "Structural Booms." *Economic Policy*, 16(32), 83–126.

Polanyí, Michael. 1962. *Personal Knowledge*. Chicago: University of Chicago Press.

Schumpeter, Joseph A. 1934 (1911). *The Theory of Economic Development*. Cambridge: Harvard University Press.

Schumpeter, Joseph A. 1939. *Business Cycles: A Theoretical, Historical, and Statistical Analysis of the Capitalist Process*. New York: McGraw-Hill.

Schumpeter, Joseph A. 1942. *Capitalism, Socialism and Democracy*. New York: Harper and Brothers.

Scott, James C. 1998. *Seeing like a State*. New Haven: Yale University Press.

Spiethoff, Arthur. 1903. *Jahrbuch für Gesetzgebung, Verwaltung und Volkswirtschaft*.

Stiglitz, Joseph E. 1994. *Whither Socialism?* Cambridge, Mass.: MIT Press.

Wiener, Martin. 1982. *English Culture and the Decline of the Industrial Spirit*. Cambridge: University Press.

4

Advance of Total Factor Productivity from Entrepreneurial Innovations

Paul A. Samuelson

Joseph Schumpeter (1883–1950), my Harvard mentor, won early fame for his 1911 *Theory of Economic Development*. However, during the fifteen years I was his Cambridge neighbor, it was Maynard Keynes (1883–1946) who, by general agreement, earned the reputation of being the greatest economist of the twentieth century. The primary reason for this was that the great global depression of 1929–1935 desperately needed a new macro paradigm like Keynes's 1936 *General Theory*.

I believe there was a grain of truth in the innuendo that Schumpeter experienced some scholarly jealousy of Keynes's celebrity. Like the entrepreneurs he praised, Schumpeter possessed a competitive personality. Because the Muse of History has an ironic sense of humor, now in the twenty-first century, Schumpeter's fame (and his citation frequency) exceeds anything he enjoyed during his lifetime, including my colleagues here who cite him authoritatively in their explorations of entrepreneurship.

It would be useful for the few surviving members of the Schumpeter Circle to record the evolutionary nuances of change in Schumpeter's own late-in-life thinking. For example, when first in September 1935 I entered his Harvard Yard graduate classroom, Schumpeter was still stressing *youthful* innovators. He then seemed to doubt that a General Electric or a Bell System Laboratory could succeed in staying at the frontier of technical and know-how discovery. But later, contemporary economic history converted him to the view that the great oligopolies of the Fortune 500 corporations deserved most credit for progress in mid-twentieth-century total factor productivity.

Has the Muse of History once again pulled the rug out from under human prophets? During World War II and its aftermath, public spending – at the Pentagon, Office of Naval Research, RAND, NIH, NSF, and so on – spawned the Silicon Valley's and Route 128's decentralized high- and low-tech venture-capital innovative firms. It was not so long ago that academic acquaintances when inventing new technology received (and expected to receive) nought in the way of monetary remuneration.

That was then, and now is now. Paradoxically, the Fortune 500 has become a revolving door bereft of much of the former oligopoly powers that it once had to share with militant trade unions. The credit or blame for that traces much to the miracle post-1950 imitative export-led growth spurts of the European Union, Japan, Hong Kong, South Korea, and Taiwan. Outside of public government employment, every union "victory" was actually a pyrrhic defeat that only accelerated the advent of global production outsourcing and factor price equalization.

No one predicted this revolutionary geography tilt toward factor price equalizations in either the *Economic Journal* or the *American Economic Review* before 1950.

Probably, scholars will write much about the role of individual innovators for this conference hosted by the Max Planck Institute of Economics and the Kauffman Foundation for Entrepreneurs. I hope and expect that there will also be recognition of *group* contributions to scientific and engineering discovery. In my limited space here, I will mostly address the evolution of economists' thinking about how "total factor productivity" grew historically and is likely to continue to grow. Society's interest in entrepreneurial innovation centers on what it does and can continue to do to enhance *total* factor productivity and thereby real standards of living. Economic history reveals that real wages are driven upward by improved technical and know-how productivity. This truth does not deny that sometimes it is owners of property rather than owners of labor who benefit the most from improving total factor productivity.

4.1. Thumbnail Sketches of Economists' Grappling with Technical Change

Modern economics can be said to go back to the Scottish Enlightenment of 1750–1850. Before and after Adam Smith's *Wealth of Nations* (1776), economic scholars were somewhat obsessed by the "law of diminishing returns." That is why Thomas Carlyle, no economist, called political economy "the dismal science." Robert Malthus (1799) epitomized this fear of diminishing returns, even before the 1812 formalized defining of that classical returns law by West, Malthus and Ricardo.

The sweep of post-A.D. 1000 economic history undergoes a sea change around 1700. For reasons not yet fully understood, China's average level of technical productivity exceeded that in Europe around 1000 A.D. Just why China's real growth subsequently fell behind that of Europe is not clear. Such change in economic fortune is not unheard of; countries in the cradle of civilization are (except for the luck of oil wells) in the lower ranks of the Penn Tables of National Per Capita Well-being (purchasing power corrected).

By 1450 it was probably the Dutch who enjoyed the greatest per capita real income, due much to their post-Columbus New World colonies. Only after what I like to call the epoch after Newton did Britain surpass the Dutch in enjoying the globe's highest per capita real income. Then, around 1900, America, Britain's one-time colony, swept past its motherland in average individual affluence.

During that same Bismarck era, Germany sought energetically to become Britain's equal. Certainly it was the outburst of scientific creativity in Wilhelmine universities that helped propel Germany into comparability to the United States and the United Kingdom. Indeed, the number of Nobel Prizes awarded to Germans between 1901 and 1933 was substantial; this number fell after Hitler came to power and has yet to return to prewar levels.

4.2. The Age of Scientific Discovery

More important than China's relative decline or the declines of the Dutch and the British is one striking fact about the documentable productivity wage rates of A.D. 1250 to 2006. Successive editions of Samuelson's introductory economics textbook contained perhaps the most interesting and most important graph of historical real wage growth in western Europe. (See, e.g., Samuelson-Nordhaus, 1995, p. 669, Figure 32.2.) Its story is striking.

Prior to 1700, wages *merely oscillate trendlessly*. A "little ice age" would show a general drop in Britain's real wages, followed by a recovery. But after 1700 – the post-Newton era – the march of science mandated a steady rise in real wages per capita, strongest in Western Europe but discernible elsewhere globally. This has to be interpreted as both result and cause of entrepreneurial know-how and practice. In the Darwinian historical record, it stands out as a new thing under the sun. Yes, Malthus had been right to worry about diminishing returns due to excessive human fertility.[1]

Paradoxically, the classical economists of the 1750–1870 period were slow to understand their own industrial revolution. Adam Smith's excellent library was light on books describing major advances in steam, iron, steel, and coal, plows, and horse harnesses – to say nothing of contemporaneous inventions in textile spinning and weaving. Smith rightly discussed how the divisions of labor could expedite pin manufacture manifold times. Of course, it was the seeming triviality of the pin that added his example's drama.

Science and industrial practice were in a two-way interaction. As has been said, Watt's steam engine did as much for the science of thermodynamic heat as science did for Watts. The same was to happen again and again: Faraday's lab findings about magnetism and electricity generated power manufacturing. High-tech nineteenth-century industry fertilized post-Faraday inventors such as Maxwell, Hertz, and Marconi.

John Stuart Mill (1806–1873), in the middle of the Victorian nineteenth century, could nevertheless still come to false results, such as "it is doubtful whether invention has ever lightened the burden of the working classes." This from Mill, the wisest of the Enlightenment's philosophers. Stanly Jevons (1835–1882), a brilliant polymath, despaired that the coal mines of Britain would soon decline.

By contrast with the pessimism of Malthus, Mill, and Jevons, Karl Marx went to the opposite extreme. In their revolutionary 1848 *Communist Manifesto*, Marx and Engels proclaimed that all human kind could *already* enjoy a good standard of living if only the capitalists' market system could be abolished. Workers allegedly had nought to lose but their chains. Technical know-how could allegedly run itself; this at a time when nineteenth-century life expectancies were less than half of those in 2006.

The duel between innovation and diminishing returns is a never-ending one. Environments are limiting and fragile. What once were rich stores of Minnesota ores and Texas oils are now depleted. Moreover, science itself creates some new perils, perils that can be ameliorated only with new scientific and engineering discoveries.

In Schumpeter's view an Edison or a Pasteur made possible Henry Fords and J. Pierpont Morgans who can organize successful new products and

---

[1] Charles Darwin reported that reading the economist Malthus had provided him with the "Eureka" moment when he realized how evolution by competitive natural selection had to be the key to biological understanding. But if Malthus had looked out his library windows he would already have seen powerful trends toward increasing productivity trends.

services. Wal-mart's Sam Walton is in the Schumpeter Hall of Fame. Even the avid imitators, who brought, by stealth, spinning and weaving to New England or who import from Detroit to Nagoya the arts of auto-making are, to the 1912 Schumpeter, heroes.

4.3. Technical Economic Paradigms

I fast forward in time to Senator Paul Douglas (1892–1976), onetime professor at the University of Chicago, my alma mater, who received the prestigious Hart Schaffner Prize for his statistical measurements of early twentieth-century macro production functions. Douglas (1934) compiled a time series of total U.S. labor supply. He also built up, by statistical estimate, a time series of "capital" – plants and equipment, for example. Using official aggregate U.S. production index data for the same sample time span, Douglas used simple regression correlation methodology, and came up with the formula:

U.S. Production Q is the following mathematical function of U.S. Labor L and U.S. "capital," K:

$$Q_t = 1.01 L_t^{75} K_t^{25}, \quad 1899 < t < 1922 \tag{1}$$

Douglas was audacious. Douglas was applauded. Also Douglas was criticized. If Nobel Prizes in economics had existed then, Douglas probably would have won one during my 1933–1934 junior year on the Chicago Midway.

I skip over many important debates. For example, L_t and K_t moved so closely together in this sample period, that a relationship like $\beta L^{1/2} K^{1/2}$ or $\beta L^{3/4} K^{1/4}$ could have given a goodness-of-fit coefficient only a bit lower than those Douglas reported.

When I left Chicago to enter Harvard's post-1935 graduate school, inevitably my new teacher Schumpeter lectured critically on the Douglas breakthrough. I paraphrase Schumpeter thus:

It is almost a *reductio ad absurdum* to ignore those vital changes that were going on in the first third of the twentieth century. Ford's assembly line. Truck competition to the railroads. Urban and rural electrification. Clearly $F[L_t, K_t]$ ought to have been replaced by $F[L_t, K_t; t]$ so that $F[L_{1922}, K_{1922}; 1922]$ would be materially greater than $F[L_{1899}, K_{1899}; 1899]$ even when the input pairs of $F[L_{1899}, K_{1899}]$ and $F[L_{1922}, K_{1922}]$ had not been too far apart.

Dynamic sciences advance by testing and correcting themselves. After the mid-1950s Robert Solow of Harvard and later MIT won a Nobel Prize by generalizing and correcting Douglas's pioneering efforts. Using cross-sectional data on wages and capital returns, Solow (1957) improved on Douglas's simple estimation regressions by bringing in yearly data on profit/wages sharing. Now for the 1909-1949 timespan Solow modified Douglas's earlier $bL^{3/4}K^{1/4}$ by the kind of exponential growth factor that Schumpeter had been looking for. Here is Solow's new approximation:

$$Q_t = (1.015)^t L_t^{5/8} K_t^{3/8} \qquad (2)$$

The factor $(1.015)^t$, representing 1.5% per year growth in total factor productivity, Solow called the innovational "residual." He reminded us contemporary economists that, as important as growth in (K/L) is to boost real productivity wage rates, so too is the residual that traces to innovations in know-how and practice. This "residual," Solow proclaimed, demonstrated that much of post-Newtonian enhanced real income had to be attributed to innovational change (rather than, as Douglas believed, being due to "deepening" of the capital/labor K/L ratio).

This is part of the reason why the 1912 Schumpeter came to be vindicated in the economic literature of the last half century.

Despite the divergent views of Malthus, Mill, Schumpeter, or Solow, if the Max Planck Institute and the Kauffman Foundation on Entrepreneurship were to nominate an honor roll for scholars who advanced our understanding of entrepreneurship, *all* their above names would deserve to be included in that Pantheon.[2]

4.4. Postwar Convergent Trends of Regional Factor Price Returns

All my above words about a single country's production apply as well to postwar 1950 economies intimately engaged in foreign exports and imports. Already, prior to Douglas or Solow, the Swedish economists Eli Heckscher (1879–1952) and Bertil Ohlin (1899–1979) discussed how and why the exchange of goods between different countries could diminish (or even wipe out) differences in their wage and profit returns much the same way that migration of people do.

When Japan's educatable low-wage population imitatively borrowed American and European know-how, it transformed its poor Asian society

---

[2] The cream of the jest is that the same Mill who belittled past inventions did in his classic 1848 *Principles* sketch a progressing society that depended not at all on net accumulation of saved capital. The funds to replace old capital could go into improved tools, and so forth, ad infinitum.

via export-led growth into a progressive advanced economy. Most economists were too slow to apprehend how globalization would be the leitmotif of the last half century.

Am I writing about the past economic history? Yes. But my words apply as well to the coming half-century, from 2006 to 2056. Just as South Korea or Taiwan or Singapore could follow in Japan's footsteps, two billion people in China and India will be able to do so too.

Not all will be sweetness and light. Schumpeter spoke of "creative capitalist destruction." Competitive market systems have no mind and no heart. Often when technical innovations expand *mean* or *average* real incomes, at the same time they may widen the gap between rich and poor – that is, between those blessed with energy, education, cleverness, and early family support versus those who by whatever combination of nature and nurture were condemned to a lower quality of life.

In addition, science's enhanced harvest of present-day globalized plenty contributes to air and water pollution, to future exhaustion of non-renewable resources, and perhaps even to terrorism and guerrilla warfare.

Going beyond factual and objective logic and empirical knowledge, we ought to remind ourselves that science itself offers us more than enough in new enlarged resources for democratic communities to be able to tackle successfully programs to limit ecological deterioration and political anarchy.

4.5. Conclusion

To sum up, economics and humanity have need for both a Keynes and a Schumpeter. Creative capital destruction can be limited by means of humane mixed economy transfers to the losers from those who are winners. Laissez-faire, by itself, will not and cannot heal the most grievous wounds of inequality that globalization will entail.

In democracies it is the voters' choices that must count. If the dynamic forces that accelerate globalized growth do, at the same time, erode electorates' feeling of altruism, then what both Schumpeter and Keynes helped to contribute – accelerated real growth and less unstable business cycles – will unequally bless our future progeny.

References

Douglas, Paul H. 1934. *The Theory of Wages.* New York: Macmillan.

Heckscher, Eli. 1919. "Effects of Foreign Trade on Distribution of Income."*Ekonomisk Tidskrift.* Reprinted in H. S. Ellis and L. Metzler, eds., *Readings in the Theory of International Trade.* Philadelphia: Blakiston, 1949.

Jevons, William S. 1865. *The Coal Question*. London: Macmillan.

Keynes, John M. 1936. "The General Theory of Employment, Interest and Money." Reprinted in The Collected Writings of John Maynard Keynes, vol. 7. London: Macmillan for the Royal Economic Society.

Maddison, Angus. 1991. *Dynamic Forces in Capitalist Development: A Long-Run Comparative View*. Oxford and New York: Oxford University Press.

Maddison, Angus. 2003. *The World Economy: Historical Statistics*. Paris: OECD.

Malthus, Thomas R. 1789. *An Essay on the Principle of Population*. Reprint. London: Macmillan, 1926.

Marx, Karl H., and Friedrich Engels. 1848. Manifest der Kommunistischen Partei. Translated into English as *Manifesto of the Communist Party*. New York: International Publishers, 1948.

Mill, John Stuart. 1848. *Principles of Political Economy, with Some of Their Applications to Social Philosophy*. London: John W. Parker.

Ohlin, Bertil G. 1933. *Interregional and International Trade*. Cambridge, Mass.: Harvard University Press.

Samuelson, Paul A. 1949. "International Factor-Price Equalization Once Again." *Economic Journal*, 59, 181–197.

Samuelson, Paul A., and William D. Nordhaus. 1995. *Economics*, 18th ed. New York: McGraw-Hill/Irwin.

Schumpeter, Joseph A. 1943 (1911). *The Theory of Economic Development*. Cambridge: Harvard University Press.

Smith, Adam. 1776. *An Inquiry into the Nature and Causes of the Wealth of Nations*. E. Cannan, ed. New York: Modern Library, 1937.

Solow, Robert M. 1957. "Technical Change and the Aggregate Production Function." *Review of Economic Statistics*, 39, 312–320.

5

Silicon Valley, a Chip off the Old Detroit Bloc

Steven Klepper

5.1. Introduction

Silicon Valley is the envy of the world, one of the most celebrated regions of economic growth in modern history. We are accustomed to thinking of it as the outgrowth of a unique confluence of ingredients. One is its roots as an early incubator of now famous electronics firms, including Hewlett Packard, Varian Associates, and Litton Industries. Another is Stanford University, led by its innovative dean of engineering and eventual provost, Frederick Terman. Yet another is its culture of vertically specialized, non-hierarchically organized firms that define a virtual network of producers. Couple all these ingredients with the growth of the semiconductor industry and the emergence of venture capitalists in Silicon Valley to support it and you get a seemingly unprecedented wave of new, spinoff enterprises in Silicon Valley formed by top employees of incumbent semiconductor firms. Today, these Silicon Valley semiconductor spinoffs are legion, including such famous firms as Fairchild Semiconductor, National Semiconductor, Advanced Micro Devices (AMD), and Intel. Indeed, according to a well-known genealogy prepared by Semiconductor Equipment and Materials International (SEMI), over 100 semiconductor spinoffs arose in Silicon Valley through 1986. Nearly all of them were descended in one way or another from Fairchild, whose direct descendants are so numerous they have been dubbed the Fairchildren.

Many have heralded these semiconductor spinoffs as representing a new form of industry and regional development. Charles Sporck, the head of

I thank Rosemarie Ziedonis for sharing longitudinal data she compiled on the sales of semiconductor producers. Joon Hwan Choi provided excellent research assistance. Support is gratefully acknowledged from the Economics Program of the National Science Foundation.

manufacturing at Fairchild during its formative era and later founder and leader of National Semiconductor, titled his recent book *Spinoff* to convey the importance of this new phenomenon. In his article on "The Splintering of the Solid-State Electronics Industry," Nilo Lindgren (1971), a senior fellow at *Innovation* magazine, was so taken by the spinoff phenomenon in semiconductors that he speculated whether it defined a whole new type of high-technology enterprise never before seen. In a recent co-authored article entitled "Learning the Silicon Valley Way," Gordon Moore, one of the traitorous eight that founded Fairchild and later went on to co-found Intel, similarly opined that "the central element in the history of Silicon Valley is the founding of a previously unknown type of regional, dynamic, high-technology economy" (Moore and Davis, 2004, p. 7) fueled by semiconductor spinoffs and entrepreneurs' willingness to pursue innovative activity, something that defines them as noted in Chapter 1.

While there is widespread agreement about the importance of semiconductor spinoffs in the emergence of Silicon Valley, there is less agreement on the circumstances that gave rise to the spinoff phenomenon. In her well-known comparison of the evolution of Silicon Valley and Route 128, AnnaLee Saxenian (1994) sees all the ingredients listed above as important contributors to the spinoff-led growth of Silicon Valley. Her views are echoed by Christopher Lécuyer (2006) in his recent book on the roots of Silicon Valley. On the other hand, Moore and Davis (2004) downgrade the importance of factors such as Stanford and Hewlett Packard and say little about the importance of a Silicon Valley culture shaped by vertically specialized, less hierarchically organized firms that Saxenian celebrates. Everyone seems to agree, though, that Silicon Valley represents a new entrepreneurial phenomenon driven by spinoffs.

It will be argued that Silicon Valley is *not* at all a new phenomenon, and recognizing this provides insights into how agglomerations like Silicon Valley emerge. Silicon Valley appears to be *sui generis* because we know little about how the geographic structure of new industries evolves. Recent work on the historical automobile industry by Klepper (2007) suggests, however, that the evolution of the auto industry around Detroit bears an uncanny resemblance to the evolution of the semiconductor industry around Silicon Valley. This is noteworthy because the automobile industry defined the Fordist method of production that is depicted as the antithesis of the "Silicon Valley way." Detroit also lacked an analog to Stanford, and while it had its share of machine shops and carriage producers, it was hardly the place the automobile industry might have been expected to flourish. Moreover, Klepper (2007) contends that the success of the

Detroit firms was confined to the spinoffs that entered there, suggesting that it was the spinoff phenomenon and not agglomeration economies that drove the agglomeration of the automobile industry around Detroit. In the parlance of Moore and Davis (2004), the lesson from Detroit is that the conditions necessary for the emergence of Silicon Valley may have been remarkably simple, albeit rare.

The argument is developed as follows. In Section 5.2, the evolution of the semiconductor industry is reviewed. Using early market share data compiled by Tilton (1971) coupled with annual data on the sales of larger merchant North American semiconductor producers from 1974 to 2002 compiled by Integrated Circuit Engineering (ICE), a private consulting firm, the role of spinoffs in the agglomeration of the semiconductor industry in Silicon Valley is traced. In Section 5.3, the spinoff process in the semiconductor industry is dissected. Various sources, including the Silicon Valley genealogy prepared by SEMI, are used to identify the spinoffs of the producers on the ICE list. Analyses are conducted of the rate at which firms spawned spinoffs and the performance of the spinoffs. The impetus for the leading spinoffs is also discussed. In Sections 5.4 and 5.5, comparable analyses of the evolution of the automobile industry and its spinoffs are conducted. In Section 5.6, parallels between the semiconductor and automobile industries are discussed and implications are drawn for how agglomerations emerge and the role that public policy can play in furthering the process.

5.2. Evolution of the Semiconductor Industry and Its Agglomeration in Silicon Valley

Semiconductor diodes and rectifiers were sold before World War II, but the transistor effectively started the semiconductor industry. It was invented in 1948 by three Bell Lab scientists, including William Shockley, who later founded the first semiconductor firm in Silicon Valley, Shockley Laboratories. Under antitrust pressure, AT&T, Bell's parent, agreed to produce transistors only for its own needs – that is, to be a captive producer. It liberally licensed its patents and held symposia to diffuse transistor technology to other firms, which led many firms to enter the merchant (i.e., non-captive) market. Tilton (1971, p. 66) presents data on the market share of the leading merchant semiconductor producers in the early years of 1957, 1960, 1963, and 1966. This is supplemented in Table 5-1 with market share data from the ICE listing for 1975, 1980, 1985, and 1990 for firms that were among the top ten producers in any of these years and also for the leaders in the earlier years.

Steven Klepper

Table 5-1. *Market shares of leading North American merchant producers,*
1957–1990

Receiving tube firms	Entry year[a]	Metropolitan location	57	60	63	66	75	80	85	90
General Electric	1951	Syracuse, NY	9	8	8	8	C	C	C	C
RCA	1951	Camden, NJ	6	7	5	7	4	3	2	
Raytheon	1951	Boston, MA	5	4	–	–	1	1	1	0.5
Sylvania	1953	New York, NY	4	3	–	–				
Westinghouse	1953	Philadelphia, PA	2	6	4	5	C	C	C	C
Philco-Ford	1954	Elmira, NY	3	6	4	3				
Other early leaders										
Texas Instruments	1953	Dallas, TX	20	20	18	17	20	19	18	15
Transitron	1953	Boston, MA	12	9	3	3	0.5			
TRW	1954	Los Angeles, CA	–	–	4	–	C	C	C	C
Hughes	1955	Los Angeles, CA	11	5	–	–	C	C	C	C
General Instrument	1955	Long Island, NY	–	–	–	4	3	2	1	0.5
Delco Radio (GM)	1956	Kokomo, IN	–	–	–	4	C	C	C	C
Motorola	1958[b]	Phoenix, AZ	–	5	10	12	8	11	13	17
Fairchild	1958	Mountain View, CA	–	5	9	13	9	7	5	A
Later leaders										
Signetics	1961	Sunnyvale, CA			–	–	5	6	5	
Analog Devices	1965	Boston, MA				–	1	1	2	2
AMI	1966	Santa Clara, CA				–	4	2	1	1
National	1967	Santa Clara, CA					10	11	10	9
Harris	1967	Melbourne, FL					2	3	3	4
Intel	1968	Santa Clara, CA					7	10	10	17
AMD	1969	Sunnyvale, CA					2	5	7	6
Mostek	1969	Dallas, TX					2	6	A	
Micron Technology	1978	Boise, ID						–	0.5	2
VLSI Technology	1979	San Jose, CA						–	1	2
LSI Logic	1980	Milpitas, CA						–	2	3
Silicon Valley Share										
Leading firms[c]			0	5	9	13	38	42	42	38
Leaders + other ICE firms[c]							43	48	49	47

– Firm was producer, but no market share data reported

Notes: C: captive producer in the listing of Integrated Circuit Engineering (ICE); A: acquired by a semiconductor producer.

[a] Dates for receiving tube firms and early leaders based on Tilton (1971).

[b] According to Tilton (1971), Motorola used semiconductors only for its own purposes before 1958.

[c] Includes Raytheon, which was based in Silicon Valley as of 1975.

Sources: See Tilton (1971) for sources for 1957, 1960, 1963, and 1966 market share data; the 1975, 1980, 1985, and 1990 market shares are based on annual compilations of ICE.

The transistor substituted for the vacuum tube in many applications. Consequently, many of the early leaders, including General Electric, RCA, Raytheon, and Sylvania, were producers of vacuum tubes and other electronics products. Most of the other leaders were also established electronics producers, including Motorola, TRW, Hughes, General Instrument, and Delco Radio. Texas Instruments (TI) was also an electronics producer, but younger and smaller than the others. Among the early leaders, only Transitron and Fairchild were new firms. Transitron was founded by two brothers, one of whom had worked at Bell Labs. Fairchild, which was the second firm in Silicon Valley, was formed by the traitorous eight employees of Shockley Laboratories, an example of entrepreneurial behavior in action.

Before the entry of Fairchild, semiconductor production was concentrated in three centers: Boston, New York, and Los Angeles. Tilton (1971, pp. 52–53) presents a list of transistor producers during the period 1951–1968, and a similar list was compiled for 1952–1980 from annual listings of transistor producers in *Thomas' Register of American Manufacturers*. Among the leaders of the industry in 1957, *Thomas' Register* listed Raytheon and Transitron in the Boston area, Sylvania and General Instrument in the New York area, and Hughes and TRW in Los Angeles. Each area also had a contingent of lesser but significant firms listed, including Hytron/CBS, Clevite, Sprague, Unitrode, and Crystalonics in the Boston area; Tung Sol, Industro Transistor, and Silicon Transistor in the New York area; and Nucleonic and Hoffman in Los Angeles. The other significant producer as of 1957 was TI, which was located in Dallas, Texas. Early semiconductors were produced from germanium, but germanium had many limitations and was eventually replaced by silicon in nearly all semiconductor devices. TI was the first producer of silicon transistors in 1954, which gave it a two- to three-year lead over its competitors that enabled it to become the industry leader with 20 percent of the market as of 1957 (Tilton, 1971, p. 65).

Prior to the entry of Fairchild, production of semiconductors in Silicon Valley was negligible. William Shockley located his firm in Silicon Valley, where he was reared, but he was a dysfunctional manager and Shockley Laboratories was not successful. Shockley was a brilliant scientist and an excellent judge of talent, however, and Fairchild was successful immediately. Along with TI, Fairchild pioneered the development of silicon transistors. It invented the planar manufacturing process, which eventually was adopted by all semiconductor producers. It also developed the integrated circuit (IC) along with TI, and was the first to produce ICs using the planar process. By 1960 Fairchild had captured 5 percent of the market, which grew to 13 percent as of 1966 with the growth in sales of ICs.[1] The other major successful firm in this era was Motorola, which based its semiconductor production in Phoenix, Arizona. Initially it produced semiconductors for its own use but then entered the merchant market around 1958 by capitalizing on developments at TI and Fairchild. It captured 5 percent of the market by 1960, which increased to 12 percent as of 1966.

Fairchild was the first spinoff in Silicon Valley and the origin of many subsequent spinoffs. The Silicon Valley genealogy compiled by SEMI was used to identify the semiconductor spinoffs in Silicon Valley, which are defined as semiconductor producers founded by employees of other semiconductor firms.[2] All of the founders of each spinoff are listed in the geneaology. The parent of each spinoff was defined as the prior employer of the first listed founder.

According to the Silicon Valley genealogy, the first spinoff in Silicon Valley after Fairchild was Rheem, which was formed in 1959 by employees of Hughes and Fairchild. Two years later it was acquired by Raytheon. The next two spinoffs in Silicon Valley were Signetics and Amelco, both of which were spinoffs of Fairchild. Seven more spinoffs entered in Silicon Valley between 1962 and 1966, including two from Fairchild. The spinoff rate then increased sharply. Three were founded in 1967, eleven in 1968, and nine in 1969. Eight of these 23 spinoffs came out of Fairchild, including National Semiconductor, Intel, and AMD, all of which became leading producers. Over the next six years through 1975 an additional 26 semiconductor producers, nearly all spinoffs, entered in Silicon Valley, including four more from Fairchild.

---

[1] In the same year, Fairchild was estimated to account for 30% of the IC market (Lécuyer, 2006, p. 249).

[2] Most of the spinoffs were new firms, but a few were organized as new subsidiaries of nonsemiconductor firms or involved a reconstitution of existing semiconductor firms in which the new "founders" were given an ownership interest. Fairchild, for example, was financed by and became a subsidiary of Fairchild Camera and Instrument, a Long Island military contractor. National Semiconductor was an example of a reconstituted firm. It was founded in Connecticut in 1959 but by 1967 was floundering, and it brought in Charles Sporck, the head of manufacturing at Fairchild, to reconstitute its efforts in Silicon Valley, effectively giving birth to a new firm. Following general practice, National was classified as a spinoff of Fairchild. MOS Technology represents a similar occurrence. It was originally founded by an employee of General Instrument and two others to produce calculator chips in Norristown, Pennsylvania. It was transformed into a producer of microprocessors after eight employees from Motorola joined it to develop a low-cost alternative to Motorola's initial microprocessor. Accordingly, MOS Technology was classified as a spinoff of Motorola.

Table 5-1 reflects the dramatic effect of the spinoffs on the agglomeration of the semiconductor industry in Silicon Valley through 1975. Fairchild was the only leading semiconductor producer based in Silicon Valley in 1966, and it accounted for 13 percent of the market. By 1975 the share of the market accounted for by the leading Silicon Valley semiconductor firms had increased to 38 percent and the joint market share of all the Silicon Valley producers on the ICE list was 43 percent. Of the eight firms that ascended to the ranks of the leaders in 1975, six were spinoffs of merchant producers. Five of them were located in Silicon Valley, including Signetics, National, Intel, and AMD, all Fairchild spinoffs, and AMI, which was a second-generation spinoff of Fairchild. The other leading spinoff, Mostek, came out of TI and was established in the Dallas area.[3] The success of the spinoffs largely came at the expense of the tube producers and diversified electronics firms, a number of which retreated into captive production.[4] The main exceptions were TI and Motorola, which remained leading producers.

After 1975 the entry of spinoffs in Silicon Valley declined for a few years and then picked up again in the 1980s. Between 1980 and 1986, which is the last year of the Silicon Valley genealogy, 49 firms entered, nearly all spinoffs. Table 5-1 indicates that this did not lead to a major change in the joint market share of the Silicon Valley firms, which increased by just a few percentage points and then topped out in 1985 at 49 percent. Three firms, all spinoffs – one from Fairchild (LSI Logic), another descended from Fairchild (VLSI Technology), and a third from Mostek (Micron Technology) – made it into the ranks of the leaders in the 1980s. However, none of these firms captured a market share of over 3 percent. Intel and secondarily AMD increased their market shares, while Fairchild, weakened by the numerous employees that had defected to found their own firms, declined and was eventually acquired by National in 1987. The other leaders, including TI, Motorola, and National, maintained their market shares.

In total, over 100 firms entered the semiconductor industry in Silicon Valley between 1957 and 1986, nearly all of which were spinoffs. Together

---

[3] The other two new leaders in 1975 were Analog Devices, which was located in the Boston area, and Harris, which produced semiconductors in Melbourne, Florida. The founder of Analog had previously started another firm in the Boston area, and before that had worked for Hewlett Packard in Silicon Valley. Harris was a diversified electronics firm.

[4] The other firm that declined sharply was Transitron. Apparently it did little R&D (Braun and MacDonald, 1978, p. 71), which soon caused it to fall behind the other leaders of the industry and eventually exit in 1986.

the Silicon Valley spinoffs captured nearly 50 percent of the market,[5] and the population of Silicon Valley (Santa Clara County) grew tremendously, increasing from 642,315 in 1960 to 1,295,071 in 1980 (Scott and Angel, 1987, p. 891). Outside Silicon Valley, spinoffs were less prominent. Among the 101 merchant producers on the ICE listings that entered by 1986, the backgrounds of 92 of them could be traced.[6] Fifty-six of the 92 were located in Silicon Valley, and 53 of these were spinoffs. In contrast, only 15 of the 36 located outside Silicon Valley were spinoffs, and many of the leaders outside Silicon Valley, such as TI, Motorola, RCA, Harris, and General Instrument, were not spinoffs. Thus, consistent with all observers, spinoffs were particularly a Silicon Valley phenomenon, and they were key to the agglomeration of the semiconductor industry there.

5.3. Spinoff Analysis

Greater insight can be developed concerning the spinoff process by analyzing which firms spawned spinoffs, the location of parents and their spinoffs, the relationship between the performance of spinoffs and their parents, and the primary reasons the leading spinoffs were formed.

5.3.1. Fertility and Location

Brittain and Freeman (1986) conducted one of the earliest studies of spinoffs, using an early version of the Silicon Valley genealogy to analyze the factors influencing the rate at which Silicon Valley semiconductor producers spawned spinoffs. Updating and expanding to encompass non-Silicon Valley firms, the data from the ICE listings were used to analyze the rate at which all 101 merchant producers on the ICE listings spawned spinoffs through 1986, the last year of the Silicon Valley genealogy. Based on the 92 ICE producers whose heritages could be traced, the spinoffs of each of the 101 merchant producers were identified. For the Silicon Valley firms, the

---

[5]   The share of semiconductor production that actually took place in Silicon Valley was considerably smaller than 50%. The leading Silicon Valley firms established production sites outside Silicon Valley and assembled components in other parts of the world to save on labor costs. Most of the captive producers were also located outside Silicon Valley, and they produced a large volume of semiconductors, led by IBM, which produced more semiconductors than any of the merchant producers in the 1970s and 1980s.

[6]   Nearly all the Silicon Valley firms could be traced from the Silicon Valley genealogy. Numerous sources were used to track the other firms, including the Web site www. antiquetech.com, which was particularly helpful. Spinoffs and their founders were defined using the same criteria that were applied to the Silicon Valley firms.

Silicon Valley genealogy was also used to identify their spinoffs that did not make it onto the ICE listings (because they were too small or entered before 1974). Thus, the list of spinoffs for the Silicon Valley firms is comprehensive,[7] whereas the list for the non-Silicon Valley firms is limited to their later and more prominent spinoffs. In total, 91 spinoffs were identified.

Table 5-2 lists the 27 firms that accounted for the 91 spinoffs. They are organized by location, number of spinoffs, and date of entry. For each firm, its total number of spinoffs, the number on the ICE list, and the number that made it into the top 20 ICE producers in one or more years are recorded, as is whether the firm itself made it into the top 20 ICE producers in one or more years.

Clearly, Fairchild stands out with 24 spinoffs. Its spinoff National also stands out with nine spinoffs. The next two most prolific parents, Intel and Signetics with six and five spinoffs, respectively, are spinoffs of Fairchild. Intersil, with four spinoffs, was not a spinoff of Fairchild, but was founded by one of the founders of Fairchild (who had previously founded two other spinoffs). Thus, it is immediately evident how influential Fairchild was in the formation of spinoffs. More generally, the top semiconductor firms dominated the spinoff process. Seventeen of the 27 parents were top 20 producers and collectively spawned 73 of the 91 spinoffs.

To convey the annual rate at which firms spawned spinoffs, a firm's total number of spinoffs is divided by the total number of years it produced semiconductors through 1986. Entry and exit years could be determined for 99 of the 101 producers on the ICE list, and among these 99 firms, 43 made it into the top 20 producers in one or more years. These 43 firms collectively produced for 695 years and the other 56 firms collectively produced for 510 years. Therefore, the annual rate at which firms spawned spinoffs was $73/695 = 0.105$ for top 20 firms and $18/510 = 0.035$ for other firms. These fractions are significantly different at the 0.01 level, as will be true for most of the comparisons reported below, and subsequently only comparisons *not* significantly different at the 0.05 level will be noted. Restricting this comparison to Silicon Valley firms (for which the listing of spinoffs is comprehensive), the analogous rates are $61/374 = 0.163$ and $18/245 = 0.073$. Thus, for each year they produced, the top 20 firms were two to three times as likely as the other firms to spawn spinoffs. Clearly, much of this differential is due to Fairchild and its 24 spinoffs. But looking

---

[7] The only spinoffs of the Silicon Valley firms that would not have been identified are those that located outside Silicon Valley and did not make it onto the ICE listings. Judging, however, from the tendency of spinoffs of Silicon Valley firms to locate in Silicon Valley, as discussed below, few spinoffs of Silicon Valley firms are likely to have been missed.

Table 5-2. *Spinoffs of merchant semiconductor producers*

Firm	Years (through 1986)	Number of spinoffs	Number of ICE spinoffs	Number of top 20 spinoffs	Top 20 firms
Silicon Valley producers					
Fairchild	1957–1986	24	14	7	Y
National	1967–1986	9	4	1	Y
Intel	1968–1986	6	6	2	Y
Signetics	1961–	5	2	1	Y
Intersil	1967	4	2	0	Y
Synertek	1973	4	3	1	Y
Semi Processes	1975	4	1	0	
AMI	1966	3	2	0	Y
AMCC	1979	3	2	1	
Seeq	1981	3	3	1	
Amelco	1961	2	0	0	Y
Micro Power	1971	2	1	0	
Raytheon/Rheem	1961	1	0	0	Y
Siliconix	1963	1	0	0	Y
Avantek	1965	1	0	0	
AMD	1969	1	1	1	Y
Exar	1971	1	1	0	
Cal-tex	1971	1	0	0	
Nitron	1972	1	0	0	
Zilog	1974	1	1	1	Y
Supertex	1976	1	0	0	
Exel	1983	1	0	0	
Non-Silicon Valley producers					
General Instrument	1960–1986	4	2	0	Y
Texas Instruments	1952–1986	3	3	2	Y
Motorola	1958–1986	2	2	1	Y
Mostek	1969	2	2	2	Y
RCA	1950–1986	1	1	0	Y

outside Silicon Valley, the annual spinoff rate was also markedly higher for the leading firms: $12/321 = 0.038$ for top 20 firms versus $0/265 = 0$ for the non-top 20 firms.

Multiple factors could explain the greater fertility of the leading producers. One is their greater size, which means they had more employees who could potentially found spinoffs. Indeed, on average the top 20 firms were well over 10 times larger than the other firms, hence they actually had a lower annual spinoff rate relative to their size than other firms. The significance of this, though, is unclear. Founders of spinoffs tended to be high-level employees, including a number of individuals who founded multiple spinoffs. If employees need high-level experience to profitably start their own firm, then it is not clear whether larger firms have more potential spinoff founders, because they surely do not have proportionately more potential spinoff founders, than other firms. One explanation for the greater fertility rate of top firms is that they have superior employees who are more likely to be able to found profitable spinoffs. Another possibility is that better firms provide superior environments for their employees to gain the organizational knowledge needed to form a profitable spinoff. These possibilities will be considered further in the analysis of the performance of the spinoffs.

Table 5-2 indicates that Silicon Valley firms dominated the spawning process, accounting for 79 of the 91 spinoffs. Standardizing by the number of years of production, the annual fertility rate of Silicon Valley firms was $79/619 = 0.128$ versus $12/586 = 0.020$ for firms outside Silicon Valley. In part, this difference is due to the more comprehensive identification of spinoffs for the Silicon Valley firms. But considering only the spinoffs that made it onto the ICE listings, the annual fertility rate was $42/619 = 0.068$ for the Silicon Valley firms versus $10/586 = 0.017$ for the firms elsewhere. Excluding Fairchild as an outlier, the Silicon Valley rate is still $28/589 = 0.048$ versus 0.017 for the firms elsewhere. Thus, it appears that Silicon Valley firms were more likely to spawn spinoffs. Restricting further the comparison to top 20 producers to control for firm quality, the fertility rate of the top 20 Silicon Valley producers is $35/374 = 0.094$ versus $10/321 = 0.031$ for the top 20 producers elsewhere. Again excluding Fairchild, the fertility rate of the top 20 Silicon Valley producers of $21/344 = 0.061$ is still nearly twice that of the top 20 producers elsewhere (but not significantly different). Moreover, among the non-top 20 firms, the fertility rate is $8/245 = 0.033$ for Silicon Valley firms versus $0/265 = 0$ for firms elsewhere. Thus, even controlling for firm quality, Silicon Valley firms had a higher fertility rate.

Again, multiple factors may have been at work. One is the blossoming of the venture capital industry in Silicon Valley (see, e.g., Kenney and Florida, 2000), which facilitated the formation of new firms there. Another is a kind of demonstration effect in which successful spinoffs induced others to form spinoffs. Another factor cited by Saxenian (1994) and others is the extent to which semiconductor firms in Silicon Valley were more vertically specialized than semiconductor firms elsewhere (see Scott and Angel, 1987), making it easier for entrants to find suppliers to complement their expertise.

Some insight can be gained about these factors from where spinoffs located vis-à-vis their parents. Most founders located their spinoffs close to home, perhaps for both economic and social reasons. This was especially true of the spinoffs of the Silicon Valley firms, nearly all of which located in Silicon Valley. Four of the 12 spinoffs of non-Silicon Valley firms also located there. Each had roots in Silicon Valley: three had non-primary founders there and the founder of the fourth previously worked for Fairchild. The fact they chose to locate in Silicon Valley is consistent with the greater availability of capital and support for start-ups there.

Most of the other spinoffs of the non-Silicon Valley firms also located close to their parents. Two prominent exceptions, both of which made it into the top 20 producers, were Micron Technology and MOS Technology. Micron, which was a spinoff of Mostek (of Dallas, Texas), was founded in a garage in Boise, Idaho, where it was subsequently able to raise capital. MOS Technology, classified as a spinoff of Motorola (of Phoenix, Arizona),[8] located in Norristown, Pennsylvania, where its "partner" fabricated its chips. On the one hand, these locations are consistent with the availability of capital and support, both abundant in Silicon Valley, being important determinants of the location of producers. On the other hand, they illustrate that it was not necessary to locate in Silicon Valley to gain access to capital or specialized suppliers. Indeed, both TI and Motorola prospered over time despite not being located in Silicon Valley, as did a host of other firms such as Analog Devices and Harris.

Further insight into the spinoff process can be gleaned by examining when firms spawned spinoffs over their lifetime. All of the spinoffs occurred during the semiconductor lifetimes of their parents. Table 5-3 reports the annual fertility rate of firms in consecutive five-year age brackets from ages 1–5 to ages 36–40. When all firms are considered, the fertility rate rises steadily into the 16–20 age bracket and then declines sharply. If the analysis is limited to the 27 firms with one or more spinoffs, as would be the case if fixed effects were used to control for firm differences, the pattern is similar but the fertility rate is much closer for the age brackets 11–15 and 16–20.[9] Similar patterns were found when the tabulations were restricted to firms that survived 15 years or longer. Thus, it appears that firms were more likely to spawn spinoffs at middle age, which occurred somewhere between ages 10 and 20.

---

[8] See note 2 for the origins of MOS Technology.

[9] For the parents, the rise from 6–10 to 11–15 and the fall from 16–20 to 21–25 is significant, whereas for all firms only the rise from 6–10 to 11–15 is significant.

Table 5-3. *Fertility rates by age bracket*

Ages	All firms	All parents
1–5	.040 (18/448)	.134 (18/134)
6–10	.062 (18/292)	.151 (18/119)
11–15	.132 (27/205)	.260 (27/104)
16–20	.162 (20/123)	.263 (20/76)
21–25	.074 (5/69)	.106 (4/47)
26–30	.077 (3/39)	.120 (3/25)
31–35	.000 (0/27)	.000 (0/10)
36–40	.000 (0/9)	.000 (0/2)

One other factor that may have influenced the timing and possibly occurrence of spinoffs is managerial frictions caused by certain types of control changes within firms. Brittain and Freeman (1986) found that spinoffs were more likely among Silicon Valley semiconductor firms after they were acquired by nonsemiconductor firms or appointed a new CEO from outside the firm. Only nine of the 27 parents were acquired, generally toward the end of the period studied, providing little basis to evaluate the effects of acquisitions on the incidence of spinoffs. Comprehensive data on CEO changes were not available to conduct an analysis comparable to Brittain and Freeman's of the effect of CEO changes on the incidence of spinoffs. But the discussion below concerning the impetus for the leading spinoffs will bring out the importance of control changes in the formation of a number of the prominent semiconductor spinoffs.

5.3.2. Performance of Spinoffs

The performance of the spinoffs can be analyzed according to the performance of their parents. Parents are divided into two groups according to whether or not they were top 20 producers. The performance of their spinoffs is measured according to the fraction that made it onto the ICE listings (this can be computed only for the Silicon Valley firms) and the fraction that were top 20 producers. These fractions are reported in Table 5-4.

Overall, the Silicon Valley firms had 43 spinoffs that made it onto the ICE listings out of a total of 79 spinoffs. The likelihood of a spinoff making it onto the ICE listings was modestly higher for the spinoffs of the leading firms: 0.574 of the spinoffs of top 20 producers in Silicon Valley made it onto the ICE listings versus 0.444 of the spinoffs of the other Silicon Valley

Table 5-4. *Performance of spinoffs and their parents*

Firm	% spinoffs on ICE list (Silicon Valley spinoffs only)	% spinoffs in top 20 firms
Top 20	.574 (35/61)	.260 (19/73)
Top 20 minus Fairchild	.568 (21/37)	.245 (12/49)
Other firms	.444 (8/18)	.111 (2/18)

producers (difference not significant). Focusing on the likelihood of spinoffs making it into the top 20 producers, the difference is much starker. Among all top 20 producers (inside and outside Silicon Valley), 19 of their 73 spinoffs, or 0.260, made it into the top 20 producers versus 2 of 18, or 0.111, of the spinoffs of non-top 20 producers (difference not significant). Standardizing by years produced, the annual rate at which firms spawned spinoffs making it into the top 20 producers was $19/695 = 0.027$ for top 20 producers versus $2/510 = 0.004$ for the other producers. Moreover, both of the spinoffs of non-top 20 producers that made it into the top 20 had founders who previously had worked at top 20 producers, which was acknowledged to have contributed to their success (McCreadie and Rice, 1989, p. 32). It would thus appear that having a founder who had worked at a top 20 producer was virtually a necessary condition for a spinoff to become a top 20 producer.

This suggests that better firms had a higher fertility rate not merely because of their greater size but also because their spinoffs were better able to compete in the industry. Multiple factors could account for the superior performance of their spinoffs. One is that better firms may have had superior employees, at least on average, which could help explain their superior performance. Indeed, some of their employees that founded leading spinoffs, such as Andrew Grove, Gordon Moore, Robert Noyce, Jerry Sanders, and Charles Sporck of Fairchild; Wilfred Corrigan, who started at Transitron, rising up through the ranks of Motorola and Fairchild; as well as L. J. Sevin of Texas Instruments, were celebrated entrepreneurial figures in the industry. It may also have been the case that working at a top firm provided distinctive lessons about organizing and competing at the highest levels, as was acknowledged regarding the two spinoffs of the lesser firms that made it into the ranks of the leaders. Either way, it seems likely that the greater fertility rate of the top 20 producers was not merely due to their greater size but also to conditions that enhanced the profitability of their spinoffs.

5.3.3. Origin of the Leading Silicon Valley Spinoffs

Further insight into the agglomeration of the semiconductor industry in Silicon Valley can be gained by tracing the origin of the spinoffs of the Silicon Valley merchant producers that attained the top 20 producers. Table 5-5 summarizes information about the impetus and main source of finance for the top Silicon Valley spinoffs whose origins could be traced.

Firms continually had to make difficult choices about which technologies to develop. Initially it was unclear whether germanium or silicon would be the best material for semiconductors. When ICs were developed, they were initially inferior to circuits composed of discrete devices and potentially infringed upon the markets of semiconductor customers. Metal oxide semiconductor (MOS) devices were slower than early, bipolar circuits and were unstable and difficult to make. Eventually, though, manufacturing problems were overcome and MOS devices proved to be superior for many applications because they enabled many more transistors to be packed onto chips. Similarly, complementary metal oxide semiconductor (CMOS) devices were extremely slow, but their low power needs ultimately facilitated even denser chips. Application-specific ICs (ASICs) initially were not economical, but MOS technology eventually changed that. Linear, or analog, devices, which are used for amplification and other nondigital applications, have always posed distinct technical and market challenges.

Initial technical and market uncertainties over these technologies led to conflicts and spinoffs in many top firms. Fairchild, for example, was formed to pursue the development of silicon transistors after Shockley abandoned this goal in favor of a new device he invented that proved to be difficult to manufacture (Lécuyer, 2006, pp. 131–139). Amelco and Signetics were formed to develop ICs after Fairchild did not pursue them aggressively due to their initial inferior performance and fear of infringing on the markets of their customers (Spork, 2001, p. 70; Lécuyer, 2006, pp. 213–218). Intel was formed in part due to Gordon Moore's frustration with Fairchild's inability to develop MOS products despite being the industry leader in MOS research, which stemmed from the separation of R&D and manufacturing at Fairchild (Bassett, 2002, pp. 172–173). Linear Technology was founded by the head of National's analog division because he felt National treated analog devices as a means of getting into a better business rather than an attractive business of its own (Wilson, 2004). Cypress was formed to exploit CMOS technology after its parent, AMD, and other established firms were not interested in CMOS (Gilder, 1989, p. 143).

Table 5-5. *Origins of leading spinoffs of Silicon Valley producers*

Spinoff	Year	Parent	Reasons	Finance
Fairchild	1957	Shockley Laboratories	Strategic disagreement (silicon transistors), management conflict	Fairchild Camera and Instrument
Amelco	1961	Fairchild	Strategic disagreement (ICs)	Teledyne
Signetics	1961	Fairchild	Strategic disagreement (ICs), management conflict	Investment banks
Electronic Arrays	1967	GME	Management conflict after acquisition by nonsemiconductor firm	N.A.
Intersil	1967	Union Carbide	Compensation practices (stock options), management conflict with nonsemiconductor parent	SSIH and Olivetti
National	1967	Fairchild	Compensation practices (stock options), management conflict with nonsemiconductor parent	National Semiconductor
Intel	1968	Fairchild	Management conflict, technical frustration (MOS)	Venture capital
AMD	1969	Fairchild	Management conflict after CEO hired from outside firm	Minimal capital ($100,000)
Zilog	1974	Intel	Personal tensions	Exxon
VLSI	1979	Synertek	Management conflict after acquisition by nonsemiconductor firm	Venture capital
LSI Logic	1980	Fairchild	Management conflict after acquisition by nonsemiconductor firm	Venture capital
Linear	1981	National	Strategic disagreement (linear circuits)	Venture capital
Cypress	1982	AMD	Strategic disagreement (CMOS)	Venture capital

N.A.: not available.

Another major challenge firms faced was how to compensate innovators and structure their organizations to harness scientific and technical advances for commercial benefit (Moore and Davis, 2004). Early on it was unclear how important stock options would prove to be in rewarding innovators and top managers. It was also unclear whether R&D should be conducted separately from manufacturing, as was common practice in other industries. Conflicts arose over these and related managerial issues, especially when firms were overseen by non-semiconductor firms that had financed or acquired them. Similar tensions arose when new management was brought in from outside the firm.

Many of these conflicts led to spinoffs and ultimately the decline of their parents. Electronic Arrays, for example, was formed after its parent, General Microelectronics was acquired by Philco, which canceled stock options and moved the company from Silicon Valley to Philadelphia (Lécuyer, 2006, p. 263). Within two years, Philco exited the industry. Intersil was similarly formed when its parent, Union Carbide, refused to give its leader stock options (Lécuyer, 2006, pp. 263–264). Union Carbide ended up selling off its semiconductor operation four years later and exiting the industry. The failure of Fairchild to grant more than meager stock options to its leading managers also figured prominently in the formation of National (Sporck, 2001, pp. 207–214; Lécuyer, 2006, pp. 259–261). Other leading spinoffs were formed after changes in top management led to friction and ultimately poor performance in incumbent firms. AMD was founded after Lester Hogan was brought in from Motorola to head Fairchild's parent, bringing new managers with him to run Fairchild (Sporck, 2001, pp. 152–157). Fairchild continued to flounder and was acquired by Schlumberger, a French firm. Schlumberger brought in its own management, which knew little about semiconductors, which led to the departure of Fairchild's CEO, Lester Corrigan, and ultimately the decline and sale of Fairchild to National (Walker and Tersini, 1992, pp. 54–57). Corrigan went on to found LSI Logic to produce ASICs, a market Fairchild had pursued earlier but then abandoned. Similarly, VLSI was formed to produce ASICs after Synertek was acquired by Honeywell, a computer manufacturer that also brought in its own management to run the company (Walker and Tersini, 1992, pp. 184–186, 195–197). Seven years later Honeywell sold Synertek and exited the industry.

The spinoffs were financed predominantly by downstream firms and venture capitalists, many of whom were past employees of successful semiconductor firms. Both had their own, distinctive sources of knowledge that they could draw on to evaluate prospective spinoffs. The leading spinoffs they financed expanded the scope of semiconductor products developed in Silicon Valley and prodded the existing firms to expand their activities. They also compensated for flaws in the way some companies such as Fairchild were designed and provided a safe haven for talented individuals caught in firms dragged down by managers from other cultures. It is especially these roles that have led numerous observers to trumpet the importance of spinoffs in the growth of the semiconductor industry in Silicon Valley (Saxenian, 1994, p. 112; Sporck, 2001, pp. 268–271; Moore and Davis, 2004).

5.4. Evolution of the Automobile Industry and Its Agglomeration in Detroit

The U.S. automobile industry is generally dated as beginning in 1895. Various sources are available to trace entrants into the industry and their backgrounds. Based on Smith (1968), a total of 725 entrants were identified from 1895 to 1966. Smith and the *Standard Catalog of American Cars* (Kimes, 1996) were used to determine the year of entry, year of exit, base location, and heritage of each entrant.[10] Firms with one or more founders who were employees of incumbent automobile firms were classified as spinoffs, which yielded a total of 145 spinoffs. Federal Trade Commission (1939) and Bailey (1971) were used to compute annual market shares of the leading firms, which are reported every five years from 1900 to 1925 in Table 5-6.

Figure 5-1 plots the annual number of entrants, exits, and producers from 1895 to 1966. Entry into the industry was concentrated in its first 15 years. From 1895 to 1900, 69 firms entered, followed by 184 firms in 1901–1905, with entry peaking at 82 in 1907. Entry remained high for the next three years and then dropped to approximately 15 firms per year from 1911 to 1922, after which only 15 firms entered through 1966. The number of firms peaked at 272 in 1909. Subsequently it fell sharply, dropping to 9 in 1941 despite enormous growth in the industry's output. The industry

---

[10] The *Standard Catalog* provides a brief description of the founding of each automobile producer. It was used to identify spinoffs. A firm was classified as a spinoff if one or more of its organizers had previously worked at another automobile producer on Smith's list. Its parent was classified as the last known automobile employer of the most influential founder (in most cases of multiple automobile founders, all of them previously worked for the same firm). See Klepper (2002) for a detailed description of the procedures followed to identify spinoffs and parents and also how acquisitions were handled in defining entrants and exiters.

Table 5-6. *Market shares of leading U.S. automobile firms, 1900–1925*

	Entry year	Entry location	1900	1905	1910	1915	1920	1925
Early entrants								
Pope	1895	Hartford, CT	36					
Stanley	1896	Watertown, MA		2				
Locomobile	1899	Bridgeport, CT	18					
Knox	1900	Springfield, MA	0.3					
Packard	1900	Warren, OH/ Detroit, MI		2	2			1
H. H. Franklin	1900	Syracuse, NY		4				
White Sewing M.	1901	Cleveland, OH	0.02	4				
Olds/GM	1901	Detroit/Lansing, MI		26		1	2	1
Cadillac/GM	1902	Detroit, MI		16	6	2	1	1
Jeffery/Nash	1902	Kenosha, WI		16			2	3
Later entrants								
Studebaker	1902	South Bend, IN			8	5	3	4
Anderson/Union	1902	Anderson, IN			2			
Ford	1903	Detroit, MI		7	18	56	22	44
Maxwell Briscoe/ Maxwell/ Chrysler	1903	Tarrytown, NY/ Detroit, MI		3	6	5	2	4
Buick/GM	1903	Flint, MI		3	17	5	6	5
Willys	1903	Terre Haute, IN			9	10	6	6
Reo	1904	Lansing, MI		4	4	2		
Stoddard	1904	Dayton, OH		1				
E. R. Thomas-Det./ Chrysler	1906	Detroit, MI			4	1		
Brush	1907	Detroit, MI			6			
Oakland/GM	1907	Pontiac, MI			2	1	2	1
Hupp	1909	Detroit, MI			3	1	1	3
Hudson	1909	Detroit, MI			3	1	2	7
Paige-Detroit	1909	Detroit, MI						1
Chevrolet/GM	1911	Flint, MI				1	6	12
Saxon	1913	Detroit, MI				2		
Chandler	1913	Cleveland, OH					2	
Dodge Brothers/ Chrysler	1914	Detroit, MI				5	7	5
Dort	1915	Flint, MI					1	
Durant	1921	New York, NY					3	
Detroit area firms			0	58	65	83	52	85

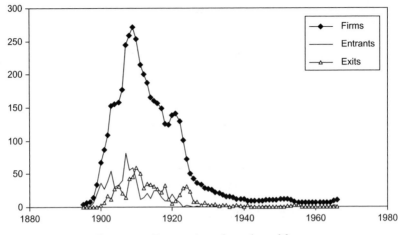

Figure 5-1. Entry, exit, and number of firms.

evolved to be a tight oligopoly dominated by three famous Detroit-based firms, General Motors, Ford, and Chrysler.

Initially the industry had little presence in Detroit. The first 69 entrants from 1895 to 1900 were concentrated in New England, New York, and the Midwest, with no firm entering in the Detroit area, which was defined as the 100-mile radius in Michigan around Detroit.[11] The initial entrants were a mixture of diversifiers and new firms with backgrounds in related industries, especially bicycles, carriages and wagons, and engines. The four leaders in 1900 listed in Table 5-6 are illustrative. Pope, which was located in Hartford, CT, was the leading U.S. producer of bicycles when it diversified into automobiles in 1895. Locomobile, which was located in Bridgeport, Connecticut, was a new firm founded by two successful businessmen. It entered by purchasing the business of the Stanley Brothers, leading producers of steam-powered automobiles located in Watertown, Massachusetts. Knox was a spinoff of another early producer, Overman, located in Springfield, Massachusetts; White Sewing Machine was a leading producer of sewing machines in Cleveland, Ohio, that diversified into automobiles. A number of the other significant early entrants were also located in New England and Cleveland, including Duryea, Stanley

[11] In addition to Detroit, the area includes the following locations in Michigan: Adrian, Chelsea, Flint, Jackson, Marysville, Oxford, Plymouth, Pontiac, Port Huron, Sibley, Wayne, and Ypsilanti. The boundaries of this region were chosen to reflect multiple locations of some of the firms and movements of others within the region.

Silicon Valley, a Chip off the Old Detroit Bloc   99

Brothers, and Waltham in New England and Winton, F. B. Stearns, Baker, and Peerless in Cleveland, making these two areas the early centers of the industry.

Initially, cars were powered by electricity, steam, or gasoline, but the internal combustion engine powered by gasoline began to dominate the industry by the early 1900s, and this provided the entrée for Detroit's rise to the top. The first great producer of a gasoline-powered car was Olds Motor Works, which was a leading engine producer located in Lansing, Michigan, not far from Detroit. Olds began producing automobiles in Lansing and Detroit in 1901. It produced a two-seater car powered by a one-cylinder gasoline engine that became the first big seller in the industry. At its peak in 1905 it produced 6,500 cars and was the leading firm in the industry, capturing 26 percent of the market. Only one of the leaders in 1900, White Sewing Machine, was still a leader of the industry in 1905, but not for long. White and Pope were producers mainly of electric automobiles and Locomobile produced steam-powered cars; the shift to the internal combustion engine hurt all three firms.

Five other firms in the Detroit area also attained the ranks of the leaders in 1905, and collectively the Detroit-area producers accounted for 58 percent of the market. Olds played a key role in the creation of four of these firms. Olds subcontracted all of its parts to local businesses. Its two main subcontractors, Leland and Faulconer and the Dodge Brothers, played a key role in the success of Cadillac and Ford Motor Company, which were the number two and number four firms in 1905. Cadillac was actually founded by Henry Ford in Detroit in 1902, but Henry Leland of Leland and Faulconer was quickly brought in to manage the company after the stockholders lost patience with Ford's slow completion of finished cars. Henry Ford went on to found the Ford Motor Company in Detroit in 1903 with help from the Dodge Brothers, who agreed to produce all of Ford's engines, transmissions, and axles in exchange for 10 percent of Ford's stock. Another one of Olds's subcontractors, Benjamin Briscoe, initially financed Buick, which was the number eight firm in 1905.[12] Reo Motor Car Company, which was tied for fifth place in 1905, was a spinoff of Olds Motor Works. It was founded by Ransom Olds, who headed Olds Motor Works but left after an argument with its top stockholder over how to organize production. Another one of the

---

[12] Buick was not successful, though, until it was taken over by William Durant, who had developed one of the leading carriage and wagon companies in nearby Flint.

leaders in 1905 that was not located in Detroit but would later move there, Maxwell Briscoe, was also descended from Olds Motor Works. It was founded by an ex-Olds employee who had co-founded his own firm, Northern Manufacturing Company, before co-founding Maxwell Briscoe with Benjamin Briscoe.[13]

In the next five years, the share of production accounted for by leading firms in the Detroit area increased to 65 percent largely driven by spinoffs of the leaders. After the departure of Ransom Olds, a number of other Olds employees left to found their own firms, and Olds Motor Works declined and dropped out of the ranks of the leaders by 1910. This was counterbalanced by the success of Ford, itself a spinoff of Cadillac, and five spinoffs from Olds, Cadillac, and Ford that made it into the ranks of the leaders: Brush, E. R. Thomas-Detroit, Hupp, Hudson, and Oakland. The other prominent Detroit-area firm was General Motors, which was formed by William Durant, the head of Buick. It combined 27 firms, including Buick, Cadillac, and Olds.[14]

Spinoffs from the leading firms helped Detroit solidify its position as the capital of the automobile industry, with Detroit-area firms increasing their market share to 83 percent over the next five years. Ford introduced the Model T in 1908, and it was a great success, enabling Ford to increase its market share to an astounding 56 percent by 1915. General Motors was disorganized; its market share declined to 8 percent and its founder, William Durant, was ousted. Durant went on to found Chevrolet, which developed a car to compete with the Model T. It captured 1 percent of the market as of 1915. Two other spinoffs of leading Detroit firms captured significant market shares. The Dodge Brothers severed their relationship with Ford after Ford declined to buy them out and founded their own firm, which by 1915 captured 5 percent of the market. Saxon was formed by the assistant general manager of E. R. Thomas-Detroit (renamed

[13] Outside the Detroit area, the leading firms were mostly experienced producers from other industries. Jeffery had been a leading bicycle producer before selling out its bicycle business and entering automobiles. H. H. Franklin produced die castings, White was a leading sewing machine company, Stoddard produced farm implements, and Packard (née Ohio Automobile Company), which would move to Detroit in 1903, was an electronics producer before entering the automobile industry.

[14] Another one of the leaders, Studebaker, actually produced its cars in Detroit for many years. Studebaker was a leading carriage company based in South Bend, Indiana. It acceded to the ranks of the leaders by purchasing E-M-F, a Detroit company that evolved out of two other Detroit companies, Northern (an Olds spinoff) and Wayne, under the direction of Walter Flanders, who had been instrumental in reorganizing Ford's production in 1907–1908. The other two new leaders in 1910 outside Detroit, Willys and Anderson/Union, grew out of established firms that were not producers of automobiles.

Chalmers-Detroit) to produce small cars, and it captured 2 percent of the market by 1915. Out of the 15 leading firms listed in 1915, 13 were located in the Detroit area, and 10 of these firms were spinoffs.

After 1915 the collective market share of the Detroit area firms fluctuated, dropping to 52 percent in 1920 and then rising to 85 percent in 1925. General Motors acquired Chevrolet, which it used to eventually displace Ford as the leading producer. Chrysler was formed from Maxwell Motors and Chalmers-Detroit, which had evolved from the spinoffs Maxwell-Briscoe and E. R. Thomas-Detroit, respectively, and later acquired the Dodge Brothers to become the number three producer in the industry. Three spinoffs, Durant Motors, Chandler, and Paige-Detroit, ascended to the ranks of the leaders, but none captured a substantial market share.[15] The big three of General Motors, Ford, and Chrysler, all of which were based in Detroit, continued to dominate the industry into the 1960s.

In total, 112 firms entered the automobile industry in the Detroit area from 1895 to 1924, and 54, or 48 percent, were spinoffs. Most of the leaders in the Detroit area were spinoffs, and by 1925 Detroit-area firms totally dominated the industry with 85 percent of the market.[16] The population of Detroit grew at an unparalleled rate for a large city, increasing from 305,000 in 1900 to 1,837,000 in 1930. Outside of Detroit, spinoffs were much less prominent. They accounted for only 15 percent of the entrants, and most of the leading firms, including the three most significant, Jeffery/ Nash, Willys, and Studebaker, were not spinoffs. Indeed, what distinguished Detroit were its spinoffs. Using longevity as a measure of performance, spinoffs in the Detroit area survived markedly longer than other Detroit area entrants and markedly longer than both spinoffs and other types of entrants elsewhere. Moreover, the longevity of non-spinoff entrants was comparable in the Detroit area and elsewhere, suggesting that the superior performance of spinoffs in the Detroit area was due to their distinctive abilities and not any benefits from locating in the Detroit area (Klepper, 2007).

---

[15] The other short-lived new firm, Dort, which was located in the Detroit area, was founded by J. Dallas Dort, who had been William Durant's partner in the carriage business and had been involved with Durant early on in Buick.

[16] The share of production that actually occurred in the Detroit area was less than the share of output accounted for by the leading Detroit firms. For example, Census figures indicate that the share of U.S. automobile production in the state of Michigan, which was concentrated around Detroit, peaked at 65% in 1914. Much of the dispersal of output was driven by the leading firms establishing branch assembly plants throughout the United States to save on transportation costs (Rubenstein, 2002).

5.5. Spinoff Analysis

As we did for the semiconductor industry, the fertility, location, perform-ance, and impetus for the leading spinoffs in the automobile industry are analyzed.

5.5.1. Fertility and Location

Nearly all entry into the automobile industry occurred by 1924, and no spinoffs entered before 1899. Accordingly, the spinoff analysis is confined to the period 1899 to 1924, during which 142 spinoffs entered the industry. This exceeds the 91 spinoffs that were identified in semiconductors, but the list of semiconductor spinoffs is not complete. It excluded spinoffs of lesser firms (which did not make it onto the ICE listings) and the lesser spinoffs of firms on the ICE listings located outside Silicon Valley.

A total of 96 firms spawned spinoffs. Not surprisingly, the majority – 68 – spawned only one spinoff. Parents are too numerous to list them all, but the 26 that spawned two or more spinoffs are listed in Table 5-7. They are ordered according to location, number of spinoffs, and year of entry. For each firm, the total number of its spinoffs and the number that were ever a leading producer (through 1925) are listed along with whether the firm itself was ever a leading producer.

Seven firms had three or more spinoffs, led by Olds Motor Works and Buick/GM, with seven spinoffs each. All seven of these firms were located in the Detroit area. Furthermore, all were related to Olds Motor Works. As noted earlier, Buick was initially financed by an Olds subcontractor and Olds's two main subcontractors were instrumental to the success of Cadillac and Ford. Northern was a spinoff of Olds that was co-founded by Jonathan Maxwell, who also co-founded Maxwell-Briscoe, making Maxwell-Briscoe a second-generation spinoff of Olds. Last, Hupp was founded by Robert Hupp of Ford, who had initially worked for Olds before moving to Ford. A number of other well-known individuals in the industry also worked for Olds during its brief life as an independent producer before being acquired by General Motors. All told, Olds Motor Works had a great impact on the industry, leading one observer of the industry to describe Ransom Olds as the "schoolmaster of motordom" (Doolittle, 1916, p. 44).

Table 5-7 reflects the dominant influence the leading automobile firms had on the spinoff process. Fifteen of the 26 firms that spawned two or more spinoffs and six of the seven that spawned three or more spinoffs were leading firms. Standardizing by the number of years of production, the

Table 5-7. *Spinoffs of automobile producers*

Firm	Years (through 1924)	Number of spinoffs	Number of leading spinoffs	Leading firm
Detroit-area producers*				
Olds	1901–1908	7	3	Y
Buick/GM	1903–1924	7	2	Y
Cadillac	1902–1908	4	3	Y
Ford	1903–1924	4	2	Y
Maxwell Briscoe/ Maxwell	1904–1924	4		Y
Northern	1902–1910	3	1	
Hupp	1909–1924	3		Y
Packard	1900–1924	2		Y
Jackson	1902–1918	2		
C. H. Blomstrom	1903–1909	2		
Imperial	1909–1917	2		
Chevrolet	1911–1916	2		Y
Saxon	1913–1922	2		Y
Non–Detroit-area producers*				
Haynes Apperson	1895–1924	2		
Duryea	1896–1907	2		Y
F. B. Stearns	1898–1924	2		Y
Berg	1902–1906	2		
Jeffery	1902–1924	2		Y
Willys	1903–1924	2		Y
Metz/American Chocolate	1903–1923	2		Y
Stoddard	1903–1910	2		Y
Lozier	1904–1915	2	1	
York	1905–1917	2		
Palmer & Springer	1907–1914	2		
Single center	1907–1909	2		
Ideal	1911–1924	2		

* Classified in Detroit area if majority of years of production there.

annual rate of spinoffs was 56/595 = 0.094 for firms that were ever a leading producer versus 86/3439 = 0.025 for the other firms. The leading firms were well over five times larger than the other firms, though, so relative to their size their spinoff rate was actually lower than other firms.

A regional breakdown of the fertility of firms indicates that Detroit-area firms were considerably more fertile than firms elsewhere. The annual

Table 5-8. *Fertility rates by age bracket*

Ages	All firms	All parents
1–5	.019 (47/2500)	.121 (47/390)
6–10	.045 (38/847)	.158 (38/241)
11–15	.031 (12/388)	.085 (12/142)
16–20	.030 (6/200)	.068 (6/88)
21–25	.024 (2/84)	.044 (2/45)
26–30	.067 (1/15)	.143 (1/7)

spinoff rate for firms in the Detroit area was 59/642 = 0.091 versus 83/ 3392 = 0.024 for other firms. This difference persists even when controlling for differences in the quality of firms in Detroit and elsewhere. Among firms that were ever a leading producer, the annual spinoff rate was 37/ 234= 0.158 for firms in the Detroit area versus 19/361 = 0.053 for firms elsewhere, and among the other firms the annual spinoff rate was 22/408 = 0.054 for Detroit-area firms and 64/3031 = 0.021 for firms elsewhere.

Spinoffs generally located close to their parents – 110 of the 145 spinoffs located within 100 miles of their parents. This was especially true for spinoffs of Detroit-area firms – 50 of these 61 spinoffs located in the Detroit area as well.

Table 5-8 reports the annual rate at which firms spawned spinoffs at different ages. In contrast to semiconductors, a number of spinoffs occurred after their parents were dated as exiting the automobile industry – thirty-six in total, with thirteen occurring one year after their parent exited, eight occurring two years after, four occurring three years after, two occurring four years after, and nine others occurring between five and eleven years after their parent exited.[17] To facilitate a comparison with semiconductors, only the 106 spinoffs that occurred during the years their parents produced automobiles are considered. Table 5-8 indicates that if all firms are included, the annual spinoff rate rises sharply from ages 1–5 to 6–10

---

[17] In part, this is due to the more comprehensive listing of automobile spinoffs. Many of the automobile firms that spawned spinoffs after they exited were short-lived producers, whereas the ICE listings did not include comparable semiconductor producers and thus their spinoffs were never identified. Second, a number of the spinoffs that occurred after exit were in firms that exited by being acquired by another automobile firm. Few instances of such acquisitions occurred among the semiconductor firms on the ICE listings. Last, in a few instances of spinoffs being founded many years after the exit of their parent firm, the identification of the parent firm may be incorrect. The founder of the spinoff might have worked at subsequent automobile firms without this necessarily showing up in the Standard Catalog.

and then drops by about a third (but not significantly) and stays roughly constant from ages 11 to 30 (combining the last two age brackets to compensate for the small number of years of production at ages 26–30 yields an annual spinoff rate of 0.030, comparable to the spinoff rate in the age brackets 11–15 and 16–20). The inclusion of all firms in the analysis depresses the spinoff rate at younger ages, however, because there are many short-lived firms in the sample and these firms had few spinoffs. Table 5-8 indicates that if the analysis is restricted to the 96 firms with spinoffs, as would be the case if fixed effects were used to control for firm differences, the annual spinoff rate rises from ages 1–5 to 6–10 (but not significantly) and then falls with age (if the last two age brackets of 21–25 and 26–30 are combined, the annual spinoff rate reaches a trough of 0.058 for ages 21–30).[18]

Smith identified all the firms that were acquired and who acquired them. Among the 713 firms, 46 were acquired (by 1925) by another automobile firm (and thus exited as independent automobile producers) and another 120 were acquired by a non-automobile firm (these firms were classified as continuing producers). This provides a large sample to assess the effects of acquisitions on the spinoff rate. For both types of acquisitions, the rate at which spinoffs occurred at the acquired firm up to one year before and two years after their acquisition was analyzed. This allows for acquisitions to have an effect before they are officially consummated and to take up to two years to affect the spinoff rate.

Consider first the 46 firms that were acquired by another automobile firm. Collectively they experienced 14 spinoffs in the four-year interval considered, for an annual spinoff rate during this period of 14/180 = 0.078.[19] The annual spinoff rate for these firms in all prior years and for firms that were not acquired by other automobile firms was 107/3854 = 0.028, suggesting that acquisitions increase the probability of spinoffs. The higher spinoff rate around the time of acquisitions could, however, be due to characteristics about acquired firms that make them more likely to have spinoffs at all times.[20] To control for this possibility, the timing of spinoffs for the 16 acquired firms that had one or more spinoffs is analyzed. They had 14 spinoffs in the four-year interval around when they were acquired,

---

[18] The fall from 6–10 to 11–15 is significant, but none of the subsequent falls is significant.

[19] Two of the firms did not have a full four-year interval because of when they exited, which is why collectively the 46 firms had only 180 rather than 184 production years in the four-year interval around their acquisition.

[20] Consistent with this, among the 46 acquired firms, 8, or 0.174, had one or more spinoffs, whereas among the other 667 firms, 88, or 0.132, had one or more spinoffs (difference not significant).

for an annual spinoff rate of 14/64 = 0.219, versus an annual spinoff rate of 13/100 = 0.130 in their prior years of production (difference not significant). This suggests that acquisitions do raise the spinoff rate.[21]

Being acquired by a non-automobile firm also seems to increase the spinoff rate. The 120 firms that were acquired by non-automobile firms experienced an annual spinoff rate in the four-year interval around their acquisition of 20/530 = 0.038.[22] In contrast, the annual spinoff rate of these firms in other years and of other firms that were not acquired by non-automobile firms is 89/3615 = 0.025 (difference not significant). Again, this differential could be due to characteristics of acquired firms that make them more likely to have spinoffs at all times.[23] Focusing on the 29 firms with spinoffs that were acquired by a non-automobile firm, their annual spinoff rate in the 34 four-year intervals around their acquisitions (some were acquired multiple times) was 20/132 = 0.152 versus an annual spinoff rate of 15/215 = 0.070 during the rest of their automobile lifetimes. Similar to acquisitions by automobile firms, this suggests that acquisitions by non-automobile firms increase the spinoff rate.

5.5.2. Performance of Spinoffs

To evaluate the relationship between the performance of spinoffs and their parents, firms are divided again according to whether they were ever a leading producer. Those that were leading producers had 56 spinoffs, 11 of which also became leading producers, for a rate of 11/56 = 0.196. The other firms spawned 86 spinoffs, and 4 of these became leading producers, for a rate of 4/86 = 0.047. Thus, the spinoffs of leading firms were themselves much more likely than the spinoffs of lesser firms to attain the ranks of the leaders. Standardizing by years of production, the annual rate at which firms spawned spinoffs that

---

[21] Alternatively, it could be that the spinoff rate was greater for all firms around the end of their automobile lifetimes. To check this, the timing of spinoffs in the 68 firms with spinoffs that exited by 1924, but not by being acquired by another automobile firm, was analyzed. These firms had an annual spinoff rate of 30/272 = 0.110 in the four-year interval around their exit year versus an annual spinoff rate of 37/380 = 0.097 in their prior years of production. This difference, which is not significant, is too small to explain the higher fertility of firms after being acquired.

[22] Some of these firms were acquired multiple times by non-automobile firms, which is why the denominator is greater than 480 years.

[23] Consistent with this, among the 120 acquired firms, 29, or 0.242, had one or more spinoffs, whereas among the other 593 firms, only 67, or 0.115, had one or more spinoffs.

became leading producers was $11/595 = 0.018$ for firms that were themselves leading producers and $4/3439 = 0.0012$ for other firms. Clearly, the likelihood of spawning a leading spinoff was much greater for the leading producers.

5.5.3. Origins of the Leading Spinoffs of Detroit-Area Firms

Klepper (2006) tracks the origins of the leading spinoffs of firms located in the Detroit area. The reasons for their formation and their sources of finance are summarized in Table 5-9. Two reasons stand out for the spinoffs: managerial conflicts and strategic disagreements.

Managerial conflicts were already noted regarding the formation of Ford, Reo, and the Dodge Brothers. Henry Ford was pushed out of Cadillac when he took longer than his stockholders desired to produce finished cars. Ransom Olds was pushed out of Olds Motor Works, the company he headed, over a dispute with his major stockholder about whether the production process should be modified to lower the defect rate of his automobiles. Ford Motor Company had been integrating backward for many years and the Dodge Brothers feared they would become obsolete. They severed their relationship with Ford when Ford dawdled over buying them out. Both of William Durant's spinoffs, Chevrolet and Durant Motors, were also the result of disputes over his management style at General Motors. Soon after he formed GM, he was ousted by its bankers because he did not attend satisfactorily to integrating the numerous firms he had acquired. He later used Chevrolet to reacquire GM, but once again was ousted after a buying spree left the company disorganized.

Many other spinoffs were formed as the result of strategic disagreements over the types of cars to produce, particularly regarding the prospects of smaller, less expensive cars that ultimately dominated the market. Olds, Cadillac, E. R. Thomas-Detroit, and General Motors all drifted over time toward the production of larger automobiles. E. R. Thomas-Detroit was founded by the chief engineer and head of sales at Olds after support for a new, smaller car they championed was withdrawn at the last minute. Subsequently, they teamed with two other Olds employees to found Hudson after the new head of E. R. Thomas-Detroit declined to produce a new, smaller car they had developed to compete with the Model T. Maxwell-Briscoe was co-founded by Jonathan Maxwell after the car he designed for Northern, an Olds spinoff that he co-founded, was abandoned in favor of a larger car. Brush and Oakland were both founded by Alanson Brush,

Table 5-9. *Origins of leading spinoffs of Detroit-area producers*

Spinoff	Year	Parent	Reasons	Finance
Ford	1903	Cadillac	Managerial/strategic disagreement (time to production)	Businessmen, Dodge Brothers
Reo	1904	Olds Motor Works	Management conflict	Past stockholders
Maxwell-Briscoe	1904	Northern	Strategic disagreement (smaller car)	Auto man
E.R. Thomas-Detroit	1906	Olds Motor Works	Strategic disagreement (smaller car)	Auto manufacturer
Brush	1907	Cadillac	Dispute over patents	Auto man
Oakland	1907	Cadillac	Dispute over patents	Carriage manufacturer
Hudson	1909	Olds Motor Works	Strategic disagreement (smaller car)	Relative
Hupp	1909	Ford	Desire to be entrepreneur	Minimal capital
Paige-Detroit	1909	Reliance Motors	Abandoned autos for trucks	Businessman
Chevrolet	1911	Buick/General Motors	Management conflict	Self financed
Saxon	1913	E.R. Thomas-Detroit (Chalmers-Detroit)	Strategic choice (smaller car)	Auto men
Chandler	1913	Lozier	Strategic conflict (smaller car)	N.A.
Dodge Brothers	1914	Ford	Management conflict	Self financed
Durant Motors	1921	Buick/General Motors	Management conflict	Past stockholders

N.A.: not available.

Cadillac's leading engineer, over a dispute concerning his patents. Both companies developed new cars that were much smaller than the luxury cars Cadillac gravitated toward over time. Saxon was founded to produce a small car that its parent, Chalmers-Detroit (the later name of E. R. Thomas-Detroit) did not want to pursue (although Hugh Chalmers, its head, did help finance Saxon). Last, Chandler was founded to produce a smaller and less expensive version of the luxury car that its parent, Lozier, was unwilling to develop.

Not surprisingly, the cars produced by spinoffs initially shared features with those of their parents, but invariably they were sufficiently different to appeal to buyers different from those of their parents' cars. This was true not only of spinoffs formed to produce smaller, less expensive cars than those favored by their parents, but also of those that resulted from management conflicts. For example, Ford concentrated on inexpensive cars for the masses while its parent, Cadillac, evolved into a producer of large luxury cars. Similarly, Reo introduced a moderately priced car, while its parent, Olds Motor Works, evolved into producing ever larger and more expensive cars. Brush and Oakland both produced much smaller cars than its parent, Cadillac. Chevrolet continued the development of smaller, less expensive cars that William Durant had initiated at Buick but that had been abandoned at General Motors after his ouster. The Dodge Brothers developed a sturdier and improved version of the Model T that appealed to buyers who wanted a better car than the Model T and were willing to pay for it.

The leading spinoffs were financed in various ways. Some were financed by experienced automobile men, such as E. R. Thomas, who headed his own automobile firm, E. R. Thomas-Detroit. The Briscoe Brothers, who were one of Olds's original subcontractors, also financed some of the leading spinoffs. Other spinoffs, including Reo and Durant, were financed by individuals who had purchased stock in the prior ventures of their founders. In other cases relatives provided finance or the founders were sufficiently wealthy from their past automobile success to finance their own ventures. Each financier had his own distinctive knowledge about the industry or the founders of the spinoffs to evaluate the prospects of these new ventures. As noted, the leading spinoffs invariably developed cars that appealed to buyers different from those who bought the cars of their parents, and in the process expanded the market for automobiles. No doubt this played an important role in the tremendous growth of the industry, which averaged over 20 percent a year from 1899 to 1924 when nearly all the spinoffs in the industry entered.

5.6. Discussion

Many parallels exist between how the automobile and semiconductor industries ended up agglomerated in Detroit and Silicon Valley.

Initially both industries were centered in areas where producers in related industries were concentrated. A fundamental shift in technology, to internal combustion engines in autos and silicon in semiconductors, opened up opportunities for new entrants, and pioneers entered Detroit and Silicon Valley. These pioneers unleashed a reproductive process in which better firms spawned more and better spinoffs, especially at middle age. With spinoffs not moving far from their geographic origins, the result was a proliferation of top firms around the original pioneers. Once this process got going, it appears to have been self-reinforcing, with firms of all qualities being more likely to spawn spinoffs in Detroit and Silicon Valley than elsewhere. The leading spinoffs were largely the result of managerial and strategic disagreements within the top firms, which were sometimes reluctant to pursue new ideas or unproductively imported practices used in other industries and firms. Spinoffs were financed by individuals and firms with their own, distinctive knowledge. They expanded the range of activities in Detroit and Silicon Valley, both of which became extraordinary engines of economic growth.

Conventional agglomeration economies related to knowledge spillovers, labor pooling, and specialized input suppliers (see Rosenthal and Strange, 2004) were not needed to tell this story. While surely beneficial, these economies may be more the result than the cause of agglomerations. Indeed, the fact that the superior performance of Detroit firms was confined to spinoffs suggests that agglomeration economies benefiting all firms were not operative in Detroit. One can only wonder whether they were important in the emergence of Silicon Valley as the center of semiconductor production.

The distinctive characteristics of Silicon Valley, including the presence of Stanford University, venture capital, and vertically specialized firms with flat hierarchal structures, however, were not integral to this story. Indeed, none of these characteristics applied to Detroit and the automobile industry, yet its development closely paralleled that of Silicon Valley. And clearly, Silicon Valley did not represent the emergence of a new type of entrepreneurial economy driven by spinoffs. In addition to Detroit, spinoffs played a key role in the evolution of Akron as the center of the U.S. tire industry at the turn of the twentieth century (Buenstorf and Klepper, 2005, 2006), and the old footwear industry as well appears to have proceeded through a similar evolution (Sorenson and Audia, 2000). It appears that this form of regional economic development is at least fifty years older than Silicon Valley.

Klepper and Thompson (2006) offer a formal theoretical model of disagreements to explain all the salient patterns regarding spinoffs in autos and semiconductors, which are shared by a number of other technologically progressive industries. In their model, spinoffs result when meritorious ideas of talented employees are rejected because of the inability of top management to recognize the value of the ideas and/or the talents of the employees. The performance of firms is based on the quality of their employees, so the best firms are the leading candidates to spawn spinoffs. The chances of such firms spawning spinoffs are greater the less able incumbent management is to judge new ideas that arise within the firm.

Fairchild and Olds exemplify these themes. Both were pioneers with many talented employees. Both were hampered by management with limited knowledge about their industries. Fairchild Semiconductor was controlled by its parent, Fairchild Camera and Instrument, which had limited insight about how to manage a semiconductor firm. This contributed to tensions over stock options, recognition of employee achievements, and poor management choices that in turn played an important role in many of the spinoffs from Fairchild. Olds Motor Works was ultimately controlled and managed by its chief stockholder and his son, neither of whom had significant manufacturing experience. This too contributed to managerial tensions and poor strategic choices, which in turn played an important role in spinoffs from Olds. Fairchild remained as a leading firm much longer than Olds and thus had many more spinoffs in total than Olds, but Olds's influence lived on through the other successful firms it indirectly influenced and through its spinoffs. The result was an extraordinary number of spinoffs in Silicon Valley and Detroit.

In Klepper and Thompson's model, spinoffs pursue ideas that originate within their parent firms but that their parents decline to develop. Because their ownership is unclear, such ideas are inherently difficult to protect from imitation. Consequently spinoffs invariably involve spillovers that benefit other firms. The development of ICs is illustrative. Amelco and Signetics were formed to push forward the technology of ICs after Fairchild did not aggressively pursue this new market. Once Fairchild saw how successful they were, it countered with its own innovative efforts and captured 30 percent of this lucrative market (Lécuyer, 2006, pp. 238–250). Sometimes the beneficiaries of spinoffs are other firms and not their parents. For example, Intel's initial innovative efforts resulted in the development of MOS computer memories, which opened up a new market that many firms subsequently entered. Parallels abound in automobiles. Chevrolet, a spinoff from General Motors, is illustrative. General Motors acquired Chevrolet five years after it was formed. Subsequently, it improved Chevrolet's operations sufficiently that it was able to use Chevrolet to displace Ford as the leading automobile producer. Eventually this even led Ford to scrap the Model T, which had grown obsolete, and to develop a new, innovative car (Hounshell, 1984, pp. 263–292).

To the extent spinoffs involve spillovers that benefit other firms, the rate at which spinoffs are created will not be socially optimal, and anything that stimulates the formation of spinoffs will be socially beneficial. Judging from the exceptional spinoff fertility of firms in Detroit and Silicon Valley, agglomerations appear to stimulate the formation of spinoffs. As such, agglomerations are as much social as regional engines of economic growth and deserve to be promoted.

More fundamentally, if spinoffs create social benefits, then it is desirable to use public policy to promote their formation. At a minimum, policies should be undertaken to prevent incumbent firms from suppressing spinoffs in antisocial ways. Incumbents naturally want to discourage spinoffs to prevent the loss of valuable employees, which was especially prevalent in the semiconductor industry. Having lived through such losses at Fairchild, the founders of Intel were determined to prevent it from recurring there. They committed to a strategy of using the threat of trade secret litigation to discourage spinoffs regardless of whether trade secrets were involved (Jackson, 1998). This clearly seems detrimental to the public interest. Perhaps constraints should be placed on the use of trade secret litigation to discourage spinoffs or special punishments should be created for firms that use trade secret litigation in this fashion.

Public policy could also be used more proactively to encourage spinoffs. One way employers can legally restrict spinoffs is by requiring employees to sign noncompete covenants. Some states, however, do not allow noncompete covenants to be enforced. California is one such state and so was Michigan after 1905, during the formative era of the automobile industry. Recent studies suggest that noncompete covenants do affect the startup rate (Stuart and Sorenson, 2003) and more generally employee mobility (Marx et al., 2007). Thus, states might want to consider restricting the use of noncompete covenants, perhaps limiting the extent to which they can be used against new firms.

Regions commonly try to galvanize economic activity by attracting firms to locate there. Whether such efforts are socially beneficial is unclear, but the findings concerning spinoffs are suggestive about the kinds of firms worth attracting. It would be best to lure firms that are more likely to spawn spinoffs. Young industries would be a natural target as they are typically characterized by greater entry and thus more spinoffs. It would be ideal to attract successful firms in such industries given their greater spinoff rate, but no doubt these are the most difficult firms to induce to move. An alternative strategy would be to encourage such firms to set up branches in a region.

Another strategy regions use to stimulate activity is to establish venture capital funds to support firms in certain strategic industries, particularly ones where spinoffs are more likely. This makes sense if capital is the key to new firm formation. At the start of the semiconductor industry, though, Silicon Valley was certainly not blessed with abundant sources of capital. Detroit was a city of substantial size, but lots of other cities had comparable sources of capital. Neither city ultimately had much trouble attracting investors. Rather, the key to both regions was the creation of firms that investors wanted to support. In the absence of such firms, greater availability of venture capital is unlikely to be productive and could even be wasteful.

The overriding lesson of Detroit and Silicon Valley is that progress in their respective industries required new firms, and the likely origin of these new firms was in the industry itself. This will hardly be true in all industries, but when it is true regions need to have in place legal and economic policies to enable talented employees to leave established firms and venture out on their own. By creating the right conditions, regions blessed with pioneers in a new industry can unleash a torrent of activity that could create the next Detroit or Silicon Valley.

References

Bailey, L. Scott. 1971. *The American Car since 1775*. New York: Automobile Quarterly, Inc.

Bassett, Ross Knox. 2002. *To the Digital Age*. Baltimore, Md.: Johns Hopkins University Press.

Braun, Ernest, and Stuart MacDonald. 1978. *Revolution in Miniature*. Cambridge, England: Cambridge University Press.

Brittain, Jack W., and John Freeman. 1986. "Entrepreneurship in the Semiconductor Industry." Mimeo.

Buenstorf, Guido, and Steven Klepper. 2005. "Heritage and Agglomeration: The Akron Tire Cluster Revisited." Mimeo.

Buenstorf, Guido, and Steven Klepper. 2006. "Why Does Entry Cluster Geographically? Evidence from the U.S. Tire Industry." Mimeo.

Doolittle, James R. 1916. *The Romance of the Automobile Industry*. New York: Klebold Press.

Federal Trade Commission. 1939. *Report on the Motor Vehicle Industry*. Washington, D.C.: U.S. Government Printing Office.

Gilder, George. 1989. *Microcosm*. New York: Simon and Schuster.

Hounshell, David A. 1984. *From the American System to Mass Production, 1800–1932*. Baltimore, Md.: Johns Hopkins University Press.

Jackson, Tim. 1998. *Inside Intel*. New York: Penguin Group.

Kenney, Martin, and Richard Florida. 2000. "Venture Capital in Silicon Valley: Fueling New Firm Formation." In *Understanding Silicon Valley*, Martin Kenney, ed., Stanford, Calif.: Stanford University Press, 98–123.

Kimes, Beverly R. 1996. *Standard Catalog of American Cars, 1890–1942*, 3rd ed. Iola, Wis: Krause Publications.

Klepper, Steven. 2002."The Capabilities of New Firms and the Evolution of the US Automobile Industry." *Industrial and Corporate Change*, 11, 645–666.

Klepper, Steven. 2007a. "Disagreements, Spinoffs, and the Evolution of Detroit as the Capital of the U.S. Automobile Industry." *Management Science*, 53, 616–631.

Klepper, Steven. 2007b. "The Organizing and Financing of Innovative Companies in the Evolution of the U.S. Automobile Industry." In *The Financing of Innovation*, Naomi Lamoreaux and Kenneth Sokoloff, eds., Cambridge, Mass.: MIT Press, 85–128.

Klepper, Steven, and Peter Thompson. 2006. "Intra-industry Spinoffs."Mimeo.

Lécuyer, Christopher. 2006. *Making Silicon Valley: Innovation and the Growth of High Tech 1930–1970*. Cambridge, Mass.: MIT Press.

Lindgren, Nilo. 1971. "The Splintering of the Solid State Industry." In *Dealing with Technological Change*. Princeton, N.J.: Auerbach, 36–51.

Marx, Matt, Deborah Strumsky, and Lee Fleming. 2007. "Noncompetes and Inventor Mobility: Specialists, Stars, and the Michigan Experiment." Harvard Business School Working Paper, No. 07–042.

McCreadie, John, and Valerie Rice. 1989. "Nine New Mavericks." *Electronic Business*, September 4, 30–38.

Moore, Gordon, and Kevin Davis. 2004. "Learning the Silicon Valley Way." In *Building High-Tech Clusters: Silicon Valley and Beyond*, Timothy Bresnahan and Alfonso Gambardella, eds. Cambridge: Cambridge University Press.

Rosenthal, Stuart S., and William C. Strange. 2004. "Evidence on the Nature and Sources of Agglomeration Economies." In the *Handbook of Urban and Regional Economics*, vol. 4, J. Vernon Henderson and Jacques Francois Thisse, eds. Amsterdam: North Holland.

Rubenstein, James M. 2002. *The Changing US Auto Industry: A Geographical Analysis*. London: Routledge.

Saxenian, AnnaLee. 1994. *Regional Advantage: Culture and Competition in Silicon Valley and Route 128*. Cambridge, Mass.: Harvard University Press.

Scott, A. J., and D. P. Angel. 1987. "The US Semiconductor Industry: A Locational Analysis." *Environment and Planning*, 19(7): 875–912.

Smith, Philip H. 1968. *Wheels within Wheels: A Short History of American Motor Manufacturing*. New York: Funk and Wagnalls.

Sorenson, Olav, and Pino G. Audia. 2000. "The Social Structure of Entrepreneurial Activity: Geographic Concentration of Footwear Production in the United States, 1940–1989." *American Journal of Sociology*, 106(2), 424–461.

Sporck, Charles E. 2001. *Spinoff: A Personal History of the Industry That Changed the World*. Saranac Lake, N.Y.: Saranac Publishing.

Stuart, Toby E., and Olav Sorenson. 2003. "Liquidity Events and the Geographic Distribution of Entrepreneurial Activity." *Administrative Science Quarterly*, 48(2), 175–201.

Tilton, John E. 1971. *International Diffusion of Technology: The Case of Semiconductors*. Washington, D.C.: The Brookings Institution.

Walker, Rob, and Nancy Tersini. 1992. *Silicon Destiny: The Story of Application Specific Integrated Circuits and Lsi Logic Corporation*. Milpitas, Calif.: C.M.C. Publications.

Wilson, Drew. 2004. "Linear Technology: Enviable position." http://www.edn.com/article/CA6253339.html?industryid=47479.

PART II

LINKING ENTREPRENEURSHIP TO GROWTH

6

Entrepreneurship and Job Growth

John Haltiwanger

6.1. Introduction and Overview

Healthy market economies are dynamic, with a high pace of churning of jobs, workers and firms. In a healthy economy like that of the United States, this churning, through entrepreneurship, is productivity-enhancing with outputs and inputs being reallocated from less productive to more productive businesses on an ongoing basis. Moreover, in a closely related manner, in following entering cohorts of businesses in the United States, the market selection dynamics are productivity-enhancing. Entering cohorts in the United States have a larger than average dispersion of productivity, but this dispersion is reduced as the cohort ages and the less productive firms exit. These patterns reflect market experimentation of new entrants, and the subsequent learning and selection dynamics for young businesses plays an important role in U.S. economic growth. Put differently, these patterns suggest entrepreneurial dynamics are critical for understanding U.S. economic growth. With "entrepreneurs" and "young businesses" treated synonymously in what follows, it is important to note that this is consistent with Schumpeter's view that entrepreneurs need new firms to exploit their ideas, as noted in Chapter 1.

The evidence for the dynamism of market economies in general and in the United States in particular has been greatly enhanced by the development of longitudinal business databases as well as longitudinal employer-employee matched data. Early evidence on this dynamism for the United

This chapter draws heavily on collaborative work with a number of colleagues (cited in text) that has been supported by a research grant from the Kauffman Foundation (Co-Principal Investigators on the grant are Steven Davis and Ron Jarmin). Thanks to Marios Michaelides for excellent research assistance. The views expressed in this chapter are those of the author and do not necessarily represent those of the census bureau. The chapter has been screened to ensure that it does not disclose any confidential information.

States and other countries was often confined to the manufacturing sector, but increasingly now there are longitudinal business data covering the private, nonfarm business sector.

While the dynamism of U.S. businesses and the role of young businesses in productivity and job growth are increasingly well understood, the literature on firm dynamics has often focused on another business characteristic closely associated with business age, namely, business size. Business size is of interest in its own right given, for example, the enormously skewed size distribution of business activity. But focusing on business size alone can be misleading. For one, as stressed by Davis and Haltiwanger (1999) and Haltiwanger and Krizan (1999), most small businesses are also relatively young. Small business dynamics should be considered together with the business life cycle, business entry and exit, and business age. Even at the most basic descriptive level, business age matters greatly. For example, the existing studies on U.S. manufacturing show that the empirical relationship between employment growth and business size is highly sensitive to the inclusion or exclusion of controls for business age (Davis and Haltiwanger, 1999). At a deeper level, the market selection process associated with business entry and exit, the acquisition of business know-how as firms age, and on-the-job skill acquisition by workers have major effects on wage and productivity dynamics at younger and, hence, smaller businesses.[1] Small business wage and productivity dynamics cannot be properly understood without recognizing their links to entry and exit, the selection process, and the business life cycle.[2]

---

[1] Jovanovic (1982) develops the seminal theoretical analysis of the business selection process and its connection to industry evolution. Ericson and Pakes (1995) develop another well-known theory of the business selection process. Aghion and Howitt (1998) provide a masterful synthesis of theoretical work on growth, innovation and creative destruction from a Schumpeterian perspective. Prescott and Visscher (1980) provide a broad theoretical analysis of organization capital and its accumulation, and Lucas (1993) provides one of the best-known treatments of learning by doing.

[2] Empirical studies find major roles for entry, exit, and selection in job creation and destruction dynamics and in productivity growth. See, e.g., Dunne, Roberts, and Samuelson (1988, 1989), Baily, Hulten, and Campbell (1992), Davis and Haltiwanger (1992), Olley and Pakes (1996), Roberts and Tybout (1996), Troske (1996), Bartelsman and Doms (2000), Aw et al. (2001), and Jarmin et al. (2001). Carroll and Hannan (2000) investigate entry and exit and business life cycle dynamics from the perspectives of sociology and organizational ecology. Bahk and Gort (1993) study the role of learning by doing in new manufacturing plants. A large literature on the relationship between business size and wages is ably surveyed by Oi and Idson (1999) and Brown, Hamilton, and Medoff (1990). A smaller literature investigates the relationship between wages and business age. See Davis and Haltiwanger (1991), Dunne (1994), Doms, Dunne, and Troske (1997), Troske (1998), and, especially, Brown and Medoff (2001).

Focusing on employer size in studying business dynamics has other limitations as well. Perhaps the most well known is that the relationship between employer size and job growth will reflect transitory shocks and in turn regression to the mean effects. That is, transitory shocks imply that businesses that have recently contracted will be measured as small and in turn will grow while businesses that have recently expanded will be measured as large and will contract. In contrast, there is no regression to the mean problem with business age. While transitory shocks obviously need to be taken into account regardless of the business characteristic under analysis, there is no analogous misclassification of age as there is with size due to transitory shocks.

This chapter reviews what we know about entrepreneurial businesses for job growth in particular but also in the context of productivity dynamics. As noted, most of the existing studies for the United States have relied on U.S. manufacturing data. We review this evidence but also take advantage of tabulations from some of the economy-wide datasets that have recently been developed for the United States. In particular, we take advantage of tabulations for the datasets created for the studies by Davis et al. (2006a) that use the Longitudinal Business Database (LBD) and the tabulations by Davis et al. (2006b) that use the extended version of the LBD (the Integrated LBD, or ILBD) that incorporates the role of non-employer businesses into the job growth dynamics of U.S. businesses. Note that by non-employer businesses we refer to the large number of businesses that do not yet employ workers but are, as we shall see, an important source of dynamism for U.S. businesses.

6.2. What Do We Know about Young and Small Business Dynamics and Their Role in Economic Performance?

Many studies consider the role of entrepreneurship in economic growth but, as noted above, with a variety of limitations. In their article for the *Handbook of Labor Economics,* Davis and Haltiwanger (1999) survey much of the literature on the dynamics of job creation and destruction. Bartelsman and Doms (2000) and Foster, Haltiwanger, and Krizan (2001) survey much of the literature on the relationship between micro and macro productivity dynamics, including the contribution of entry and exit to productivity growth. Mainly because of data limitations, most analyses for the United States and other countries on the relationship between productivity and growth dynamics at the micro level focus on the manufacturing sector.[3]

---

[3] Exceptions include Foster et al. (2002), who explore the micro-macro productivity dynamics of the retail trade industry.

Our discussion here is not comprehensive but is intended to provide some understanding of the results in the existing literature.

Several patterns have emerged in previous research. One key fact is that small businesses are often young businesses. Thus, it is often useful to study and discuss results in terms of small and young businesses and also, as feasible, to separate out the influences of size and age.

In terms of employment dynamics, small and young businesses exhibit high rates of job creation and destruction and high rates of entry and exit. Job destruction for young and small businesses is disproportionately accounted for by business exit. The relationship between net employment growth and business size is sensitive to measurement and statistical issues (e.g., regression to the mean). Net employment growth is decreasing in business age. Controlling for business age, it is often difficult to find a systematic relationship between net employment growth and size.

In terms of productivity dynamics, there is a burgeoning literature on the relationship between entry and exit and productivity dynamics at the micro and macro levels. Based on work mainly for the manufacturing sector, upon entry new businesses have on average about the same or slightly lower productivity than incumbents, but this average conceals tremendous heterogeneity.[4] Low-productivity entrants have very high rates of exit. Thus, part of the reason for the slightly below average productivity of entering businesses is that an entering cohort contains a highly heterogeneous group of businesses. Put differently, the U.S. entry process is characterized by a high rate of market experimentation. In this respect, market experimentation appears to be greater in the United States than in Europe. There is also evidence of important "learning by doing" for young businesses. Conditional on survival, young businesses exhibit more rapid productivity growth than incumbents.

The contribution to overall (industry) productivity growth from entry and selection is substantial. Whether measured in terms of labor or total factor productivity, net entry accounts for roughly 30 percent of productivity growth in U.S. manufacturing industries over a ten-year horizon. In U.S. retail trade, net entry accounts for almost all labor productivity growth over a ten-year horizon. These findings refer to entry and exit of establishments. The patterns of entry and exit vary by sector in interesting

---

[4] A further complicating factor is that micro estimates of productivity are typically better thought of as real revenue per unit of input since plant level prices are typically not observed. Foster, Haltiwanger, and Syverson (2005) find, for a sample of products where plant-level prices are observed, that entering plants have low prices and higher physical productivity than would be inferred from measured revenue productivity.

ways. For example, in retail trade much of the action in the 1990s involved the entry of new establishments associated with large multi-unit firms and the exit of small independents.

While many of these findings show up in several studies, there are major gaps in our knowledge. First, most of the available evidence is based on studies of the U.S. manufacturing sector. Second, extending the analysis beyond manufacturing especially for productivity dynamics is challenging because statistical agencies often collect less detailed data on inputs and outputs for nonmanufacturing businesses, and because there are difficult conceptual issues involved in measuring output for service industries. Third, there has been considerable attention in the popular press and in the recent academic literature on changes in the pace of firm volatility. Most of the latter are based on publicly traded firms. The latter are interesting in their own right given that the financing of their operations is substantially different from the financing for privately held firms. Still, it is important to consider the role of privately held firms in considerations of firm level volatility. Fourth, most previous studies have no data or extremely crude data on non-employer businesses, which means that they miss a major component of the small business sector. Since there are a huge number of businesses with no current employees (roughly 20 million in the United States), their contribution to economic performance and the young and small business sector is an open question in the literature.

6.3. Job Flows for the U.S. Private Sector

Both the Bureau of the Census and the Bureau of Labor Statistics (BLS) have recently developed longitudinal business databases covering the entire private sector. The BLS Business Employment Dynamics (BED) series provide quarterly job flow statistics for the nonfarm private sector from U.S. establishments with at least one employee with detailed breakdowns by industry, region, and employer size class with historical series dating back to 1992.[5]

---

[5] Statistics from the BED can be accessed at http://www.bls.gov/bdm/home.htm. Statistics by employer size have recently been released by BLS (see http://www.bls.gov/news.release/pdf/cewbd.pdf). The definition of a firm with the BED is different from the definition of a firm under the LBD. For the BED, a firm is defined as one with a Federal Employer Identification Number. In the LBD, a firm is defined as all establishments under the common operational control of an enterprise. Note that many firms have multiple EINs for purposes of filing income and payroll taxes. BED firm size statistics also take advantage of a dynamic sizing method so that gross job flows at the micro level are allocated to different sized classes as the firm passes through these size classes. We note that even with these methodological and measurement differences the key patterns of gross job flows by employer size reported here are similar to those reported for the BED.

The Bureau of the Census Longitudinal Business Database (LBD) has been developed at the Center for Economic Studies and provides longitudinal business data with information on employment, payroll, industry, and geography from 1975 to 2001 for establishments and firms with at least one employee.[6] The LBD is being extended with non-employer businesses in the manner described in Davis et. al. (2006b) (with the resulting data product called the ILBD). A related data infrastructure project at the census bureau integrates employer and employee data (the Longitudinal Employer Household Dynamics project, or LEHD) from unemployment insurance wage records. The BED, LBD and LEHD are all rich new sources of business dynamics for the United States. In the analysis that follows, we focus on tabulations from the LBD. The primary reason is that the LBD offers the longest time horizon over which to characterize U.S. business dynamics and as such permits exploration of the role of employer age as well as changes in the pace of business dynamics over time. One other advantage of the LBD is that businesses can be defined in an internally consistent manner on both an establishment (a physical location of activity) and a firm (all establishments under operational control of the same enterprise) basis. For many purposes, both establishment and firm level business dynamics are of interest. For the present purpose, we focus on firms as opposed to establishments. In addition, we use some tabulations from the ILBD.

The empirical results focus on measuring business dynamics via job flows. The concepts for job flows are defined as follows. The net employment growth for a business is measured as the change in employment from one period to the next divided by the average employment in the two periods. As discussed in detail in Davis, Haltiwanger, and Schuh (1996), this net growth rate measure has several advantageous properties: (1) it accommodates entry and exit; (2) it is symmetric for employment gains and losses; (3) it is a second-order approximation of the log first difference. Using this growth rate measure, job creation and destruction rates for businesses with some observable characteristic (e.g., industry or size) are measured as follows. Job creation (JC) for a firm of a given type measures the gross employment gains from all expanding businesses

---

[6] A precursor to the LBD is the LEEM dataset developed jointly by the Census Bureau and SBA. A number of studies emerged from the LEEM (e.g., Acs, Armington and Robb, 1999) studying patterns of job flows by employer size and age. The advantage of the LBD relative to the LEEM is the number of years that are covered, the improved longitudinal linkages (see Jarmin and Miranda, 2002, for discussion), and the much improved measurement of employer age. Still, a number of the findings reported in this chapter from the LBD have antecedents in the findings from the LEEM (again, see Acs et al., 1999).

(including contribution from entry) of that type, while job destruction (JD) measures the gross employment gains from all contracting businesses for employers of that type. In both cases, these measures are converted to rates by dividing by average employment in the current and prior period for firms of the type in question. By construction, the net growth rate (NET) for any given type of firms is given by the difference between creation and destruction.

It is also useful to consider auxiliary related measures of job dynamics. The total job reallocation rate (SUM) is a measure of the total rate of all jobs reallocated in a period and is given by the sum of job creation and destruction. Each of these concepts can be further decomposed into the contribution from continuing businesses and the contribution from entering and exiting businesses. In what follows, we denote as ENTRY the job creation coming from entering businesses, EXIT the job destruction coming from exiting businesses, and FIRM TURNOVER as the sum of ENTRY and EXIT. Note that these terms correspond to standard definitions of entry, exit, and turnover as job creation from entering businesses is simply an employment-weighted measure of firm entry and so on.

The LBD permits measuring each of these concepts on an annual basis where the employment concept is the number of workers on the payroll for the payroll period including March 12 of each year. The tabulations from the LBD used in this chapter are derived from statistics developed in Davis et al. (2006a) that focus on changing patterns of firm volatility in the United States. In addition, some of the tabulations in this paper are based on an extension of the LBD to include non-employer businesses. Nonemployer businesses are businesses with positive revenue but no employees. Many (indeed most) sole proprietors are nonemployer businesses. The ILBD is an ongoing database infrastructure project at CES. In this chapter, tabulations from the ILBD are drawn from Davis et al. (2006b), who explore the role of nonemployer businesses for understanding U.S. business dynamics.

Details about the database construction including a discussion of longitudinal linkages can be found in Davis et al. (2006a, 2006b).

6.4. The Role of Employer Size and Age

To start, we present basic summary statistics by employer size, employer age, and both together. The contribution here is that these statistics are from a comprehensive longitudinal database covering the entire U.S. private sector for a substantial period of time. Figure 6-1 presents statistics by

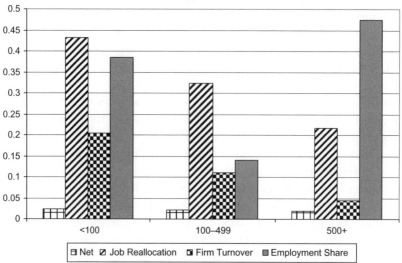

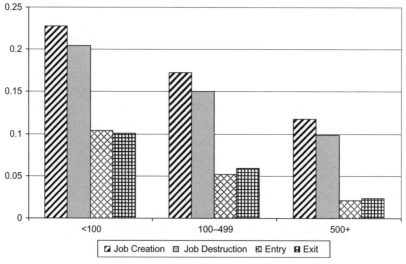

Figure 6-1. Job flows by employer size. Source: Tabulations from LBD (based on Davis et al., 2006a).

employer size. Employer size for a business is based on the average employment in the current and the prior period. As Davis et al. (1996) emphasize, using this type of measure mitigates some of the regression to the mean problems with measures of employer size.[7] It is also worth emphasizing again that this measure is for firm size, not establishment size. Three firm size classes are considered: firms with fewer than 100 employees, with between 100 and 499 employees, and with more than 500 employees.

The top panel of Figure 6-1 shows the patterns of net employment growth, job reallocation (SUM), firm turnover, and employment shares by employer size class (with averages across the 1981–2001 period).[8] Some basic and reasonably well-known patterns are confirmed. First, about half of employment is with firms with fewer than 500 employees. Second, gross job flows as measured by job reallocation dwarf net growth rates. Third, job reallocation and firm turnover are sharply decreasing in employer size. Fourth, net growth exhibits a modest inverse relationship with employer size. For this time period, the inverse relationship is quite modest with the average net growth rate of the firms under 100 employees at 2.27 percent and the average net growth rate for firms larger than 500 at 1.95 percent.

The lower panel of Figure 6-1 shows the underlying patterns of job creation, job destruction, and employment-weighted entry and exit. Almost half of the job creation and destruction for small firms comes from entry and exit. In contrast, less than one third of the job creation and destruction of larger businesses comes from entry and exit.

Figure 6-2 reports analogous statistics for employer age. Employer age is measured in the LBD as the age of the oldest establishment. Two age classes are examined: firms less than five years old and firms five or more years old. Given left censoring in the LBD in 1975, all of the tabulations in this chapter using the LBD start in 1981.

The patterns by this simple age breakdown are stark and striking. Young firms have much higher net growth rate than mature firms. The annual average net growth rate of young firms is over 20 percent. The high net growth is accompanied by very high volatility, with firm turnover of almost 50 percent each year. These rapidly growing, volatile young firms

---

[7] Regression to the mean problems are the most problematic using base size measures of size classes. The BLS method of dynamic sizing overcomes many of the problems associated with transitory shocks. We note that the basic patterns that we focus on here also appear to hold with the BED using dynamic sizing methods.

[8] The 1981–2001 period is used since this permits measuring young (less than five years old) and mature firms (five or more years old) on a consistent basis.

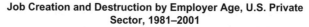

Net Growth, Job Reallocation, and Firm Turnover by Employer Age, U.S. Private Sector, 1981–2001

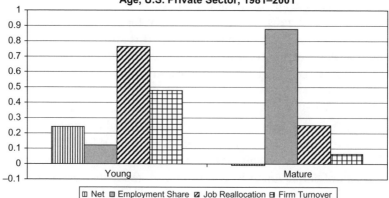

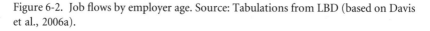

Job Creation and Destruction by Employer Age, U.S. Private Sector, 1981–2001

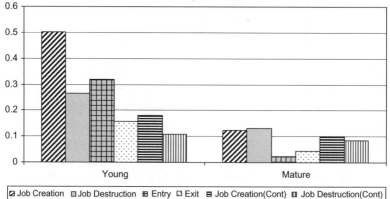

Figure 6-2. Job flows by employer age. Source: Tabulations from LBD (based on Davis et al., 2006a).

account for a relatively small share of total employment in the United States (around 10 percent).

The lower panel shows the underlying patterns of job creation and destruction. In this panel, we show the job creation and destruction rates as well as the contributions of continuing firms and entering and exiting firms. The young firms are striking in that over 60 percent of the job creation is from entry and about half of the job destruction is due to exit. However, the high net growth rate and high volatility is also driven by young continuing firms with job creation from continuing firms almost at

20 percent and substantially above the job destruction rate of around 10 percent.

Mature firms in contrast have a modest negative net growth rate with entry and exit accounting for only about 25 percent (still a large percent) of the gross flows. Interestingly, the negative net growth is associated with the entry rate being less than the exit rate; while conditional on survival, mature firms exhibit positive but modest net growth. Of course, the higher exit than entry rate for mature firms is almost by construction as in some ways it is surprising to see any "entry" for mature firms. It turns out that there are some mature firms that have periods of inactivity, so entry should really be interpreted as going from zero to positive activity from year $t-1$ to t.[9]

Figure 6-3 shows the patterns of job flows for U.S. businesses with employer size and employer age combined. Holding size constant, young businesses have much higher net growth rates than mature businesses and are much more volatile. Again, holding size constant, the job creation and destruction of young businesses is driven in large part by entry and exit, but considering the overall rates of job creation and destruction relative to entry and exit it is clear that young continuing businesses also exhibit considerable volatility.

Holding age constant, smaller businesses are more volatile, but there is no systematic relationship between employer size and net growth. For young businesses smaller businesses have a modestly higher net employment growth than large businesses. For mature businesses, the lowest net growth rate is for the smallest ones.

It is also important to pay attention to shares in considering age and size effects together. The largest employment share is accounted for by large, mature businesses (over 40 percent). The smallest employment share is accounted for by large, young businesses. That is, conditional on being young, small businesses have the largest share of employment. Still, as noted, the high pace of volatility of young medium and large firms (even though they account for only a small share of activity) is striking.

Combining the insights of Figures 6-1 to 6-3, the basic message that emerges is that business age is a critical factor in accounting for differences in net growth and volatility for U.S. businesses. Employer size has more modest effects even if one focuses only on size; after controlling for age there are less dramatic and less systematic patterns by employer size.

---

[9] Alternatively, there are some new firms with old establishments. For the most part, such entities would not be measured as new firms but in some cases this might happen.

Net Growth, Job Reallocation, and Firm Turnover by Employer Size and Age, U.S. Private Sector, 1981–2001

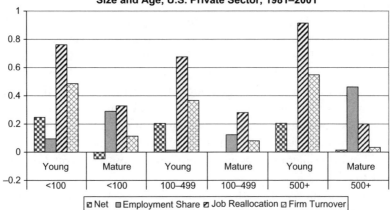

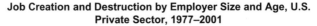

Job Creation and Destruction by Employer Size and Age, U.S. Private Sector, 1977–2001

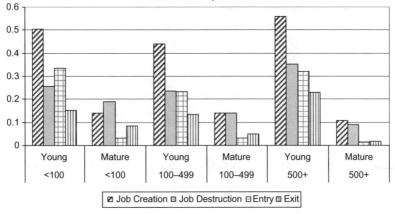

Figure 6-3. Job flows by employer size and age. Source: Tabulations from LBD (based on Davis et al., 2006a).

In many ways, these patterns confirm findings in the existing literature on the U.S. manufacturing sector.

What should we make of these patterns? First, it is clear from Figures 6-1 to 6-3 and the existing literature that U.S. businesses exhibit tremendous volatility with resulting high churning of jobs. Second, much but not all of this volatility is associated with high volatility of young businesses both via entry and high exit rates for young businesses. Third, even for large, mature businesses there is considerable volatility.

Returning to Figure 6-3, the job reallocation rate for large, mature businesses is 20 percent. Much of that is driven by the reallocation among continuing firms but this nevertheless represents considerable churning of jobs.

6.5. Privately Held versus Publicly Traded Firms: Growth and Changing Volatility[10]

The results in the prior section highlight the role of employer age in U.S. business dynamics. Young businesses grow fast on average but are very volatile. These patterns are consistent with creative destruction models of economic fluctuation where entry and exit play a large role because of market experimentation, learning and selection effects. A related potential difference between young and mature firms is the financing for firm operations. While the LBD does not have much information about the sources of financing, it is possible in the LBD to identify publicly traded versus privately held firms, as the COMPUSTAT data have been merged with the LBD.[11] Publicly traded firms by their very nature have access to equity financing not feasible for privately held firms.

Differences in the size, age, growth, and volatility of privately held versus publicly traded firms can be measured using the LBD. Privately held versus publicly traded status is of course endogenous so caution must be used in drawing causal inferences from the simple cross-tabulations presented here. Still, as will become apparent, they show rich differences in the patterns of privately held vs. publicly traded firms indicating that understanding the role of financing for the dynamics of young and small businesses is a rich area for future analysis with the LBD and the ILBD.

Figure 6-4 shows the average shares of employment by employer age, size, and publicly versus privately held. Small businesses are overwhelmingly privately held whether young or mature. Large, mature businesses are the only employer size/age category with the share of publicly traded larger than the share of privately held. Nevertheless, the latter category – large,

---

[10] As noted, all of the tabulations in section 6.5 are derived from tabulations used in Davis et al. (2006a). The latter focuses on changes in the patterns of firm volatility especially between privately held and publicly held firms. Thus, this section relies very heavily on that paper.

[11] See Davis et al. (2006a) for details about the integration of the LBD and COMPUSTAT data.

John Haltiwanger

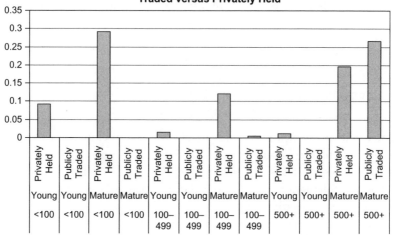

Figure 6-4. Share of employment by employer size, age, and publicly traded versus privately held. Source: Tabulations from LBD (based on Davis et al., 2006a).

mature, privately held businesses – accounts for more than 20 percent of U.S. private sector employment. The clear message from Figure 6-4 is that publicly traded businesses are large and mature as well.

Figure 6-5 shows the patterns of net growth and job flows by privately held versus publicly traded. Given the patterns in Figure 6-3 and Figure 6-4, the patterns in Figure 6-5 are not surprising. Publicly traded firms are much less volatile than privately held firms. Moreover, interestingly, publicly traded firms have higher net growth than privately held firms. The latter might at first glance be surprising given Figure 6-4, which shows that publicly traded firms are larger and more mature.

To explore these patterns further, Figure 6-6 shows the patterns of net growth and volatility (measured by job reallocation) by employer size, age, and publicly traded versus privately held status. In every size/age cell, publicly traded firms have higher net growth than privately held firms, and in some cases the differences in net growth are substantial (such as for young firms). Young privately held firms grow more rapidly than other firms, but young publicly traded firms still grow much faster.

Holding age and size constant, there is less of a systematic relationship between volatility and publicly traded status. For large firms (regardless of

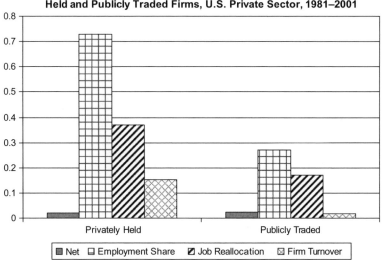

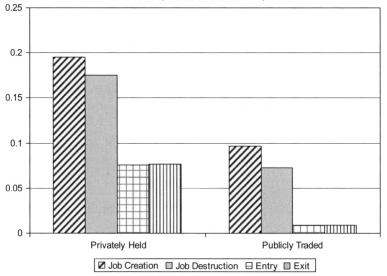

Figure 6-5. Job flows by privately held versus publicly traded firms. Source: Tabulations from LBD (based on Davis et al., 2006a).

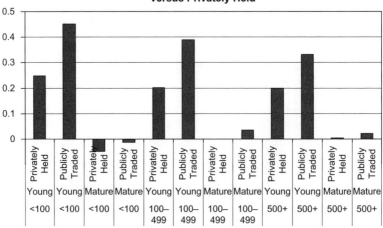

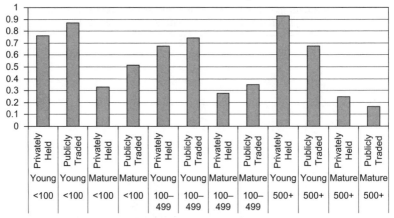

Figure 6-6. Net growth and volatility by employer size, age and privately held vs. publicly traded. Source: Tabulations from LBD (based on Davis et al., 2006a).

age), publicly traded firms are less volatile than privately held firms. However, for small- and medium-sized firms, publicly traded firms are slightly more volatile than privately held firms.

An interesting feature of publicly versus privately held status is that the patterns of volatility have changed substantially over time. As emphasized by Comin and Phillipon (2005) and Davis et al. (2006a), publicly traded

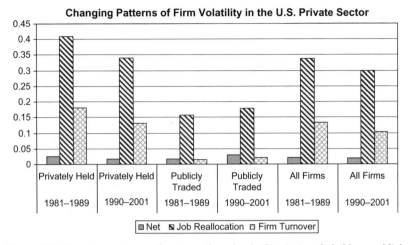

Figure 6-7. Changing patterns of net growth and volatility (privately held vs. publicly traded). Source: Tabulations from LBD (based on Davis et al., 2006a).

firms have become more volatile over time.[12] This latter pattern is confirmed in Figure 6-7, which shows that the pace of job reallocation for publicly traded firms increased in the 1990s. However, as emphasized by Davis et al. (2006a), overall firm level volatility has declined over this same period. The latter is driven by a large decline in firm level volatility for privately held firms between the 1980s and the 1990s, which in turn is driven by a large decline in firm turnover over this same period for all firms and especially for privately held firms.[13]

Returning to employer size and age effects, Figure 6-8 examines the changing degree of volatility by employer size and age. Job reallocation and firm turnover fall noticeably for small firms (whether young or mature) and medium-sized mature firms. Job reallocation and firm

---

[12] These papers have a much more extensive analysis of changes in firm level volatility including a rich set of alternative measures of firm volatility including measures of the cross-sectional dispersion of firm level growth rates as well as measures of within firm growth volatility. Interestingly, the patterns for these alternative measures are similar to the patterns emphasized here on job reallocation. This makes sense as job reallocation can be interpreted as an absolute deviation measure of dispersion with the absolute deviations deviated from zero.

[13] Both the metric of firm volatility and the simple classification of the pre-1990 and the post-1990 period yield an understatement of the decline in volatility reported in Davis et al. (2006a). Job reallocation is a measure of dispersion of the cross-sectional distribution of growth rates. Davis et al. (2006a) show that this measure declines but also show greater declines in a measure of within firm volatility calculated as the square root of the moving ten-year average of within firm squared deviations of growth rates.

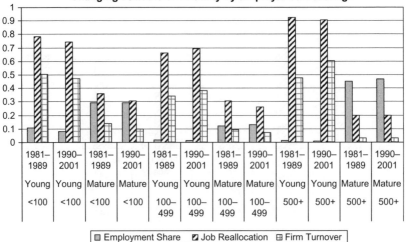

Figure 6-8. Changing patterns of volatility by employer size and age. Source: Tabulations from LBD (based on Davis et al., 2006a).

turnover rises for young and medium-sized firms. Firm turnover also increases for young and large firms.

Putting the pieces together, Figure 6-9 examines changing patterns of net growth and firm volatility by employer size, age, and privately versus publicly traded. For net growth the patterns show a pattern of modest decline for many but not all privately held age/size groups and a pattern of an increase in the net growth for most but not all publicly traded age/size groups. Turning to volatility, for privately held firms, small firms (whether young or mature), medium-sized, mature, and large mature firms exhibit declines in job reallocation. For publicly traded, the results appear to be more mixed with medium-sized/mature and large/mature firms exhibiting an increase.

To fully understand the patterns in Figure 6-9 compared with those in Figure 6-7, it is important to return to examining shares. Figure 6-10 shows the changing pattern of employment shares. Observe that for publicly traded firms there is a shift away from large, mature firms. It is still the dominant type but shows a reduction of the share by about 3 percent. Given that the large, mature, publicly traded firms have the lowest volatility on average (see Figure 6-9), this shift away from large, mature firms helps contribute to the rising volatility among publicly traded ones. The opposite pattern is observed for privately held firms. In particular, the share of small, young privately held firms has been decreasing, while

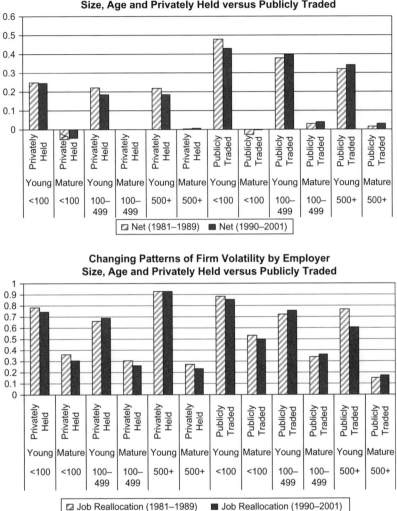

Figure 6-9. Changing patterns of net growth and firm volatility. Source: Tabulations from LBD (based on Davis et al., 2006a).

the share of the large, mature privately held firms has been increasing. The former group has much higher volatility than the latter group and this contributes to the decline in overall volatility for privately held firms.

To conclude this section, we note that the patterns of net growth and firm volatility by employer size and age are closely linked to the patterns of net growth and firm volatility by privately held and publicly traded

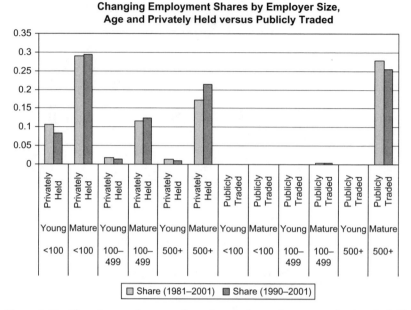

Figure 6-10. Changing employment shares by employer size, age, and privately held versus publicly traded. Source: Tabulations from LBD (based on Davis et al., 2006a).

characteristics. One basic message is that publicly traded firms have more rapid growth than privately held firms even and especially holding age and size constant. However, the strong growth from young firms holds for privately held as well as publicly traded. Another basic message is that young, small, and privately held firms are especially volatile relative to large, mature, publicly traded firms. However, interestingly, these patterns appear to be changing over the last couple of decades; not changing enough to reverse these patterns, but the volatility of the young, small, privately held firms is declining while the volatility of the large, mature, publicly traded firms is rising. Moreover, compositional shifts among publicly traded and privately held firms are further reducing the difference in volatility between publicly traded and privately held firms.

Several patterns may be at work here in terms of accounting for the changing volatility. For one, the overall decline in firm turnover and firm volatility is consistent with findings that the shift in key sectors such as retail trade away from small, single unit establishment firms to large, national chains has reduced firm turnover.[14] While this phenomenon

---

[14] See Foster et al. (2006) and Jarmin, Klimek, and Miranda (2001) for further discussion.

seems especially tied to retail trade, the shift to multi-unit firms is an area worth further investigation for all sectors. Second, there is accumulating evidence consistent with Figure 6-9 that publicly traded firms have become younger and riskier. Fama and French (2004) and Davis et al. (2006a) document that more recent cohorts of publicly traded firms are much more volatile than prior cohorts. The speculation (not confirmed) is that it has become easier to go public, so that riskier firms now do so. This speculation might account for both the privately held and publicly traded patterns since it may be that some types of risky firms that in prior decades were more likely to be privately traded are now increasingly publicly traded.

6.6. Pre-History of Young Employer Firms

One of the key messages from the findings in the prior sections is that young firms in particular exhibit high growth and are very volatile. The high growth and volatility of young firms is driven in part by entry and exit and also by the rapid but volatile growth of continuing young firms.

Given the importance of young firms in accounting for growth and volatility, it is of interest to understand the dynamics of entry and young firms on a variety of dimensions. Recent analysis (e.g., Davis et al., 2006a) has highlighted the role of micro businesses without employees as being part of the testing ground for new employer businesses. Figure 6-11 shows why such micro businesses are likely to be important for understanding the dynamics of young and small businesses. Of the roughly 20 million businesses in the United States, about 75 percent of them do not have employees (denoted as "non-employers" in Figure 6-11). Most of the latter are sole proprietors (denoted as "person ID businesses" in Figure 6-11). The 15 million or so nonemployer businesses are interesting in their own right simply because of the high number, and in a related way these reflect individuals who have at least some self-employment income. Of course, many of these micro businesses are truly micro in that the share of revenue accounted for by these non-employer businesses is quite small. About 96 percent of gross revenue from U.S. businesses, according to the lower panel of Figure 6-11, derives from businesses with employees and most of the latter comes from multi-establishment (MU) firms.

It turns out that not only are there large numbers of micro businesses but some of them transit to employer businesses. Put differently, a substantial fraction of young employer businesses have a prehistory as a non-employer business. Figure 6-12 shows that for a selected set of

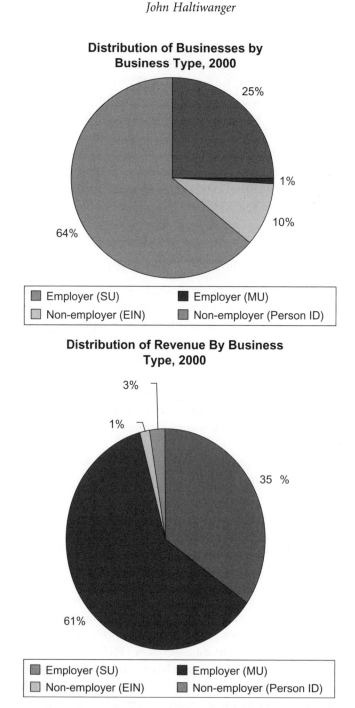

Figure 6-11. Comparisons of employer and nonemployer businesses. SU; MU: multi-establishment firms. Source: Tabulations from ILBD (based on Davis et al., 2006b).

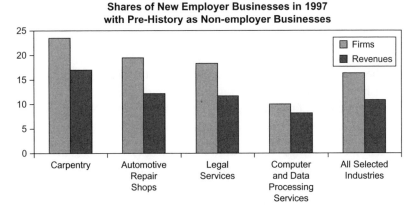

Figure 6-12. Shares of new employer businesses in 1997 with prehistory as non-employer businesses. Source: Tabulations from ILBD (based on Davis et al., 2006b).

industries more than 15 percent of young employer firms and more than 10 percent of revenue of young employer firms have a prehistory as a nonemployer.

6.7. Concluding Remarks

To conclude, we highlight the key findings and then discuss their implications. Key findings for the U.S. private sector include:

- Young businesses have much higher net growth and much higher volatility than mature businesses. These patterns hold both with and without controls for employer size.
- An important component of the net growth and volatility of young businesses is entry and exit but young continuing businesses also exhibit high net growth and volatility.
- Once age is controlled for, there is not much of a systematic relationship between employer size and net growth. Controlling for age, small businesses are more volatile than larger businesses.
- Publicly traded businesses exhibit higher net growth and less volatility than privately held businesses. The net growth pattern is enhanced after controlling for employer size and age since privately held firms are more likely to be young and small. Young, publicly traded firms grow much more rapidly than young, privately held firms, which in turn grow much more rapidly than mature firms.

- There has been a decline in overall firm volatility in the United States over the last couple of decades. This is driven by a decline in firm volatility for privately held firms that more than offsets an increase in firm volatility for publicly traded firms. Privately held firms have become somewhat larger and older over the last couple of decades, while the opposite is true for publicly traded firms.
- A nontrivial fraction of young employer firms have a prehistory as non-employer firms.

All of these findings point toward a picture of U.S. business dynamics as being characterized by constant change and churning, with young firms exhibiting rapid net growth and high volatility. Caution needs to be used in using these findings to make statements along the lines of "young firms create the most jobs" or "young firms disproportionately create jobs." Such caution is required for both accounting and conceptual reasons. For accounting reasons, the high pace of churning of jobs means that gross job flows dwarf net job creation. As such, many groups like young businesses both create and destroy many jobs. With the same group exhibiting both expansion and contraction it is potentially quite misleading to portion out the share of net job growth accounted for any given group.

For conceptual reasons, the high net growth and high volatility of young firms points toward creative destruction interpretations of U.S. growth dynamics. While not the focus of this chapter, recent studies have shown that in the United States this high pace of churning especially among young firms is productivity-enhancing. Even with this latter finding, considerable caution needs to be used in attributing growth to young firms and in a related way to the entry and exit dynamics. Instead, it is the process of creative destruction that is contributing to growth. With creative destruction, there is ongoing innovation and market experimentation with a high degree of churning contributing to growth. Of course, this implies that some firms are successful and grow while others are not successful and contract (and perhaps exit). Among young firms, since both outcomes are likely it is hardly appropriate to target young firms as the sources of growth. Rather again, the high net growth and volatility of young firms is a feature of healthy creative destruction dynamics ongoing among U.S. businesses.

While caution is required in attributing growth to or targeting young businesses per se, it is of course of interest to explore which factors make young businesses grow rapidly and exhibit such volatility. Put differently, it is of interest to understand the market structure and institutions that underlie a healthy creative destruction process. An obvious issue in this context is the credit market. Young businesses and especially micro businesses (without employees) are likely to face difficulties obtaining financing. Given the observed volatility this is hardly surprising. Put differently and in a closely related way, being a young and small business implies by its very nature that the business will not have had the time or resources to have established a reputation for credit markets. But we have also found that those businesses that have gone public grow especially rapidly, including the young businesses that have gone public. The direction of causality here is unclear. It may be that it is precisely those young businesses that have been especially innovative in their product, process, and/ or location of activity (where the latter is potentially tied to both product and process innovation) that grow rapidly, attract market attention, and go public. Still, somehow those young businesses that have gone public have attracted the attention of financial markets, and it is important to understand how such connections are generated.[15] In this context, one must emphasize that there are a vast array of micro businesses, most of which never even hire a worker, with only a small fraction making the transition to an employer and an even smaller fraction making the transition to going public. So understanding the nature of and the factors influencing these transitions is of importance for growth. In other words, these findings highlight the importance of understanding the role of entrepreneurship for growth.

[15] So, for example, the role of venture capital and/or angel financing is of interest in this context.

References

Acs, Zoltan J., Catharine Armington, and Alicia Robb. 1999. "Measures of Job Flow Dynamics in the U.S. Economy." Center for Economic Studies, U.S. Census Bureau, Working Papers.

Aghion, Phillipe, and Peter Howitt. 1998. *Endogenous Growth Theory.* Cambridge, Mass.: MIT Press.

Aw, Bee Yan, Xiaomin Chen, and Mark J. Roberts. 2001. "Firm-Level Evidence on Productivity Differentials and Turnover in Taiwanese Manufacturing." *Journal of Development Economics,* 66(1), 51–86.

Bahk, Byong-Hyong, and Michael Gort. 1993. "Decomposing Learning by Doing in New Plants." *Journal of Political Economy,* 101(4), 561–583.

Baily, Martin, Charles Hulten, and David Campbell. 1992. "Productivity Dynamics in Manufacturing Plants." *Brookings Papers on Economic Activity, Microeconomics,* 187–267.

Bartelsman, Eric J., and Mark Doms. 2000. "Understanding Productivity: Lessons from Longitudinal Data."Board of Governors of the Federal Reserve System, Finance and Economics Discussion Series number 2000–19.

Brown, Charles, Jay Hamilton, and James Medoff. 1990. *Employers Large and Small*. Cambridge, Mass.: Harvard University Press.

Brown, Charles, and James Medoff. 2001. *"Firm Age and Wages."* NBER Working Paper 8552.

Carroll, Glenn R., and Michael T. Hannan. 2000. *The Demography of Corporations and Industries*. Princeton: Princeton University Press.

Comin, Diego, and Thomas Philippon. 2005. "The Rise in Firm level Volatility: Causes and Consequences." NBER Working Paper 11388.

Commerce Clearing House. Various years. *U.S. Master Sales and Use Tax Guide*. Chicago: CCH Incorporated.

Davis, Steven J., and John Haltiwanger. 1991. "Wage Dispersion Between and Within U.S. Manufacturing Plants, 1963–1986." *Brookings Papers on Economic Activity, Microeconomics*, 115–200.

Davis, Steven J., and John Haltiwanger. 1992. "Gross Job Creation, Gross Job Destruction and Employment Reallocation." *Quarterly Journal of Economics*, 107(3), 819–863.

Davis, Steven J., and John Haltiwanger. 1999. "Gross Job Flows." In Orley Ashenfelter and David Card, eds., *Handbook of Labor Economics*, vol. 3. Amsterdam: Elsevier Science.

Davis, Steven J., John C. Haltiwanger, and Scott Schuh. 1996. *Job Creation and Destruction*. Cambridge, Mass.: MIT Press.

Davis, Steven J., John Haltiwanger, Ron Jarmin, and Javier Miranda. 2006a. "Volatility and Dispersion in Business Growth Rates: Publicly Traded vs. Privately Held Firms." NBER Working Paper 12354.

Davis, Steven J., John Haltiwanger, Ron Jarmin, C. J. Krizan, Javier Miranda, Alfred Nucci, and Kristin Sandusky. 2006b. "Measuring the Dynamics of Young and Small Businesses: Integrating the Employer and Nonemployer Universes." Paper provided by Center for Economic Studies, U.S. Census Bureau, working paper 06–04.

Doms, Mark, Timothy Dunne, and Kenneth Troske. 1997. "Workers, Wages, and Technology." *Quarterly Journal of Economics*, 112(1), 253–290.

Dunne, Timothy. 1994. "Plant Age and Technology Use in U.S. Manufacturing Industries." *Rand Journal of Economics*, 25(3), 488–499.

Dunne, Timothy, Mark Roberts, and Larry Samuelson. 1988. "Patterns of Firm Entry and Exit in U.S. Manufacturing." *Rand Journal of Economics*, 19(4), 495–515.

Dunne, Timothy, Mark Roberts, and Larry Samuelson. 1989. "The Growth and Failure of U.S. Manufacturing Plants," *Quarterly Journal of Economics*, 104(4), 671–698.

Ericson, Richard, and Ariel Pakes. 1995. "Markov Perfect Industry Dynamics: A Framework for Empirical Work." *Review of Economic Studies*, 62(1), 53–82.

Fama, Eugene F., and Kenneth R. French. 2004. "New Lists: Fundamentals and Survival Rates." *Journal of Financial Economics*, 73(2), 229–269.

Foster, Lucia, John Haltiwanger, and C. J. Krizan. 2001. "Aggregate Productivity Growth: Lessons from Microeconomic Evidence." In Edward Dean, Michael Harper, and Charles Hulten, eds., *New Directions in Productivity Analysis*. Chicago: University of Chicago Press.

Foster, Lucia, John Haltiwanger, and C. J. Krizan. 2002. "The Link Between Aggregate and Micro Productivity Growth: Evidence from Retail Trade." NBER Working Paper 9120.

Foster, Lucia, John Haltiwanger, and Chad Syverson. 2005. "Reallocation, Firm Turnover, and Efficiency: Selection on Productivity or Profitablity." NBER Working Paper W11555.

Haltiwanger, John, and C. J. Krizan. 1999. "Small Business and Job Creation in the United States: The Role of New and Young Businesses." In *Are Small Firms Important? Their Role and Impact*, Zoltan Acs, ed. Boston: Kluwer Academic Publishing.

Jarmin, Ron S., and Javier Miranda. 2002. "The Longitudinal Business Database." Center for Economic Studies, U.S. Census Bureau, Working Papers.

Jarmin, Ron S., Shawn Klimek, and Javier Miranda. 2001. "Firm Entry and Exit in the U.S. Retail Sector, 1977–1997." Center for Economic Studies, U.S. Census Bureau, Working Papers.

Jovanovic, Boyan. 1982. "Selection and the Evolution of Industry." *Econometrica*, 50(3), 649–670.

Lucas, Robert E., Jr. 1993. "Making a Miracle." *Econometrica*, 61(2), 251–272.

Oi, Walter, and Todd Idson. 1999. "Firm Size and Wages." In Orley Ashenfelter and David Card, eds., *Handbook of Labor Economics*, vol. 3. Amsterdam: Elsevier Science.

Olley, G. Steven, and Ariel Pakes. 1996. "The Dynamics of Productivity in the Telecommunications Equipment Industry." *Econometrica*, 64(6), 1263–1297.

Prescott, Edward C., and Michael Visscher. 1980. "Organization Capital." *Journal of Political Economy*, 88(3), 446–461.

Roberts, Mark J., and James R. Tybout. 1996. *Industrial Evolution in Developing Countries: Micro Patterns of Turnover, Productivity and Market Structure*. Oxford: Oxford University Press.

Troske, Kenneth. 1996. "The Dynamic Adjustment Process of Firm Entry and Exit in Manufacturing and Finance, Insurance and Real Estate." *Journal of Law and Economics*, 39(2), 705–735.

Troske, Kenneth R. 1998. "The Worker-Establishment Characteristics Database." In J. Haltiwanger and M. Manser, eds., *Labor Statistics Measurement Issues*. Chicago: University of Chicago Press.

U.S. Bureau of the Census. 1988 and 1994. *County and City Data Book* [machine-readable data files]. Washington, D.C.: U.S. Bureau of the Census.

7

Entrepreneurship at American Universities

Nathan Rosenberg

Innovations, almost by definition, are one of the least analyzed parts of economics, in spite of the verifiable fact that they have contributed more to per capita economic growth than any other factor.

Ken Arrow

7.1. Some Historical Perspectives

My central concern in this chapter is with innovation in the American university community. I have chosen to begin with the term "innovation" rather than "entrepreneurship" because I propose to deal with issues that take us well beyond "entrepreneurship," as that term is ordinarily used. I by no means ignore the traditional entrepreneur, but I also address larger themes such as the creation and the institutionalization of new academic disciplines and the roles that they have played, in turn, in the discovery and the diffusion of (potentially) useful knowledge.

The trajectory taken in the United States versus Europe owes a great deal to the political system in which it occurs. After the Napoleonic Wars, institutions of higher education in much of continental Europe became, overwhelmingly, public. In effect, they were nationalized, with extensive centralized control as the inevitable accompaniment of centralized funding. University faculty became civil servants.

Higher education in the United States was shaped by a very different set of political forces, the most distinguishing feature of which was an aversion to the centralization of power. The federalization of the country in the last

This chapter was originally prepared for presentation at the Kauffman Foundation–Max Planck Gesellschaft Conference on "Entrepreneurship and Economic Growth," Munich, Germany, May 8–9, 2006. The author wishes to acknowledge the Merck Company Foundation for support in the preparation of this manuscript.

two decades of the eighteenth century translated into the localization of decision making as well as financial support of the educational system. This hostility to centralization has had its reflection in the fact that, to this day, there is no major public research university located in the nation's capital, despite numerous proposals over the years as well as the availability of superb library and archival collections. Support for establishing a national university in Washington, D.C., goes back to Hamiltonian proposals that were advanced almost immediately after the American Revolution, but they were rejected out of a fear of the possibility of concentrating excessive power in a centralized authority. Perhaps even more pertinent is the fact that the United States has never had a ministry of education!

In the absence of a reliable source of revenue, a prerequisite for the success of an American university has always been its ability to raise funds, and the leadership of universities has therefore required the critical entrepreneurial skill of fund-raising. In a small number of cases, some of America's most eminent universities were founded with substantial endowments by entrepreneurs who had already acquired great wealth: Johns Hopkins University, Cornell University, Vanderbilt University, Stanford University, Carnegie Mellon University, and the University of Chicago (the latter was, of course, founded with Rockefeller money, but in 1891 it was thought unwise to prejudice the future of a newly born university with the name of a robber baron). But for the vast majority of private institutions, and even for institutions that started life with sizable benefactions, the president of a university has had to be a skillful and determined fundraiser, on par with the entrepreneur scraping funds from whatever sources will listen to his or her pitch.

In this context, the older, elite American universities paid little attention to more "practical" disciplines, such as science and engineering, until the incentive of a private endowment was forthcoming. Harvard established the Lawrence Scientific School in 1847. Yale created the Sheffield Scientific School in response to a gift by a private entrepreneur in 1858. MIT was established on April 10, 1861, through the leadership of a group of Boston industrialists (two days before Fort Sumter was bombarded and the Civil War was begun).[1]

State universities might, on first consideration, appear to have been exempt from the need for entrepreneurial leadership, but this was actually

---

[1] UNIDO, "Capability Building for Catching-Up," UNIDO, Vienna, 2005, p. 46. See also Karl Wildes and Nilo Lindgren, *A Century of Electrical Engineering and Computer Science at MIT, 1882–1982*, pp. 378–379.

not the case. Although the Morrill Act, passed by Congress in 1862, was the enabling "land grant" legislation that gave rise to a national network of state universities, control and the subsequent financing of these universities was placed in the hands of each state. Because there are many states, as well as an even larger number of private universities, it was never obvious why a public institution of higher education was necessary in each state, to be supported by revenues raised by the state's taxpayers. Thus, to persuade state legislators to appropriate the necessary tax revenues, it was essential to demonstrate that the state university was providing uniquely valuable services to the business, agricultural, and industrial interests of each state, a sort of knowledge capital. Convincing legislators required considerable entrepreneurial skills of a political and rhetorical sort.

At state universities both teaching curricula and research activities came to be specialized in ways that would accommodate the changing needs of local industry and business. The Morrill Act referred to the need for these new institutions to advance the interests of "agriculture and the mechanic arts." The subsequent Hatch Act, passed by Congress in 1887, twenty-five years after the Morrill Act had established the land grant state university system, established state agricultural experiment stations that subsequently played a crucial role in the developing improved agricultural technologies. As the country expanded westward and underwent industrialization, university teaching and research programs grew in terms of their diversity and extent of specialization. Indeed, the ease with which these activities could be altered became, and has remained, an essential feature that distinguished American universities from their European counterparts.

Thus, after World War I, a college of engineering might offer undergraduate degrees in a bewildering variety of highly specialized engineering subjects, specializations of somewhat doubtful social benefit. In Illinois, a state heavily dependent on railroads, an engineering student entering the University of Illinois found that he or she might take an undergraduate degree in architectural engineering, ceramic engineering, mining engineering, municipal and sanitary engineering, railway civil engineering, railway electrical engineering, and railway mechanical engineering. As one observer wryly observed at the time, "Nearly every industry and government agency in Illinois had its own department at the state university in Urbana-Champaign."[2]

American universities, especially state universities, have been a cornucopia of useful technologies for local industry – critical knowledge capital that

---

[2] Levine, 1986.

improved the local economy. The Babcock test, developed by an agricultural research chemist at the University of Wisconsin and introduced in 1890, provided a cheap and simple method for measuring the butterfat content of milk, and thus an easy way to determine the adulteration of milk, a matter of no small consequence in a state dominated by dairy farmers. In Ohio, the University of Akron, a public urban university, supplied skilled personnel for the local rubber industry and later came to excel in research on rubber processing; even later, it "graduated" into a research center in polymer chemistry. The University of Minnesota developed at its own Mines Experiment Station, a processing technique for the efficient exploitation of low-grade iron ores, after the rich hematite deposits of the Mesabi Range had been largely exhausted. Similarly, for many years the University of Oklahoma has distinguished itself for its research in the field of petroleum, and the universities of Kentucky and North Carolina have worked intensively on devising technologies that have been employed in the post-harvest processing of tobacco. In the early 1980s there were no fewer than thirty-seven universities in the United States that were performing research for local and regional forest products industries. The main focal points of such research were "wood moisture relations, wood chemistry including pulp and paper, mechanical properties, reconstituted products, and wood anatomy/microscopy."[3]

But American universities in the twentieth century also moved gradually, yet decisively, beyond these highly specialized research projects for the benefit of local industry. In the first half of the twentieth century American universities began to focus heavily, in both research and teaching, on new disciplines in several fields of engineering and applied sciences. A striking feature here was that these subjects were institutionalized, acquiring departmental status, very early and quickly, even when the related scientific discipline had been developed earlier in Europe, and even when European contributions to the science remained far more advanced than the contributions coming from America. This was conspicuously the case with respect to the engineering disciplines that had been built upon electricity, chemistry, and aerodynamics (fluid mechanics).[4]

---

[3] Resch et al., 1985, p. 584.

[4] In one important dimension, public universities in recent years are becoming more like private universities: "Public universities in general, which used to cover most of their budgets from state money, now get only 15–20% from that source. Their costs are rising rapidly, especially where new technology and health-care expenses are concerned. To fill the gap, many of them are looking to the private sector for help. But can they do this and still stay loyal to their old public responsibilities?" *The Economist*, June 2, 2001.

What I propose to do now is to examine a number of episodes in which American universities took innovative actions within the academic world that resulted in significant benefits for the performance of the American economy. In some of these episodes, federal funds served as a powerful facilitator; in other cases it was the comparative ease with which American faculty could cross the boundaries between the academy and industry. In most cases there were organizational changes that redefined the responsibilities and the opportunities of the academic participants.

I must confess that I offer no sweeping general principles, but I take refuge in a simple, declarative statement by one of our greatest economic theorists, Kenneth Arrow: "Where innovation is concerned, we are all historians."

For this presentation I am going to look at the histories of several diverse fields, starting with aeronautical engineering, chemical engineering, and then computing. Then I look at health care and the development of diagnostic devices, including endoscopes, computed tomography (CT), and magnetic resonance imaging (MRI). This is followed with some concluding observations.

7.2. Aeronautical Engineering

Aircraft design became a subject of great importance in the second decade of the twentieth century. Germany completely dominated the underlying science, the theory of aerodynamics, under the towering leadership of Ludwig Prandtl at Göttingen University. Prandtl was a professor at Göttingen from 1904 until his death in 1953. His articulation of the boundary-layer hypothesis in 1904, which emerged out of his earlier interest in the flow of liquids, eventually became the most fundamental concept of aerodynamic theory, a theory further elaborated primarily in Germany during the interwar years.

Research in aeronautical engineering in the United States, where the main contributors worked at Cal Tech, Stanford, and MIT, drew heavily on Prandtl's fundamental research. However, more knowledge was required for successful aircraft design, knowledge that was not deducible from the science of aerodynamics. Extensive experimentation was essential. Consider W. F. Durand and E. P. Lesley's propeller tests at Stanford that ran for fully ten years, from 1916 to 1926. These protracted experimental tests were necessary because there was no way in which the body of scientific knowledge would permit a more direct determination of the optimal design of a propeller, given the fact that "the propeller operates in combination with both engine and airframe . . . and it must be compatible with the power-output characteristics of the former and the flight requirements of the latter."[5]

The Stanford experiments led to a better understanding of how to approach the whole problem of aircraft design. In this sense, a critical output of these experiments was a form of generic technological knowledge that lies at the heart of the modern discipline of aeronautical engineering. "Though less tangible than design data, such understanding of how to think about a problem also constitutes engineering knowledge. This knowledge was communicated both explicitly and implicitly by the Durand-Lesley reports."[6]

The greater degree of sophistication in aeronautical research methods that resulted from the Stanford experiments made an important contribution to the maturing of the American aircraft industry in the 1930s, a maturity crowned by the emergence of the DC-3 in the second half of that decade. But the success of the DC-3, the most popular commercial transport plane ever built, also owed an enormous debt to another educational institution, the California Institute of Technology. The Guggenheim Foundation had established an aeronautical laboratory at Cal Tech that made possible research that was decisive to the success of Douglas Aircraft, located in nearby Santa Monica. Both technical features, such as durability and reliability of components, and economically essential features, such as passenger carrying capacity, were largely the product of Cal Tech Guggenheim Aeronautical Laboratory research, highlighted also by their use of multicellular construction. The wind tunnel testing at this lab eventually led to an accumulation of numerous improvements in the DC-3.

Thus, the emergence of the DC-3 was an innovation that represents the beginning of the modern commercial aircraft industry. It was an innovation that was the product of joint extensive research and cooperation across the university-industry interface. The scale of this innovation may be simply stated: By 1938, DC-3s were carrying more than 95 percent of all commercial air traffic in the United States, and these aircraft were being used by thirty foreign airlines.[7] It should be emphasized that the DC-3 did not incorporate any truly major technological improvements that were not already available to the aircraft industry in the first half of the 1930s. Rather, its superior performance and its low operating costs were the

---

[5] Vincenti, 1990, p. 141.
[6] Ibid., p. 158.
[7] Miller and Sawers, 1970, p. 102.

product of numerous small modifications and design improvements based on the existing state of aeronautical engineering knowledge at the time.[8]

Of course, World War I and its turbulent aftermath had a great deal to do both with Germany's failure to fully exploit its early leadership in aerodynamics as well as with the transatlantic transfer of that body of scientific knowledge. This transfer was facilitated when Prandtl's most distinguished student, Theodore von Karman, a Hungarian Jew, accepted an invitation to join the faculty of Cal Tech in 1930. Von Karman's leadership played a critical role in Cal Tech's subsequent contributions to the design of the DC-3.[9]

Still, it is far from clear that the sophisticated aerodynamic concepts developed at Göttingen would have had as rapid a commercial application in Germany as in the United States, even if the times and the circumstances had been more propitious. Prandtl regarded himself as someone working in the domain of "applied physics," but it is clear in context that he conducted experiments in order to confirm theory, not to apply it. It is doubtful that he would have participated in the very practical aircraft design exercises that von Karman became so extensively involved in for Douglas Aircraft, beginning in 1932.[10] Von Karman wrote in his autobiography that he "enjoyed climbing into the ten-foot wind tunnel with a wad of putty, and imagining myself being the airplane I tried to feel where I might be pressed by an element of air." Such practical applications were far beneath the dignity of a German university professor at the time. Perhaps it is worth recalling that Germany had introduced the *Technische Hochschule* in the second half of the nineteenth century in order to teach technical subjects that were regarded as unfit to be taught by university professors, and they did not receive the right to award doctoral degrees until Kaiser Wilhelm decreed so in 1900.[11]

7.3. Chemical Engineering

American leadership in introducing a new engineering discipline into the university curriculum, even at a time when the country was far from the

---

[8] For a broader discussion of some of these issues, see Rosenberg, 1982, chap. 6.

[9] See Hanle, 1982, and Goodstein, 1991. Von Karman has been described by an authoritative source as "probably the leading aerodynamicist of the 1920–1960 time period" (Anderson, 1997, p. 5).

[10] See Karman and Edson, 1967, p. 170.

[11] See Hanle, 1982, chaps. 3–5, for a useful examination of the cultural environment in which Prandtl was immersed.

frontier of scientific research, was nowhere more conspicuous than in the discipline of chemical engineering early in the twentieth century.

At the beginning of the twentieth century Germany was the world leader in the science of chemistry, particularly organic chemistry. For the first forty years of the twentieth century, the Nobel Prizes tell much of the story. Germany was, overwhelmingly, the dominating recipient. Up to 1939, only three Americans received Nobel Prizes in chemistry, compared with 15 for Germany and six apiece for the the United Kingdom and France. Between 1949 and 1994, however, 36 Americans received the chemistry prize; Britons were second with 17, Germans third with 11, and the French received just one.

The spectacular growth of the automobile industry in the United States in the second and third decades of the twentieth century, along with the subsequent demand for liquid fuels, led to the need to design and to operate chemical process plants at increasing volumes of output and thus to the emergence of research and teaching programs in American universities.[12]

For present purposes, it is essential to see the parallelism of the discipline of chemical engineering with that of aeronautical engineering. Chemical engineers are concerned with the design, construction, and operation of large-scale chemical-process plants.[13] But chemical engineering does not and cannot achieve these goals through an application of the science of chemistry. Chemical engineering is not applied chemistry. New products in the chemical industries have, historically, typically emerged out of laboratory research conducted by bench chemists making use of small beakers, test tubes, and retorts. However, such laboratory research does not provide the information required for scaling up to commercial production. In the most practical sense, scaling up the original equipment to a size appropriate for commercial production is, usually, physically impossible and hardly ever economically feasible. One cannot, for example, readily scale up with glass containers. Instead, scaling up requires recourse to apparatus of an entirely different sort, involving entirely different materials that can sustain extremely high pressures and temperatures, as well as the use of pumps, compressors, piping, and vats of a very large scale.

---

[12] For a discussion of the role played by differences between the United States and Germany in the composition of demand for chemical-based products, and how these differences influenced the approach in each country to the discipline of chemical engineering, see Rosenberg, 1998.

[13] See Landau, 1966.

Consequently, what constitutes an optimal scale for commercial production requires experimentation of a sort that is entirely different from that which led to the original development of the product. Optimal plant size cannot, for many reasons, be achieved by a simple linear extrapolation from a small-scale model. The key experimental tool of the chemical engineer is therefore the pilot plant and inferences drawn from experimental data provided by such plants. Such optimal size will be found to differ from one chemical product line to another.

The central concept in the discipline of chemical engineering, when it first made its appearance in an academic context, was that of "unit operations." A. D. Little presented this concept in a report to the Corporation of the Massachusetts Institute of Technology in December 1915. In Little's words:

> Any chemical process, on whatever scale conducted, may be resolved into a coordinated series of what may be termed "unit actions," as pulverizing, mixing, heating, roasting, absorbing, condensing, lixiviating, precipitating, crystallizing, filtering, dissolving, electrolyzing, and so on. The number of these basic unit operations is not very large and relatively few of them are involved in any particular process…. Chemical engineering research … is directed toward the improvement, control and better coordination of these unit operations and the selection or development of the equipment in which they are carried out.[14]

A critical feature of the concept of unit operations is that it went well beyond the purely descriptive approaches of industrial chemistry by calling attention to a small number of distinctive processes that were common to many product lines. This act of intellectual abstraction laid the foundations for a more rigorous and, eventually, more quantitative discipline. It is tempting to call Little's manifesto an attempt to provide a general purpose technology for the chemical sector.[15]

Chemical engineering was now in a position to be able to accumulate a set of methodological tools that could be refined and that could provide the basis for a wide range of problem-solving activities connected with the design of chemical-process plants. Not least important, it now had the basis for a curriculum that could be taught. In 1920, just a few years after Little's formulation, chemical engineering achieved the status of a separate, independent department at MIT, under the chairmanship of W. K. Lewis.

The teaching of chemical engineering was organized around the concept of unit operations for the next few decades, but the concept underwent

---

[14] Little, 1933, p. 7.
[15] Rosenberg, 2000.

substantial alteration in its intellectual content, almost from the very beginning. An academic environment created strong pressures toward analytical rigor, internal consistency, and generality. An engineer trained in terms of unit operations could mix and match these operations as necessary in order to produce a wide variety of distinct final products. Such an engineer was much more flexible and resourceful in his or her approach to problem solving. Of key importance was that he was well equipped to take techniques and methods from one branch of industry and to transfer them to another. Experience in one place could now be readily transferred to other, apparently unrelated places. This capability was especially valuable in the innovation process – particularly as new materials and new products emerged.

Thus, research that improved the efficiency of any one process was now likely to be more quickly employed in a large number of places. Putting the point somewhat differently, the identification of a small number of unit operations common to a large number of industries meant that it was now possible to identify specific research topics for which new findings could be confidently expected to experience widespread utilization. Needless to say, this point is of great significance in the growth of an engineering discipline. Chemical processing plants existed in many industries in addition to the chemical industry proper.[16]

Although the episode is not well known, these recently acquired technical skills of the chemical engineer played a crucial role in the introduction of penicillin, probably the most important medical innovation of the twentieth century. Alexander Fleming's brilliant theory, that common bread mold was responsible for the bactericidal properties that he had observed in his Petri dish came in 1928. Nevertheless, penicillin remained unavailable at the outbreak of the Second World War. Producing penicillin on a commercial scale during the war required a crash program in which the eventual solution came not, as would normally be expected, from the pharmaceutical chemist but rather from chemical engineers who designed and operated a pilot plant. These engineers successfully demonstrated how the technique of aerobic submerged fermentation, which became the dominant production technology, could be made to work by solving apparently intractable problems of heat and mass transfer.[17]

---

[16] Some of the larger ones included petroleum refining, rubber, leather, coal (by-product distillation plants), food processing, sugar refining, explosives, ceramics and glass, paper and pulp, cement, and various metallurgical industries.

[17] See Elder, 1970.

An important aspect of the relationship between the scientific and technological realms should be noted here. Industrial progress has often proceeded in a sequence in which fundamental science first opened new product categories but then had to await further development until the appropriate methods of manufacturing were worked out. In the case of the modern petrochemical industry, which emerged during and especially after the Second World War, many of the processing methods had already been developed in the interwar years, largely in the petroleum-refining industry. The modern postwar petrochemical industry had indeed had its origins in fundamental research on long-chained molecules by Hermann Staudinger in Germany in the 1920s. Thus, when the fruits of this earlier scientific research finally became available after that war in the form of new products made possible by plastics, synthetic fibers, and synthetic rubber, the basic processing technologies were already at hand as a result of the earlier accomplishments of the chemical engineers who had developed the methods of producing the necessary chemical feedstocks (ethylene and polyethylene) before and during the Second World War.

The transformation of the American chemical industry, as it existed in 1920, into the petrochemical industry that matured after World War II was in large measure the achievement of the chemical engineering profession, and especially the newly formed chemical engineering department at MIT. Beginning in the 1920s, "The major oil companies quickly hired large numbers of MIT chemical engineers, and for a number of years these men practically dominated the industry. The chemical engineering senior faculty at MIT was almost completely hired as consultants or permanent employees by Exxon."[18]

The development of the discipline of chemical engineering offers interesting evidence into how the interaction between industry and academia can, at least in some instances, provide valuable, powerful spillovers to both. In chemical engineering, the interface between university and industry was unusually intimate – to the extent that MIT students undertook research topics drawn from the immediate needs at the technology frontier that their professors brought back from their consultancy excursions. It was in this context that two MIT graduate students came to play a critical role in the design and development of one of the most valuable innovations in the history of petroleum refining: fluidized catalytic cracking. This newly designed process was rapidly adopted and went on to play a significant role in the Second World War in increasing the production of

---

[18] Weber, 1980, p. 26.

high-octane gasoline. The technique was, in a sense, generalized into the fluidized solids technique, which had a wide range of applications in synthetic rubber and plastics and a gradually expanded range of industrial processes.[19]

At the same time, the most significant findings drawn from the consulting experiences of the MIT faculty were quickly transmitted to students through swift changes in the content of the teaching curriculum. As long as professors maintained an active role in a teaching capacity, it was only natural to apply the knowledge acquired from their problem-solving activities as consultants, in a larger and more general context. This meant fitting that knowledge together in an internally consistent way with other knowledge that made up their discipline. When reverting to their teaching roles, they needed to systematize their knowledge as an essential precondition for writing textbooks, articles, and so on. This systematization had profound implications for the diffusion of new technological knowledge, not only because open universities "naturally" diffuse their knowledge, but also because the need to systematize knowledge for teaching purposes meant that professors had to spend time and sustained effort in further activities that inevitably facilitated the spread of useful knowledge.[20]

The prominent role played by an academic institution devoted to teaching as well as research was of great importance for a related reason. Even though students in chemical engineering programs went to work in different firms or organizations, they had all been taught a common language of concepts, theories and methods. This shared language facilitated the development of a professional community of people who could readily communicate with and learn from one another, and vastly reduced the barriers to the diffusion of technical knowledge across organizational boundary lines. This ability was precisely what made chemical engineers, soon after the introduction of the concept of unit operations, so different from the earlier industrial chemists, who tended to speak in idiosyncratic industry-specific or even firm-specific languages.

Of course, the fact that the discipline of chemical engineering was located in universities in the United States had other, longer-term consequences. In the years immediately following Little's formulation of the concept of unit operations, research in chemical engineering sought to acquire a deeper understanding of each operation, in order to establish mathematical regularities that would improve the efficiency of the design

---

[19] See Enos, 1962. See also Jahnig, Martin and Campbell, 1983.
[20] See Arora and Gambardella, 1994.

process as well as lower the cost of operating the equipment that was eventually designed.[21]

Eventually these separate operations were reduced to more inclusive and more rigorous concepts such as fluid mechanics and heat transfer. In time, chemical engineers attempted to codify the basic physical phenomena underlying momentum (viscous flow), energy transport (heat conduction, convection, and radiation), and mass transport (diffusion). It was continual advances such as these that led in recent years to the claim that chemical engineering has finally achieved the status of an "engineering science." Beginning with the concept of unit operations as a way of abstracting from the particularities of specific artifacts, it eventually moved to a deeper level: expressing the processing activities of chemical plants in terms of basic molecular and transport phenomena, and eventually introducing the fundamental concept of thermodynamics. As a result, much of the designing activity of chemical engineers is now understood at a more fundamental level, while the design of chemical processing equipment still draws on empirical regularities that have stood the test of time, even when these regularities could not be accounted for at a fundamental level that would satisfy the more rigorous demands of the scientist.

Thus, a critical achievement of the initial concept of unit operations was that it clarified the objectives of research. By providing an intellectual platform for science, it eventually altered the nature of the platform itself. Consequently, it can be said of chemical engineering that it did not emerge out of prior science, but rather, as it matured, it increased the opportunity to focus the scientific concepts and methodologies for the problems it dealt with. As a result, chemical engineering eventually became more scientific. But it is crucial to understand that it was the earlier maturation of chemical engineering that made the application of science possible.

7.4. Computing

The emergence of the computer in the immediate postwar period involved the dissolution of many of the traditional boundaries between universities, private industry and the federal government. This needs to be seen, at least partly, in terms of a perceived strategic crisis within the context of the Cold War that was felt immediately after the Soviet Union's successful

---

[21] See the enormously influential textbook by three members of the MIT faculty: W. Lewis, W. McAdams, and W. Walker, *Principles of Chemical Engineering*, 1923. This book took a long step forward from Little's initial formulation of unit operations to a methodology of far greater quantitative and mathematical rigor.

launching of *Sputnik* in 1957. But America's early dominance owed a great deal to the outcome of the Second World War. Pioneering research had, of course, been conducted outside the United States during the war itself, especially by Alan Turing in Great Britain and Konrad Zuse in Germany. Manchester and Cambridge Universities were actively engaged in computer development immediately after the end of the war, and in 1948 Manchester developed the first computer, the Mark I, that made use of a magnetic drum memory. Zuse, of Berlin University, worked extensively on electromechanical calculators, one of which was installed in the German plant that manufactured the V-2 rockets that were sent over London in the closing months of the war. However, partly due to the impact of the war and its immediate aftermath, the emergence of a practical electronic, digital computer was largely the direct outcome of research activities carried out at American universities, especially in its schools of engineering.

In the case of hardware, the ENIAC, generally considered to be the first fully electronic digital computer, was created at the end of the war at the Moore School of Electrical Engineering at the University of Pennsylvania; it was financed under a contract with the Aberdeen Proving Grounds in Maryland, which was anxious to improve the accuracy of its ballistics tables. The machine was essentially a more powerful version of something called the "differential analyzer," an analog machine that had been built and operated in the peaceful 1930s at MIT, under the direction of Vannevar Bush. Bush, an electrical engineer, had developed the machine in an attempt to simulate the operation of large and complex electric power grids, especially in the analysis of the problems associated with transient stability as electric power systems became increasingly interconnected.

The original ENIAC was "hard-wired" and made no use of software in its problem-solving activities. John von Neumann was an occasional adviser to the ENIAC project, and his ideas were incorporated in a subsequent machine, the EDVAC, which represented the first stored-program computer. The EDVAC's instructions were stored in memory, and therefore were much more readily modified. Von Neumann chaired an influential Advisory Panel on University Computing Facilities that, in 1956, endorsed the idea of establishing a National Science Foundation (NSF) program devoted to the support of university research in computer science.

The American commercial computer industry may be said to have been launched when Eckert and Mauchly, the University of Pennsylvania engineering professors who invented the ENIAC, established their own firm in 1946. It was an inauspicious beginning. They were dismissed from their professorial positions when they informed the university administration of their intention to undertake the entrepreneurial role of commercializing the computer. Their firm, the Eckert-Mauchly Corporation, quickly experienced financial problems and failed. The firm was acquired by Remington Rand in 1950.

Many of the subsequent contributions of American universities to the development of an enhanced computer capability were achieved as "by-products" of projects undertaken on contract to the federal government. Some of the key innovations in the strategic air-defense systems of the 1950s (Whirlwind and SAGE, or Semi-Automatic Ground Environment), in which MIT (including Lincoln Labs) played a central role, produced general principles as well as specific technologies that soon found much broader applications.[22] SAGE was a computerized, command-and-control early-warning system that was developed and eventually deployed in the 1950s. SAGE was the first widespread computer network, the first extensive digital data communications system, and the first real-time transaction processing system. Although the system had been rendered obsolete by the introduction of ICBMs by the time it was completed, it produced much that was of later use. Concepts that were developed on the SAGE system formed the basis for later commercial applications such as airline reservation systems, automated teller machines for IBM, and high-speed communication networks that were eventually deployed by AT&T. Far from the least important contribution of SAGE was its role in educating a huge number of systems programmers. The insufficient supply of such skills has been a persistent handicap to European competitiveness in the computer industry.[23]

The role of the federal government in the emergence of the software industry was also heavily influenced by strategic and military concerns, which were dramatically heightened by the Soviet launch of *Sputnik* in the fall of 1957. It should be remembered that the federal government, especially the military, has always been a major purchaser of the output of the software industry.[24]

In the fifteen years after the *Sputnik* launch, the NSF provided $85 million to more than 200 universities to allow them to purchase computer

---

[22] MIT's Lincoln Laboratories were established by the Air Force in 1950 in order to develop the country's air-defense system.

[23] For a more detailed treatment of the role of MIT in computer development, see Wildes and Lindgren, 1985.

[24] For an excellent treatment of the role of the federal government in the development of the U.S. software industry, see Langlois and Mowery, 1996. See also Steinmueller, 1996.

hardware. The "transactions" between the universities and private industry were particularly illuminating. The early participants in the computer industry understood that there was a potentially huge commercial advantage to establishing a high degree of visibility on college campuses, and IBM, Burroughs, Sperry Rand, Bendix, and Royal McBee all sponsored university donation programs, although those of IBM were by far the largest. Concerns were expressed by some observers at the time, no doubt with some justice, that IBM's impact on university curricula overemphasized practical applications while neglecting the more theoretical dimensions.[25]

Nevertheless, the self-interested behavior of computer firms in introducing their own computers onto college campuses in this early period undoubtedly played a major role in America's head start, not only in the computer industry but also in the creation of the new discipline of computer science.

The most important response to *Sputnik*, in terms of the eventual impact on the role played by American universities in the development of computers, was without question the federal Advanced Research Projects Agency (ARPA), founded in 1958. ARPA's research focused on problems connected with ballistic missile defense, nuclear test detection, propellants, and materials. It built programs in new, complex fields dealing with issues of long-term significance, making extensive use of (mostly) promising young scientists who came in typically on a two-year rotation basis from academia and industry. ARPA's Information Processing Techniques Office (IPTO) focused on aspects of command and control problems, but with special attention to the fundamental problems within the realm of computing that, when solved, would contribute to solutions or improvements in command and control systems.[26]

ARPA was allowed a great deal of discretion and freedom of action. As opposed to the NSF system of peer review of small grants to individual researchers, along with a strong political sensitivity to the geographic distribution of its awards, ARPA was free to "concentrate its resources on centers of scientific and engineering excellence (such as MIT, Carnegie Mellon University and Stanford University) without regard for

---

[25] "The strongest impulse for introducing computers on campuses in the mid-1950s did not come from the schools themselves or from any federal agency, but instead from IBM. Through its educational program, the company donated its Model 650 computer to more than 50 schools by 1959, with the stipulation that the schools offer courses in data processing and numerical analysis." Aspray and Williams, 1994, p. 61.

[26] See *Funding a Revolution* (National Academy Press 1999), pp. 98–105 (no author).

geographical distribution questions with which NSF had to be concerned."
Moreover, it was free to award block grants on a multiple-year basis,
on projects of an avowedly high-risk nature. It was allowed, in short,
"the luxury of a long-term vision to foster technologies, disciplines, and
institutions."[27] The vision at the center of ARPA's definition of its
responsibilities, combined with its aggressive leadership and the federal
government's substantial funding, created not only the essential research
infrastructure but a new academic discipline of computer science. In the
early years of the emergence of this new discipline ARPA was, overwhelmingly, the main source of federal support.

Federal support for university research in computer science increased
from about $76 million in 1976 to $500 million in 1995. This funding,
primarily from ARPA and NSF, accounted for about 70 percent of all
funding for universities in the field of computer science over the period.
A key aspect to notice here is that the government's funds were directed
toward the development of an entirely new academic discipline. Participating researchers were, inevitably, concerned with improving their status
in the academic community and saw ARPA support as a way of enhancing
their academic reputations so as to ensure future research funding and
tenure at prestigious academic institutions. ARPA funds were regarded as
incentive compatible with the longer-term professional goals of its academically oriented researchers.

Moreover, college students were also responding to market signals, as
there was a huge and growing demand for computer science education,
which further strengthened the prospects of the researchers for achieving
their long-term professional goals. This would have been less likely in a
system where education and research in computer science were not conducted by the same people.

The growth in human resources that were committed to computer
science, post-*Sputnik*, was remarkable by almost any standard: As late as
1959, there were virtually no formal programs in the field; the vast majority of people came to computing with training in other areas, especially
mathematics and engineering, and became computer scientists through
on-the-job experience. But by 1965 the Association for Computing Machinery reported that computer science had become a "distinct academic

---

[27] Ibid., p. 100. As Mowery has astutely observed: "Paradoxically, the national security
rationale for much of the DoD and ARPA funding of university 'centers of excellence,'
may have insulated these programs, which did not operate solely via peer review, from
the distributional politics that otherwise might have forced the use of very different
criteria for allocation." Mowery, 1996, p. 75.

discipline," with doctorates being offered at more than fifteen universities, master's degrees at more than thirty, and bachelor's degrees at about seventeen. By 1967, computer science was taught in separate departments at Carnegie Mellon, Cornell, the University of Illinois, the University of Michigan, the University of North Carolina, Notre Dame, the University of Pennsylvania, Pennsylvania State University, Purdue, Stanford, the University of Texas, the University of Toronto, and the University of Wisconsin.[28]

The number of bachelor's degrees awarded in computer science at American universities grew from 89 in 1966 to 42,000 in 1986. Between 1987 and 1995 there was a sharp decline as the market absorbed the huge supply increase of the previous years. At the same time, the award of a master's degree in computer science continued to grow, at an annual rate of 14.4 per year for the period 1966 to 1995, and the number of doctoral degrees awarded accelerated sharply in the mid-1980s.

Perhaps an even more significant indicator of IPTO's impact on the progress of computer science within the academic community can be derived from data on tenured faculty members at the top forty U.S. computer science departments.

At the beginning of the 1990s, more than 26 percent of the tenured members of those select computer science departments had received their Ph.D. degrees from one of the three main IPTO-sponsored institutions: MIT, Stanford, and Carnegie Mellon. This shows a remarkable penetration of IPTO in the computer education process. An even greater number, 42 percent, of the tenured faculty members in the ten top-ranked departments had received their Ph.D. degrees from one of the three schools, and more than 53 percent of the nontenured faculty members did.[29]

These academic "production" figures provide strong evidence of the ability of American universities, with directed federal funding, to respond rapidly and effectively to newly emerging needs of the private sector. This achievement stands in sharp contrast to Japan and Western Europe, which continually suffered from shortages of skilled personnel.

But the full extent of the contribution of American universities to the computer industry over the past four decades is not adequately captured by the numbers just cited. In addition, "U.S. universities provided important channels for cross-fertilization and information exchange between industry and academia, and also between defense and civilian research

---

[28] Norberg and O'Neill, 1996, pp. 289–90. The listing of universities may not be complete.
[29] Ibid., p. 190.

efforts in software and in computer science generally."[30] It is difficult to find comparable forces at work in the history of Japan, Western Europe, or the Soviet Union, in their university systems or in government, that might have provided the organizational innovations that facilitated such changes in the role of universities, or provided incentive mechanisms from competitive market forces that contributed so much to the American success story in the realm of computer science.

Langlois and Mowery also make the important observation that the U.S. military did not attempt to restrict access to information concerning computers but, on the contrary, took positive steps to encourage their diffusion.

The U.S. armed forces, from the earliest days of their support for the development of computer technology, were surprisingly eager for technical information about the innovation to reach the widest possible audience, in contrast to the military in Great Britain or the Soviet Union. The Office of Naval Research (ONR) organized seminars on automatic programming in 1951, 1954, and l956. Along with similar conferences sponsored by computer firms, universities, and the meetings of the fledgling Association for Computing Machinery (ACM) the ONR conferences circulated ideas within a developing community of practitioners who did not yet have journals or other formal channels of communication. The ONR also established the Institute for Numerical Analysis at UCLA, which made important contributions to the overall field of computer science.[31]

Thus, the story of the involvement of American universities in generating powerful new computer-based technologies is an account in which university research, with generous federal government funding, produced a series of innovations in software, computer architecture, and computer networking. These innovations led, in turn, from the ARPANET to the NSFNET, which, in turn, came to underpin national and international electronic mail. The global communications network at the turn of the century, the Internet and the World Wide Web, trace their origins directly back to the undertaking, by ARPANET, to link more closely together the activities of four universities (Carnegie Mellon, MIT, Stanford, and the University of California at Berkeley). Each of these universities was, at the time, performing research for the Department of Defense. The remarkable degree of openness and accessibility that characterize today's Internet and World Wide Web must owe a great deal to the fact that they were

---

[30] Langlois and Mowery, 1996, p. 60.
[31] Ibid.

developed primarily in a university context. It is most unlikely that this technology would have developed in the directions that it has, and as quickly as it has, if it had originated in a commercial environment in which proprietary considerations loomed large.

The software sector of the computer industry has experienced spectacular growth in the past twenty five years. By June 1997 there were 5,806 software firms in the United States that had come into existence since 1980 and were still in existence as of June 1997. The corresponding number for firms producing computer hardware was 2,179.[32]

7.5. Diagnostic Devices

In the post–World War II period, technological innovation in the American medical world became increasingly concentrated in university hospitals, or academic medical centers (AMCs). This was full of consequences for the medical research process, inasmuch as it established the possibility for close interactions between the clinical community and the worlds of science and engineering.[33] This closer proximity was especially consequential for one particular category of medical devices: diagnostic technologies.

The American medical device industry has, in the recent past, consisted of at least 10,000 firms, the vast majority of which have been very small. But it has also included a small number of large firms that produce a wide range of medical products, such as Johnson & Johnson and U.S. Surgical, as well as a number of large, multi-product, multi-national firms that have important medical departments – General Electric, Philips, Siemens, and Sony. There is also evidence that the contribution of small firms to medical device innovation has been concentrated in the early stages of developing a new class of devices, but these small firms (and sometimes single individuals) have failed to derive the (expected) benefits of first-mover advantages.

---

[32] Table 2, "US High-Tech Business Formations, by Technology Area," *NSFD Issue Brief*, March 4, 1999, available at http://www.nsf.gov/sbe/srs/issuebrf/ib.htm. The computer industry, moreover, has been dominating venture capital disbursements in recent years, but what is even more striking is the shift that has occurred with respect to such venture capital disbursements within the industry. In 1987, disbursements for computer hardware exceeded that for computer software and services ($631 million to $527 million; all figures in current dollars). By 1990 software exceeded hardware, and subsequently venture capital disbursements for software grew far more rapidly than for hardware. By 1996 software was fully five times larger than hardware ($2510.2 million to $493.7 million) (Venture Economics Investor Services, 1997, as reported in "Venture Capital Investment Trends in the United States and Europe," *NSF Issue Brief*, October 16, 1998].

[33] For valuable international institutional comparisons, see Braun, 1994.

Within the university community, medical device innovations have been dependent not only on clinicians in AMCs who are frequently co-inventors of new devices, but also on faculty in departments of applied physics or electrical engineering. Indeed, many of the diagnostic breakthroughs of the past half-century have involved precisely such collaborations.

Three diagnostic technologies that are examined here have some common features: (1) The development of their innovative technologies was intensely interdisciplinary – indeed, it would be plausible to say that the early stages of R&D (i.e., up to the development of a working prototype) were inherently interdisciplinary. That is to say, advances in engineering and the physical sciences needed to be integrated with those in medicine. In recent years such programs have been institutionalized in bioengineering – as is the case at Stanford. Stanford now has a Department of Bioengineering. Stanford's University Bulletin states that the mission of this department is "to create a fusion of engineering and the life sciences that promotes scientific discovery and the invention of new technologies and therapies through research and education .... The discipline [of bioengineering] embraces biology as a new science base for engineering." (2) The early exploratory research involved prominent roles played by university faculty at AMCs and by electrical engineers, although, at the early stage, crucial contributions were made from a "rank outsider" to the medical world: Electrical and Musical Industries Ltd. (EMI). (3) The early contributors to the development of the diagnostic technology usually failed after the technology successfully reached the working prototype stage.

The diagnostic imaging technologies that have emerged since the 1950s include the most technologically sophisticated products in the medical device realm in recent decades: the fiber optic endoscope, CT, and MRI. CT and MRI also represent two of the highest fixed costs in the entire realm of medical devices. It is important to remember that both of these technologies, which have revolutionized medical diagnosis since the early 1970s, would have been inconceivable in the absence of prior and ongoing improvements in computer technology.

CT and MRI were totally dependent on the powerful mini computers that became available in the early 1970s, as well as on microelectronics generally. Huge advances in microelectronics had been achieved during the pressure cooker circumstances of World War II, including such inventions as radar. Each of the three imaging technologies (the endoscope, CT, and MRI) was brought to the working prototype stage within the university community, in this case within the larger, Anglo-American university community. A feature common to both the American and British scenes in the case of CT and MRI was the close cooperation, at the R&D stages, between the AMCs and university physics or electrical engineering departments. But also of great significance has been the international mobility of key personnel as well as collaborative arrangements that now routinely cross international boundaries between Western Europe (especially the United Kingdom) and North America. In particular, postdoctoral fellowships have proven to be a key mechanism for the transatlantic transfer of information that has been pertinent to innovation in diagnostic technologies.

7.5.1. The Endoscope

The fiber optic endoscope was invented in the mid-1950s by a young South African gastroenterologist, Basil Hirschowitz, who was at the University of Michigan on an American Cancer Society fellowship. The immediate stimulus was his reading of two articles published simultaneously in *Nature* in 1954 by A.C.S. van Heel of Holland and H. H. Hopkins and N. S. Kapany in the department of physics at the Imperial College of London. These articles suggested the possibility of transmitting images along an aligned bundle of flexible glass fibers. On reading these articles, Hirschowitz decided to explore the possibilities for developing a flexible device as a substitute for the extremely unsatisfactory rigid GI endoscope that was then in use. Hirschowitz joined forces with a young assistant professor of physics and an undergraduate. The eventual product of their development work was taken to American Cystoscope Makers, Inc., which agreed to manufacture endoscopes under license. Although ACMI had filed patents in the United States and Europe, it had neglected to file one in Japan, which was most ironic, in view of the extremely high incidence of gastric cancer in that country (Japanese death rates from gastric cancer were more than six times higher than those in the United States). Two Japanese firms, Olympus Corporation and Machida Instrument Company, thus began manufacturing the endoscope. Olympus, exercising its considerable skills in miniaturization and photography, became the dominant firm. In recent years it has controlled over 75 percent of the world market for upper GI endoscopes.[34]

The remarkable story of the endoscope is that Hirschowitz's initial successes at the University of Michigan opened up a wide range of surgical

---

[34] For more details, see Gelijns and Rosenberg, 1995.

improvements in which a minimally invasive diagnostic technology was transformed into a minimally invasive therapy. These new therapies drastically reduced hospitalization time, lowered the frequency of post-surgical infection, and accelerated the speed of patient recovery over a wide range of what were previously much longer and more painful surgical procedures. Fiber-optic colonoscopy originated in the 1960s at the AMC of the University of Michigan where Hirschowitz had done his earlier work. Endoscopies were rapidly applied in gynecological procedures, but in many areas adoptions of new technologies were slow because they were considered to be contrary to the culture of surgery. In the 1990s, however, drastic changes became obvious, as in the removal of gallstones, which was the first major surgical practice to be transformed into a laparoscopic procedure. In fact, more than half of all 33,000 general surgeons in the United States acquired the necessary skills in an eighteen-month period, a breathtakingly rapid adoption of a new medical procedure by any historical standard. Adoption rates were a good deal slower in Europe and a great deal slower in Japan.

7.5.2. Computed Tomography

The CT scanner makes use of x-rays but uses mathematical techniques and computer technology to produce images from which one can derive three-dimensional information.[35] The concept and the techniques of tomography had been developed by European radiologists, although the scanner itself had rather eclectic origins. As early as 1961, W. H. Oldendorf of UCLA had developed and patented a tomographic device that would provide cross-sectional images of the head, but he was unable to secure funding for its further development. Alan Cormack, a nuclear physicist at Tufts University, conducted critical experiments measuring the amount of x-ray energy that was absorbed by the body, and used this information to calculate linear absorption coefficients.

In the late 1950s Godfrey Hounsfield, an engineer who worked at the central research laboratory of Britain's Electrical & Musical Industries Ltd. (EMI) on issues of pattern recognition and computer storage techniques, conceived and patented a CT scanner (Hounsfield received some financial support from Britain's Department of Health and Social Security). The scanner was first commercialized in 1973 by EMI, and it was the dominant firm for five years but left the market in 1980. Although EMI was, briefly,

---

[35] See Klug and Crowther, 1972.

highly successful, it lacked the huge financial resources that further development required. But, even more to the point, EMI lacked the technical know-how and the necessary feedback from early users to maintain its early but brief leadership through frequent redesign of the equipment. EMI did not survive the eventual "shake-out" and was sold to Thorn Electrical Industries. By 1981 General Electric had emerged as the dominant firm, with 60 percent of the huge American market, a market that, in turn, accounted for more than 50 percent of the world market for CT scanners.[36] The need for further development work on the CT scanner was critical because, as it was initially designed, it could scan only the head and not the entire human body, and it was absolutely essential to reduce imaging time. Robert Ledley, a professor of physiology, biophysics, and radiology at Georgetown University Medical School in Washington, D.C., set out to develop a device that would scan the whole body and be relatively inexpensive. He developed a prototype, patented it, and established a company to bring it to market. The pharmaceutical firm Pfizer, which was conducting clinical trials with one of their drugs at Georgetown University, heard about the device and, wanting to diversify into medical devices, licensed it. Pfizer introduced its scanner into clinical practice in 1975, but the firm's attempt to enter the market proved to be short-lived.[37]

By the mid-1970s the CT scanner market contained as many as twenty firms and scanning time had been reduced from many minutes to less than five seconds. Participants in this improvement process were primarily American but included European firms such as Siemens and Philips as well. As further evidence of the eclectic nature of the contributors, the National Cancer Institute of the National Institutes of Health awarded a contract to the small aerospace company, American Science and Engineering (AS&E) to develop a CT scanner in collaboration with investigators from Columbia-Presbyterian Medical Center and Bell Labs. AS&E could rely on its core competence in electronics and airport x-ray equipment to introduce the first fourth-generation scanner in 1976, which also generated images in less than 5 seconds.

7.5.3. Magnetic Resonance Imaging

MRI had its origins entirely within the university research community, where it had been widely used in the 1950s and 1960s as a way of

---

[36] See the excellent study by Trajtenberg, 1990.
[37] See Gelijns and Rosenberg, 1999.

identifying the chemical composition of materials. Nuclear magnetic resonance (NMR) spectroscopy was first perceived as a potential imaging technology by Raymond Damadian's observation, in 1970, that NMR signals could distinguish between cancerous and noncancerous tissue. Damadian, a medical doctor, was at that time an assistant professor of biophysics at the State University of New York's Downtown Medical Center in Brooklyn. His findings, reported in an article in *Science* in 1971, quickly attracted the interest of universities and private industry, mostly in the United States and the United Kingdom. In 1971, Paul Lauterbur, a member of the Chemistry Department at the State University of New York in Stony Brook, generated a two-dimensional image from a series of one-dimensional projections of two tubes of water, which was reported in *Nature* in 1973.

Entry into the nascent MRI industry took a variety of forms. Several of the universities where earlier research had been carried out gave birth to new single-product firms: the State University of New York (Fonar Corporation), University of Aberdeen (M&D Technology Ltd.), University of Nottingham (Nalorac Cryogenics), and University of California, Los Angeles (OMR Technology). At the same time, the British government supported EMI's entry into the industry but also provided financial support for the university-based R&D at the universities of Nottingham and Aberdeen. The West German government provided grants to Bruker Instrument, Philips, and Siemens, after they had started development programs with their own funds. Other large firms accelerated market entry through the purchase of technology and the acquisition of other firms. Some firms (GE, Philips, Siemens, and Technicare) marshalled their own considerable R&D resources. GE, for example, which did not begin its development of the MRI scanner until 1980, relied heavily on William Edelstein, a Harvard physics Ph.D., who took a postdoc at the University of Glasgow after completing his graduate work. Edelstein spent more than six years in postdoctoral positions at the universities of Glasgow and Aberdeen, where some of the key physics research in NMR imaging was being conducted. He was recruited by GE in 1980 and joined their corporate laboratory in Schenectady, becoming a central figure in the firm's rapid entry into MRI. GE also hired Paul Bottomley, a member of the relevant research group at the University of Nottingham.

By 1983, each of the eleven companies that had developed prototypes or, at least, engineering models, also had a close collaborative relationship with a university or medical school. These connections were critical for clinical testing and also as a source of feedback for further product modification and improvement. By 1988, MRI had become an established technique worldwide, and the 1300 units that had been sold by that time were located in major university schools and large hospitals where, to a considerable extent, they had originated.

Thus, the origin of MRI may be regarded as primarily the result of a convergence of the research capabilities of physics departments and AMCs in the United States and the United Kingdom, along with the indispensible capabilities of the computer. The contribution of universities, however, was by no means limited to "pure" research but also included a considerable part of the development work, all the way to the working prototype and final testing stages.

Universities and AMCs have come to play a central role in generating the new diagnostic technologies that have been considered here: the fiber optic endoscope, CT, and MRI. At the same time, these institutions have become, to a considerable extent, internationalized, with "traffic" now flowing in both directions. European multinationals now "tap into" American AMCs and large American firms tap into British AMCs and have recruited key personnel who have worked at those institutions. Siemens and Philips have had collaborative programs not only with German and Dutch AMCs, but also with numerous U.S. AMCs as well.

Start-up firms (as well as some older firms that came from outside the industry, such as EMI) have played a strategic role in developing the new diagnostic technologies that have originated in university contexts. These firms, however, have usually failed in undertaking entrepreneurial roles – that is, they seldom achieved commercial success, even when they possessed patent protection. Damadian's experience, although by no means typical, is nevertheless symptomatic. Damadian established a new firm, Fonar, based on his MRI patent for the work he had carried out at Downtown Medical Center. In 1980 Fonar was responsible for the very first commercial placement of an MRI instrument outside the company's own plant. Nevertheless, Fonar, a start-up with only modest financial resources, was simply elbowed aside by much larger multinational firms. This elbowing, however, did not occur without penalty. In 1997 the court supported Damadian's patent suit against GE and ordered the firm to pay Fonar $128.7 million. Fonar also successfully sued Hitachi, Johnson & Johnson, Philips, and Siemens for patent infringement, and each of these firms settled out of court for undisclosed sums of money. Although Damadian eventually won his case, as well as a large sum of money, Fonar has not been a significant presence in the MRI sector and Damadian's patent proved ultimately unworkable!

7.6. Some Concluding Observations

Commercial success in medical diagnostics requires huge financial resources to spend on R&D for frequent product improvement and modification, as well as a high degree of marketing and manufacturing sophistication. New entrants into these product lines have seldom possessed such capabilities. But, even more important, the industry is one in which established reputations of suppliers for the maintenance of quality, credibility as to equipment performance, and long-term support loom very large. These considerations constitute serious obstacles to successful entry into the industry. Thus, although small firms have frequently played a valuable role as originators of medical diagnostic technologies, they have seldom managed to convert this inventive advantage into that of a major participant in the market.

But there is yet another dimension of reputation in the market for health-care products:

[I]nformation on the experience of individuals with medical equipment flows rapidly and widely within the medical community. Thus, abusing the firm's reputation in one market at one time is very likely to affect badly the performance of the firm in other markets and over a long period of time. In plain words, a hospital that finds a CT scanner to be inferior to its expected quality, having formed its expectations – inter alia – on the basis of price, is not likely to purchase x-ray machines, or intensive care units, or perhaps even pharmaceuticals from the same manufacturer.[38]

Thus, although small firms have frequently played a valuable role as originators of medical diagnostic technologies, they have seldom managed to convert this inventive advantage into that of a major participant in the market.

These considerations apply equally well not only to manufacturers of MRI machines and CT scanners, but also to the multiproduct firms that play a large role in medical devices, such as GE, Johnson & Johnson, Philips, and Siemens.

Commercial success with respect to MRI machines and CT scanners has turned very heavily on certain trajectories that became relevant only after the development of a working prototype – indeed, this consideration goes a long way toward explaining why first movers seldom achieved the status of successful entrepreneurship. For example, learning how to drastically reduce the scanning times of these highly expensive machines without simultaneously losing some of the sharpness of the resolution was critical to the firm's competitive status.

---

[38] Trajtenberg, 1990, p. 147.

AMCs are now, by far, the largest generator of patent royalties among American universities, although the rank order is subject to sudden changes – frequently through the expiration of a single lucrative patent.[39] However, one must not conclude that patent royalties are necessarily good measures (or even good proxies) for the contribution of American universities to the improved economic performance of the economy. In fact, there are only a small number of industrial sectors where it can be said that patent revenues provide some useful measure of the contribution of university research to economic improvement. To begin with, the findings of basic research are – at least in principle – not patentable at all, although barriers to such a practice have begun to erode in recent years. It is still the case, however, that fundamental breakthroughs in science become public knowledge very quickly. In any case, as already suggested, the great bulk of revenues from university patenting are heavily concentrated in pharmaceuticals and the biomedical sector. But useful findings from university research may be channeled into the economy through conferences, consulting activities, publications in professional journals, and, perhaps most important in the long run, through useful new knowledge that is carried into industry via the hiring of university graduates.

It will be recalled that, early on in this chapter, I assured you that I would not end up with some general principles, and I believe that I have fulfilled that promise.

But there is at least a common denominator that runs through many of the historical episodes that I have discussed, even if they do not rise to the level of general principles. That is to say, a common theme is that a breakthrough in the realm of science has eventually provided the basis for some significant breakthrough in the realm of technology. But in my various episodes (although not all of them) the scientific breakthrough was achieved in Europe, whereas the eventual successful innovation took place in the United States. An Aristotelian might reply by saying that it is in the "nature" of American culture to succeed in the marketplace. There is, of course, something to the Aristotelian observation. It is an interesting observation, and a sharp-eyed young French aristocrat, de Tocqueville, said something like this more than 150 years ago after a lengthy visit to the United States. The trouble is that the observation, by itself, is not very interesting. It provides little explanatory value. What we really want to know is: What were the specific organizational and structural changes that accounted for these American successes?

---

[39] See Mowery, 2004.

References

Anderson, John D., Jr. 1997. *A History of Aerodynamics*. Cambridge, Mass.: Cambridge University Press.

Arora, Ashish, and Alfonso Gambardella. 1994. "The Changing Technology of Technical Change: General and Abstract Knowledge and the Division of Innovative Labour."*Research Policy*, 23.

Arora, Ashish, Ralph Landau, and Nathan Rosenberg. 1998. *Chemicals and Long-Term Economic Growth: Insights from the Chemical Industry*. New York: John Wiley & Sons.

Aspray, William, and Bernard O. Williams. 1994. "Arming American Scientists: NSF and the Provision of Scientific Computing Facilities for Universities, 1950–1973." *IEEE Annals of the History of Computing*, 16(4), 60–74.

Braun, Dietmar. 1994. *Structure and Dynamics of Health Research and Public Funding: An International Institutional Comparison*. Dordrecht: Kluwer Academic Publishers.

Elder, Albert. 1970. *The History of Penicillin Production*. New York: American Institute of Chemical Engineers.

Enos, John L. 1962. *Petroleum Progress and Profits: A History of Process Innovation*. Cambridge, Mass.: MIT Press.

Gelijns, Annetine, and Nathan Rosenberg. 1995. "From the Scalpel to the Scope: Endoscopic Innovations in Gastroenterology, Gynecology, and Surgery." In *Sources of Medical Technology: Universities and Industry*, A. Gilijns and N. Rosenberg, eds. National Academies Press, chap. 4.

Gelijns, Annetine, and Nathan Rosenberg. 1999. "Diagnostic Devices: An Analysis of Comparative Advantages." In *Sources of Industrial Leadership*, David Mowery and Richard Nelson, eds. Cambridge, Mass.: Cambridge University Press, chap. 8.

Goodstein, Judith R. 1991. *Millikan's School: A History of the California Institute of Technology*. New York: W.W. Norton.

Hanle, Paul A. 1982. *Bringing Aerodynamics to America*. Cambridge, Mass.: MIT Press.

Jahnig, C. E., H. Z. Martin, and D. L. Campbell. 1983. "The Development of Fluid Catalytic Cracking." In *Heterogeneous Catalysis: Selected American Histories*, Burton Davis and William Hettinger, eds. American Chemical Society.

Karman, Theodore von, and Lee Edson. 1967. *The Wind and Beyond*. Boston: Little, Brown.

Klug, A., and R. A. Crowther. 1972. "Three-Dimensional Image Reconstruction from the Viewpoint of Information Theory." *Nature*, 238, 435–440.

Landau, Ralph. 1966. *The Chemical Plant: From Process Selection to Commercial Operation*. New York: Reinhold Publishing.

Langlois, Richard N., and David C. Mowery. 1996. "The Federal Government Role in the Development of the U.S. Software Industry." In *The International Computer Software Industry: A Comparative Study of Industry Evolution and Structure*, David C. Mowery, ed. New York: Oxford University Press, 53–85.

Levine, David O. 1986. *The American College and the Culture of Aspiration, 1915–1940*. Ithaca, N.Y.: Cornell University Press.

Lewis, Warren K., William H. Walker, and William H. McAdams. 1923. *Principles of Chemical Engineering*. New York: McGraw-Hill.

Little, Arthur D. 1933. "Chemical Engineering Research." In *Twenty-five Years of Chemical Engineering Progress*, S. D. Kirkpatrick, ed. American Institute of Chemical Engineers, chap. 1.

Miller, Ronald, and David Sawers. 1970. *The Technical Development of Modern Aviation*. New York: Praeger.

Mowery, David C. 1996. *The International Computer Software Industry: A Comparative Study of Industry Evolution and Structure*. New York: Oxford University Press.

Mowery, David C. 2004. *Ivory Tower and Industrial Innovation: University-Industry Technology Transfer Before and After the Bayh-Dole Act*. Stanford, Calif.: Stanford University Press.

National Academy of Science. 1999. *Funding a Revolution: Government Support for Computing Research*. Washington, D.C.: National Academy Press.

Norberg, Arthur, and Judy O'Neill. 1996. *Transforming Computer Technology: Information Processing for the Pentagon, 1962–1986*. Baltimore: Johns Hopkins University Press, 289–90.

Resch, Helmuth, Paul R. Blankenhorn, John G. Haygreen, and Warren S. Thompson. 1985. "Forest Products Research at U.S. Universities in 1982." *Wood and Fiber Science*, 17(4), 568–584.

Rosenberg, Nathan. 1982. *Inside the Black Box: Technology and Economics*. Cambridge, Mass.: Cambridge University Press.

Rosenberg, Nathan. 1998. "Technological Change in Chemicals: The Role of University-Industry Relations." In *Chemicals and Long-Term Economic Growth*, A. Arora, R. Landau, and N. Rosenberg, eds. New York: John Wiley & Sons.

Rosenberg, Nathan. 2000. "Chemical Engineering as a General Purpose Technology." In *Schumpeter and the Endogeneity of Technology: Some American Perspectives*, Nathan Rosenberg, ed. London: Routledge, chap. 5.

Steinmueller, W. Edward. 1996. "The U.S. Software Industry: An Analysis and Interpretive History." In *The International Computer Software Industry: A Comparative Study of Industry Evolution and Structure*, David C. Mowery, ed. New York: Oxford University Press, 15–52.

The Stanford Bulletin 2006–07. *Publication of the Office of the University Registrar*, Stanford University. Available at: http://www.stanford.edu/dept/registrar/bulletin/current/index.html.

Trajtenberg, Manuel. 1990. *Economic Analysis of Product Innovation: The Case of CT Scanners*. Cambridge, Mass.: Harvard University Press.

UNIDO. 2005. *Capability Building for Catching-up*. UNIDO, Vienna, 46.

Vincenti, Walter. 1990. *What Engineers Know and How They Know It*. Baltimore: Johns Hopkins University Press, 141.

Walker, William H., Warren K. Lewis, and William H. McAdams. 1937. *Principles of Chemical Engineering*. New York: McGraw-Hill.

Weber, Harold C. 1980. *The Improbable Achievement: Chemical Engineering at MIT*. Cambridge, Mass.: MIT Press.

Wildes, Karl, and Nilo Lindgren. 1985. *A Century of Electrical Engineering and Computer Science at MIT, 1882–1982*. Cambridge, Mass.: MIT Press, 378–379.

Scientist Commercialization and Knowledge Transfer?

David B. Audretsch, Taylor Aldridge, and Alexander Oettl

8.1. Introduction

How and why do scientists decide to commercialize their scientific research? The answers to these questions are important not only to institutions and scientists engaged in research, but also to policymakers trying to promote economic growth. New Endogenous Growth models and theories highlight the central role that investments in scientific research, or knowledge, play in generating economic growth (Romer, 1986; and Lucas, 1993). More recently, policymakers, serving local communities, states and nations have observed that these investments in knowledge do not automatically generate economic growth. Rather, what Acs et al. (2004) and Audretsch et al. (2006) term the knowledge filter prevents or slows employment creation and economic growth that could otherwise result from public and private investments in science and research. The combination of large investments in research with low rates of economic growth and employment generation, first found in Sweden, was called the Swedish Paradox. Later as it was found in other European nations, the problem was redubbed the European Paradox. Acs et al. (2004) and Audretsch et al. (2006) identify the commercialization of science and research as the missing link in the process of economic growth. In the absence of scientist commercialization of research, investments in science and research will not generate economic growth or jobs.

The purpose of this study is to understand how and why scientists commercialize research. We do this by analyzing the propensity of

The authors would like to offer our thanks to Lesa Mitchell, Vice President of Advancing Innovation at the Ewing Marion Kauffman Foundation, for her invaluable comments and suggestions. We would also like to thank Melanie Fabich for her tireless research assistance.

scientists receiving National Cancer Institute (NCI) grants to commercialize their research. As the second section of this chapter makes clear, there is no single path for scientist commercialization of research. Thus, in the third section, three distinct measures of scientist commercialization are introduced and explained: patents, Small Business Innovation Research (SBIR) awards, and licenses. These three modes of commercialization are used to identify the main determinants of scientist commercialization of research in the fourth section. Finally, in the last section, a summary and conclusion are provided. In particular, the results of this study suggest that while scientists receiving NCI funding commercialize their research, the modes of commercialization are quite heterogeneous in terms of both prevalence and determinants. Reliance on publicly accessible databases, such as patents and SBIR, represent, at best, a fragment of the commercialization activities by NCI scientists. Other important commercialization modes, such as licenses, can be measured and analyzed only by creating new systematic and comprehensive sources of data.

8.2. Scientist Commercialization of University Research

How and why do scientists decide to commercialize their scientific research? One answer to the question of "why" was provided by Stephan and Levin (1992), who suggest that a scientist will choose to commercialize research if it furthers his or her goals. But how do scientists best appropriate the value of their human capital? That is, which mode of commercialization is most appropriate for a scientist with a given stock of knowledge and scientific human capital? Alternatives abound, such as working full-time or part-time with an existing firm, licensing the knowledge to an existing firm, or starting a new firm as an entrepreneur, what Schumpeter, as noted in Chapter 1, would describe as the best approach.

Previous studies identified several major modes of scientist commercialization. Ownership of intellectual property, in the form of patented inventions, is an important step in the commercialization process (Jaffe, Trajtenberg, and Henderson, 1993; Henderson, Jaffe, and Trajtenberg, 1998; Jaffe and Lerner, 2001). Meanwhile, Jensen and Thursby (2001), Thursby, Jensen, and Thursby (2001), and Thursby and Jensen (2005) found that both patents and the licensing of patents are important modes of scientist commercialization. In particular, Thursby and Jensen (2004) employ a principal-agent framework in which the university administration is the principal and the faculty scientist is the agent, and identify that the "question is whether or not the researcher remains in the university, and if so her choice of the amount of time to spend on bias applied research, is complicated by the fact that she earns license income and prestige both inside and outside the university."

Several studies have identified the important role that the Small Business Innovation (SBIR) program can play as a mode of scientist commercialization (Lerner, 1999; Audretsch, Link, and Scott, 2002; Audretsch, 2003). Toole and Czarnitzki (2005) found that only 8 percent of the unique principle investigators (PIs) were awarded an SBIR grant from the Department of Health and Human Services between 1983 and 1996, which suggests that the SBIR may perhaps be an important instrument of public policy but not a common mechanism for commercializing scientist research.

8.3. Measurement Issues

This study examines scientists at universities in the United States who were awarded a research grant by the NCI between 1998 and 2002. Of those research grant awards, the largest 20 percent, which included 1,693 scientist grantees, were taken to form the database used in this study. These 1,693 grantees received more than $5.3 billion from the NCI in this time frame.

Since our focus is on the propensity for scientists to commercialize their research, commercialization must be operationalized and measured. Based on the literature identified in the previous section, three principal measures of scientist commercialization are used, which reflect the three different modes by which scientists can and do commercialize their research. These are (1) patenting inventions, (2) receiving an SBIR grant to obtain funding for an innovative small business, and (3) licensing a patent. There certainly are other modes of commercialization unexplored by this study: employmenet in the private sector, being awarded consulting contracts, starting up a private company without SBIR assistance, and informal interactions. The absence of these modes of commercialization of university research by scientists in this study does not mean that they are unimportant, but rather that they are difficult to measure.

Based on these three different measures reflecting distinct modes of scientist commercialization of research, the NCI grantee database was used to determine the answer to the question, Why do some scientists commercialize, while others do not?

8.3.1. Patents

The first measure of commercialization by NCI recipients are numbers of inventions patented. The propensity for NCI recipient scientists to patent was analyzed by obtaining patent data from the United States Patent and Trade Office (USPTO) covering 1975 to 2004. The inventor patent data included identification of the invention's patent number, the name and address of the inventor, and the inventor sequence number.

A total registered 3.25 million patentees were recorded from 1975 to 2004. To match the patent records with any of the 1,692 NCI recipient scientists, a Structured Query Language (SQL) program was created to analyze the data. Matches between the patentee and NCI awardee databases were considered positive if the following four conditions were met:

1. A positive match was made with the first, middle, and last name. If no middle name was listed in either the NCI award database or the patent database, matches were made using only the first and last names.
2. The second criterion involved matching the relevant time periods between the two databases. Observations from both databases were matched over the time period 1998–2004, which corresponds to the initial year in which observations were available to us from the NCI database (1998–2002) and the final year in which patents were recorded in the patent database (1975–2004).
3. The third criterion was based on location. If the patentee resided within a radius of approximately 45 miles from the geographic location of the university, the third condition was fulfilled.
4. The fourth criterion involved verifying the patent title. Only those patent titles constituting scientific content fulfilled the fourth condition.

Based on these four criteria, a subset of 606 distinct issued patentees were identified between 1998 and 2004. NCI-award scientists commercializing through patents varied from those not commercializing in several important ways. As Table 8-1 shows, scientists who commercialized had a higher propensity to be located at a university in New England or California, to be employed at an Ivy League university (as opposed to a public institution), to have a slightly greater value of the NCI grant award, to have a higher number of citations in scientific journals, and to be male.

Figure 8-1 shows that the geographic distribution of patentees varied both across regions as well as by gender. In some regions, such as New

Table 8-1. *Commercialization of NCI scientists*

Variables	NCI scientists	Patentees	Licensers	SBIR
Sample size	1649	606		8
New York	9.45%	8.42%	10.00%	13.00%
Minnesota	3.01%	1.82%	0.00%	0.00%
Great Lakes	13.11%	11.06%	12.50%	25.00%
Mid-Atlantic	16.18%	16.50%	22.50%	38.00%
South	10.28%	10.23%	10.00%	13.00%
New England	9.27%	12.21%	12.50%	0.00%
California	13.76%	17.33%	12.50%	0.00%
Northwest	5.26%	3.63%	0.00%	0.00%
Texas	7.86%	8.09%	20.00%	0.00%
Other geographic region	11.99%	10.73%	5.00%	13.00%
Ivy League	10.34%	12.21%	15.00%	13.00%
Public institution	53.75%	49.67%	50.00%	38.00%
NCI award	$3,155,232	$3,216,702	$2,905,668	$2,506,598
Star scientist	10%	11.72%	12.50%	25.00%
Papers published	8491	84.84	108.93	46.66
Mean scientist citations	1316.44	3770.00	1741.19	1500.34
Patentee	36%	100%	100%	37.50%
Male	78%	86.80%	82.50%	75.00%
Associate's colleges	0%	0.00%	0.00%	0.00%
Specialized other	0%	0.00%	0.00%	0.00%
Specialized medical	16%	16.01%	27.50%	12.50%
Research extensive	77%	77.39%	62.50%	87.50%
Master's colleges	0%	0.00%	0.00%	0.00%
Research intensive	7%	6.60%	10.00%	0.00%

York, the Mid-Atlantic, the Northwest, and Texas, the propensity for females to patent exceeded that of their male colleagues. By contrast, in other regions, such as California, New England, and the Great Lakes, male scientists had a greater propensity to patent.

Gender also clearly played a role in a number of other dimensions. For example, Figure 8-2 shows that the mean amount of the NCI grant was considerably greater for male scientists who patented than for their female counterparts.

8.3.2. Small Business Innovation Research

The second measure of scientist commercialization involves scientists awarded SBIR grants to provide finance for the small business. Creation

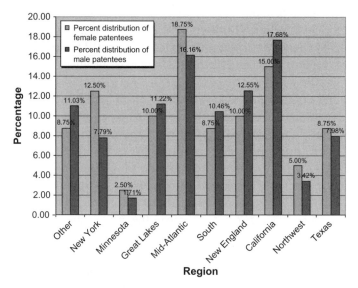

Figure 8-1. Patents by region and gender.

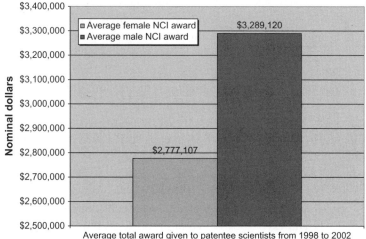

Figure 8-2. NCI grant award by gender for patenting scientists.

of the SBIR in the early 1980s was a response to the loss of American competitiveness in global markets. Congress mandated that each federal agency allocate about 4 percent of its annual budget to funding innovative small firms as a mechanism for restoring American international competitiveness (Wessner, 2000). The SBIR provides a mandate to the major R&D agencies in the United States to allocate a share of the research budget to innovative small firms. In 2001 the SBIR program amounted to around $1.4 billion. Consisting of three phases, the SBIR program provides increasing support to ideas that show commercial promise and pass certain thresholds.

The SBIR represents about 60 percent of all public entrepreneurial finance programs. Taken together, the public small-business finance is about two-thirds as large as private venture capital. In 1995, $2.4 billion was provided through and guaranteed by public programs, which amounted to more than 60 percent of the total funding disbursed by traditional venture funds in that year. Equally as important, the emphasis on SBIR and most public funds is on early-stage finance, which is generally ignored by private venture capital. Some of the most innovative American companies received early stage financing from SBIR, including Apple Computer, Chiron, Compaq, and Intel.

There is compelling evidence that the SBIR program has had a positive impact on economic performance in the United States (Lerner, 1999; Wessner, 2000; Audretsch, Weigand and Weigand, 2002; Audretsch, 2003). The relevant agency awarding SBIR grants to scientists for commercialization of science involving cancer research is the National Institutes of Health (NIH), although this does not preclude the possibility that scientists engaging in cancer research have not received SBIR awards from other agencies. The SBIR award data from the NIH from 1998 to 2002, including a wealth of details ranging from the amount of the award to the people involved, is listed on the NIH Web site.[1]

Between 1998 and 2002, some 6,461 SBIR awards were granted to 3,230 distinct scientists by the NIH. The PI of each SBIR award was then matched to the 1,693 NCI scientists using an SQL program. Only those scientists who were included in both the SBIR database as a PI and an NCI award recipient, and where there was a match of last and first names, were considered for this study. The resulting thirty-four matches were then subjected to a location criterion. The address of the PI listed in the SBIR grant was then matched to the NCI scientists using a fifty-mile radius around the respective university. If the location was outside a fifty-mile radius, the match was considered invalid. For example, there are four scientists with the name David Johnson listed in the NIH SBIR database as having been awarded an SBIR. Their addresses are given as Hamilton, Montana; Lawrence, Kansas; San Diego,

---

[1] http://grants.nih.gov/grants/funding/award_data.htm.

California; and Seattle, Washington. None of these matched the two NCI recipients named David Johnson from Houston, Texas, or Nashville, Tennessee. The geography criterion reduced the number of confirmed SBIR-NCI recipients to eight. Thus, one of the most striking insights to emerge in this study is that use of the SBIR is not a prevalent or even common mode of commercialization by scientists receiving NCI awards.

The most striking feature of the small group of SBIR scientists is that they tend to be highly accomplished in terms of research output and reputation. As shown, one-quarter of them are classified as "star scientists," in that they were among the top 10 percent of scientists in terms of numbers of publications. In fact, the mean number of publications of SBIR scientists was five times greater. Similarly, their citations were about three times as great as the overall group of NCI scientists. Most of the SBIR scientists are employed at universities classified by the Carnegie Higher Education Classification as being "Research Extensive."[2] Interestingly, the mean value of their NCI award was relatively low. Thus, there are considerable reasons to view those scientists funded by the NCI who also obtain an SBIR grant as outliers.

8.3.3. Licenses

The third mode of scientist commercialization involves licenses. Unlike the patent and SBIR databases, which are publicly available, there is no such public database that identifies and measures licensed intellectual property. Thus, we created a new database of NCI awardees who engaged in licensing by surveying those NCI awardees who were also in the USPTO patent database. The survey instrument was designed with two criteria in mind:

1. Maximize the information obtained without placing too great of a burden in terms of time on some of the nation's top medical scientists. (By minimizing scientists' time requirements, we believed we would improve the response rate.)
2. Maximize the information shedding light on knowledge creation and subsequent commercialization through modes other than patents, such as SBIR grants and licenses.

A survey consisting of twelve questions generated from these two criteria was designed and implemented. The questions were divided into four subgroups focusing on commercialization and on personal characteristics.

---

[2] "Research Extensive" universities award at least 50 doctoral degrees annually across at least three disciplines, or at least 20 doctoral degrees annually. http://www.carnegie foundation.org/Classification/downloads/cc2000-public.zip.

The first category focused on licensing and contained questions concerning the number of licenses issued and the types of companies receiving the license. The second category included questions about the actual contribution made and role played by the NCI grant.

Contact information, including e-mail and telephone numbers, for the 606 patenting scientists were obtained using the Google search engine. Most records were easily found, and a database of the resulting details was created.

Scientists were initially contacted via telephone, and if there was not a positive response, they were then sent an email requesting participation in the survey. Of the 606 patenting NCI scientists who were contacted, completed responses were obtained from 75 scientists. Of those 75 scientists providing responses, 41 licensed intellectual property. In addition, four scientists engaged in the sale of full ownership of their patent.

Those NCI scientists licensing intellectual property also exhibited distinct differences from the overall sample of NCI awardees. In particular, as shown in Table 8-1, they were more likely to be located in either the Mid-Atlantic region or Texas, to be a star scientist, to have a greater number of papers published and citations in scientific journals, and to be employed by a university classified by Carnegie as a "Specialized Medical Institution," which is defined as a university that awards most of their professional degrees in medicine and related fields. By contrast, those NCI awardees licensing their intellectual property tended to have a somewhat lower grant award than did the overall sample of NCI awardees.

Figure 8-3 shows that the mean NCI award for scientists engaging in licensing was considerably greater for males than for females. Similarly, Figure 8-4 shows that in certain regions, such as New York and California, the women had a greater propensity for licensing, while in other regions, such as the Great Lakes, New England, Texas, and the Mid-Atlantic, the men had a greater propensity for licensing.

Responses to the survey suggested that, at least in terms of licensee size, there is no difference between genders. As Figure 8-5 shows, gender seemed to play no role in whether the licensee tends to be a large or small company.

8.4. Determinants of Scientist Commercialization

8.4.1. Main Factors

A number of theories and hypotheses have posited why some scientists choose to commercialize research while others do not, and some compelling insights have been garnered through previous empirical studies. These

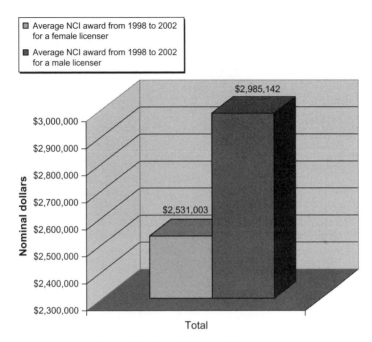

Figure 8-3. Mean NCI award by gender.

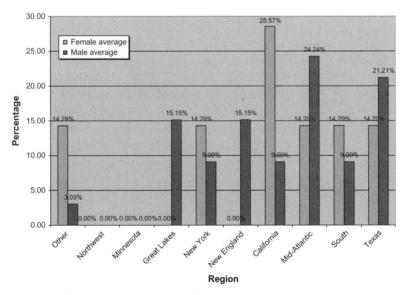

Figure 8-4. Distribution of licenses by region and gender.

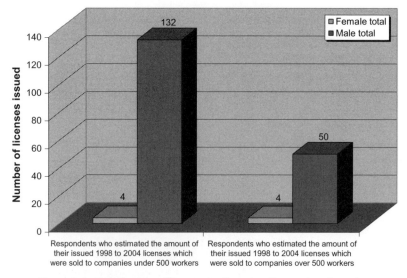

Figure 8-5. Distribution of licenses by firm size (licensee) and gender.

include the scientist life cycle, which highlights the role of age, experience, and reputation; the knowledge production function, which highlights the role of scientific human capital and resources; and the regional and university contexts, which highlight the role of geographically bounded spillovers and institutional incentives.

Scientist Life Cycle

A large literature has emerged focusing on what has become known as the appropriability problem. The underlying issue revolves around how firms that invest in the creation of new knowledge can best appropriate the economic returns from that knowledge (Arrow, 1962). Audretsch (1995) proposed shifting the unit of observation away from exogenously assumed firms to individuals – agents with endowments of new economic knowledge. When the lens is shifted away from the firm to the individual as the relevant unit of analysis, the appropriability issue remains, but the question becomes: How can scientists with a given endowment of new knowledge best appropriate the returns from that knowledge? Levin and Stephan (1991) suggest that the answer depends on both the career trajectory as well as the stage of the life cycle of the scientist.

The university or academic career trajectory encourages and rewards the production of new scientific knowledge. Thus, the goal of the scientist in the university context is to establish *priority*. This is done most efficiently through publication in scientific journals (Audretsch and Stephan, 2000). By contrast, with a career trajectory in the private sector, scientists are rewarded for the production of new economic knowledge, or knowledge that has been commercialized in the market, but not necessarily new scientific knowledge per se. In fact, scientists working in industry are often discouraged from sharing knowledge externally with the scientific community through publication. As a result of these different incentive structures, industrial and academic scientists develop distinct career trajectories.

The appropriability question confronting academic scientists can be considered in the context of the model of scientist human capital over the life cycle. Scientist life-cycle models suggest that early in their careers scientists invest heavily in human capital in order to build a scientific reputation (Levin and Stephan, 1991). In the later stages of their career, the scientist trades or "cashes in" this reputation for economic return. Thus, early in his or her career, the scientist invests in the creation of scientific knowledge in order to establish a reputation that signals the value of that knowledge to the scientific community.

With maturity, scientists seek ways to appropriate the economic value of the new knowledge. Thus, academic scientists may seek to commercialize their scientific research within a life-cycle context. The life-cycle model of the scientist implies that, *ceteris paribus*, a scientist's age should play a role in the decision to commercialize. In the early stages of a scientist's career, he or she will tend to invest in his or her scientific reputation. As the scientist evolves toward maturity and the marginal productivity of his or her scientific research starts to hit diminishing returns, the incentive for cashing in through commercialization becomes greater.

Scientists working in the private sector are arguably more fully compensated for the economic value of their knowledge. This will not be the case for academic scientists, unless they cash out, in terms of Dasgupta and David (1994), by commercializing their scientific knowledge. This suggests that academic scientists seek commercialization within a life-cycle context. This life-cycle context presents two distinct hypotheses: both age and scientific reputation should influence the decision of a university scientist to engage in commercialization activities.

Knowledge Production Function – Resources

The question of why some contexts generate more innovative activity than others has been the subject of considerable research in economics. While the conventional approach to analyzing innovative output at the micro-economic level has been at the level of the firm, it conceivably can apply to the unit of analysis of the individual knowledge worker, such as a scientist. The fundamental questions addressed in this literature are "What do firms do to generate innovative output?" and "Why are some firms more innovative than others?" For the unit of observation of the individual scientist, this question translates into, "What do scientists do to generate innovative output?" and "Why are some scientists more engaged in commercialization of scientific activity than others?"

In what Zvi Griliches (1979) formalized as the *model of the knowledge production function*, knowledge-generating inputs are linked to innovative outputs. Griliches, in fact, suggested that it was investments in knowledge inputs that would generate the greatest yield in terms of innovative output. This might suggest a hypothesis that the propensity for a scientist to engage in commercialization activity is positively related to the amount of the award, on the grounds that a greater award amount, *ceteris paribus*, represents a greater investment in new knowledge.

Scientific Human Capital

An implication of the knowledge production function is that those scientists with a greater research and scientific prowess have the capacity for generating a greater scientific output. But how does scientific capability translate into observable characteristics that can promote or impede commercialization efforts? Because the commercialization of scientific research is particularly risky and uncertain (Audretsch and Stephan, 2000), a strong scientific reputation, as evidenced through vigorous publication and a formidable number of citations, provides a greatly valued signal of scientific credibility and capability to any anticipated commercialized venture or project. This suggests a hypothesis linking measures of the quality of the scientist, or his or her scientific reputation as measured by publications and citations, to commercialization.

Locational and Institutional Contexts

Scientist location can influence the decision to commercialize for two reasons. First, as Jaffe (1989), Audretsch and Feldman (1996, Glaeser, Kallal, Scheinkman, and Shleifer (1992), and Jaffe, Trajtenberg, and Henderson (1992) show, knowledge tends to spill over within geographically bounded regions. This implies that scientists working in regions with a high level of investments in new knowledge can more easily access and generate new scientific ideas. This suggests that scientists working in knowledge clusters should tend to be more productive than their counterparts who are geographically isolated. As Glaeser et al. (1992, p. 1126) have observed, "Intellectual breakthroughs must cross hallways and streets more easily than oceans and continents."

A second component of externalities involves not the technological knowledge, but rather behavioral knowledge. As Feldman and Desrochers (2004) show for a study based on the commercialization activities of scientists at Johns Hopkins and Duke University, the likelihood of a scientist engaging in commercialization activity, which is measured as disclosing an invention, is shaped based on the commercialization behavior of the doctoral supervisor in the institution where the scientist was trained, as well as the commercialization behavior and attitudes exhibited by the chair and peers at the relevant department. Similarly, based on a study of 778 faculty members from forty universities, Louis et al. (1989) find that it is the local norms of behavior and attitudes toward commercialization that shape the likelihood of an individual university scientist to engage in commercialization activity, in their case by starting a new firm.

Thus, the locational and institutional contexts can influence the propensity for scientists to engage in commercialization activities by providing access to spatially bounded knowledge spillovers and by shaping the institutional setting and behavioral norms and attitudes toward commercialization.

8.4.2. Estimation of a Logit Model

To shed light on the question "How do some scientists commercialize their scientific research, while others do not?" a logit model was estimated for the unit of observation of the scientist identified in the NCI database where the dependent variable takes on the value of one if he or she has commercialized over the time period 1998-2004 and zero if he or she has not. As the previous section emphasized, there is no singular mode for scientist commercialization. Rather, scientists select across multiple modes of possible commercialization. Thus, the logit model was estimated for each of the main modes of commercialization – patents and licenses (including selling a license). Each of these measures of commercialization is described and defined in Table 8-2. Because the sample size is large enough to warrant empirical estimation of the logit model, only two of the measures of commercialization – patents and licensing – could be used. SBIR data was omitted due to the small sample size.

Table 8-2. *The modes of commercialization*

Commercialization mode	Description
Patenting scientist	Number of National Cancer Institute grant recipient Scientists who patented from 1998 to 2004 ($N = 606$)
Selling a license	Number of scientists who sold full ownership of their patents (from a respondent sample of, 75, $N = 4$)
SBIR grant	Number of scientists awarded an SBIR grant ($N = 8$)

The previous section suggests five different factors shaping the decision by a scientist to commercialize her research: resources, personal characteristics, scientific human capital (quality), nature of the university, and location. These factors are empirically operationalized through the following measures:

Resources

Award Amount: This variable is the mean total NCI awarded to the scientist between 1998 and 2002. The award amount was obtained from the original NCI award spreadsheet. If external funding of scientific research is conducive to commercialization, a positive coefficient of the Award Amount would be expected.

Gender

Male: This is a dummy variable assigned the value of one for males (1,310) of the overall 1,693 included in the NCI database. Scientist gender was determined during the Google search process. The estimated coefficient will reflect whether the gender of the scientist influences the propensity to commercialize research.

Location

Ten different locational dummy variables were created taking on the value of one for Texas, California, New York, Minnesota, Great Lakes (Ohio, Indiana, Illinois, Michigan and Wisconsin), Northwest (Oregon and Washington), New England (Maine, Vermont, New Hampshire, Connecticut, Rhode Island, and Massachusetts), South Atlantic (Virginia, North Carolina, South Carolina, Georgia and Florida), Mid-Atlantic (Washington, Maryland, Pennsylvania), and other (Arizona, Alabama, New Mexico,

Colorado, Nebraska, Hawaii, and Iowa). Those regions that have tended to have greater investments in research and science and that have developed a culture more encouraging to university and scientist commercialization, such as California and New England, might be expected to have a positive coefficient.

University Type

- *Ivy League*: A dummy variable was created taking on the value of one for all scientists employed at Brown University, Cornell University, Columbia University, Dartmouth College, Harvard University, Princeton University, the University of Pennsylvania, and Yale University.
- *Public universities*: A dummy variable was created taking on the value of one for scientists employed at public universities and zero otherwise. Because they are at least partially financed by the public, state universities tend to have a stronger mandate for outreach and commercialization of research. This may suggest a positive coefficient.
- *Carnegie classifications*: *The Carnegie Classification of Universities* (2000) provides a comprehensive study classifying universities by types of degree offered. Each type of institution is defined according to the types and numbers of degrees offered in different fields. The categories are:
  1. Special Medical Institution (graduate only, that specializing in medical degrees (i.e., doctors and nurses))
  2. Research-Intensive University (grants doctoral degrees in three fields and fewer than 50 annually)
  3. Research-Extensive University (grants doctoral degrees in more than three fields and more degrees than 50 annually)
  4. Bachelor's and Master's College (grants only BA/BS and masters degrees but no Ph.Ds)
  5. Associate's College (two-year institution)

Scientist Human Capital (Quality)

- *Citations*: A computer program was designed to measure the citations of the 1,693 scientists through the "Expanded Science Citation Index." A higher number of citations reflects a higher level of human capital and scientific reputation (Audretsch and Stephan, 2000).

A positive coefficient would reflect that the likelihood of commercialization is greater for more productive scientists.

- *Publications*: A specific computer program was designed to measure the publications of the scientist, which should also reflect the level of human capital and scientific reputation (Audretsch and Stephan, 2000).
- *Star Scientist*: A scientist is classified as being a star if he or she is in the top 10 percent of citations per publication. A dummy variable was created taking on the value of one for those scientists with a star classification and zero otherwise. Star scientists may be able to attract resources for commercialization, suggesting a positive coefficient (Audretsch and Stephan, 1996).

Finally, two additional dummy variables were included to reflect the impact that receiving an NCI grant had on the likelihood of commercialization. These dummy variables were assigned the value of one if the scientist answered affirmatively to the question posed in the survey, "Did the NCI grant help you to patent?" and "Did the NCI grant help you to license?"

The definitions of the explanatory variables are summarized in Table 8-3. Table 8-4 shows the simple correlation coefficient between the different variables.

The results from estimating the logit model using the patent measure for scientist commercialization are provided in Table 8-5.

There is no evidence suggesting that the size of the grant award influences the likelihood of the scientist to file for a patent. The various measures of scientist human capital, or scientist quality, are highly correlated, and therefore including them in the same estimated model may result in multi-collinearity. Thus, the first column presents results when the measure of star scientist is used, while the second column includes the measure of publications, and the third and fourth column show citations. As the positive and statistically significant coefficient of star scientist suggests, those scientists with a prolific publication record tend to have a higher propensity to commercialize research through patents. Similarly, those scientists with greater citations also have a greater likelihood of filing for a patent.

There is also considerable statistical evidence suggesting that the gender of a scientist influences the likelihood of commercialization in the form of patents. In particular, being male increases the propensity for a scientist to patent. The evidence concerning the impact on university type on the

Table 8-3. *Independent variables and definitions*

Independent variables	Description
Total	Aggregate sum of money given to Scientist from 1998 to 2002
Male	Where a Male = 1
Texas	Binary variable of whether Scientists' University is in Texas, Texas = 1
California	Binary variable of whether Scientists' University is in California, California = 1
New York	Binary variable of whether Scientists' University is in New York, New York = 1
Minnesota	Binary variable of whether Scientists' University is in Minnesota, Minnesota = 1
Great Lakes	Binary variable of whether Scientists' University is in Ohio, Indiana, Illinois, Wisconsin, or Michigan, Great Lakes = 1
Northwest	Binary variable of whether Scientists' University is in Oregon or Washington, Northwest = 1
New England	Binary variable of whether Scientists' University is in New England (ME, NH, VT, MA, CT, or RI), New England = 1
South	Binary variable of whether Scientists' University is in the South Eastern Atlantic (VA, NC, SC, GA, or Fl), South = 1
Mid-Atlantic	Binary variable of whether Scientists' University is in the Mid-Atlantic (NY, PA, DE, MD, or DC), New England = 1
Ivy league	Binary variable of whether Scientists' University is an Ivy League School, Ivy League School = 1
Public	Binary variable of whether Scientists' University is Public, Public = 1
Papers	Papers published by scientist from 1998 to 2004
Star	Binary variable of top decile Scientists who published papers
Citations	Citations of scientist from 1998 to 2004
Patentee	Binary Variable of whether scientist patented or not, Patentee = 1
Number of patents	Aggregate number of Patents from Scientist from 1998 to 2004
Did the NCI grant help you license	Respondents who said yes = 1
Did the NCI grant help you patent	Respondents who said yes = 1
Star scientist	Scientists who were the top 10% of our sample
Male	Gender of Scientist, where Male = 1
Associate's college	Binary Variable of where Scientist's institution grants a two year degree
Bachelor's and Master's college	Binary Variable of where Scientist's institution grants a four year degree

(continued)

Table 8-3 (*Continued*)

Independent variables	Description
Special medical institution	Binary Variable, where Scientist's University award most of their professional degrees in medicine. In some instances, they include other health professions programs, such as dentistry, pharmacy, or nursing
Research-intensive university	Binary Variable, where Scientist's University awards at least ten doctoral degrees per year across three or more disciplines, or at least 20 doctoral degrees per year overall
Research-extensive university	Binary Variable, where Scientist's University awards 50 or more doctoral degrees per year across three or more disciplines, or at least 20 doctoral degrees per year overall

patenting activities of scientists is weaker and more ambiguous. There is at least some evidence suggesting that being employed in a public university may actually reduce the likelihood of a scientist patenting. Finally, the region in which the scientist is located apparently influences his or her propensity to patent. In particular, those scientists located in California and New England exhibit a greater likelihood of patenting, even after controlling for the other main factors, such as scientist quality and gender.

The measure of licensing for scientist commercialization is used in estimating the log model, and the regression results are presented in Table 8-6. As for the measure of patents, the award amount does not appear to influence the likelihood of scientist licensing. However, in contrast to the measure of patents, none of the measures of scientific human capital, or scientist quality, plays a role in the decision to license. Similarly, scientist gender does not influence the likelihood of licensing. However, age apparently does play a role in the decision to license. Those scientists who are older have a higher propensity to license their intellectual property.

The nature of the scientist's university also influences licensing behavior. Those scientists employed at a medical university have a greater likelihood of licensing, as do those scientists located in Texas.

There is evidence that obtaining a NCI award also facilitates licensing activity. Those scientists who responded that the NCI grant helped them to patent, to license, and to create a business all exhibited a higher likelihood of licensing.

Table 8-4. *Correlation matrix between variables*

	Patentee	Male	Medical	Extensive	Intensive	Star	Citations	Papers	Total	Public	Ivy League
Patentee	1.000										
Male	0.163	1.000									
Medical	0.005	0.010	1.000								
Extensive	0.006	0.009	-0.794	1.000							
Intensive	0.001	-0.036	-0.115	-0.486	1.000						
Star	0.045	0.026	0.041	-0.007	-0.040	1.000					
Citations	0.089	0.054	0.041	-0.035	0.005	0.514	1.000				
Papers	0.000	0.029	0.036	-0.023	-0.008	0.529	0.865	1.000			
Total	0.014	0.042	-0.009	0.014	-0.009	-0.026	0.059	-0.026	1.000		
Public	-0.061	-0.001	0.057	-0.103	0.093	0.027	-0.027	0.022	-0.059	1.000	
Ivy League	0.046	-0.014	-0.147	0.111	0.036	-0.009	-0.009	-0.026	0.005	-0.366	1.000
Texas	0.006	-0.002	0.621	-0.504	-0.069	0.028	0.032	0.019	0.013	0.148	-0.099
Northwest	-0.054	0.024	-0.015	0.053	-0.062	-0.016	-0.026	-0.024	-0.042	0.219	-0.080
California	0.077	0.016	-0.173	-0.007	0.268	-0.006	0.005	-0.029	0.037	0.106	-0.136
New England	0.076	0.029	-0.138	0.097	0.047	0.003	0.040	0.016	-0.015	-0.263	0.293
South	-0.001	0.022	-0.098	0.120	-0.082	-0.021	-0.016	-0.007	0.009	0.041	-0.115
Mid-Atlantic	0.006	-0.019	0.004	-0.008	0.020	-0.039	-0.014	-0.016	0.008	-0.191	0.199
Great Lakes	-0.046	-0.028	-0.144	0.154	-0.039	0.017	-0.003	0.046	-0.004	0.104	-0.132
Minnesota	-0.052	-0.039	0.170	-0.118	-0.047	0.034	0.017	0.018	0.005	-0.017	-0.060
New York	-0.026	-0.041	-0.024	0.022	-0.012	0.001	-0.008	-0.011	-0.039	-0.304	0.222
Other	-0.029	0.036	-0.030	0.085	-0.098	0.017	-0.019	-0.005	0.004	0.193	-0.125

(continued)

Table 8-4 (*continued*)

	Texas	Northwest	California	New England	South	Mid-Atlantic	Great Lakes	Minnesota	New York	Other
Texas	1.000									
Northwest	−0.069	1.000								
California	−0.117	−0.094	1.000							
New England	−0.093	−0.075	−0.128	1.000						
South	−0.099	−0.080	−0.135	−0.108	1.000					
Mid-Atlantic	−0.128	−0.104	−0.176	−0.141	−0.149	1.000				
Great Lakes	−0.113	−0.092	−0.155	−0.124	−0.132	−0.171	1.000			
Minnesota	−0.052	−0.042	−0.070	−0.056	−0.060	−0.077	−0.069	1.000		
New York	−0.094	−0.076	−0.129	−0.103	−0.109	−0.115	−0.126	−0.057	1.000	
Other	−0.108	−0.087	−0.148	−0.118	−0.125	−0.162	−0.143	−0.065	−0.119	1.000

Table 8-5. *Logit results for scientist commercialization – patents*

	(1)	(2)	(3)
Male	.884(6.33)**	.896(6.43)**	.878(6.29)**
Medical university	.248(1.52)	–	–
Extensive university	–	.020(0.14)	–
Intensive university	−.140(0.63)	–	–
Star scientist	.298(1.75)*	–	–
Citations	–	–	.644(2.96)**
Papers published	–	−.010(−0.05)	–
NCI total award	.992(0.951)	−.342(0.02)	−.003(−0.19)
Public institutions	−.182(1.44)	−.202(1.62)	−.209(−1.69)*
Ivy league	.219(1.13)	.171(0.89)	–
Texas	–	.191(0.438)	.259(1.11)
Northwest	−.361(1.29)	−.406(1.48)	−.283(−0.97)
California	.597(3.00)**	.485(2.80)**	.587(2.97)**
New England	.463(0.04)**	.375(1.73)*	.526(2.31)**
South	.134(0.64)	–	.169(0.78)
Mid-Atlantic	.090(0.47)	−.137(1.57)	.184(0.94)
Great Lakes	–	–	–
Minnesota	−.659(1.79)*	−.580(1.57)	−.510(−1.35)
New York	−.162(0.70)	−.211(0.95)	−.062(0.27)
Other			0.033(0.874)
Intercept	−1.388(6.41)**	−1.286(5.44)**	−1.432(6.82)**
Pseudo R^2	0.04	.037	.041
>Chi-squared	0.000	0.000	0.000
Sample size	1683	1683	1683

Notes: *t-statistic in brackets.*
* Statistically significant at the two-tailed test for 90 percent level of confidence.
** Statistically significant at the two-tailed test for 95 percent level of confidence.

8.5. Conclusions

This chapter found that scientists whose research is supported by grants from the National Institute of Cancer are active in commercialization. However, the extent and nature of scientist commercialization is shaped by the particular mode of commercialization pursued by the individual scientist. In particular, this study has found that, when it comes to commercializing research, the modes considered here – patents, licensing, and SBIR – are anything but interchangeable or homogeneous. Rather, each mode represents a distinct and unique conduit for commercializing science. While just over one-third of the NCI scientists had filed for a patent,

Table 8-6. *Logit results for scientist commercialization – licensing*

	(1)	(2)
Grant help patentee	3.450(3.85)**	2.944(3.68)**
Grant help licenser	2.962(2.13)**	3.263(2.29)**
Age	0.023(0.55)	–
Extensive universe	–	−0.674(0.67)
Medical universe	1.472(1.27)	–
Male	−0.333(0.36)	−0.530 (−0.62)
Citations	–	–
Papers published		−0.003(0.86)
Star scientist	−0.147(0.10)	–
Total NCI award	−0.107(0.53)	−0.177 (0.90)
Public institution	−0.087(0.10)	0.655(0.64)
Ivy League	−1.288(1.03)	–
Texas	–	3.251(1.67)*
South	−1.880(1.30)	–
Mid-Atlantic	–	1.388(1.18)
California	0.034(0.03)	1.183(0.831)
New England	0.338(0.25)	0.944(0.60)
New York	−1.538(0.76)	–
Great Lakes	−2.223(1.50)	−0.253(021)
Intercept	−1.829(0.69)	−1.884(0.83)
Pseudo R²	0.445	0.458
>Chi-squared	0.000	0.000
Sample size	75	75

Notes: *t-statistic in brackets.*
* Statistically significant at the two-tailed test for 90 percent level of confidence.
** Statistically significant at the two-tailed test for 95 percent level of confidence.

slightly over half of the patenting scientists responding to the survey reported that they had licensed their intellectual property. By contrast, only eight of the entire 1,693 scientists had been awarded an SBIR grant. Thus, the prevalence of commercializing science varies substantially across the different commercialization modes.

Similarly, the heterogeneity of scientist commercialization applies not just to the prevalence of commercialization across the different modes, but also to those factors conducive to commercialization. The empirical evidence from this study suggests that factors conducive to scientist commercialization of research, such as gender, age, scientific human capital and quality, and institutional and geographic contexts, are strikingly specific to the particular mode of commercialization.

The heterogeneity of scientist commercialization of research with respect to both prevalence and determinants is particularly important for public policy. The perception of scientist commercialization of research and those specific factors conducive to scientist commercialization should not be based on a singular mode of commercialization. Policy conclusions reached from studies focusing on a singular mode of commercialization may actually obscure as much as they reveal about how and why scientists commercialize their research.

This would suggest that future research designed to guide public policy should not be limited to those modes of commercialization that are publicly available and can be relatively and easily accessed at low cost. While scientist patent activity and participation in the SBIR program are certainly important modes of commercialization, their ease of access should not lead to the conclusion that they are even the most important and prevalent forms of commercialization. Rather, as this study has shown, other modes of commercialization for which no systematic comprehensive public sources of data exist, such as scientist licensing, may also be a highly prevalent and important form of scientist commercialization. Future research needs to explore other modes of commercialization, and painstaking data collection needs to be undertaken to provide systematic measurement and analysis of commercialization conduits such as the start-up of new firms. It is imperative that comprehensive and systematic new sources of measurement be created by directly interacting with the scientists themselves to gauge the extent, nature, determinants, and impact of scientist commercialization of research. If the commercialization of science represents one of the missing links of economic growth, job creation, and competitiveness in global markets, then undertaking the painstaking measurement and analysis is essential to guide public policy in both understanding and promoting this important source of economic growth.

References

Acs, Zoltan J., and Catherine Armington. 2006. *Entrepreneurship, Geography and American Economic Growth.* Cambridge: Cambridge University Press.

Acs, Zoltan J., David B. Audretsch, Pontus Braunerhjelm, and Bo Carlsson. 2004. "The Missing Link: The Knowledge Filter and Entrepreneurship in Economic Growth." *CERP* working paper 4783.

Arrow, Kenneth J. 1962. "Economic Welfare and the Allocation of Resources for Invention." In Richard Nelson, ed., *The Rate and Direction of Inventive Activity.* Princeton: Princeton University Press, 609–626.

Association of University Technology Managers. 2004. "Recollections: Celebrating the History of AUTUM and the Legacy of Bayh-Dole."

Audretsch, David B. 1995. *Innovation and Industry Evolution*. Cambridge, Mass.: MIT Press.

Audretsch, David B. 2003. "Standing on the Shoulders of Midgets: The U.S. Small Business Innovation Research Program (SBIR)." *Small Business Economics*, 20(2), 129–135.

Audretsch, David B., and Maryann P. Feldman. 1996. "R&D Spillovers and the Geography of Innovation and Production." *American Economic Review*, 86(3), 630–640.

Audretsch, David B., and Paula E. Stephan. 2000. *The Economics of Science and Innovation*. London: Edward Elgar.

Audretsch, David B., and Paula E. Stephan. 1996. "Company-Scientist Locational Links: The Case of Biotechnology." *American Economic Review*, 86(3), 641–652.

Audretsch, David B., Albert N. Link, and John T. Scott. 2002. "Public/Private Technology Partnerships: Evaluating SBIR-Supported Research." *Research Policy*, 31(1), 145–158.

Audretsch, David B., Max C. Keilbach, and Erik E. Lehmann. 2006. *Entrepreneurship and Economic Growth*. New York: Oxford University Press.

Audretsch, David B., Jürgen Weigand, and Claudia Weigand. 2002. "The Impact of the SBIR on Creating Entrepreneurial Behavior." *Economic Development Quarterly*, 16(1), 32–38.

Dasgupta, Partha, and Paul A. David. 1994. "Toward a New Economics of Science." *Research Policy*, 23(5), 487–521.

Feldman, M. P., and P. Desrochers. 2004. "Truth for Its Own Sake: Academic Culture and Technology Transfer at the Johns Hopkins University." *Minerva*, 42(2), 105–126.

Glaeser, Edward, Hedi Kallal, Jose Scheinkman, and Andrei Shleifer. 1992. "Growth in Cities." *Journal of Political Economy*, 100(6), 1126–1152.

Griliches, Zvi. 1979. "Issues in Assessing the Contribution of R&D to Productivity Growth." *Bell Journal of Economics*, 10(1), 92–116.

Henderson, Rebecca, Adam B. Jaffe, and Manuel Trajtenberg. 1998. "Universities as a Source of Commercial Technology: A Detailed Analysis of University Patenting, 1965–1988." *Review of Economics & Statistics*, 80(1), 119–127.

Jaffe, Adam. 1989. "Real Effects of Academic Research." *American Economic Review*, 79(5), 957–970.

Jaffe, Adam, and Josh Lerner. 2001. "Reinventing Public R&D: Patent Policy and the Commercialization of National Laboratory Technologies." *Rand Journal of Economics*, 32(1), 167–198.

Jaffe, Adam, Manuel Trajtenberg, and Rebecca Henderson. 1993. "Geographic Localization of Knowledge Spillovers as Evidenced by Patent Citations." *Quarterly Journal of Economics*, 108(3), 577–598.

Jensen, Richard, and Marie Thursby. 2001. "Proofs and Prototypes for Sale: The Licensing of University Inventions." *American Economic Review*, 91(1), 240–259.

Lerner, Josh. 1999. "The Government as Venture Capitalist: The Long-Run Impact of the SBIR Program." *Journal of Business*, 72(3), 285–318.

Levin, Sharon G., and Paula E. Stephan. 1991. "Research Productivity over the Life Cycle: Evidence for Academic Scientists." *American Economic Review*, 81(1), 114–132.

Louis, Karen S., David Blumenthal, Michael E. Gluck, and Michael A. Stoto. 1989. "Entrepreneurs in Academe: An Exploration of Behaviors among Life Scientists." *Administrative Science Quarterly*, 34, 110–131.

Lucas, Robert E. 1993, "Making a Miracle." *Econometrica*, 61(2), 251–272.

Mowery, David C., Richard R. Nelson, Bhaven N. Sampat, and Arvids Ziedonis. 2004. *Ivory Tower and Industrial Innovation*. Stanford, Calif.: Stanford University Press.

Mowery, David C. 2005. "The Bayh-Dole Act and High-Technology Entrepreneurship in U.S. Universities: Chicken, Egg, or Something Else?" In Gary Liebcap, ed., *University Entrepreneurship and Technology Transfers*. Amsterdam: Elsevier, 38–68.

Romer, Paul M. 1986. "Increasing Returns and Long-Run Growth." *Journal of Political Economy*, 94(5), 1002–1037.

Shane, Scott. 2004. *Academic Entrepreneurship: University Spinoffs and Wealth Creation*. Cheltenham, U.K.: Edward Elgar Publishing.

Stephan, Paula E., and Sharon G. Levin. 1992. *Striking the Mother Lode in Science*. New York: Oxford University Press.

Thursby, Jerry, and Marie C. Thursby. 2005. "Gender Patterns of Research and Licensing Activity of Science and Engineering Faculty." *Journal of Technology Transfer*, 30(4), 343–353.

Thursby, Jerry, Richard Jensen, and Marie C. Thursby. 2001. "Objectives, Characteristics and Outcomes of University Licensing: A Survey of Major U.S. Universities." *Journal of Technology Transfer*, 26, 59–72.

Thursby, Marie, and Richard Jensen. 2004. "Patent Licensing and the Research University." *NBER* Working Paper 10758.

Toole, Andrew, and Dirk Czarnitzki. 2005. "Biomedical Academic Entrepreneurship through the SBIR Program." *NBER Working Paper* 11450.

Wessner, Charles. 2000. *The Small Business Innovation Research Program (SBIR)*. Washington, D.C.: National Academy Press.

Zucker, Lynn G., and Michael R. Darby. 1998. "Intellectual Human Capital and the Birth of U.S. Biotechnology Enterprises." *American Economic Review*, 88, 290–306.

Why Entrepreneurship Matters for Germany

Max Keilbach

Entrepreneurship is the active and constructive element in the whole capitalist society.

J. M. Keynes (1920, chap. 6)

9.1. Introduction

While entrepreneurship has long been mentioned in the economic literature as one of the most important or even the most important elements in economic activity, it has recently regained considerable attention in the economic literature as a vital force that drives innovation and economic growth. In the same spirit as Keynes, William Baumol emphasized nearly fifty years later, "It has long been recognized that the entrepreneurial function is a vital component in the process of economic growth" (Baumol, 1968, p. 65), and Lazear (2002) claimed more recently, "The entrepreneur is the single most important player in the economy."

In this chapter, we aim to investigate the fundamentals of these statements. In particular, we investigate the hypothesis that entrepreneurship drives innovation and economic growth. To do so, we lay out different aspects of entrepreneurship in Section 9.2. Then we discuss how entrepreneurship drives innovation and consequently economic performance. Section 9.4 presents empirical evidence for Germany and Section 9.5 concludes.

9.2. What Is the Economic Function of Entrepreneurship?

While the above quotes are rather recent, the role of the entrepreneur as major driver in the economy has long been acknowledged. However, different functions and different aspects of entrepreneurship have been emphasized.

Walras (1874) and Kirzner (1973) considered the entrepreneur as the agent who seeks and identifies arbitrage opportunities, which consist of a mismatch of supply and demand for existing products or technologies. By realizing these opportunities, the entrepreneur increases supply and satisfies demand of the product where the arbitrage opportunity existed. As such, the entrepreneur is the driving force behind the *tâtonnement* process that leads to the general equilibrium in the Walrasian model. Since the Walrasian entrepreneur acts within a framework of existing products or technologies, entrepreneurial opportunities consist in the mere mismatch of supply and demand on these markets; the Walrasian entrepreneur is static in the sense that it does not explicitly consider the creation of new products. Once the equilibrium is attained, the entrepreneur is devoid of function. Consequently, the Walrasian analysis of equilibria is independent of the entrepreneurial function.

Schumpeter (1934, 1950) saw the function of the entrepreneur in the "recognition and realization of new economic opportunities." In this view, opportunities are not only arbitrage opportunities but potential new products, potential new production processes and opportunities in marketing and reorganization, including, for example, processes involved in production. Hence, Schumpeter extends the notion of opportunity recognition from arbitrage on markets for existing products to the development of new economic knowledge into new products or technologies, or, put differently, the search for "innovation."

Hence, in this view, the function of entrepreneurship in the innovation process is to "explore" new technologies or techniques, rather than to "exploit" existing ones, a definition consistent with that introduced in Chapter 1 in the discussion of how new opportunities are discovered and implemented. If exploration is into unknown fields, there is a risk of failure. Von Mangoldt (1855) argued that entrepreneurial profit is a reward for uninsurable risk. Along the same lines, Clark (1892) argued that innovation leads to a comparative advantage, which is rewarded by excess returns. On the other hand, returns in excess of a riskless rate were due to mere monopolistic advantage rather than compensation for risk.

Knight (1921) developed this work and distinguished between risk (which is known or can potentially be known and therefore is calculable) and uncertainty (which cannot be known and therefore is incalculable). Consequently, Knight saw the main function of the entrepreneur as dealing with the uncertainty implied by introducing new goods to a market – taking the responsibility and the control for this activity.

Correspondingly, Sarasvathy, Dew, Velamura, and Venkataraman (2002) discuss three different levels of how entrepreneurs deal with opportunity. For them, with increasing level of activity, the entrepreneurial function is to recognize opportunity, to discover opportunity, or even to create opportunity. These three views integrate the three types of Knightian uncertainty with the three types of market processes that Buchanan and Vanberg (1991) describe, that is, the market as an allocative process, the market as a discovery process, and the market as a creative process. Note that according to the literature quoted above, all three processes are driven by entrepreneurs.

Marshall (1920) also devotes a part of his *Principles* to the economic function of entrepreneurship. He considers the entrepreneurial function as equally important as the role of what we know as the "production factors." In the fourth book, he considers four "agents of production": land, labor, capital, and organization. He understood "organization" in two senses: first a structural sense evoked by "industrial organization" and second in the sense of an activity. Referring to entrepreneurs as "business men" or "undertakers," he states that:

> They "adventure" or "undertake" its risks [i.e., the risks of production]; they bring together the capital and the labour required for the work; they arrange or "engineer" its general plan, and superintend its minor details. Looking at business men from one point of view we may regard them as a highly skilled industrial grade, from another as middlemen intervening between the manual worker and the consumer. (Marshall, 1920, 244)

Hence for Marshall, the function of the entrepreneur is to organize and control the production process and to bear the risks involved with it.

Summarizing this literature, three major economic functions can be allocated to entrepreneurship:

Opportunity Recognition. Entrepreneurs are the agents who discover or create new economic opportunities. These can be arbitrage opportunities or they can be related to new products, technologies, or techniques.

Opportunity Exploration. Beyond recognition, entrepreneurs are the agents who are actually exploring new opportunities. They organize the necessary resources and manage the implied processes.

Risk Processing. By exploring new and unknown territories, entrepreneurs risk failure. Entrepreneurial activity implies taking on this risk.

In short, entrepreneurs are the agents of change, starting new firms. In an innovation-oriented or knowledge-based economy, the function of opportunity recognition and taking the risk of realizing it becomes more prominent. The act of the entrepreneur is no longer a short preface to static equilibrium but a driving force in shaping the dynamics in the economic system.

9.3. Entrepreneurship and the Innovation Process

9.3.1. Background

The traditional model of economic development by Solow (1956) formalizes economic growth as the result of accumulating production capital through investment. The failure to explain U.S. growth using that model, however, made Solow himself conclude that productivity growth through innovation, not capital accumulation, must be the engine of long-run growth in modern economies. The endogenous growth theory (Romer, 1986; Lucas, 1988; Romer, 1990; Grossman and Helpman, 1991; Aghion and Bolton, 1992) explicitly models a knowledge-generating sector, which generates innovations (the R&D sector) or increases human capital, the stock of productive skills and capabilities embodied in labor, through education. One of the main assumptions underlying this theory is that knowledge behaves like a public good in that it is non-exhaustive and non-excludable. This implies that the stock of existing knowledge and the newly created knowledge is available (i.e., spills over) automatically to all economic agents. In that respect, the properties of knowledge differ fundamentally from the "traditional" production factors, capital and labor.

The public goods assumption implicitly suggests that it is possible to fully commercialize all new knowledge, hence that it can fully be applied to the production process. However, as Arrow (1962) pointed out, new knowledge differs from the traditional production factors not only by its public goods characteristics; it is also inherently uncertain. By uncertainty, Arrow understood the fact that it is a priori unknown if newly generated knowledge can be transferred successfully into a viable innovation, be it a new product or any other innovation.

Indeed, one can think of the stream of new knowledge arriving at a certain time period as involving different levels of uncertainty. For some of the new knowledge, its usefulness, hence the possibility of transforming it into a new product is obvious to agents involved in the production process. Think of quality improvements or improved properties of existing products as prime examples of this. At the other end of the "uncertainty scale" is new knowledge whose usefulness is not obvious at all because the knowledge is disconnected from existing products. Here, we can think of new knowledge as either very useful, indeed potentially revolutionizing,[1] or useless, indeed potentially inapplicable.

With the increasing uncertainty of new knowledge, the risk of exploiting and developing a marketable product from that new knowledge increases. This uncertainty plays on two levels:

Firms encounter a *technological uncertainty*, or the uncertainty that a new product is not feasible or feasible only at significantly higher costs.

There is a *market-oriented uncertainty*, the uncertainty that, once the product is developed, it will not fulfill demand on the consumer side; hence there is no market for the product, or the market develops later than expected by the firm.

Of course these uncertainties translate into a financial risk for the firm that attempts exploiting the uncertain new knowledge. A failure of either the technology or marketing might ultimately cause firm failure. Of course, a higher uncertainty implies a higher probability of failure of the project or even the whole venture. This failure feeds back information to other agents who realize that the product or technology was not viable in this form, thus generating a positive external effect on the society.

The fact that periods of strong exploration of new technologies are connected with high business start-up and high exit rates is supported by empirical evidence and by the literature on industry life cycle (Klepper, 1996). This literature suggests that early phases in the life cycle of an industry are characterized by a low market size and by large numbers of business start-ups and firm exits. With the establishment of a dominant design and increasing market size, market concentration starts and entry rates decline. Caves (1998) observes that strong correlation of entry and exit rates have consistently been found in a large number of time-series and cross-section studies for different countries, industries, and time periods. We will investigate further the relation between entry and exit in Section 9.4.

Since high uncertainty implies higher risk of failure, incumbent firms tend to concentrate on the application of new knowledge to their existing product portfolio, innovating their existing technologies (Baumol, 2002a). Therefore, not all of the newly created knowledge is developed by incumbent firms. Acs et al. (2004) call this process the *knowledge filter*. This filter implies that both the assumption that new knowledge is fully fed back into

---

[1]   In the extreme case, these are technologies that are able to start up a new innovation life cycle in the sense of Gort and Klepper (1982).

the economy and the assumption that knowledge spills over without restriction into the economy made by the endogenous growth theory are false and that the endogenous growth theory actually overstates the impact of knowledge creation on growth.

9.3.2. Uncertain New Knowledge and Entrepreneurial Vision

Uncertainty of new knowledge implies that it is unknown a priori whether the new knowledge is applicable, that is, whether it is possible to exploit this new knowledge economically and, if yes, what returns it can generate. This means that with increasing uncertainty of the new knowledge, the *variance* of the value of new knowledge increases. The increasing variance of this value implies that there will be divergent views on the usefulness of the new knowledge. While some agents will consider bits of new knowledge useless, others will form new ideas. This is the function of *Entrepreneurial Vision.* The archetypal story of any major invention is that it had been envisioned by someone who as entrepreneur subsequently developed it despite strong skepticism or even resistance by experts in the respective industries. Consider the Ford Model T (Tedlow, 2001) or the dry copy (Xerox) machine, to suggest just two examples.

If entrepreneurs, as implied in Chapter 1, develop new and uncertain knowledge, they are the agents who bear the risk that is implicit in the unknown outcome of the exploration of new opportunity, even as they push against the resistance of experts.

Therefore they play a central role in the innovation process of an economy. Baumol (2002b) distinguishes this entrepreneurial function explicitly from the role of larger incumbent corporations who are rather involved into routine processes of large-scale innovation. These processes seem quantitatively more important as they are easier to measure. R&D expenditure and the number of patents generated are larger and so are the resulting job creation and value added. However, a number of systematic studies[2] have provided evidence that breakthroughs and new products are rather introduced by small and young firms, or entrepreneurs. In that sense Baumol (2002b) refers to innovation as an integrated process based on a division of labor between small firms, who launch new products and introduce new technologies, and large firms, who take on these ideas and

---

[2] See, e.g., Scherer (1980) and CHI Research, Inc. (2002). The U.S. Small Business Administration (1995, p. 114) enumerates some seventy important innovations by small firms in the twentieth century, ranging from low-tech innovations such as the zipper or Bakelite to high-tech ones such as the nuclear magnetic resonance scanner or the microprocessor.

further develop them. Hence entrepreneurial firms and large firms co-exist in the innovation process in what Baumol (2002a) calls a "David-Goliath symbiosis." This discussion has made obvious that entrepreneurship plays an important part in the innovation process of an economy.

If entrepreneurs co-exist with larger innovative firms and play an important part in the innovation process, they will generate new knowledge that can potentially be beneficial for other agents of the economy. One of the external effects of their innovative activity is new knowledge about the viability of new technologies or new products. Indeed, very often, a product that has successfully been launched by an entrepreneur is quickly copied by other agents. As unwanted as this might be for the first entrepreneur, this process speeds up the diffusion of the new product or technology and therefore is beneficial to the economy as a whole. In that respect, entrepreneurship generates external effects that can play an important role for the economic performance of an economy.

9.3.3. The Knowledge Spillover Theory of Entrepreneurship

The discussion above states that entrepreneurship drives innovation and therefore economic performance. However, another mechanism is implicit in this discussion: A higher level of (uncertain) new economic knowledge will *ceteris paribus* correspond to a higher number of agents who regard this knowledge as economic opportunities and will be tempted to do so by starting up a new venture.

These two mechanisms have been summarized by the Knowledge Spillover Theory of Entrepreneurship suggested by Audretsch (1995) and Audretsch, Keilbach, and Lehmann (2006). Put shortly, this theory suggests that:

High knowledge contexts (industries or regions) imply a higher level of newly created knowledge. Since new knowledge is uncertain, it is not fully exploited by incumbent firms, leaving a higher level of knowledge-based opportunities. Therefore, knowledge-based entrepreneurship is higher in high knowledge contexts.

By exploring otherwise unexploited knowledge, entrepreneurship plays an important role in the innovation process. Hence high levels of entrepreneurship are correlated with high levels of economic performance.

Figure 9-1 summarizes the discussion of this section. R&D activity generates new knowledge, which comes with different levels of uncertainty. According to the level of uncertainty, the actual innovation process differs. While incumbent firms use the more established bits of knowledge (those

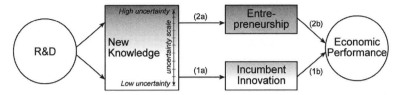

Figure 9-1. Entrepreneurship in a knowledge-based economy.

with lower uncertainty), their innovation activity generates economic performance through processes well described by the endogenous growth theory. This path is illustrated with arrows 1a and 1b.

The less established bits of knowledge (those with higher levels of uncertainty) are taken on by entrepreneurs who are less tied to established production processes and therefore can more easily develop new visions based on this less established knowledge. By the processes described above, this process will drive economic performance. This path is illustrated by arrows 2a and 2b in Figure 9-1. Both processes coexist and this David-Goliath symbiosis in the exploitation of new knowledge is described by arrows 1a and 2a.

9.4. Empirical Evidence for Germany

In this section, we aim to provide empirical evidence for the arguments given in the Knowledge Spillover Theory of Entrepreneurship. At the same time, we aim to investigate the relation between new firm entry as a response to knowledge-oriented opportunities and firm failure as a side effect of the exploration of uncertain knowledge

We use data for 428 German regions, from 2000, unless otherwise specified. The data are published and updated annually by the German Federal Statistical Office on the CD-ROM "Statistik Regional."

9.4.1. New Knowledge as Driver of Entrepreneurship

To estimate the impact of knowledge on entrepreneurship (arrow 2a in Figure 9-1), we regress the R&D intensity, measured as R&D employees relative to all employees (labor) on the entry rates, that is, start-ups in all industries relative to population. We take this intensity measure of business start-ups as a proxy variable for the regional level of entrepreneurship.

The first column of Table 9-1 shows the results. We find a positive correlation of R&D intensity with the regions' entry rates. We take this

Table 9-1. *Determinants of entry and exit rates (p-values in brackets;*
a parameter estimate is significant at α = 0.05 if p ≤ 0.05)

Dependent variable	Entry rates 2001	Exit rates 2001
Exit rates 2000	0.6729(0.000)	
Entry rates 2000		0.7761(0.000)
R&D intensity	0.8221(0.008)	−0.9045(0.004)
GDP growth rate	0.1445(0.000)	−0.0859(0.015)
Unemployment rate	−0.0128(0.000)	0.0079(0.000)
Social diversity	−0.1088(0.037)	0.3405(0.000)
Industrial diversity	−0.3271(0.000)	−0.1268(0.018)
Constant	−1.9142(0.000)	−1.2064(0.000)
R^2	0.7516	0.7307

as evidence for our argumentation in Section 9.3.2 that R&D activity
creates new economic knowledge that is not completely exploited by
incumbent firms, thus leaving opportunities for new firms.

A more general measure of opportunity is the GDP growth rate. Strong
GDP growth implies a generally increasing market size hence new business
opportunities. The estimated sign and significance level of GDP growth
corresponds to this argument.

There is a longstanding debate on whether unemployment is conducive
to start-ups or rather obstructive, and indeed, there is empirical evidence
for both (Evans and Jovanovic, 1989; Evans and Leighton, 1990; Yamawaki, 1990; Storey, 1991; Reynolds et al., 1994; Reynolds, Miller, and Maki,
1995). In our data, we find a negative relationship between unemployment
rate and start-up intensity. Given the regional context of our data, we
interpret unemployment rate as a proxy for economic activity level, where
low regional unemployment rate corresponds to a strong economic situation. Hence, regions with high unemployment rates have a low propensity to entrepreneurship because the general economic situation is weak.

Florida (2002) argues that social diversity in a society is a proxy for the
openness of this society with respect to new ideas. Such openness is important in an environment where new ideas are transformed into business
ideas and ultimately to new firm start-ups. We measure social diversity by
an entropy index of the regions of voting behavior on the occasion of the
1998 parliamentary vote. The measure takes into account not just all the
major political parties but also the smaller ones. Given the estimated sign
and significance level of this variable, unlike Florida (2002), we find that
social diversity obstructs entrepreneurship.

In the 1990s there was a debate (Ellison and Glaeser, 1997; Henderson, 1997) over what type of spatial industry concentration serves as the stronger "engine to growth": strong concentration of industries, leading to "Marshall-Arrow-Romer" type of externalities, or strong variety of industries, leading to "Jacobs" type of externalities. The empirical literature did not come to a unanimous conclusion, suggesting that both effects are important, depending on the stage of the industy's life cycle. We find a positive relationship between industrial concentration and the start-up intensity, suggesting that strong regional concentration of industries is conducive to entrepreneurship. The variable "exit rates" and the second column of Table 9-1 are discussed in Section 9.4.4.

9.4.2. Entrepreneurship and Economic Performance

To estimate the impact of entrepreneurship on economic performance (arrow 2b in Figure 9-1), different approaches have been used (see Audretsch, Keilbach, and Lehmann, 2006, for a summary). Here, we estimate a Cobb–Douglas production function for 428 German regions that includes labor and capital as principal regressors but is augmented by R&D intensity and entrepreneurship. R&D intensity and entrepreneurship are measured as described in Section 9.4.1. Table 9-2 shows the results of this regression.

The results for capital, labor, and R&D intensity are in the usual range (e.g., Mankiw, Romer, and Weil, 1992). The estimate for entrepreneurship is positive and significant, suggesting that higher level of entrepreneurship is correlated with higher levels of GDP. Although the underlying functional form of this estimation is a reduced one, together with the results of Section 9.3.2 we consider this result as evidence in favor of our hypothesis discussed in Section 9.3.1.

9.4.3. Entrepreneurship, Start-ups, and Failure

The discussion in Sections 9.4.1 and 9.4.2 emphasized that one function of entrepreneurship bear the risk of exploring new opportunities for products or technologies. Indeed, it is a stylized fact that high entry rates come with high exit rates and low entry rates with low exit rates (Caves, 1998). This pattern is also present in our dataset on German regions, where we find significant correlation coefficients of 0.99 for entry and exit rates of years 2000 and 2001.

There are at least three possible hypotheses why entry and exit rates are strongly correlated. Let us denote the first as the "survival hypothesis," the

Table 9-2. *Results of a regression of an augmented Cobb-Douglas production function for 428 German regions, including R&D intensity and Entrepreneurship (p-values in brackets)*

Dependent variable	GDP
Capital	0.1209(0.000)
Labor	0.7647(0.000)
R&D intensity	0.0288(0.000)
Entrepreneurship	0.2478(0.000)
Constant	0.0343(0.902)
R^2	0.9431

second as the "replacement hypothesis," and the third as the "market size hypothesis."

In early periods of a market, different firms enter, suggesting different varieties of the concerned good. With increasing market size, the emergence of a dominant design and the emergence of a large-scale production process, a shakeout process sets in that results in a concentration of the number of firms. The more firms entering the market, the more exits will be caused by this process, *ceteris paribus*.

The second hypothesis is that firms that enter the market will replace existing ones that have lower performance or inferior products. This process would imply immediate spatial correlation of entry and exit, that is, entry in t would imply exit in $t+1$ (see Audretsch 1995 for a discussion).

The market size hypothesis states that exiting firms leave potential markets for new entrants. This hypothesis implies that exit in t is correlated with entry in $t+1$.

The regressions in Table 9-1 show consistently a positive impact of entry in t on exit in $t+1$ and of exit in t on entry in $t+1$. We consider this as evidence in favor of hypotheses 2 and 3. The interesting result shown in Table 9-1 is that the estimates for entry and exit rates have the same significance level; however, the signs of most of the variables are inverted: Regions with a high R&D intensity have lower exit rates; regions with a strong GDP growth have lower exit rates, regions with higher unemployment rates also have higher exit rates; and regions with higher social diversity have higher exit rates.

Hence overall, dynamic regions with a high R&D intensity and low unemployment rates show strong net firm foundation rates, while weak regions show stronger net exit rates. However for all regions, firm entry and firm exit is strongly positively related.

9.5. Summary and Policy Implications

In this chapter, we argue that R&D generates new knowledge, which comes with varying levels of uncertainty. Those bits that correspond to more established knowledge are taken on by incumbent (or larger) firms that tend to innovate along their established product or technology portfolio. This implies that the less established bits (i.e., the more uncertain parts) of knowledge are unexploited by these firms. This leaves knowledge-based opportunities for entrepreneurs who are less tied to established production processes and who are willing to take on the risk of developing uncertain knowledge into new products.

By doing so, entrepreneurs introduce not only new products or technologies to the market, they also generate external effects not only through the generation of new technological knowledge, which corresponds to the mechanisms described in the endogenous growth theory, but also through the generation of knowledge on the viability or nonviability of new products or technologies. Hence, entrepreneurship plays a double role in the important process by (1) transforming otherwise untouched bits of knowledge into new products and (2) creating new knowledge. Then, a high level of entrepreneurship within either a region or industry will generate a positive impact on the level of economic performance.

We also argued that a higher level of uncertain new economic knowledge will, *ceteris paribus*, correspond to a higher number of agents who regard this knowledge as posing economic opportunities and who are tempted to start up a new venture.

Using data on 428 German counties, we were able to provide empirical evidence in favor of both arguments. We therefore conclude that entrepreneurship is conducive to economic performance. Apparently, this insight has increasingly diffused among policymakers. This is the reason why an increasing number of regions aim to foster entrepreneurship by subsidizing start-up activities or by offering an "entrepreneurship of the year" prize.

However, we have also provided evidence that the risk involved with entrepreneurship has a downside. High business start-up rates induce high failure rates. This holds for economically strong regions but also for economically weak regions. Hence a policy that creates entrepreneurship and drives start-ups will have to deal with the other aspect of entrepreneurship: the failure of firms. More specifically, it must be able to handle the economic consequences of firm failure and, because failure is a learning experience, somehow discourage the stigmatization of entrepreneurs who experience failure. Because entrepreneurial failure cannot be separated from any other entrepreneurial activity, a society that does not acknowledge failure as integral part of the process will never become an entrepreneurial one.

References

Acs, Z., D. Audretsch, P. Braunerhjelm, and B. Carlsson. 2004. *The Missing Link: The Knowledge Filter and Endogenous Growth*. Discussion Paper. Stockholm: Center for Business and Policy Studies.

Aghion, P., and P. Bolton. 1992. "An Incomplete Contracts Approach to Financial Contracting." *Review of Economic Studies*, 59, 473–494.

Arrow, K. 1962. "Economic Welfare and the Allocation of Resources for Invention. In *The Rate and Direction of Inventive Activity*. Princeton: Princeton University Press, pp. 609–626.

Audretsch, David B. 1995. *Innovation and Industry Evolution*. Cambridge: MIT Press.

Audretsch, David B., Max C. Keilbach, and Erik E. Lehmann. 2006. *Entrepreneurship and Economic Growth*. New York: Oxford University Press.

Baumol, William J. 1968. " Entrepreneurship in Economic Theory." *American Economic Review*, 58(2), Papers & Proceedings, 64–71.

Baumol, William J. 2002a. "Entrepreneurship, Innovation and Growth: The David-Goliath Symbiosis."*Journal of Entrepreneurial Finance and Business Ventures*, 7(2), 1–10.

Baumol, William J. 2002b. *Free Market Innovation Machine: Analyzing the Growth Miracle of Capitalism*. Princeton: Princeton University Press.

Buchanan, James M., and Viktor J. Vanberg. 1991. "The Market as a Creative Process." *Economics and Philosophy*, 7, 167–186.

Caves, Richard E. 1998. "Industrial Organization and New Findings on the Turnover and Mobility of Firms." *Journal of Economic Literature*, 36, 1947–1982.

Clark, John B. 1892. "Insurance and Business Profit." *Quarterly Journal of Economics*, 7(1), 40–54.

Ellison, G., and E. Glaeser. 1997. "Geographic Concentration in the U.S. Manufacturing Industries: A Dartboard Approach." *Journal of Political Economy*, 105, 889–927.

Evans, David, and Boyan Jovanovic. 1989. "Estimates of a Model of Entrepreneurial Choice under Liquidity Constraints." *Journal of Political Economy*, 97(4), 808–827.

Evans, David, and Linda S. Leighton. 1990. "Small Business Formation by Unemployed and Employed Workers." *Small Business Economics*, 2, 319–330.

Florida, Richard. 2002. *The Rise of the Creative Class*. New York: Basic Books.

Grossman, G., and E. Helpman. 1991. *Innovation and Growth in the Global Economy*. Cambridge: MIT Press.

Henderson, J. Vernon. 1997. "Externalities and Industrial Development." *Journal of Urban Economics*, 42, 449–470.

Keynes, John M. 1920. *The Economic Consequences of the Peace*. New York: Harcourt, Brace and Howe.

Kirzner, I. Mayer. 1973. *Competition and Entrepreneurship*. Chicago: University of Chicago Press.

Klepper, Steven. 1996. "Entry, Exit, Growth, and Innovation over the Product Life Cycle."*American Economic Review*, 86(3), 562–583.

Knight, Frank H. 1921. *Risk, Uncertainty and Profit.* Boston and New York: Houghton Mifflin.

Lazear, Edward. 2002. "Entrepreneurship." NBER Working Paper No. 9109.

Lucas, Robert E. 1988. "On the Mechanics of Economic Development." *Journal of Monetary Economics,* 22(1), 3–42.

Mankiw, G., David Romer, and David N. Weil. 1992. "A Contribution to the Empirics of Economics and Growth." *Quarterly Journal of Economics,* 107, 407–437.

Marshall, Alfred. 1920. *Principles of Economics,* 8th ed. London: Macmillan. Reprint 1994.

Reynolds, Paul, David Storey, and Paul Westhead. 1994. "Cross-National Comparisons of the Variation in New Firm Formation Rate." *Regional Studies,* 28, 443–456.

Reynolds, Paul, Brenda Miller, and Wilbur R. Maki. 1995. "Explaining Regional Variation in Business Births and Deaths: U.S. 1976–1988." *Small Business Economics,* 7, 389–407.

Romer, Paul M. 1986. "Increasing Returns and Long-Run Growth." *Journal of Political Economy,* 94(5), 1002–1037.

Romer, Paul M. 1990. "Endogenous Technical Change." *Journal of Political Economy,* 98, 71–102.

Sarasvathy, Saras D., Nick Dew, Rama Velamuri, and S. Venkataraman. 2002. *"Three Views of Entrepreneurial Opportunity."* In *International Handbook of Entrepreneurship,* Audretsch and Acs (eds.). Kluwer Academic Publishers.

Schumpeter, Joseph A. 1934 (1911). *The Theory of Economic Development.* Cambridge: Harvard University Press.

Schumpeter, Joseph A. 1950 (1942). *Capitalism, Socialism and Democracy.* New York: Harper and Row.

Storey, David J. 1991. "The Birth of New Firms – Does Unemployment Matter? A Review of Evidence." *Small Business Economics,* 3, 167–178.

Tedlow, Richard S. 2001. *Giants of Enterprise: Seven Business Innovators and the Empires They Built.* New York: Collins Business.

von Mangoldt, H. 1855. *Die Lehre vom Unternehmensgewinn.* Stuttgart: Verlag von Julius Maier.

Walras, Léon. 1874. *Eléments d'Economie Politique Pure ou Théorie de la Richesse Sociale.* Lausanne: Corbaz.

Yamawaki, Hideki. 1990. *"The Effects of Business Conditions on Net Entry: Evidence from Japan."* In *Entry and Market Contestability: An International Comparison.* Oxford: Basil Blackwell.

PART III

POLICY

10

Entreprenomics
Entrepreneurship, Economic Growth,
and Policy

Roy Thurik

10.1. Introduction

In his *Theory of Economic Development,* Schumpeter (1934) emphasizes the role of the entrepreneur as prime cause of economic development. He describes how the innovating entrepreneur challenges incumbent firms by introducing new inventions that make current technologies and products obsolete, thus driving them out of the market. This process of creative destruction is the main characteristic of what has been called the Schumpeter Mark I regime. Schumpeter developed his ideas during the first decades of the 20th century when small businesses were considered a vehicle for entrepreneurship and a source of employment and income, setting the stage as defined in Chapter 1.

However, the economies of scale and scope present in production, distribution, management, and R&D dictated increasing firm size from the 1930s onward (Chandler, 1990). Moreover, the growing level of economic development, together with high price elasticities stimulating price competition, favored large-scale production. The increasing presence and role of large enterprises in the economy during this period is well documented

The author would like to thank David Audretsch, Philipp Koellinger, Adam Lederer, and the participants of the Kauffman-Max Planck Conference on Entrepreneurship and Economic Growth (Ringberg Castle, Rottach Egern, May 8–9, 2006) for comments. This chapter is an extended version of the author's introduction at this conference called "Entrepreneurship and Economic Growth: A Wrap Up." It also draws on earlier or related work such as Audretsch et al. (2002a), Thurik and Wennekers (2004), Audretsch and Thurik (2004), Carree and Thurik (2006b), and Audretsch et al. (2007). Financial assistance from the Ewing Marion Kauffman Foundation is gratefully acknowledged. The views expressed are those of the author.

(Audretsch, Thurik, Verheul, and Wennekers, 2002a). The importance of small business seemed to fade. At the same time it was recognized that the small business sector needed protection for social and political reasons, but not on the grounds of economic efficiency (Audretsch and Thurik, 2000).

In the years following the Second World War large firms had not yet gained the powerful position of the 1960s and 1970s and small businesses were still the main suppliers of employment and hence of social and political stability (Thurik and Wennekers, 2004). Scholars such as Schumpeter (1942), Galbraith (1956), Bell (1960), and Chandler (1977, 1990) were convinced that the future was in the hands of large corporations and that small business would fade away as the victim of its own inefficiencies. In their classic work, Berle and Means (1932) investigated the then modern firm with its increasing size and role, hierarchy of management, and divide between management and control. The U.S. policy response to the rise of large corporations was aimed at a careful support of the small business sector for social and political reasons. The influence of the Great Depression emphasized this support. The passage of the Robinson-Patman Act (providing some measure of protection to small independent retailers and their independent suppliers from unfair competition from vertically integrated, multi-location chain stores) and the creation of the Small Business Administration (and a number of predecessor agencies) were aimed at protecting less efficient small businesses and maintaining their viability. These policy responses are typical for a Schumpeter Mark II regime. In *Capitalism, Socialism and Democracy*, Schumpeter (1942) focuses on innovative activities by large and established firms. He describes how large firms outperform their smaller counterparts in the innovation and appropriation process through a strong positive feedback loop from innovation to increased R&D activities. This process of creative accumulation is the main characteristic of the Schumpeter Mark II regime.

In the last twenty years of the twentieth century, the joint effect of globalization and the ICT revolutions drastically reduced the cost of shifting both capital and information out of the high-cost locations of Europe and North America into low-cost locations around the world. Economic activity in a high-cost location is no longer compatible with routinized tasks. Rather, globalization has shifted the comparative advantage of high-cost locations to knowledge-based activities that cannot be transferred around the globe without significant cost. Knowledge as an input into economic activity is inherently different from the more traditional inputs such as land, capital, and labor. It is characterized by high uncertainty and high asymmetries across people and is costly to transact. The response to a trend establishing knowledge as the main source of comparative advantage is the re-emergence of the *Entrepreneurial Economy*. In Audretsch and Thurik (2001, 2004) the two Schumpeterian regimes are used in the framework of two broad concepts of economic organization: the *Managed Economy* and the *Entrepreneurial Economy*. They introduce the concept of the "managed economy," which flourished for most of the last century. It was based on relative certainty in outputs, which consisted mainly of manufactured products and which were brought forward by the traditional inputs of labor, capital and land. They contrast it to the model of the "entrepreneurial economy," based on entirely different elements such as flexibility, turbulence, diversity, creativity and novelty, and new forms of linkages and clustering.

Entrepreneurship has emerged as an important element in the organization of economies. It has re-emerged from an era where mainstream thinking dictated a future where ever bigger organizational hierarchies would dominate. This emergence did not occur simultaneously in all developed countries. Differences in growth perspectives are often attributed to differences in the speed countries evolve from the managed to the entrepreneurial economy. The recognition that entrepreneurship helps to foster growth led to the political mandate to promote entrepreneurship. Hence, a clear and organized view is needed of what the determinants of entrepreneurship are. Entrepreneurship, its drivers, and its consequences can be best understood using the model of the "entrepreneurial economy," which explains the functioning of the modern economy. This functioning of the economy should provide the basis for an "Entrepreneurship Policy Framework" in which determinants of entrepreneurship and the ways of public intervention are the essential elements.

The study of the role of entrepreneurship in the modern economy I label "Entreprenomics." The field is rooted in economics but has a distinctly eclectic flavor (Thurik, Wennekers, and Uhlaner, 2002; Wennekers, Uhlaner, and Thurik, 2002; Audretsch and Thurik, 2004). It has the rapt attention of policymakers. Often, it attempts to introduce the variable "entrepreneurship" in subfields of economics such as labor economics, economics of growth and economic development, industrial organization, enterprise policy, applied micro economics, and business economics. Although the specific implementation of the variable varies, all attempt to measure the process by which new opportunities are discovered and implemented, what is termed entrepreneurship, as introduced in Chapter 1.

The purpose of the present contribution is to provide such an Entrepreneurship Policy Framework. It describes the managed economy and the emergence of the entrepreneurial economy in terms of data and conceptual material in Section 10.2. The models of the managed and the entrepreneurial economy are compared in Section 10.3, distinguishing among different groups of characteristics, including underlying forces, external environment characteristics, internal or firm characteristics, and policy characteristics. In Section 10.4 the focus is on the links between entrepreneurship and growth, while Section 10.5 tries to provide an account of why Europe reacted slower to the challenges of the entrepreneurial economy than the United States. The policy guidelines are in Section 10.6, where on the basis of an Entrepreneurship Policy Framework six channels of policy interventions to foster entrepreneurship and to bridge the gap between the managed economy to the entrepreneurial economy are proposed. These channels will be linked to the fourteen dimensions of the entrepreneurial economy described in Section 10.3. Section 10.7 contains some concluding remarks.

10.2. The Era of the Managed Economy and the Emergence of the Entrepreneurial One

The large enterprise was clearly the dominant form of organization until the 1980s. Not surprisingly, Robert Solow (1956) suspected capital and labor as the main sources of growth, which in his later empirical work appeared to be the case only to a limited degree and which led to the introduction of the "Solow residual." Capital and labor, however, were factors best utilized in large-scale production. Also, the increasing level of transaction costs (Coase, 1937) incurred in large-scale production demanded increasing firm size. Statistical evidence, gathered from both Europe and North America, points toward an increasing presence and role of large enterprises in the economy in this period (Caves, 1982; Brock and Evans, 1989; Teece, 1993). This was the era of mass production when economies of scale seemed to be the decisive factor in dictating efficiency. This was the world described by John Kenneth Galbraith (1956) in his theory of countervailing power, where the power of "big business" was balanced by that of "big labor" and "big government." Stability, continuity, and homogeneity were the cornerstones of the managed economy (Audretsch and Thurik, 2001).

Large firms dominated this economy while small firms and entrepreneurship were viewed as a luxury. They were viewed as something Western countries needed in order to ensure decentralized decision making, obtained at the unfortunate cost of efficiency. A generation of scholars has investigated this perceived trade-off between economic efficiency, on the one hand, and political and economic decentralization, on the other (Williamson, 1968). These scholars have produced a large number of studies focusing mainly on three questions: (1) What are the gains to size in general and large-scale production in particular? (2) What are the economic and welfare implications of an oligopolistic market structure? and (3) What are the public policy implications?

Many stylized facts were discovered about the role of small business in the postwar economies of North America and Western Europe. Four of these stylized facts will be mentioned here: *Small businesses are generally less efficient than their larger counterparts.* Studies from the United States in the 1960s and 1970s revealed that small businesses produced at lower levels of efficiency than larger firms (Pratten, 1971; Weiss, 1976). *Small businesses are characterized by lower levels of employee compensation.* Empirical evidence from both North America and Europe found a systematic and positive relationship between employee compensation and firm size (Brown and Medoff, 1989; Brown, Hamilton, and Medoff, 1990). *Small businesses are only marginally involved in innovative activity.* Based on R&D measures, small businesses accounted for only a small amount of innovative activity (Acs and Audretsch, 1990; Chandler, 1990; Scherer, 1991; Audretsch, 1995). *The relative importance of small businesses is declining over time in both North America and Europe* (Scherer, 1991).

Given the careful documentation that large-scale production was driving out entrepreneurship, it came as a surprise when scholars first began to document that the alleged inevitable demise of small business began to reverse itself in the 1970s. Loveman and Sengenberger (1991) and Acs and Audretsch (1993) carried out analyses examining the re-emergence of small business and entrepreneurship in North America and Europe, and two major findings emerged. First, the relative importance of small business varies largely across countries, and, second, in most European countries and North America the importance of small business increased since the mid-1970s.

Acs and Audretsch (1993) were among the first to provide systematic data showing the increasing importance of small businesses. They show that the employment share in manufacturing of small firms in the Netherlands increased from 68 percent in 1978 to 72 percent in 1986. In the United Kingdom this share increased from 30 percent in 1979 to 40 percent in 1986; in Western Germany from 55 percent in 1970 to 58 percent by 1987; in Portugal from 68 percent in 1982 to 72 percent in 1986; in the north of Italy from 44 percent in 1981 to 55 percent in 1987, and in the south of Italy from 61 percent in 1981 to 68 percent in 1987. A study by

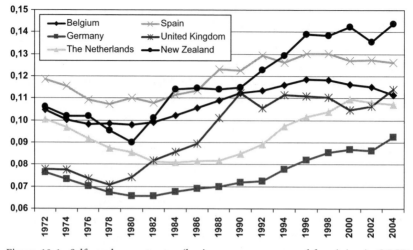

Figure 10-1. Self-employment rates (business owners per workforce) in six OECD countries. Source: Compendia 2004.2; see also van Stel (2005).

EIM (2002) documents how the relative importance of small firms in nineteen European countries, measured in terms of employment shares, has continued to increase between 1988 and 2001. See Figure 10-1 for the development of the self-employment rates (business owners per workers) in a selection of OECD countries taken from van Stel (2005). A U-shape can be observed for these countries when the reversal happened in the early 1980s. This trough marks the beginning of what Audretsch and Thurik (2001) call the entrepreneurial economy. Recently, the upward trend of self-employment leveled off in such countries as the United Kingdom, Belgium, Spain, and Portugal (van Stel, 2005). In the United Kingdom this may be due to policy measures favoring incumbent businesses over start-ups (Thurik, 2003). In Belgium this may be due to the high level of economic development and to the shake-out of industries that are in a more advanced stage than in other modern OECD countries. In Spain it may be explained by the relatively high start-up costs (Verheul, van Stel, Thurik, and Urbano, 2006). In Portugal consolidation and "shake-out" occurred in some markets leading to a reduction in the business ownership rate as the economy became more integrated into the EU market (Baptista and Thurik, 2006).

As the empirical evidence documenting the re-emergence of small businesses increased, scholars began to look for explanations and to develop theoretical underpinnings. Acs and Audretsch (1993) and Carlsson (1992) provide evidence of manufacturing industries in many countries. Carlsson advances two explanations for the shift toward smallness. The first deals with fundamental changes in the world economy from the 1970s onward that relate to the intensification of global competition, the increase in the degree of uncertainty and the growth in market fragmentation. The second explanation deals with the introduction of flexible automation that effected a shift from large to smaller firms. The pervasiveness of changes in the world economy, and in the direction of technological progress, resulted in a structural shift affecting the economies of all industrialized countries. Piore and Sabel (1984) argue that the instability of markets in the 1970s resulted in the demise of mass production and promoted flexible specialization. This fundamental change in the path of technological development led to the occurrence of vast diseconomies of scale. In other words, the level of transaction costs fell dramatically.

Brock and Evans (1989) show that this trend away from large firms has been economy-wide at least for the United States, and they provide four additional reasons why it has occurred: the increase of labor supply, particularly in the higher education levels, leading to lower real wages; changes in consumer tastes; relaxation of entry and labor market regulations; and the fact that the economic world went through a period of creative destruction. Loveman and Sengenberger (1991) point at two additional trends of industrial restructuring: that of horizontal and vertical disintegration (the breaking up of large plants and businesses) and that of the formation of new business communities. These intermediate forms of market coordination thrive owing to declining costs of transaction and exploit the virtues of learning and selection. Furthermore, they emphasize the role of public and private policies promoting the small business sector. Audretsch and Thurik (2000) suggest that the shift toward the knowledge-based economy is the driving force behind the shift from large to smaller businesses. Also, this economy works best when the inherent uncertainties and asymmetries of knowledge creation are absorbed by groups of small firms rather than by one dominant firm (Audretsch and Thurik, 2001, 2004). Carree and Thurik (2003) try to explain the transition from increasing average firm size to decreasing firm size in a framework of ten key mechanisms: scale, scope, experience, organization, transportation, market size, adjustment, effectiveness, control, and culture. The former four obstruct declining firm size, while the latter six promote it. Overseeing all these sources, one may conclude that the re-emergence of small businesses is largely a consequence of new technological opportunities enabled by the information-technology revolution.

While entrepreneurs undertake a definitive action, that is, they start a new business, this action cannot be viewed in a vacuum. Entrepreneurship is shaped by a portfolio of forces and factors, including legal, institutional, and social factors (Audretsch et al., 2002a). This chapter devotes particular attention to the policy component in this portfolio. See Audretsch, Grilo, and Thurik (2007) for some remarks on the economic rationale of public intervention.

10.3. Contrasting the Entrepreneurial and Managed Models

The era of the managed economy was driven out with the emergence of the entrepreneurial economy. This suggests two contrasting models with important but different roles of entrepreneurship. While both the managed economy and the entrepreneurial economy models strive to explain how economic growth occurs, the foundations of said growth vary substantially. In the managed economy, economic growth happens through stability, specialization, homogeneity, scale, certainty, and predictably, while flexibility, turbulence, diversity, novelty, innovation, linkages, and clustering drive the entrepreneurial economy (Audretsch and Thurik, 2004). The models distinguish among different groups of characteristics, including underlying forces, external environment characteristics, internal or firm characteristics, and policy characteristics. These forces are contrasted in Table 10-1.

The term "model" may suggest that different economic laws are valid in the managed and the entrepreneurial economy. But the laws have not changed; what changed was the framework: the ubiquitous application of information technologies, the political context that marked the end of the cold war, and the lowering of trade barriers. Table 10-1 also provides a column called "channels of government intervention." These six channels, described below, refer to six distinct ways in which policies can facilitate or discourage entrepreneurship. The column indicates which channel influences which dimension of the entrepreneurial economy.

The first group of characteristics contrasts the forces underlying the models of the managed and entrepreneurial economy: localization versus globalization, change versus continuity, and jobs with high wages versus jobs or high wages. The second group of characteristics contrasts the external environment characteristics of the models of the managed and the entrepreneurial economy. Turbulence, diversity, and heterogeneity are central to the model of the entrepreneurial economy. By contrast, stability, specialization and homogeneity are the cornerstones in the model of the managed economy. The third group of characteristics contrasts firm behavior of the models of the managed and the entrepreneurial economy:

Table 10-1. *Fourteen dimensions of the difference between the model of the entrepreneurial and the managed economy and the channels of government intervention*

Category	Entrepreneurial economy	Managed economy	Channel of government intervention
Underlying forces			
	Localization	Globalization	G2
	Change	Continuity	G1
	Jobs with high wages	Jobs or high wages	G1, G5, G6
External environment			
	Turbulence	Stability	G5, G6
	Diversity	Specialization	G5, G6
	Heterogeneity	Homogeneity	G3, G4
How firms function			
	Motivation	Control	G4
	Market exchange	Firm transaction	G6
	Competition with cooperation	Competition or cooperation	G6
	Flexibility	Scale	G5, G6
Government policy			
	Enabling	Constraining	G4, G6
	Input targeting	Output targeting	G3, G5
	Local locus	National locus	G2
	Entrepreneurs	Incumbents	G5

Source: Audretsch and Thurik (2004).

control versus motivation, firm transaction versus market exchange, competition and cooperation as substitutes versus complements, and scale versus flexibility. The final group of contrasting dimensions of the models of the managed and the entrepreneurial economy refers to government policy, including whether the goals of the policy are enabling versus constraining, whether the target of policy works with inputs versus outputs, whether the locus of policy is local versus national, and whether the financing policy supports entrepreneurs versus incumbents.

The fourteen dimensions describing the difference between the models of the managed and entrepreneurial economy are discussed in detail in Audretsch and Thurik (2004). Building on Audretsch and Thurik (2001), these contrasting models provide a lens through which economic events can be interpreted and policy formulated. Using the wrong lens leads to the wrong policy choice. For example, under the model of the managed economy firm failure is viewed negatively, representing a drain on society's resources. In the model of the managed economy resources are not invested in high-risk ventures. In the model of the entrepreneurial economy firm failure is viewed differently. It is seen as an experiment, an attempt to go in a new direction in an inherently risky environment (Wennekers and Thurik, 1999). An externality of failure is learning. In the model of the entrepreneurial economy the process of searching for new ideas is accompanied by failure. Similarly, the virtues of long-term relationships, stability, and continuity under the model of the managed economy give way to flexibility, change, and turbulence in the model of the entrepreneurial economy. What is a liability in the model of the managed economy is, in some cases, a virtue in the entrepreneurial economy model.

10.4. Consequences of Entrepreneurship

While the switch from a managed economy regime to one of an entrepreneurial economy has been the subject of a multitude of investigations, the consequences of this regime change are yet another area of research. Acs (1992) began the discussion in an intuitive fashion. He claimed that small firms play an important role in the economy by serving as agents of change with their entrepreneurial action, which generates innovative activity, stimulates industry evolution, and creates new jobs. Acs and Audretsch (1990) were the first to evaluate the new role of smallness in the process of innovative activities. Baumol (1993) looked at the role of entrepreneurial activities and its possible effects. After these initial forays a huge amount of research developed showing the often positive relationship between smallness, entrepreneurship, or a related indicator and any dimension of economic performance (Carree and Thurik, 2003, 2006a).

Since the last decade of the twentieth century, small and, in particular, new businesses are seen more than ever as vehicles for entrepreneurship, contributing not just to employment and social and political stability but also to innovative and competitive power (Wennekers and Thurik, 1999). The focus shifted from small businesses as a social good that should be maintained at an economic cost to small businesses as a vehicle for entrepreneurship and economic growth. Baumol was one of the first to justify the re-introduction of the entrepreneur into mainstream economics thinking after its virtual removal in the first few decades after the Second World War (Baumol, 1968). Indeed, recent econometric evidence suggests that entrepreneurship is a vital determinant of economic growth (Carree and Thurik, 1999; Audretsch and Fritsch, 2002; Audretsch, Carree, van Stel, and Thurik, 2002b; Carree, van Stel, Thurik, and Wennekers, 2002, 2007; Audretsch and Keilbach, 2004; van Stel, Carree, and Thurik, 2005; Thurik, Carree, van Stel, and Audretsch 2008). According to Audretsch et al. (2002b), a lack of entrepreneurship will lead to reduced economic growth. The positive link between entrepreneurship and economic growth has now been verified across a wide spectrum of units of observation, spanning the establishment, the enterprise, the industry, the region, and the country (Carree and Thurik, 2003).

Below three options are provided to better understand this positive link between entrepreneurship and economic growth. All three consist of three main arguments. The first is the shift from the managed to the entrepreneurial economy view (Audretsch and Thurik, 2001), with its empirical support. The second is the historical view of entrepreneurial roles (Carree and Thurik, 2003), and the third is the entrepreneurial capital view (Audretsch and Keilbach, 2004; Audretsch and Thurik, 2004; Audretsch, Keilbach and Lehman, 2006).

The shift from the managed to the entrepreneurial economy has many consequences. The most important is the changing and growing role of entrepreneurship and small firms as drivers of growth. The role of smallness in the process of innovative activities is investigated extensively by Acs and Audretsch (1990) and Audretsch (1995). A discussion of the relation between the role of small firms and industry dynamics can be found in Audretsch (1995). Foelster (2000) and Acs and Armington (2004) are among many who show the job generation effect of entrepreneurship. An alternative and wide view of the impact of the regime change is that of the institutional change that makes the difference between high and low performance. For example, Saxenian (1990, 1994) attributes the superior performance of Silicon Valley to a high capacity for promoting entrepreneurship.

The role of innovations, of the job generation process, and of institutional environments are examples of why the entrepreneurial economy works differently from the managed economy. Using Global Entrepreneurship Monitor (GEM) data and a model controlling for several alternative drivers of growth, van Stel, Carree, and Thurik (2005) find that entrepreneurial activity affects economic growth, but that this effect depends on the level of per capita income in that entrepreneurship has a negative impact on GDP growth for developing countries and a positive one for developed countries. In other words: entrepreneurship has a different role in the managed versus the entrepreneurial economy. Using OECD data of twenty-three developed countries, Carree, van Stel, Thurik, and

Wennekers (2002) show that there is some evidence of a U-shaped relation between economic development and the rate of entrepreneurship (business owners per workers). This evidence is weaker in their 2007 update (Carree, van Stel, Thurik, and Wennekers, 2007). They suggest that a "Schumpetarian Regime Switch" occurred. Piore and Sabel (1984) call it an "Industrial Divide," while Jensen (1993) refers to the "Third Industrial Revolution." After economic regime change, whatever it is called, there is a positive relation between entrepreneurship and economic development.

Carree and Thurik (2003) focus on three entrepreneurial roles, emphasized by Schumpeter, Kirzner, and Knight, respectively. The first is the role of innovator. Schumpeter was the economist who has most prominently drawn attention to the innovating entrepreneur who carries out "new combinations we call enterprise; the individuals whose function it is to carry them out we call entrepreneurs" (Schumpeter 1934, p. 74). The second is the role of perceiving profit opportunities, labeled Kirznerian (or neo-Austrian) entrepreneurship (Kirzner, 1997). The third role is that of assuming the risk associated with uncertainty, labeled Knightian entrepreneurship or "neo-classical entrepreneurship" (Shane, 2000). In the neo-classical framework, entrepreneurship is explained by fundamental attributes of people (such as "taste" for uncertainty). When an individual introduces a new product or starts a new firm, this can be interpreted as an entrepreneurial act in terms of at least one of the three types of entrepreneurship. The individual is an innovator, has found a previously undiscovered profit opportunity and takes the risk that the product or venture may turn out to be a failure. A lack of entrepreneurial activity or alertness is therefore directly connected to low rates of innovation, unused profit opportunities, and risk-averse attitudes. These are important barriers preventing healthy economic development.

Audretsch and Thurik (2004) have a different approach and distinguish three ways in which entrepreneurial capital affects growth (see also Audretsch, Keilbach, and Lehman, 2006). The first way is by creating knowledge spillovers. Romer (1986), Lucas (1988, 1993), and Grossman and Helpman (1991) established that knowledge spillovers help to drive economic growth. Insight into the process of knowledge spillovers is important, especially since a policy implication commonly drawn from new economic growth theory is that, due to the increasing role of knowledge and the resulting increasing returns, knowledge generators, such as R&D, should be publicly supported. The literature identifying the creation of knowledge spillover mechanisms (the way knowledge is transmitted across firms and individuals) is underdeveloped. However, some of the transmission mechanisms of entrepreneurship have been identified. Cohen and Levinthal (1989) suggest that firms develop the capacity to adapt new technology and ideas developed in other firms and are therefore able to appropriate some of the returns accruing to investments in new knowledge made externally, that is, outside their own organizations. Audretsch (1995) proposes a shift in the unit of observation away from exogenously assumed firms toward individuals, such as scientists, engineers, or other knowledge workers. When the focus is shifted from the firm to the individual, the appropriability issue remains, but the question shifts, becoming: How can economic agents with a given endowment of new knowledge best appropriate the returns from that knowledge? In this spillover process, where a knowledge worker may exit the firm or university in order to create a new company, the knowledge production function is reversed. Knowledge is exogenous and embodied in a worker; the firm is created endogenously through the worker's effort to appropriate the value of his or her knowledge by way of innovative activity. Hence, entrepreneurship serves as a mechanism by which knowledge spills over to a new firm in which it is commercialized.

The second way in which entrepreneurship capital generates economic growth is through augmenting the number of enterprises and increasing competition. Jacobs (1969) and Porter (1990) argue that competition is more conducive to knowledge externalities than local monopolies. By local competition Jacobs (1969) is referring not to competition within product markets as traditionally envisioned by the industrial organization literature, but rather to the competition for new ideas embodied in economic agents. Not only does an increase in the number of firms enhance the competition for new ideas, but greater competition across firms also facilitates the entry of new firms specializing in a particular new product niche. This is because the necessary complementary inputs are more likely available from small specialist niche firms than from large, vertically integrated producers. Glaeser, Kallal, Scheinkman, and Shleifer (1992) as well as Feldman and Audretsch (1999) found empirical evidence supporting the hypothesis that an increase in competition within a city, as measured by the number of enterprises, is accompanied by higher growth performance of that city. Van Stel and Nieuwenhuijsen (2004) found that this competition effect may prevail in particular for manufacturing industries.

A third way in which entrepreneurship capital generates economic output is by providing diversity among firms (Cohen and Klepper, 1992). Not only does entrepreneurship capital generate a greater number of firms, it also increases the variety of firms in a geographic space. There has been a series of theoretical arguments suggesting that the degree of diversity, as opposed to homogeneity, will influence the growth potential of a geographic environment. The basis for linking diversity to economic performance is provided by Jacobs (1969), who argues that the most important sources of knowledge spillovers are external to the industry in which the firm operates and that cities are a source of considerable innovation because there the diversity of knowledge sources is greatest (Jaffe, Trajtenberg, and Henderson, 1993; Audretsch and Feldman, 1996). According to Jacobs the exchange of complementary knowledge across diverse firms and economic agents yields an important return on new economic knowledge. In her view, the geographic environment is essential for promoting knowledge externalities that lead to innovative activity and subsequent economic growth. In this environment, entrepreneurship capital can contribute to growth by injecting diversity and serving as a conduit for knowledge spillovers, leading to increased competition. The entrepreneurial economy is characterized by a high reliance on this third role of entrepreneurship capital because it serves as the basis for the first two roles.

10.5. The Response of Europe

Thus, while entrepreneurship has always mattered to policymakers, the way in which it has mattered has drastically changed. Audretsch and Thurik observe that "entrepreneurship has emerged as the engine of economic and social development throughout the world" (2004, p. 144). Confronted with increasing concerns over unemployment, job creation, economic growth and international competitiveness in global markets, policymakers have responded to this new evidence with a new mandate promoting new business creation, that is, entrepreneurship (Reynolds, Hay, Bygrave, Camp, and Autio, 2000). Initially, European policymakers were relatively slow to recognize these links but since the mid-1990s have rapidly built momentum in crafting appropriate approaches (EIM/ENSR, 1993–1997; Audretsch et al., 2002a). Yet without a clear and organized view of where and how entrepreneurship manifests itself, policymakers do not know how to promote it. This explains the variation in their responses (European Commission, 2003; Audretsch et al., 2002a). The so-called Green Paper on Entrepreneurship of the European Commission (European Commission, 2003) was the first EU document extolling the virtues of entrepreneurship as the most important driver in the economy and paving the way for Union-wide stimulation programs. Currently, it is deeply embedded in European policy that the creativity and independence of entrepreneurs contribute to higher levels of economic activity. Indeed, "the challenge for the European Union is to identify the key factors for building a climate in which entrepreneurial initiative and business activities can thrive. Policy measures should seek to boost the Union's levels of entrepreneurship, adopting the most appropriate approach for producing more entrepreneurs and for getting more firms to grow" (European Commission, 2003, p. 9).

It is generally believed that the United States has been much quicker to absorb the merits of entrepreneurship than Europe, based on the different growth rates of the United States when compared with European nations over the last twenty years. Indeed, the European countries have been relatively slow to follow suit. Clearly, the European response varied across countries. Nevertheless, by and large five distinct stages can be discerned in the European stance toward the entrepreneurial economy (Audretsch et al., 2002a, p. 4–6).

The first stage was denial. During the 1980s and early 1990s, European policymakers looked to Silicon Valley with disbelief. Europe was used to facing a competitive threat from the large well-known multinational American corporations, not from nameless and unrecognizable start-up firms in exotic industries such as software and biotechnology. Twenty years ago the emerging firms such as Apple Computer and Intel were interesting but were irrelevant competitors in the automobile, textile, machinery, and chemical industries, then the obvious engines of European competitiveness.

The second stage, during the mid-1990s, was recognition. Europe recognized that the entrepreneurial economy in Silicon Valley delivered a sustainable long-run performance. But it held to its traditional products while embracing the theory of comparative advantage and channeling resources into traditional moderate technology industries. During this phase Europe's most important economy, Germany, provided the automobiles, textiles, and machine tools. The entrepreneurial economy of Silicon Valley, Route 128, and the Research Triangle produced the software and microprocessors. Each continent specialized in its comparative advantage and traded with each other.

The third stage, during the second half of the 1990s, was envy. As Europe's growth stagnated and unemployment soared, the capacity of the American entrepreneurial economy to generate both jobs and higher wages became the object of envy. The United States and Europe adhered to different doctrines: as the entrepreneurial economy diffused across the United States, European policymakers, particularly in large countries such as Germany and France, despaired that European traditions and values were simply inconsistent and incompatible with the entrepreneurial economy. They should have concluded that the concept of comparative advantage had yielded to the different, but better, concept of dynamic competitive advantage.

The fourth stage, during the last years of the twentieth century, was consensus. European policymakers reached a consensus that – in the terminology of Audretsch and Thurik (2001) – the new entrepreneurial economy was superior to the old managed economy and that a commitment had to be forged to creating a new entrepreneurial economy. A broad set of policies was instituted to create a new entrepreneurial economy. European policymakers looked across the Atlantic and realized that if places such as North Carolina, Austin, and Salt Lake City could implement targeted policies to create the entrepreneurial economy, European cities and regions could as well. After all, Europe had a number of advantages and traditions, such as a highly educated and skilled labor force, world-class research institutions, and a variety of cultures and hence approaches to new products and organizations. These phenomena would provide a perfect framework for absorbing the high levels of uncertainty inherent to the entrepreneurial economy (Audretsch and Thurik, 2001).

The fifth stage is attainment. There are signs that an entrepreneurial economy is finally emerging in Europe. Consider the Green Paper on Entrepreneurship of the European Commission (European Commission, 2003), which aims to stimulate debate among policymakers, businesses, representative organizations, journalists, and scientific experts on how to shape entrepreneurship policy. It analyzes a range of policy options and asks, within the proposed context for entrepreneurship policy, a number of questions suggesting different options on how to progress (see Audretsch et al., 2002a, for further information on the five stages and some country studies on the determinants of entrepreneurship; see Grilo and Thurik, 2005a, for comparative studies of entrepreneurial engagement levels in Europe and Grilo and Thurik (2005b, 2006) for the state of latent and actual entrepreneurship in Europe, respectively).

10.6. An Entrepreneurship Policy Framework Including Six Channels of Intervention

The scientific recognition that entrepreneurship helps to foster growth led to the political mandate to promote entrepreneurship. Policymakers, however, need a clear and organized view of the determinants of entrepreneurship. Entrepreneurship, its drivers, and its consequences can be best understood using the model of the entrepreneurial economy which is concerned with the functioning of the modern economy. The determinants of entrepreneurship and the ways of public intervention are the essential elements of the Entrepreneurship Policy Framework.

One of the reasons that policymakers and scholars have traditionally had little guidance in understanding why entrepreneurship varies temporally and geographically is that it is an interdisciplinary subject. Because it encompasses individuals, groups, enterprises, cultures, geographic locations, industries, countries, and particular episodes of time, it is exceptionally difficult to capture adequately. Researchers in a broad range of fields, including management, finance, psychology, sociology, economics, political science, and geography can all stake a claim as entrepreneurial experts. However, while any particular discipline may be well suited to analyze some unit of observations, none is equipped to analyze them all. These multidimensional aspects of entrepreneurship include both stock and flow variables (the number of business owners and the change of the number of entrants or exits) and cover many qualitative aspects (mom and pop entry, high growth ventures, cutting-edge technological firms, etc.). Moreover, there is a discrimination between occupational and behavioral entrepreneurship (Wennekers, 2006) because entrepreneurial activity (defined for instance as behavior concentrating on opportunities) may occur not only in businesses – both small and large – but also outside the business world (Stevenson and Gumpert, 1991; Low, 2001; Davidsson, 2004).

Below an Entrepreneurship Policy Framework of the determinants of entrepreneurship will be presented that integrates the different strands from the relevant fields of enquiry. Thus the framework is inspired by the earlier works of Verheul, Wennekers, Audretsch, and Thurik (2002), as well as Wennekers et al. (2002) but leans most heavily on Audretsch et al. (2007). It explains the level of entrepreneurship by making a distinction between the supply side of entrepreneurship (the labor market perspective where the capabilities are the outcome) and the demand side of entrepreneurship (product market perspective where the carrying capacity of the market in terms of business opportunities is the outcome) while integrating those factors shaping the demand for entrepreneurship, on the one hand, with those influencing the supply of entrepreneurs, on the other. While both the demand and supply sides are influenced by many factors, what results is a level of entrepreneurship that is determined by these two sides. The second goal of the Entrepreneurship Policy Framework is to create insight into the role of government policy by identifying six channels of intervention and policy instruments. See Figure 10-2.

Three levels of analysis are distinguished when explaining entrepreneurship: the micro, industry, and macro level covering, respectively, the individual entrepreneur or business, sectors or regions of industry, and the national economy. Studies at the micro level focus on the decision processes of individuals and their motives for becoming self-employed (Parker, 2004; Grilo and Irigoyen, 2006). They are concerned with personal factors: psychological traits, formal education and other skills, financial assets, family background, and previous work experience. Studies at the industry (regional) level of entrepreneurship focus on the market-specific determinants of entrepreneurship, such as profit opportunities and opportunities for entry and exit (Carree and Thurik, 1999). The macro perspective focuses on a range of environmental factors, such as technological, economic, and cultural variables as well as government regulation (Wennekers et al., 2002).

Technology developments and shifts in demand given resource availability thus generate new business opportunities. These can be exploited either by existing firms or through the creation of new ventures by new entrepreneurs entering the market. When this exploitation of opportunities takes place in large incumbent firms it is commonly referred to as "corporate entrepreneurship" or "intrapreneurship." Although intrinsically part of the entrepreneurial economy this form of entrepreneurial behavior is not discussed here further. The extent to which incumbents rather than new firms fill the market gap created by technological or preference evolution depends on a variety of elements, some of which can be influenced by governmental intervention. Competition policy, protection of intellectual property rights, product, and labor market regulatory environment are examples of interventions influencing this partition of the exploitation of opportunities between incumbent firms and potential new entrants. In Figure 10-2, the box "Business Opportunities" and its dotted line schematically represent this.

Potential entrepreneurs must recognize business opportunities, possess the ability and resources to pursue them and be willing to do so rather than keep present employment positions or take up outside options such as alternative employment or unemployment. The box labeled "Capabilities" in Figure 10-2 represents the individual characteristics of potential entrepreneurs, their abilities, their access to resources necessary to start a business, and their intrinsic preferences between leisure and income, as well as their attitudes toward risk.

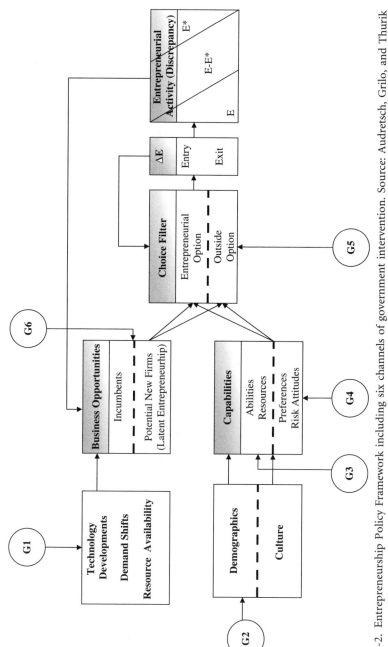

Figure 10-2. Entrepreneurship Policy Framework including six channels of government intervention. Source: Audretsch, Grilo, and Thurik (2007).

The individual decision process that potential entrepreneurs experience when confronted with the choice between the entrepreneurial venture based on the opportunities (that best matches their capabilities) and the best "outside" option is central in the Entrepreneurship Policy Framework. This process is covered by the box labeled "Choice Filter." The risk reward profile of each available option will depend on the entrepreneur's abilities and resource access, while the final arbitrage between the entrepreneurial option and the outside option will depend on individual preferences and, in particular, on risk attitudes. This is represented by the arrows linking "Capabilities" to "Choice Filter." Figure 10-2 shows two arrows from "Business Opportunities" to "Choice Filter" because the spectrum of available opportunities influences not only the risk reward profile of the "best to the individual" entrepreneurial venture but also the profile of the outside option. This second link takes into consideration the effect that opportunities taken up either by incumbent firms or by other potential entrepreneurs may have on alternative employment possibilities (the so-called outside options).

The "Business Opportunities" box represents the demand conditions for entrepreneurship, while the "Capabilities" box illustrates the supply conditions of entrepreneurship. The "Capabilities" box is fed with factors that are not individually specific but rather aggregate characteristics of the society to which the individual belongs. These factors have a quantitative demographic dimension as well as a qualitative cultural one. Nevertheless, they are also important in shaping the supply conditions of entrepreneurship. These demand and supply conditions should not be confused with the stricter demand and supply sides in regular economic modeling. At this point in the setup entrepreneurs of course are not commodities that can be sold or bought in a market. Instead, they are people who act as potential suppliers in particular product markets. That is why the occupational choice filter is introduced.

Entry and exit rates of entrepreneurship at the aggregate level follow directly from the occupational choices made at the individual level: There is an arrow from the "Choice Filter" box to the box "ΔE" (entry and exit). People have various employment alternatives to evaluate. Employed people can exchange their wage jobs (or unemployment) for self-employment; they can remain in the category of employment they are currently in, or they can exit from self-employment. These occupational decisions determine the actual level of entrepreneurship, E, in the "Entrepreneurial Activity (Discrepancy)" box. It is assumed that there is a feedback effect where entry and exit impact the occupational choice made in the "Choice Filter."

This "demonstration effect" represents the influence that entry and exit exert on the (perceived) attractiveness of self-employment for individuals. In other words: if many people enter self-employment other people may be persuaded to also make that choice, independent of the regular evaluation of the entrepreneurial option versus the outside option on the basis of capabilities and business opportunities for new firms.

The actual rate of entrepreneurship may deviate from the "equilibrium" rate of entrepreneurship, E^*, in the "Entrepreneurial Activity (Discrepancy)" box. Carree et al. (2002, 2007) present evidence of a long-term relationship between the stage of economic development and the "equilibrium" level of business ownership and suggest that countries where the business ownership rate does not equal the equilibrium rate suffer from a lower rate of macro-economic growth. See also Audretsch, Carree, van Stel, and Thurik (2002b), who introduce the term "growth penalty." In this respect the equilibrium level should be interpreted as a "normative" or "average" level and not as derived in the formal economics context. The 'discrepancy' between the actual number of entrepreneurs and the long-term equilibrium rate ($E-E^*$ in the box "Entrepreneurial Activity (Discrepancy)") may be the result of cultural forces and institutional settings. Examples are the regulation of entry, incentive structures, and the functioning of the capital market (Davis and Henrekson, 1999; Henrekson and Johansson, 1999; Carree et al., 2002, 2007). The "discrepancy" can be removed through either market forces or government intervention. The capacity of the market to remove the "discrepancy" works through the valuation of the number and type of business opportunities. Therefore, there is a feedback loop from the "Entrepreneurial Activity (Discrepancy)" box to the "Business Opportunities" box to reflect the fact that a surplus or lack of business opportunities may be the consequence of the entry and exit of entrepreneurs in earlier periods. A high level of unemployment can push people into self-employment due to the relatively low opportunity costs of entrepreneurship (Evans and Leighton, 1989; Storey, 1991; Audretsch and Thurik, 2000). Moreover, a number of business owners in excess of the "equilibrium" rate will lower profitability due to higher competition, resulting in higher exit or failure rates and lower entry.

The dynamics set in motion by market forces as described above will bridge the gap between actual and long-term "equilibrium" entrepreneurship. Moreover, one can also take a more normative stance and discuss the concept of E^* from the perspective of the policy-making government: E^* can be viewed as the (government-)perceived "optimal" or target entrepreneurship. Its level depends on the social choice function of the government, on its perception of existence of market failures and distortions, and on its beliefs concerning the leeway to correct these market failures. These elements will determine the extent to which the government is willing to intervene in the economy and the channels through which it wants to intervene. See Audretsch et al. (2007) for a discussion of these elements. In short, depending on the nature of the (assumed) discrepancy, the government can try to intervene through policies fostering or restricting entrepreneurship. Below six channels of policy intervention, G1 through G6, are distinguished (Audretsch et al., 2007).

"Channel 1" public intervention (as represented by arrow G1 in Figure 10-2) deals with the demand side of entrepreneurship and is meant to affect the type, number, and accessibility of entrepreneurial opportunities. A distinction is made between demand side policies creating room for entrepreneurship (policies stimulating technological developments and income policy) and policies affecting the accessibility of markets (competition policy and establishment legislation). The latter type of intervention enables entrepreneurs to make use of the available room and is dealt with under "Channel 6." Technological advancements create opportunities for entrepreneurial ventures through new ideas or new application processes. These advancements can be stimulated by the government through (subsidizing) expenditures on R&D. Income policy can create opportunities for entrepreneurship because, for instance, a higher wealth or income disparity level may stimulate the demand for tailor-made products and services, thereby stimulating demand for entrepreneurship (Wennekers et al., 2002). "Channel 1" public intervention aims in particular at the "change" and "jobs with high wages" dimensions of the entrepreneurial economy model as described in Table 10-1.

"Channel 2" public intervention (as represented by arrow G2) deals with the supply side of entrepreneurship and is meant to impact the number of potential and future entrepreneurs at the aggregate (population). G2 intervention policies range from immigration policy to regional development policy (dealing with sub-urbanization processes), influencing the composition and the dispersion of the population, respectively. Moreover, the fiscal treatment of families with children, including family allowances or child benefits, may influence the age structure of the population and the number of potential entrepreneurs in the long run. "Channel 2" public intervention aims in particular at the "localization" and "local locus" dimensions of the entrepreneurial economy model as described in Table 10-1.

"Channel 3" public intervention (as represented by arrow G3) is meant to influence the abilities and resources of potential entrepreneurs.

Government policy can help to bridge financial and knowledge gaps by making available financial and informational resources, respectively. For example, policies aimed at the development of the venture capital market can help to improve the access of business owners to the financial capital needed to start or expand a business. Direct financial support, such as subsidies, grants, and loan guarantees, can also increase the availability of resources of (potential) entrepreneurs. The skill and knowledge base of (potential) entrepreneurs can be influenced through the direct provision of relevant "business" information, such as advice and counseling, or through the educational system. However, innate characteristics, such as learning capacity and personality traits, are difficult to develop through education and training. G3 policies can be typified as input-related policies, because they refer to inputs in the entrepreneurial process that are both material, such as financial capital, and immaterial, such as knowledge. "Channel 3" public intervention aims in particular at the "heterogeneity" and "input targeting" dimensions of the entrepreneurial economy model as described in Table 10-1.

"Channel 4" public intervention (as represented by arrow G4) works through the preferences of individuals to become entrepreneurs. Preferences of people, including their evaluation of risks, are developed during their upbringing. Values and attitudes are the expression of these preferences, and because, to a large extent, they are determined by cultural background, they are difficult to influence or modify (Freytag and Thurik, 2007). G4 policies are typically characterized by their pervasive but indirect and lagged effect on society. This is often referred to as "fostering an entrepreneurial culture." For example, entrepreneurial values and attitudes can be shaped by introducing entrepreneurial elements in the educational system and by paying attention to entrepreneurship in the media. "Channel 4" public intervention aims in particular at the "heterogeneity," "motivation," and "enabling" dimensions of the *Entrepreneurial Economy* model as described in Table 10-1.

"Channel 5" public intervention (as represented by arrow G5) is directed at the decision-making process of individuals, that is, potential entrepreneurs. Given opportunities, abilities, resources, and preferences, the evaluation of the entrepreneurial option versus outside options such as unemployment and employment can be influenced by this type of government intervention. Relevant policies are taxation influencing business earnings, social security arrangements influencing the willingness of people to give up their present state of employment to become entrepreneurs, and labor market legislation regarding hiring and firing, thereby determining the flexibility of the business and the attractiveness to start or continue a business. Bankruptcy policy can also influence the risk-reward profile. For example, people may shy away from self-employment when legal consequences of bankruptcy are severe. "Channel 5" public intervention aims in particular at the "jobs and high wages," "turbulence," "diversity," "flexibility," "input targeting," and "entrepreneurial" dimensions of the entrepreneurial economy model as described in Table 10-1.

"Channel 6" public intervention (as represented by arrow G6) involves the demand side of entrepreneurship and influences the accessibility of markets. Whereas G1 policies influence the size of the markets, G6 policies such as competition policy are meant to improve the accessibility of markets. For instance, G6 policies aim at reducing the market power of large firms and at lowering barriers to entry for small businesses. Protection of property rights and the regulatory environment of product and labor markets are further examples. Last, through establishment and bankruptcy legislation the government can influence the accessibility of markets. When establishment requirements and bankruptcy legislation are strict and opaque, potential entrepreneurs can be discouraged to exploit business opportunities and to fill in the market gaps. "Channel 6" public intervention aims in particular at the "jobs with high wages," "turbulence," "diversity," "market exchange," "competition with cooperation," "flexibility," and "enabling" dimensions of the entrepreneurial economy model as described in Table 10-1.

10.7. Concluding Remarks

Entrepreneurship has emerged as an important element in the organization of economies. Its role has changed dramatically over the last half-century. "Entrepreneurship has emerged as the engine of economic and social development throughout the world" (Audretsch and Thurik, 2004, p. 144). This emergence did not occur simultaneously in all developed countries. Using survey data Grilo and Thurik (2005b) give a detailed account of the differences in the actual and latent entrepreneurship rates in the fifteen old member states of the European Union. They show that four times as many Greeks than French people answer positively to the question of whether they are involved in some form of entrepreneurship. Similarly, twice as many Portuguese than Finnish citizens answer that they want to be entrepreneurs (latent entrepreneurship). A quickly developing literature shows that differences in national growth rates are often attributed to differences in the speed with which countries embrace entrepreneurial energy.

The increased importance of entrepreneurship is clearly recognized by politicians and policymakers. For example, it is deeply embedded in the current European policy approach that the creativity and independence of entrepreneurs can contribute to higher levels of economic activity. Indeed, "the challenge for the European Union is to identify the key factors for building a climate in which entrepreneurial initiative and business activities can thrive. Policy measures should seek to boost the Union's levels of entrepreneurship, adopting the most appropriate approach for producing more entrepreneurs and for getting more firms to grow" (European Commission, 2003, p. 9). Hence, clear and organized views are needed of what the determinants and consequences of entrepreneurship are.

The increased importance of entrepreneurship is also recognized in the domain of scientific research. In the last decade or so the field of economics contributed significantly to providing views of what the determinants and consequences of entrepreneurship are. The Kauffman-Max Planck Conference on Entrepreneurship and Economic Policy (Rinberg Castle, Rottach Egern, May 8–9, 2006) and the present book are among the many examples of this contribution. Earlier in this chapter I termed this approach "entreprenomics."

The present contribution tries to provide an example of such a view. Entrepreneurship, its drivers, and its consequences can be best understood using the model of the entrepreneurial economy which explains the functioning of the modern economy. It is argued that the model of the managed economy is the political, social, and economic response to an economy dictated by the forces of large-scale production, reflecting the predominance of the production factors of capital and (unskilled) labor as the sources of competitive advantage. By contrast, the model of the entrepreneurial economy is the political, social, and economic response to an economy dictated not just by the dominance of the production factor of knowledge – which is often identified as replacing the more traditional factors as the source of competitive advantage – but also by a very different, but complementary, factor: entrepreneurship capital, or the capacity to engage in and generate entrepreneurial activity. Knowledge or R&D can spill over to the advantage of the entire economy only in the context of generous entrepreneurial activity.

The functioning of the entrepreneurial economy provides the basis for an Entrepreneurship Policy Framework in which determinants of entrepreneurship and the ways of public intervention are described. The purpose of the Entrepreneurship Policy Framework is to provide a unified framework for understanding and analyzing what determines entrepreneurship. The Entrepreneurship Policy Framework of entrepreneurship integrates the different strands from the relevant fields into a unifying, coherent framework. At the heart of the Entrepreneurship Policy Framework is the assumption that the level of entrepreneurship can be explained by making a distinction between the supply side (labor market perspective) and the demand side (product market perspective; carrying capacity of the market) of entrepreneurship. While both the demand and supply sides are formed by many factors, what results is a level of entrepreneurship that is equilibrated by these two sides. In this equilibration the entrepreneurial choice filter plays a crucial role covering the individual decision process experienced by potential entrepreneurs evaluating the entrepreneurial option against "outside" options. The Entrepreneurship Policy Framework also creates insight into the role of government policy through identifying six channels influencing the demand side, the supply side, and the characteristics of the choice filter by policy instruments.

References

Acs, Zoltan J. 1992. "Small Bbusiness Economics: A Global Perspective." *Challenge*, 35, 38–44.

Acs, Zoltan J., and Catherine Armington. 2004. "Employment Growth and Entrepreneurial Activity in Cities." *Regional Studies*, 38, 911–927.

Acs, Zoltan J., and David B. Audretsch. 1990. *Innovation and Small Firms*. Cambridge, MA: MIT Press.

Acs, Zoltan J., and David B. Audretsch. 1993. "Conclusion." In Z. J. Acs and D. B. Audretsch (eds.), *Small Firms and Entrepreneurship: An East-West Perspective*. Cambridge, U.K.: Cambridge University Press, 227–231.

Audretsch, David B. 1995. *Innovation and Industry Evolution*. Cambridge, Mass.: MIT Press.

Audretsch, David B., and Maryann P. Feldman. 1996. "R&D Spillovers and the Geography of Innovation and Production." *American Economic Review*, 86(3), 630–640.

Audretsch, David B., and Michael Fritsch. 2002. "Growth Regimes over Time and Space." *Regional Studies*, 36(2), 113–124.

Audretsch, David B., and Max Keilbach. 2004. "Entrepreneurship Capital and Economic Performance." *Regional Studies*, 38(8), 949–959.

Audretsch, David B., and A. Roy Thurik. 2000. "Capitalism and Democracy in the 21st Century: From the Managed to the Entrepreneurial Economy." *Journal of Evolutionary Economics*, 10(1), 17–34.

Audretsch, David B., and A. Roy Thurik. 2001. "What's New about the New Economy? From the Managed to the Entrepreneurial Economy." *Industrial and Corporate Change*, 10(1), 267–315.

Audretsch, David B., and A. Roy Thurik. 2004. "The Model of the Entrepreneurial Economy." *International Journal of Entrepreneurship Education*, 2(2), 143–166.

Audretsch, David B., A. Roy Thurik, Ingrid Verheul, and Sander Wennekers, eds. 2002a. *Entrepreneurship: Determinants and Policy in a European-U.S. Comparison.* Boston/Dordrecht: Kluwer Academic Publishers.

Audretsch, David B., Martin A. Carree, André J. van Stel, and A. Roy Thurik. 2002b. "Impeded Industrial Restructuring: The Growth Penalty." *Kyklos,* 55(1), 81–98.

Audretsch, David B., Max C. Keilbach, and Erik E. Lehmann. 2006. *Entrepreneurship and Economic Growth.* New York: Oxford University Press.

Audretsch, David B., Isabel Grilo, and A. Roy Thurik. 2007. "Explaining Entrepreneurship and the Role of Policy." In D. B. Audretsch, I. Grilo, and A.R. Thurik, *Handbook of Entrepreneurship Policy.* Cheltenham, U.K., and Brookfield, U.S.: Edward Elgar Publishing Limited.

Baptista, Rui, and A. Roy Thurik. 2006. "The Relationship between Entrepreneurship and Unemployment: Is Portugal an Outlier?" *Technological Forecasting and Social Change,* 74(1), 75–89.

Baumol, William J. 1968. "Entrepreneurship in Economic Theory." *American Economic Review,* 58(2), 64–71.

Baumol, William J. 1993. *Entrepreneurship, Management and the Structure of Payoffs.* Cambridge, Mass.: MIT Press.

Bell, D. 1960. *The End of Ideology: On the Exhaustion of Political Ideas in the Fifties.* Glencoe, Ill.: Free Press.

Berle, Adolf A., and G. C. Means. 1932. *The Modern Corporation and Private Property.* New York: Macmillan Company.

Brock, Willim A., and David S. Evans. 1989. "Small Business Economics." *Small Business Economics,* 1(1), 7–20.

Brown, Charles, and James Medoff. 1989. "The Employer Size-Wage Effect." *Journal of Political Economy,* 97(5), 1027–1059.

Brown, Charles, Jay Hamilton, and James Medoff. 1990. *Employers Large and Small.* Cambridge, Mass.: Harvard University Press.

Carlsson, Bo. 1992. "The Rise of Small Business: Causes and Consequences." In W. J. Adams (ed.), *Singular Europe: Economy and Policy of the European Community after 1992.* Ann Arbor: University of Michigan Press, 145–169.

Carree, Martin A., and A. Roy Thurik. 1999. "Industrial Structure and Economic Growth." In D. B. Audretsch and A. R. Thurik (eds.), *Innovation, Industry Evolution and Employment.* Cambridge, U.K.: Cambridge University Press, 86–110.

Carree, Martin A., and A. Roy Thurik. 2003. "The Impact of Entrepreneurship on Economic Growth." In D. B. Audretsch and Z. J. Acs (eds.), *Handbook of Entrepreneurship Research.* Boston and Dordrecht: Kluwer Academic Publishers, 437–471.

Carree, Martin A., and A. Roy Thurik, eds. 2006a. *The Handbook of Entrepreneurship and Economic Growth (International Library of Entrepreneurship).* Cheltenham, U.K., and Brookfield, U.S.: Edward Elgar Publishing Limited.

Carree, Martin A., and A. Roy Thurik. 2006b. "Understanding the Role of Entrepreneurship for Economic Growth." In M. A. Carree and A. R. Thurik (eds.), *The Handbook of Entrepreneurship and Economic Growth (International Library of Entrepreneurship).* Cheltenham, U.K., and Brookfield, U.S.: Edward Elgar Publishing Limited.

Carree, Martin A., André J. van Stel, A. Roy Thurik, and Sander Wennekers. 2002. "Economic Development and Business Ownership: An Analysis Using Data of 23

OECD Countries in the Period 1976–1996." *Small Business Economics*, 19(3), 271–290.

Carree, Martin A., André J. van Stel, A. Roy Thurik, and Sander Wennekers. 2007. "The Relation between Economic Development and Business Ownership Revisited."Tinbergen Institute Discussion Paper No. TI 2007-022/3.

Caves, Richard. 1982. *Multinational Enterprise and Economic Analysis.* Cambridge: Cambridge University Press.

Chandler, Alfred D., Jr. 1977. *The Visible Hand: The Managerial Revolution in American Business.* Cambridge, Mass.: Harvard University Press.

Chandler, Alfred D., Jr. 1990. *Scale and Scope: The Dynamics of Industrial Capitalism.* Cambridge, Mass.: Harvard University Press.

Coase, Ronald H. 1937. "The Nature of the Firm." *Economica*, 4(16), 386–405.

Cohen, Wesley M., and Steven Klepper. 1992. "The Trade-off between Firm Size and Diversity in the Pursuit of Technological Progress." *Small Business Economics*, 4(1), 1–14.

Cohen, Wesley M., and Daniel A. Levinthal. 1989. "Innovation and Learning: The Two Faces of R&D." *Economic Journal*, 99(3), 569–596.

Davidsson, Per. 2004. *Researching Entrepreneurship (International Studies in Entrepreneurship).* Boston: Springer.

Davis, Steven J., and Magnus Henrekson. 1999. "Explaining National Differences in the Size and Industry Distribution of Employment." *Small Business Economics*, 12(1), 59–83.

EIM. 2002. *SMEs in Europe: Report Submitted to the Enterprise Directorate General by KPMG Special Services.* Zoetermeer: EIM Business and Policy Research.

EIM/ENSR. 1993. *The European Observatory: First Annual Report.* Zoetermeer: EIM Business and Policy Research.

EIM/ENSR. 1994. *The European Observatory: Second Annual Report.* Zoetermeer: EIM Business and Policy Research.

EIM/ENSR. 1995. *The European Observatory: Third Annual Report.* Zoetermeer: EIM Business and Policy Research.

EIM/ENSR. 1996. *The European Observatory: Fourth Annual Report.* Zoetermeer: EIM Business and Policy Research.

EIM/ENSR. 1997. *The European Observatory: Fifth Annual Report.* Zoetermeer: EIM Business and Policy Research.

European Commission. 2003. Green Paper on Entrepreneurship in Europe. http://ec.europa.eu/enterprise/entrepreneurship/green_paper/index.htm.

Evans, David S., and Linda S. Leighton. 1989. "The Determinants of Changes in U.S. Self-employment, 1968–1987." *Small Business Economics*, 1(2), 111–119.

Feldman, Maryann P., and David B. Audretsch. 1999. "Innovation in Cities: Science-based Diversity, Specialization and Localized Monopoly." *European Economic Review*, 43, 409–429.

Foelster, Stefan. 2000. "Do Entrepreneurs Create Jobs?" *Small Business Economics*, 14(2), 137–148.

Freytag, Andreas, and A. Roy Thurik. 2007. "Entrepreneurship and Its Determinants in a Cross-country Setting." *Journal of Evolutionary Economics*, 17(2), 117–131.

Galbraith, John K. 1956. *American Capitalism: The Concept of Countervailing Power.* Boston: Houghton Mifflin.

Glaeser, Edward, Hedi Kallal, Jose Scheinkman, and Andrei Shleifer. 1992. "Growth in Cities." *Journal of Political Economy*, 100(6), 1126–1152.

Grilo, Isabel, and Jesus M. Irigoyen. 2006. "Entrepreneurship in the EU: To Wish and Not to Be." *Small Business Economics*, 26(4), 305–318.

Grilo, Isabel, and A. Roy Thurik. 2005a. "Entrepreneurial Engagement Levels in the European Union." *International Journal of Entrepreneurship Education*, 3(2), 143–168.

Grilo, Isabel, and A. Roy Thurik. 2005b. "Latent and Actual Entrepreneurship in Europe and the US: Some Recent Developments." *International Entrepreneurship and Management Journal*, 1(4), 441–459.

Grilo, Isabel, and A. Roy Thurik. 2006. "Entrepreneurship in the Old and the New Europe." In E. Santarelli (ed.), *Entrepreneurship, Growth and Innovation: The Dynamics of Firms and Industries*. New York: Springer, 75–103.

Grossman, Gene M., and Elhanan Helpman. 1991. *Innovation and Growth in the Global Economy*. Cambridge, MA: MIT Press.

Henrekson, Magnus, and Dan Johansson. 1999. "Institutional Effects on the Evolution of the Size Distribution of Firms." *Small Business Economics*, 12(1), 11–23.

Jacobs, Jane. 1969. *The Economy of Cities*. New York: Vintage Books.

Jaffe, Adam, Manuel Trajtenberg, and Rebecca Henderson. 1993. "Geographic Localization of Knowledge Spillovers as Evidenced by Patent Citations." *Quarterly Journal of Economics*, 108(3), 577–598.

Jensen, Michael C. 1993. "The Modern Industrial Revolution, Exit, and the Failure of Internal Control Systems." *Journal of Finance*, 48(3), 831–880.

Kirzner, Israel M. 1997. "Entrepreneurial Discovery and the Competitive Market Process: An Austrian Approach." *Journal of Economic Literature*, 35(1), 60–85.

Loveman, Gary, and Werner Sengenberger. 1991. "The Re-emergence of Small-scale Production: An International Comparison." *Small Business Economics*, 3(1), 1–37.

Low, Murray B. 2001. "The Adolescence of Entrepreneurship Research: Specification of Purpose." *Entrepreneurship: Theory and Practise*, June, 25(4), 17–25.

Lucas, Robert E. 1993. "Making a Miracle." *Econometrica*, 61(2), 251–272.

Lucas, Robert E. 1988. "On the Mechanics of Economic Development." *Journal of Monetary Economics*, 22, 3–39.

Parker, Simon C. 2004. *The Economics of Self-Employment and Entrepreneurship*. Cambridge: Cambridge University Press.

Piore, Michael, and Charles Sabel. 1984. *The Second Industrial Divide: Possibilities for Prosperity*. New York: Basic Books.

Porter, Michael. 1990. *The Competitive Advantage of Nations*. New York: Free Press.

Pratten, C. F. 1971. *Economies of Scale in Manufacturing Industry*. Cambridge: Cambridge University Press.

Reynolds, Paul D., William D. Bygrave, Erkko Autio, Larry W. Cox, and Michael Hay. 2002. "Global Entrepreneurship Monitor: 2002 Executive Report." Ewing Marion Kauffman Foundation.

Romer, Paul M. 1986. "Increasing Returns and Long-run Growth." *Journal of Political Economy*, 94(5), 1002–1037.

Saxenian, AnnaLee. 1990. "Regional Networks and the Resurgence of Silicon Valley." *California Management Review*, 33, 89–111.

Saxenian, AnnaLee. 1994. *Regional Advantage: Culture and Competition in Silicon Valley and Route 128*. Cambridge, Mass.: Harvard University Press.

Scherer, F. M. 1991. "Changing Perspectives on the Firm Size Problem." In Z. J. Acs and D. B. Audretsch (eds.), *Innovation and Technological Change: An International Comparison*. Ann Arbor: University of Michigan Press, 24–38.

Schumpeter, Joseph A. 1934. *The Theory of Economic Development*. Cambridge, Mass.: Harvard University Press.

Schumpeter, Joseph A. 1942. *Capitalism, Socialism and Democracy*. New York: Harper and Row.

Shane, Scott. 2000. "Prior Knowledge and the Discovery of Entrepreneurial Opportunities." *Organization Science*, 11(4), 448–469.

Solow, Robert M. 1956. "A Contribution to the Theory of Economic Growth." *Quarterly Journal of Economics*, 70, 65–94.

Stel, André van. 2005. "COMPENDIA: Harmonizing Business Ownership Data across Countries and over Time."*International Entrepreneurship and Management Journal*, 1(1),105–123.

Stel, André van, and Henry R. Nieuwenhuijsen. 2004. "Knowledge Spillovers and Economic Growth: An Analysis Using Data of Dutch Regions in the Period 1987–1995." *Regional Studies*, 38(4), 393–407.

Stel, André van, Martin Carree, and A. Roy Thurik. 2005. "The Effect of Entrepreneurial Activity on National Economic Growth." *Small Business Economics*, 24(3), 311–321.

Stevenson, Howard H., and David E. Gumpert. 1991. "The Heart of Entrepreneurship." In W. A. Sahlman and H. H. Stevenson (eds.), *The Entrepreneurial Venture*. Boston: McGraw-Hill.

Storey, David J. 1991. "The Birth of New Firms – Does Unemployment Matter?" *Small Business Economics* 3, 167–178.

Teece, David J. 1993. "The Dynamics of Industrial Capitalism: Perspectives on Alfred Chandler's 'Scale and Scope.'" *Journal of Economic Literature*, 31(1), 199–225.

Thurik, A. Roy. 2003. "Entrepreneurship and Unemployment in the UK." *Scottish Journal of Political Economy*, 50(3), 264–290.

Thurik, A. Roy, and Sander Wennekers. 2004. "Entrepreneurship, Small Business and Economic Growth." *Journal of Small Business and Enterprise Development*, 11(1), 140–149.

Thurik, A. R., S. Wennekers, and L. M. Uhlaner. 2002. "Entrepreneurship and Economic Performance: A Macro Perspective." *International Journal of Entrepreneurship Education*, 1(2), 157–179.

Thurik, A. Roy, Martin A. Carree, André J. van Stel, and David B. Audretsch. 2008. "Does Self-employment Reduce Unemployment?" *Journal of Business Venturing*, 23(6), 673–686.

Verheul, Ingrid, André van Stel, A. Roy Thurik, and David Urbano. 2006. "The Relationship between Business Ownership and Unemployment in Spain: A Matter of Quantity or Quality?" *Estudios de Economía Aplicada*, 24(2), 435–457.

Verheul, Ingrid, Sander Wennekers, David B. Audretsch, and A. Roy Thurik. 2002. "An Eclectic Theory of Entrepreneurship: Policies, Institutions and Culture." In D. B. Audretsch, A. R. Thurik, I. Verheul, and Sander Wennekers (eds.), *Entrepreneurship: Determinants and Policy in a European–US Comparison*. Boston and Dordrecht: Kluwer Academic Publishers, 11–82.

Weiss, L. W. 1976. "Optimal Plant Scale and the Extent of Suboptimal Capacity." In R. T. Masson and P. D. Qualls (eds.), *Essays on Industrial Organization in the Honor of Joe S. Bain*. Cambridge, Mass.: Ballinger, 126–134.

Wennekers, Sander. 2006. *Entrepreneurship at the Country Level: Economic and Non-economic Determinants*. Rotterdam: ERIM Ph.D. Series Research in Management no. 81.

Wennekers, Sander, and A. R. Thurik. 1999. "Linking Entrepreneurship and Economic Growth." *Small Business Economics*, 13(1), 27–55.

Wennekers, Sander, Lorraine Uhlaner, and A. Roy Thurik. 2002. "Entrepreneurship and Its Conditions: A Macro Perspective." *International Journal of Entrepreneurship Education*, 1(1), 25–64.

Williamson, Oliver E. 1968. "Economies as an Antitrust Defence: The Welfare Trade-offs." *American Economic Review*, 58(1), 18–36.

The Bayh-Dole Act and High-Technology Entrepreneurship in the United States during the 1980s and 1990s

David C. Mowery

11.1. Introduction

Assessments of the economic contributions of high-technology entrepreneurs and entrepreneurship to U.S. economic growth and competitiveness have shifted somewhat since the 1980s. During the 1990s, the era of the "New Economy," numerous observers hailed the resurgent economy in the United States as an illustration of the power of high-technology entrepreneurship. The new firms that a decade earlier had been criticized by such authorities as the MIT Commission on Industrial Productivity[1] for their failure to compete successfully against non-U.S. firms were seen as important sources of economic dynamism and employment growth. Indeed, the transformation in U.S. economic performance between the 1980s and 1990s is only slightly less remarkable than the failure of experts in academia, government, and industry to predict it.

University–industry research collaboration and technology transfer, especially the licensing by U.S. universities of patented inventions, was cited by a number of accounts as a central cause of U.S. economic resurgence in the 1990s, and the Bayh-Dole Act of 1980 has been credited for growth in such collaboration.[2] Implicit in many of these characterizations was the argument that university patenting and licensing have enhanced high-technology entrepreneurship and the economic contributions of

---

[1]   See Dertouzos et al. (1989); for an assessment of the Commission's critique, see Mowery (1999).

[2]   "Regulatory reform in the United States in the early 1980s, such as the Bayh-Dole Act, have [sic] significantly increased the contribution of scientific institutions to innovation. There is evidence that this is one of the factors contributing to the pick-up of US growth performance" (OECD, 2000, p. 77).

U.S. university research.[3] Similar characterizations of the effects of the Bayh-Dole Act have been articulated by the President of the Association of American Universities[4] and the Commissioner of the U.S. Patent and Trademark Office.[5]

But few of these assessments of the effects and importance of the Bayh-Dole Act cite much evidence in support of their arguments. Indeed, if the criticism of high-technology start-ups that was widespread in the gloomy analyses of the late 1980s and early 1990s was overstated, the more recent emphasis on patenting and licensing as the essential ingredient in university–industry collaboration, knowledge transfer, and new-firm formation seems to be equally overstated. Among other things, the emphasis on the Bayh-Dole Act as a catalyst to these interactions ignores the long history, extending to the earliest decades of the twentieth century, of research collaboration and technology transfer between universities and industry in the United States.

This chapter reviews the evidence on university–industry interactions and technology transfer, focusing in particular on the role of the Bayh-Dole

---

[3] "Possibly the most inspired piece of legislation to be enacted in America over the past half-century was the Bayh-Dole Act of 1980. Together with amendments in 1984 and augmentation in 1986, this unlocked all the inventions and discoveries that had been made in laboratories throughout the United States with the help of taxpayers' money. More than anything, this single policy measure helped to reverse America's precipitous slide into industrial irrelevance. Before Bayh-Dole, the fruits of research supported by government agencies had gone strictly to the federal government. Nobody could exploit such research without tedious negotiations with a federal agency concerned. Worse, companies found it nigh impossible to acquire exclusive rights to a government-owned patent. And without that, few firms were willing to invest millions more of their own money to turn a basic research idea into a marketable product" ("Innovation's Golden Goose," 2002).

[4] "In 1980, the enactment of the Bayh-Dole Act (Public Law 98-620) culminated years of work to develop incentives for laboratory discoveries to make their way to the market-place promptly, with all the attendant benefits for public welfare and economic growth that result from those innovations. Before Bayh-Dole, the federal government had accumulated 30,000 patents, of which only 5% had been licensed and even fewer had found their way into commercial products. Today under Bayh-Dole more than 200 universities are engaged in technology transfer, adding more than \$21 billion each year to the economy."

[5] "In the 1970s, the government discovered the inventions that resulted from public funding were not reaching the marketplace because no one would make the additional investment to turn basic research into marketable products. That finding resulted in the Bayh-Dole Act, passed in 1980. It enabled universities, small companies, and nonprofit organizations to commercialize the results of federally funded research. The results of Bayh-Dole have been significant. Before 1981, fewer than 250 patents were issued to universities each year. A decade later universities were averaging approximately 1,000 patents a year."

Act in (allegedly) transforming this relationship. I also summarize some case studies of the transfer of specific academic inventions to commercial firms during the post-1980 period, to illustrate the complexity of this process and the different channels of university–industry interaction within the broader process of technology transfer and commercialization. I discuss recent criticism by established industrial firms of U.S. university licensing policies and practices, to illustrate the tensions that have developed between universities and some U.S. industrial firms over these policies during the twenty-five years since the passage of the Bayh-Dole Act. The history of U.S. university–industry collaboration before and after the Bayh-Dole Act, as well as these recent debates between industry and U.S. universities over technology-transfer policies, offer some cautionary implications for other national governments seeking to develop policies similar to Bayh-Dole, an issue that I briefly consider before concluding.

11.2. How Does Academic Research Influence Industrial Innovation? A Review of Recent Studies

A number of studies based on interviews and surveys of senior industrial managers in industries ranging from pharmaceuticals to electrical equipment have examined the influence of university research on industrial innovation. All of these studies (Levin et al., 1987; GUIRR, 1991; Mansfield, 1991; Cohen, Nelson, and Walsh, 2002) emphasize differences among industries in the relationship between university and industrial innovation. In particular, university research advances affect industrial innovation more significantly and directly in the biomedical field than in other sectors.

In these other technological and industrial fields, universities have occasionally contributed relevant "inventions," but most commercially significant inventions have come from non-academic research. The incremental advances that were the primary focus of firms' R&D activities in these sectors were largely the domain of industrial research, problem solving, and development. University research contributed to technological advances by enhancing knowledge of the fundamental physics and chemistry underlying manufacturing processes, product innovation, and experimental techniques, including instrumentation.

The studies by Levin et al. (1987) and Cohen et al. (2002) summarize industrial R&D managers' views on the relevance to industrial innovation of various fields of university research (Table 11-1 summarizes the results

Table 11-1. *The relevance of university science to industrial technology*

Science	Number of industries with "relevance" scores		Selected industries for which the reported "relevance" of university research was large (≥ 6)
	≥ 5	≥ 6	
Biology	12	3	Animal feed, drugs, processed fruits/vegetables
Chemistry	19	3	Animal feed, meat products, drugs
Geology	0	0	None
Mathematics	5	1	Optical instruments
Physics	4	2	Optical instruments, electronics
Agricultural science	17	7	Pesticides, animal feed, fertilizers, food products
Applied math/operations research	16	2	Meat products, logging/sawmills
Computer science	34	10	Optical instruments, logging/ sawmills, paper machinery
Materials science	29	8	Synthetic rubber, nonferrous metals
Medical science	7	3	Surgical/medical instruments, drugs, coffee
Metallurgy	21	6	Nonferrous metals, fabricated metal products
Chemical engineering	19	6	Canned foods, fertilizers, malt beverages
Electrical engineering	22	2	Semiconductors, scientific instruments
Mechanical engineering	28	9	Hand tools, specialized industrial machinery

discussed in Levin et al., 1987). Virtually all of the fields of university research that were rated as "important" or "very important" for their innovative activities by industrial respondents in both surveys were related to engineering or applied sciences, fields of U.S. university research with a long history of university–industry collaboration. Interestingly, with the exception of chemistry, few basic sciences appear on the list of university research fields deemed by industry respondents to be relevant to their innovative activities. The absence of fields such as physics and mathematics in Table 11-1, however, should not be interpreted to mean that academic research in these fields does not contribute to technical advance in industry. Instead, these results reflect the fact that the effects on industrial innovation of basic research findings in such areas as physics, mathematics, and the physical sciences are realized only after a considerable lag. Moreover, application of academic research results often requires that these advances be incorporated into the applied sciences, such as chemical engineering, electrical engineering, and material sciences.

The survey results summarized in Cohen et al. (2002) indicate that in most industries, university research results play a minor role in triggering new industrial R&D projects; instead, the stimuli originate with customers or from manufacturing operations. Pharmaceuticals is an exception, since university research in this field often triggers industrial R&D projects. Cohen et al. (2002) further report that the results of "public research" performed in government laboratories and universities were used more frequently by U.S. industrial firms (on average, in 29% of industrial R&D projects) than prototypes emerging from these external sources of research (used in an average of 8.3% of industrial R&D projects). A similar portrait of the relative importance of different outputs of university and public-laboratory research emerges from this study's summary of responses to questions about the importance to industrial R&D of various information channels (Table 11-2). Although pharmaceutical executives assign greater importance to patents and license agreements involving universities and public laboratories, even respondents from this industry rated research publications and conferences as a more important source of information.

Table 11-2. *Importance to industrial R&D of sources of information on public R&D (including university research)*

Information source	% rating it as "very important" for industrial R&D
Publications & reports	41.2
Informal Interaction	35.6
Meetings & conferences	35.1
Consulting	31.8
Contract research	20.9
Recent hires	19.6
Cooperative R&D projects	17.9
Patents	17.5
Licenses	9.5
Personnel exchange	5.8

Source: Cohen et al. (2002).

For most industries, patents and licenses involving inventions from university or public laboratories were reported to be of little importance, compared with publications, conferences, informal interaction with university researchers, and consulting.

The consistency in the findings of the Levin et al. study and the more recent survey conducted by Cohen and colleagues is striking – the "New Economy" notwithstanding, the late 1990s do not contrast sharply with the late 1970s. At the same time, the coverage of these surveys is limited to R&D within established firms. The Levin study in particular focuses primarily on manufacturing, excluding such important service sector industries as software, which scarcely existed at the time of the Levin survey. Additional research on the relationship between the innovative activities of smaller firms, especially those in knowledge-intensive industries, and better coverage of innovation in the nonmanufacturing sector is needed. We also lack comparably detailed information on the relationship between academic research and firms' innovative activities in other industrial economies.

Nonetheless, these studies indicate that the relationship between academic research and industrial innovation in the biomedical field differs from that in other knowledge-intensive sectors. This work also suggests that academic research rarely produces "prototypes" of inventions for development and commercialization by industry – instead, academic research informs the methods and disciplines employed by firms in their R&D facilities. Industrial R&D managers also rely on a variety of channels for learning about and exploiting the results of academic research. Finally, the channels rated by industrial R&D managers as most important in this complex interaction between academic and industrial innovation rarely include patents and licenses. Perhaps the most striking aspect of these survey and interview results is their limited influence on the design of U.S. policy initiatives to enhance the contributions of university research to industrial innovation.

11.3. The Bayh-Dole Act and Academic Patenting in the United States

11.3.1. The "Pre-Bayh-Dole" Era

To provide some context for interpreting the effects of the Bayh-Dole Act on U.S. university patenting and licensing, a brief overview of university activities in this sphere before the passage of the Act is essential. U.S.

universities have been active patentees (and licensors) of research results for much of the twentieth century. The pre-1980 patenting activities of U.S. universities built on research collaborations between university and industrial researchers that spanned many channels of technology and knowledge exchange, including publishing, training of industrial researchers, and faculty consulting.

University–industry collaboration in turn was facilitated by the unusual structure of the U.S. higher education system (especially in comparison with those of other industrial economies). The U.S. higher education system was significantly larger, included a heterogeneous collection of institutions (religious and secular, public and private, large and small), lacked any centralized national administrative control, and encouraged considerable interinstitutional competition for students, faculty, resources, and prestige (see, e.g., Trow, 1979, 1991; Geiger, 1986, 1993). In addition, the reliance by many public institutions of higher education on "local" (regional or state-level) sources for political and financial support enhanced their incentives to develop collaborative relationships with regional industrial and agricultural establishments. The structure of the U.S. higher education system thus strengthened incentives for faculty and academic administrators to collaborate in research and other activities with industry (and to do so through channels extending beyond patenting and licensing) long before the Bayh-Dole Act.

Although U.S. universities were patenting faculty inventions as early as the 1920s, few institutions had developed formal patent policies prior to the late 1940s, and a number of these policies embodied considerable ambivalence toward patenting. For example, despite the adoption by a growing number of universities of formal patent policies by the 1950s, many medical schools prohibited patenting of inventions. A number of universities active in patenting chose not to manage patenting and licensing themselves, in many cases because of concern over the political consequences of a visible role in profiting from faculty inventions, and in other cases because of fears that their nonprofit tax status could be jeopardized.[6]

---

[6] Etzkowitz's discussion of the debate within MIT over institutional patent policies during the 1930s (1994, p. 404) notes that "in 1936, the committee on patents of the institute put forward the view that: 'There is recognized to be danger in deriving any income whatever from inventions, first because of possible influence upon our tax exempt status, and second because of possible criticism of our methods leading to ill will among those upon whom we must depend for support. The first difficulty seems to be avoided if the actual handling of our affairs is delegated to some other organization.'"

World War II and the Cold War that followed transformed the structure of the U.S. national innovation system (Mowery and Rosenberg, 1998). Nowhere was this transformation more dramatic than in U.S. universities. Previously funded largely by state governments, the U.S. Agriculture Department, and industry, academic research experienced a surge of federal funding. As the growth in university–industry research links had done during the 1920s and 1930s, increased federal funding of university research strengthened two motives for university involvement in patenting. First, the expanded scale of the academic research enterprise increased the probability that universities would produce patentable inventions. Second, many federal research sponsors required the development of a formal patent policy.

One important "independent" manager of the patenting and licensing activities for U.S. research universities from the 1930s through the 1960s was the Research Corporation, founded in 1912 by Frederick Cottrell, a University of California chemistry professor who wished to use the licensing revenues from his patents to support scientific research.[7] Although many of the patents whose licensing it managed during the 1920s and 1930s were donated by philanthropic faculty, by the 1940s, the Corporation had become an important "independent" manager of patenting and licensing for such universities as MIT, Princeton, and Columbia. The Research Corporation's role as a patent manager grew during the 1950s and 1960s, as more universities signed "Invention Administration Agreements" (IAAs) with the Corporation. As of 1940, only three of the nation's eighty-nine "Research Universities" (as classified by the Carnegie Commission's 1973 taxonomy) had signed IAAs with the Research Corporation. By 1950 this number had increased to twenty, and by the mid-1960s, nearly two-thirds of the Carnegie Commission's Research Universities were Research Corporation clients.

Well into the 1960s, many U.S. universities continued to avoid direct involvement in patent administration, and others maintained a "hands off" attitude toward patents altogether. Columbia's policy left patenting to

---

[7] In addition to wishing to use the proceeds from licensing of his inventions for philanthropic purposes, Cottrell was concerned about the implications of involving the administration of the University of California in managing his patents: "A danger was involved, especially should the experiment prove highly profitable to the university and lead to a general emulation of the plan. University trustees are continually seeking for funds and in direct proportion to the success of our experiment its repetition might be expected elsewhere . . . the danger this suggested was the possibility of growing commercialism and competition between institutions and an accompanying tendency for secrecy in scientific work" (Cottrell, 1932, p. 222).

the inventor and patent administration to the Research Corporation, stating that "it is not deemed within the sphere of the University's scholarly objectives" to hold patents; Harvard, Chicago, Yale, and Johns Hopkins adopted similar positions. All of these universities, as well as Ohio State and the University of Pennsylvania, discouraged or prohibited medical patents. Other universities allowed patents on biomedical inventions only if it could be established that such patenting would advance the public interest.[8] This institutional ambivalence toward patenting began to change during the 1960s, although the prohibitions on medical patenting at Columbia, Harvard, Johns Hopkins, and Chicago were not dropped until the 1970s. The pace of change accelerated during the 1970s, in response to federal initiatives in R&D funding and patent policy.

11.3.2. Sources of Growth in University Patenting during the 1970s

The growth of university patenting during the 1970s reflected changes in the sources of academic research funding and advances in biomedical research. Reductions in the rate of growth in federal funding of university research during this time, especially at some leading private U.S. research universities, heightened the interest of university faculty and administrators in the potential revenues associated with licensing these research advances.[9] Universities' increased interest in licensing revenues resulted in the entry by a number of institutions (particularly private universities) into direct management of their patenting and licensing. Increased university interest in managing patents and licenses was facilitated by new federal policies that supported the negotiation of agency-specific waivers for patent rights.

In 1968, the federal Department of Health, Education and Welfare (HEW), which housed the National Institutes of Health, established

---

[8] Columbia University's policy stated, "It is recognized, however, that there may be exceptional circumstances where the taking out of a patent will be advisable in order to protect the public. These cases must be brought to [the University administration] for its consideration and approval" (cited in Palmer 1957, p. 175).

[9] During 1968–1974, "Research I" public universities (as defined by the Carnegie Commission on Higher Education) saw a 29.5% increase in federal research dollars per faculty member, while "Research I" private universities saw a 10.5% decline. Research II public universities enjoyed a 15.4% increase in federal research funding per faculty member, while such funding declined by 12.6% during this period at Research II private universities (Graham and Diamond, 1997, p. 105). These shifts in federal research funding reflected cutbacks in defense-related funding programs during the end of the Vietnam conflict, as well as the effects of the Mansfield Amendment, which restricted federal support for research deemed less directly relevant to defense applications.

Institutional Patent Agreements (IPAs) that gave universities with "approved technology transfer capability" the right to retain title to agency-funded patents.[10] Along with creating IPAs, HEW began to act more quickly on requests from universities and other research performers for title to the intellectual property resulting from federally funded research. Between 1969 and 1974 the agency approved 90 percent of petitions for title and negotiated IPAs with seventy-two universities and non-profit institutions (Weissman, 1989). The National Science Foundation (NSF) instituted a similar IPA program in 1973, and the Department of Defense had already begun in the mid-1960s to allow universities with approved patent policies to retain title to inventions resulting from federally funded research.

Approximately one-quarter (49 of 212) of the Carnegie Research and Doctoral Universities had IPAs with either HEW or NSF during the 1970s. These institutions accounted for 73 percent of university patenting during the 1970s, and continued to account for 55 percent of university patenting during the 1980s. Another twenty-seven of these universities petitioned the government for title during 1974–1980 (as indicated by acknowledgments in the "government interest" section of their patents). Together, institutions that either petitioned for rights or had IPAs accounted for 92 percent of patents during the 1970s, and 85 percent of university patents during the 1980s. Many of the most active patentees in the post–Bayh-Dole era were among the leaders in patenting government-funded research during the 1970s.

Declines in Department of Defense support for academic research during the 1970s were partially offset by growth in research funding from the National Institutes of Health, reflecting the Nixon administration's "War on Cancer" and the growing political influence of interest groups lobbying for expanded research on specific diseases. The NIH share of federal support for academic research grew from 37 percent in 1971 to 47 percent by 1981. Expanded biomedical research funding, combined with significant scientific advances in molecular biology, led to an increase in academic patenting in biomedical technologies during the 1970s.

---

[10] HEW had instituted an IPA program in 1953 and 18 universities had negotiated IPAs with the agency by 1958. But after 1958, no additional requests for IPAs were approved by HEW, because "opinions of responsible agency officials differed concerning the value of such agreements" (U.S. General Accounting Office, 1968, p. 24). Pharmaceutical companies also complained that these IPAs failed to define the scope of licensees' exclusive rights.

Overall, the decade of the 1970s represented a watershed in the growth of U.S. university patenting and licensing. The institutional ambivalence that had prevented many universities from direct involvement in management of patenting subsided, for reasons that are not well understood, and a number of universities entered into direct management of patenting and licensing. Private universities in particular expanded their patenting and licensing during this decade: Their share of university-assigned patents grew from 14 percent in 1960 to 45 percent in 1980. U.S. universities' share of overall U.S. patenting more than doubled during the decade (albeit from a very low level, increasing from 0.2 percent to 0.5 percent of U.S. patents), and biomedical technologies' share of U.S. university patents almost doubled, increasing from 17 percent in 1970 to 30 percent in 1980. The increased share of biomedical disciplines within overall federal academic R&D funding, the dramatic advances in biomedical science that occurred during the 1960s and 1970s, and the strong industrial interest in the results of this biomedical research all affected the growth of biomedical patenting by U.S. universities during the 1970s.

The decision by a growing number of universities to manage their patenting and licensing activities directly reduced the role of the Research Corporation during the 1970s. Along with some apparent increase in the willingness of universities to expose themselves to the risks and political criticisms that previously had led many to avoid direct involvement in patenting and licensing, entry by universities into this activity reflected dissatisfaction with the performance of the Research Corporation. The Research Corporation's status as a manager of the patents of research universities had long been a source of considerable tension and dissatisfaction among several of its leading clients. In 1962, a dispute among the Research Corporation, IBM, and MIT over the terms for a license to Jay Forrester's magnetic core memory patents led MIT to cancel its IAA with the Corporation, severing the Corporation's ties to a leading academic patentee.

The Research Corporation also contributed to its own demise by encouraging and assisting its client universities during the 1960s and 1970s in the development of organizations to manage the early stages of the technology transfer process, particularly invention screening and evaluation. These activities appear to have led at least some client universities to "cherry-pick" their emergent invention portfolios, directly managing patenting and licensing for the most promising commercial prospects and leaving the Research Corporation with the remainder (Mowery and Sampat, 2001a).

11.3.3. Origins of the Bayh-Dole Act

By the 1970s, the developments described above meant that most U.S. universities were able to patent the results of federally funded research via agency-specific IPAs or similar programs at the Defense Department, as well as through case-by-case petitions. But HEW policy discussions in the late 1970s triggered concern among U.S. research universities that their ability to patent and license government-funded inventions might be curtailed. These concerns, along with growing dissatisfaction within Congress and the industrial community over the lack of uniformity in patent rights to inventions resulting from federally funded research, provided the impetus for the introduction in 1978 of the bill that eventually became the Bayh-Dole Act.

In August 1977, HEW's Office of the General Counsel expressed concern that university patents and licenses, particularly exclusive licenses, could contribute to higher health-care costs (Eskridge, 1978). The department ordered a review of its patent policy, including a reconsideration of whether universities' rights to negotiate exclusive licenses should be curtailed.[11] During the ensuing twelve-month review by HEW of its patent policies, the agency deferred decisions on thirty petitions for patent rights and three requests for IPAs.

In response to HEW's review of its patent policies, "universities got upset and complained to Congress" (Broad, 1979a, 476). A former Purdue University patent attorney, Norman Latker, who had been an architect of the changes in HEW's patent policies in 1968 that led to the creation of IPAs, was fired from HEW after denouncing the agency's subsequent review of these policies. Latker asked Senator Birch Bayh of Indiana to develop legislation liberalizing and rationalizing federal policy toward university patents on federally funded research.[12] In September 1978, Senator Robert Dole (R-KS) held a press conference where he criticized HEW for "stonewalling" university patenting (commenting, "rarely have we

---

[11] The purpose of the HEW review was "to make sure that assignment of patent rights to universities and research institutes did not stifle competition in the private sector in those cases where competition could bring the fruits of research to the public faster and more economically," according to the testimony of Comptroller General Elmer Staats during the Bayh-Dole hearings (United States Senate Committee on the Judiciary 1979, p. 37).

[12] Latker returned to the HEW's patent office in 1978, after his dismissal was overturned by a civil service review board on procedural grounds. Reporting on these events in *Science*, Broad (1979a) noted, "The reinstatement is timely. Support is now building for the Bayh-Dole patent bill, and Latker's return to the HEW is seen by many university researchers and patent transfer fans, to whom Latker is something of a hero, as a shot in the arm for their cause" (p. 476).

witnessed a more hideous example of overmanagement by the bureaucracy") and announced his intention to introduce a bill to remedy the situation (Eskridge, 1978, 605). On September 13, 1978, Senators Birch Bayh (D-IN) and Dole introduced S.414, the University and Small Business Patent Procedures Act.

The Act proposed a uniform federal patent policy that gave universities and small businesses rights to any patents resulting from government-funded research.[13] The bill lacked provisions that had been included in most IPAs, including the requirement that a participating university must have an "approved technology transfer" capability. In contrast to the language of many IPAs between universities and HEW, the bill imposed no restrictions on the negotiation by universities and other research institutions of exclusive licensing agreements.[14]

Many members of Congress had long opposed any federal grant of ownership of patents to research performers or contractors (Broad, 1979b). The Bayh-Dole bill nevertheless attracted little opposition. The bill's focus on securing patent rights for only universities and small business weakened the argument that such patent-ownership policies would favor big business.[15] The bill's introduction in the midst of debates over U.S. economic competitiveness also proved crucial to its passage. An article in *Science* discussing the debate on the Bayh-Dole bill observed:

The critics of such legislation, who in the past have railed about the "giveaway of public funds," have grown unusually quiet. The reason seems clear. Industrial innovation has become a buzzword in bureaucratic circles ... the patent transfer

---

[13] Identical legislation (H.R. 2414) was introduced in the House of Representatives by Rep. Peter Rodino (D-NJ) in 1979.

[14] "Another IPA restriction dropped in the Dole-Bayh bill is the requirement that grantees and contractors try first to offer non-exclusive licenses. "It's too hard and inefficient a process," a Bayh aide said. "Universities don't have the financial capability to beat the bushes and try to find someone who is willing to accept a license on a nonexclusive basis" (Henig, 1979, p. 281).

[15] A contemporary account noted that limiting the bill to universities and small businesses was "a tactical exclusion taken to ensure liberal support" (Henig 1979, p. 282). A Senate aide commented, "We'd like to extend [the policy] to everybody ... but if we did the bill would never have a chance of passing" (Broad, 1979b, p. 474). The original bill also included several provisions designed to defuse criticism that it would lead to "profiteering" at the expense of the public interest, including a recoupment provision requiring that institutions pay back a share of licensing income or sales to funding agencies. The final version of the Bayh-Dole Act eliminated this provision, "because there was no agreement on whether the funds would be returned to the agencies or to general revenue, or how the collection and auditing functions would be conducted" and "fears that the costs of the infrastructure required to administer such a program would exceed the amounts collected." See http://www.nih.gov/news/070101wyden.htm.

people have latched onto this issue. It's about time, they say, to cut the red tape that saps the incentive to be inventive. (Broad 1979b, 479)

A number of universities, including Harvard, Stanford, the University of California,[16] and MIT, lobbied for passage of the bill. Witnesses from universities active in patenting (including Stanford, Purdue, and Wisconsin) testified in support of the bill, as did representatives from various university associations (including the American Council on Education, the Society for University Patent Administrators, and the National Association of College and University Business Officers) and the Research Corporation. The prominent role of research universities already active in patenting in supporting passage of the Act highlights the extent to which the Bayh-Dole Act was a response to increased university patenting during the 1970s, rather than an exogenous "cause" of the post-1980 growth in patenting and licensing.

The Bayh-Dole Patent and Trademark Amendments Act of 1980 provided blanket permission for performers of federally funded research to file for patents on the results of such research and to grant licenses for these patents, including exclusive licenses, to other parties. The Act facilitated university patenting and licensing in at least two ways. First, it replaced a web of IPAs that had been negotiated between individual universities and federal agencies with a uniform policy. Second, the Act's provisions were indicative of congressional support for the negotiation of exclusive licenses between universities and industrial firms for the results of federally funded research.

The passage of the Bayh-Dole Act was one part of a broader shift in U.S. policy toward stronger intellectual property rights.[17] Among the most important of these policy initiatives was the establishment of the Court of Appeals for the Federal Circuit (CAFC) in 1982. Established to serve as

---

[16] As Kevles (1994) points out, the University of California also filed an *amicus curiae* brief in the *Diamond v. Chakrabarty* case, in which the U.S. Supreme Court ruled that patents on life forms were valid. Had the Chakrabarty patent not been upheld as valid, the Reimers patenting and licensing strategy for the Cohen-Boyer invention would have been utterly useless. Indeed, much of the post-1980 growth in university licensing rests on an array of other policy initiatives and judicial decisions during the 1980s that strengthened patent-holder rights overall and in such new areas as computer software and biotechnology (see below and Mowery et al., 2004, for further discussion).

[17] According to Katz and Ordover (1990), at least 14 congressional bills passed during the 1980s focused on strengthening domestic and international protection for intellectual property rights, and the Court of Appeals for the Federal Circuit created in 1982 has upheld patent rights in roughly 80% of the cases argued before it, a considerable increase from the pre-1982 rate of 30% for the Federal bench.

the court of final appeal for patent cases throughout the federal judiciary, the CAFC soon emerged as a strong champion of patent-holder rights.[18] But even before the establishment of the CAFC, the 1980 U.S. Supreme Court decision in *Diamond v. Chakrabarty* upheld the validity of a broad patent in the new industry of biotechnology, facilitating the patenting and licensing of inventions in this sector. The effects of Bayh-Dole thus must be viewed in the context of these changes in overall U.S. policy toward intellectual property rights.

11.3.4. The Effects of Bayh-Dole

How did the Bayh-Dole Act affect patenting by U.S. universities? Since overall patenting in the United States grew during this period, indicators of university patenting need to be normalized by overall trends in patenting or R&D spending. Figure 11-1 depicts U.S. research university patenting as a share of domestically assigned U.S. patents during 1963–1999, in order to remove the effects of increased patenting in the United States by foreign firms and inventors during the late twentieth century. Universities increased their share of patenting from less than 0.3 percent in 1963 to nearly 4 percent by 1999, but as I noted earlier, this share began to grow before 1980.

Increased university patenting reflected growth in patenting by institutions with considerable pre-1980 experience in patenting and licensing, as well as entry into this activity by universities with little experience.[19] As Figure 11-2 shows, by 1992, universities that had received ten or more patents during the 1970s accounted for 64 percent of total patenting, down from their share of nearly 85 percent in 1975. Universities with little or no experience in patenting had increased their share from slightly more than 13 percent in 1975 to 36 percent in 1992. Entry by less experienced

---

[18] See Hall and Ziedonis (2001) for an analysis of the effects of the CAFC and related policy shifts on patenting in the U.S. semiconductor industry.

[19] The Bayh-Dole Act did not dramatically affect the patenting and licensing activities of universities that had long been active in this area, such as Stanford University and the University of California. Indeed, the biomedical patents and licenses that dominated these institutions' licensing revenues during the 1980s and 1990s had begun to grow before the passage of the Bayh-Dole Act. Columbia University, an institution with little experience in patenting and licensing before 1980 (and an institution that prohibited the patenting of inventions by medical faculty until 1975), also had filed for its first "blockbuster" patent before the effective date of the act. Nevertheless, the act did increase patenting of faculty inventions at both Stanford and the University of California, although many of these patents covered inventions of marginal industrial value and did not yield significant licensing royalties.

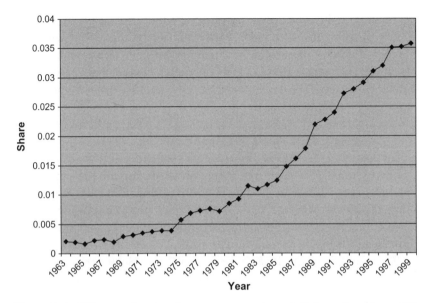

Figure 11-1. U.S. research university patents: percentage of all domestic-assignee U.S. patents, 1963–1999.

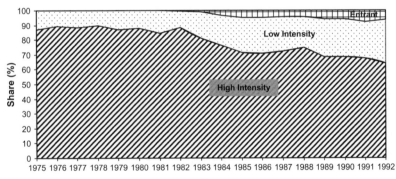

Figure 11-2. Shares of all U.S. university patents by "high intensity," "low intensity," and "entrant" university patenters, 1975–1992.

institutional patentees appears to have affected the quality of university patenting, based on analyses of citations to university patents by other patents (see Henderson et al., 1998a, 1998b; Mowery and Ziedonis, 2002). Although new entrants had narrowed the "quality gap" between their patents and those of experienced institutional patentees by the early 1990s, these effects of entry reflected the need for universities to develop strategies for managing their patenting activities, effectively to "learn to patent." Having initially pursued a rather indiscriminate approach to patenting, a number of entrant universities became more selective in patenting faculty inventions, in many cases doing so only after interest was expressed by potential licensees. The development of more effective licensing programs also required these newly created offices to develop considerable technological, commercial, and legal expertise, all of which relied on hiring specialists who were in very short supply and commanded high salaries.

Another issue of interest in academic patenting is the distribution among technology fields of university patents during the pre- and post–Bayh-Dole periods. Figure 11-3 displays this information for U.S. research university patents during 1960–1999, and highlights the growing importance of biomedical patents in the patenting activities of the leading U.S. universities during the period. Nonbiomedical university patents increased by 90 percent from the 1968–70 period to the 1978–80 period, but biomedical university patents increased by 295 percent. And as was noted earlier, the growth in the share of biomedical technologies in university patenting began in the 1970s, well before the Bayh-Dole Act.

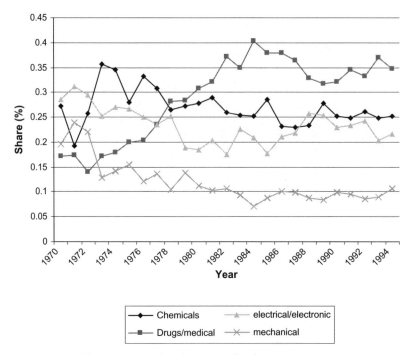

Figure 11-3. University patents by class, 1970–1995.

By 2002, according to the Association of University Technology Managers (2003), gross licensing revenues for all U.S. universities exceeded $1.2 billion. Licensing data from the University of California nine-campus system, Stanford University, and Columbia University, all of which have been ranked among the institutions reaping the highest gross licensing income, show that biomedical patents accounted for more than 66 to 85 percent of the gross licensing revenues of these academic institutions for much of the 1980s and 1990s (Mowery et al., 2004). Even for these relatively successful academic licensors, however, licensing revenues (especially net licensing revenues that flow to the institution) represent a remarkably small share of overall academic operating budgets. To cite only one example, the annual net licensing revenues of the University of California system after deduction of operating expenses and payments to inventors averaged roughly $16 million during fiscal 2001–2004, less than 0.5 percent of the system's annual research expenditures of nearly $3 billion and well below the $235 million in industry-sponsored research at the University of California in fiscal 2003. Inasmuch as the U.C. system reports relatively high gross licensing revenues (averaging nearly $76 million annually during FY2001–2004), it seems likely that the financial contributions to most university operating budgets from patent licensing are modest at best, and negative for a great many institutions. Moreover, these financial inflows appear to be dwarfed by those associated with industry sponsorship of academic research.

Revenues, of course, are not the only motive for university licensing programs. Other important motives include retention of faculty who wish to see their inventions patented and licensed, the transfer of university inventions to commercialization, regional or state-level economic development, and (in the wake of the 2003 *Madey v. Duke* decision of the Court of Appeals for the Federal Circuit, which eliminated the informal "experimental use" defense against claims of patent infringement) the preservation of the freedom of academic scientists to conduct research. This array of potential goals for patenting and licensing activities, however, creates some challenges for management. First, these goals are not entirely compatible – for example, support for regional economic development may entail an acceptance of lower royalty rates on licenses for firms active in the vicinity of the university. Technology licensing thus will involve some trade-offs among these goals. Second, in spite of these trade-offs, as well as the evidence above on the relatively modest scale of net revenues at many university technology licensing offices, a recent survey of technology licensing officers (Thursby et al., 2001) indicates that these individuals cite licensing revenues as the most important goal of their activities.

Another aspect of universities' licensing activities that is relevant to discussions of the role of universities in high-technology entrepreneurship concerns the characteristics of the firms that are licensing university patents. Although many of the positive evaluations of the economic effects of the Bayh-Dole Act highlight the role of small-firm start-ups as beneficiaries of these licensing transactions, the data compiled by the Association of University Technology Managers (AUTM, 2001, 2002) suggest that firms founded specifically to commercialize licensed university technologies account for a minority of licensees. The AUTM annual reports for 2001 and 2002 indicate that 14 to 16 percent of university patent licensees in these years were start-up firms founded to exploit the licensed inventions. More than half (50 to 54%) of academic licensees during this period were small firms (with fewer than 500 employees) already in existence, while roughly a third of licensees were large firms. The emphasis in recent academic research (DiGregorio and Shane, 2003) on the role of university "spinoffs" in the licensing activities of U.S. universities thus needs to be qualified by a recognition that such start-ups account for a much smaller share of university licensing activity than large firms.

The characterizations of the catalytic effects of the Bayh-Dole Act that were mentioned in the Introduction to this chapter cite little evidence in support of their claims beyond simple counts of university patents and licenses. But growth in both university patenting and licensing predates Bayh-Dole and is rooted in internationally unique characteristics of the U.S. higher education system. Nor does evidence of increased patenting and licensing by universities alone indicate that university research discoveries are being transferred to industry more efficiently or commercialized more rapidly, as Mowery et al. (2004) and Colyvas et al. (2002) point out. Current research thus provides mixed support at best for a central assumption of the Bayh-Dole Act, that is, the argument that patenting and licensing are necessary for the transfer and commercial development of university inventions.

11.4. Case Studies of University-Industry Technology Transfer

Additional insight into the actual processes involved in university-industry technology transfer and commercialization is provided by case studies of the transfer and commercialization of patented university inventions that were licensed to firms. These case studies thus do not highlight the other channels of technology transfer discussed earlier in this chapter; but in almost all of the cases, these "nonpatent" channels for interaction and knowledge exchange are important complements to the licensing trans-actions. The case studies also underscore the field-specific and invention-specific differences in the technology transfer process. There is substantial variation across the cases in the importance of patents and licenses, the role of the university, the reputation and involvement of the academic inven-tor, and even the direction and characteristics of the knowledge flows between university and industry.

The five case studies are the following:

- *Cotransformation:* a process to transfer genes into mammalian cells (Columbia University)
- *Gallium nitride:* a semiconductor with both military and commercial applications (University of California)
- *Xalatan:* a glaucoma treatment (Columbia University)
- *Ames II tests:* a bacteria assay for testing potential carcinogenic prop-erties of pharmaceuticals and cosmetics (University of California)
- *Soluble CD4:* a prototype for a drug to fight AIDS (Columbia University).[20]

Previous work on university–industry technology transfer has high-lighted the importance of inventor cooperation in developing embryonic technologies (Jensen and Thursby, 2001) and inventions associated with considerable know-how or tacit knowledge (Lowe, 2001; Shane, 2002). These five cases, however, reveal considerable variety in the role of the university inventor in technology commercialization. In three of the five cases (gallium nitride, the Ames II tests, and soluble CD4), inventor-founded start-up firms played a role in commercialization, and inventors were heavily involved. In the Xalatan case, the efforts of established firms to exploit the university invention were aided by the inventor. In the cotransformation case, by contrast, licensees required no assistance from the inventor, since industrial firms possessed sufficient "absorptive capacity" to exploit the invention as a result of having invested in R&D in similar fields.

Industry R&D investment clearly influenced the transfer and "absorp-tion" by industry of university-generated inventions and knowledge in most

---

[20] See Mowery et al. (2004, chap. 8) for a fuller description and discussion of these five cases. Professor Robert Lowe of Carnegie-Mellon University co-authored the chapter, along with David C. Mowery and Bhaven Sampat.

of these cases. Although the role of R&D investment in the development of firm-specific "absorptive capacity" is widely acknowledged (Cohen and Levinthal, 1990), its consequences for the technology licensing strategies of universities have received less attention. These case studies suggest that the amount and extent of prior industrial R&D activity influences the technology transfer process and can affect the role of patents and licensing. The gallium nitride, cotransformation, and soluble CD4 inventions were exploited by industrial firms that did not license the relevant patents; the university research advances represented important "proofs of concept" that directed well-informed industrial researchers to pursue related research.

In the cotransformation case, firms had the capabilities and incentives to use the invention in the absence of exclusive licenses (or, indeed, in the absence of any formal license at all). In this case, it appears that technology transfer occurred in spite of rather than because of the patents, licenses, and involvement of the university technology transfer office. Columbia's non-exclusive licensing agreements for the cotransformation patent, like the equally renowned (and lucrative) Cohen-Boyer patent jointly licensed by the University of California and Stanford University, do not appear to have accelerated or otherwise made feasible the commercial development of this invention. Instead, these licensing agreements were used by Columbia to levy a tax on the commercialization of an invention that almost certainly would have been commercially developed in the absence of licensing, once the technical information was published.[21]

Industry R&D activities also may affect the academic research agenda, as in the gallium nitride (GaN) case. Much of the early research activity in gallium nitride applications was undertaken within industry in the United States, Europe, and Japan. Sustained university patenting activity began only in the 1990s, nearly two decades after the first industrial patents. Knowledge and technology flowed from industry to the university as well as the reverse, in contrast to the frequent portrayal of this flow as dominated by university–industry knowledge transfers. The GaN case, like that of cotransformation, is one in which patents per se were not essential for university–industry technology transfer. Unlike the Axel cotransformation patents, however, the GaN patents generated little licensing income for the University of California's Santa Barbara campus (UCSB). The contrasting

---

[21] Neils Reimers, the first head of Stanford's Office of Technology Transfer and manager of the licensure of Cohen-Boyer, subsequently noted, "whether we licensed it or not, commercialization of recombinant DNA was going forward. As I mentioned, a nonexclusive licensing program, at its heart, is really a tax ... [b]ut it's always nice to say [technology transfer]" (Reimers, 1998).

licensing history of the GaN and cotransformation patents reflect differences in the level of demand for the technologies they respectively supported, as well as underlying differences in the legal strength and economic value of patents in the biomedical and electronics fields. Another important contrast with the Axel case was the role of the inventors in technology transfer–only when established industrial firms expressed no interest in licensing the GaN patents did the UCSB engineering faculty who had developed these technologies start their own firm. Moreover, this firm did not license the GaN patents, although it was acquired three years after its foundation by another firm that had licensed the GaN patents.

The Xalatan case differs from the cotransformation and GaN cases in that patents were important to the transfer and commercialization of this technology. This invention resembled the "prototypes" discussed by Jensen and Thursby (2001) in that a lengthy and costly period of development was necessary to bring this invention to market. The inventor's know-how and involvement also were indispensible to this development process, in contrast to the cotransformation patents. But the Xalatan case illustrates another challenge for university licensing managers that surfaces in the soluble CD4 case as well. Although a firm may be willing to sign an exclusive licensing agreement with the university (and although most such agreements include "due diligence" or "best efforts" clauses that commit a licensee to invest in the development of an invention), it is difficult for any licensor, let alone an academic licensor, to ensure that a licensee will develop the technology in a timely fashion. The licensee for the Xalatan patents (Pharmacia) was slow to develop the technology, and a combination of rising interest in the technology by other firms and pressure from the inventor and Columbia University were important in revitalizing the licensee's development efforts.

The commercialization of the Ames II tests presents some interesting similarities and contrasts with the GaN and Xalatan cases. Like GaN and Xalatan, inventor involvement in development and commercialization was important and reflected the importance of tacit know-how for the inventions' applications. It seems likely that without the participation of the inventor, a license alone would not have sufficed to commercialize the Ames II tests. But in contrast to GaN, patent protection and an exclusive license for the invention aided the start-up firm/licensee that undertook commercial development to obtain venture-capital financing.

The CD4 case illustrates the commercial and technical uncertainties involved in bringing an embryonic invention, even one that appears to have great commercial potential, from laboratory to marketplace. This case also provides some evidence that exclusive licenses may not be necessary, even for embryonic inventions, if their potential profitability is sufficiently large and downstream innovations can themselves be patented. Moreover, the case highlights the risks associated with exclusive licensing agreements for such innovations, since it is often difficult for licensing professionals to determine which of several potential licensees (in the rare cases in which several firms are interested in licenses to the invention) is most likely to bring the invention to market successfully. Finally, this case (like the cotransformation case) suggests that in contexts where firms have strong links with the relevant scientific and technological communities, inventor involvement may be less critical for commercialization.

A central premise underpinning the Bayh-Dole Act is the belief that patenting and licensing are necessary to facilitate the development and commercialization of publicly funded university inventions. Although the act does not mandate that universities follow any single specific policy in patenting and licensing faculty inventions, university administrators and technology licensing officers frequently assume that the technology transfer process is essentially similar for all technologies and industries. But these case studies reveal considerable heterogeneity within even a small sample of technologies. There are significant differences among these cases in the role of intellectual property rights in inducing firms to develop and commercialize university inventions, in the role of the inventor in post-license development and commercialization, and in the relationship between academic and industrial research activities in different technical fields. University technology licensing offices should develop more flexible licensing policies that can accommodate these interindustry differences in the role of patents.[22]

The nature of feedback between industrial and academic research differs among these cases. Bayh-Dole was implicitly based on an assumption of a "linear model" of innovation, in which universities perform basic research with little concern for application and private firms invest in applied

---

[22] Recent initiatives within the technology licensing programs at the University of California represent one effort to develop such "differentiated" policies. In 2000, the U.C. President's Office authorized the negotiation of royalty-free licenses with industrial sponsors of campus research in electrical engineering and computer science (University of California Office of the President, 2002). Another reflection of the changing priority assigned to licensing royalties relative to other goals at U.C. Berkeley is the "socially responsible licensing initiative," which negotiates royalty-free licenses on inventions sold in low-income economies. Although promising, these initiatives could prove to be very difficult to manage. For example, intellectual property resulting from industrially sponsored research is likely to be difficult to separate from the results of publicly funded research in many university laboratories.

research and commercialization. In this view, patent-based incentives are essential to link universities, inventors, and industry in the commercialization process. But this assumption does not accurately describe university–industry interactions, before or after Bayh-Dole, in many technical fields. In most of the cases discussed in this chapter, there was considerable overlap between the scientific and industrial communities in the nature of research activities (including publication). Consistent with the work of Zucker, Darby, and colleagues on biotechnology (Zucker and Darby, 1998; Zucker et al., 2002), as well as the survey evidence discussed earlier in this paper, these cases show that technology transfer from universities to firms operates through a range of channels, including labor mobility and research collaboration. There is also little evidence of significant delays in the disclosure or publication by academic researchers of their research advances. All of these inventions were the subject of published papers, and in a majority of the cases the publications appeared before patent applications were filed.

These case studies do suggest that patents may be important for start-up firms in their search for financing. Consistent with previous studies, the evidence from this small sample of cases suggests that university patenting and licensing were more important for the biomedical inventions than for the electronics inventions included. But there is considerable heterogeneity in the technology transfer process within the biomedical field, further underscoring the importance of flexibility in the management of licensing policies.

11.5. Industry Criticism of U.S. University Licensing Policies

Our 2004 monograph on the Bayh-Dole Act and U.S. university–industry technology transfer argued that university patenting and licensing could well become a "source of friction" rather than a facilitator for university–industry research collaboration. Recent criticisms of university licensing policies by a number of U.S. firms suggest that such frictions have indeed increased. Much of this criticism has come from established firms in fields such as information technology, including firms with histories of collaboration with university researchers. A senior R&D manager from Hewlett Packard, a U.S. firm with long-established ties with faculty at many U.S. universities, stated in testimony before the U.S. Senate Commerce Committee's Subcommittee on Science, Technology and Space that

largely as a result of the lack of federal funding for research, American Universities have become extremely aggressive in their attempts to raise funding from large corporations .... Large US based corporations have become so disheartened and

disgusted with the situation they are now working with foreign universities, especially the elite institutions in France, Russia and China, which are more than
willing to offer extremely favorable intellectual property terms. (Testimony of R.
Stanley Williams, September 17, 2002; statement reproduced at http://www.me-
magazine.org/contents/current/webonly/webex319.html; accessed April 2, 2005)

Although biomedical firms have been less prominent critics, the NIH
Director's Working Group on Research Tools stated in its 1998 report that

if there was one point on which virtually every private firm that we spoke to was in
agreement, it was that universities take inconsistent positions on fair terms of
access to research tools depending on whether they are importing tools or export-
ing them. Over and over again, firms complained to us that universities "wear the
mortarboard" when they seek access to tools developed by others, yet they impose
the same sorts of restrictions when they enter into agreements to give firms access
to their own tools. As one lawyer for a small biotechnology firm put it, "Universities want it both ways. They want to be commercial institutions when it comes
to licensing their technology, but to be academic environments when it comes to
accessing technology that others have developed . . . . They throw the same things
in the way of small companies." (National Institutes of Health, 1998, p. 15)

A more sweeping (and arguably exaggerated) assessment was presented
at a 2003 conference organized by the Government University Industry
Research Roundtable at the National Academy of Sciences:

the universities' approach of securing iron-clad protection for intellectual property
seems to be yielding diminishing returns, even within the narrow confines of the
licensing activity itself . . . . The requisite legal negotiations for IP-that-will-ulti-
mately-prove-to-be-useless are laborious, individualized and negotiated between
universities and companies on a case-by-case basis. The up-front legal negotiations
can easily cost more than the total cost of the research project being conducted,
and/or extend past the time when the company has interest in the technology path
being pursued . . . . In summary, the uncertainty of the true value of university-
generated intellectual property, combined with a litigious culture, have combined
to make the university-industry working relationship – one that has historically
contributed greatly to graduate education – unaffordable and nearly unsustainable
within the U.S. (Government University Industry Research Roundtable, 1991, p. 2)

These criticisms have triggered considerable discussion among large
industrial firms (many of which are in the information technology sector)
and U.S. research universities over licensing policies. In December 2005,
four large IT firms (Cisco, Hewlett Packard, IBM, and Intel) and six
universities (Carnegie Mellon, Rensselaer Polytechnic, UC Berkeley, Stanford, University of Illinois at Champaign-Urbana, and University of
Texas-Austin) agreed on a "statement of principles" for collaborative
research on open-source software that emphasizes liberal dissemination

of the results of collaborative work funded by industrial firms.[23] The Government University Industry Research Roundtable conference mentioned earlier is one of a series of meetings involving industrial firms, the Industrial Research Institute (representing R&D directors of large U.S. firms), and the National Conference of University Research Administrators that produced a set of principles for patent and licensing policies at the "Re-engineering the Partnership" Conference, held in April 2006.

Most of the tensions that have received considerable press and some attention from policymakers involve relationships between established firms and universities – indeed, in some respects, the economic interests of established firms with large patent portfolios may differ from those of small start-up firms that are owners or licensees of far fewer patents. Moreover, the industrial critics of universities are largely firms outside the biomedical sector, reflecting the fact that the value of individual patents in industries such as information technology typically is lower than is true of biomedical research. Nevertheless, the current controversies and discussions among U.S. industrial firms (some of which, as was noted earlier, contrast U.S. university Intellectual Property (IP) rights policies unfavorably with those of universities outside the United States) and U.S. research universities may result in a rethinking by universities of the role of patents in collaborative research relationships with U.S. industry.[24] The evidence cited earlier on the relative magnitude of industry-sponsored research and net licensing revenues suggests that "royalty-maximizing" policies may serve universities poorly in relationships with established firms in sectors such as information technology.

---

[23] The "Open Collaboration Principles" cover "just one type of formal collaboration that can be used when appropriate and will co-exist with other models, such as sponsored research, consortia and other types of university/industry collaborations, where the results are intended to be proprietary or publicly disseminated." According to the "Principles," "The intellectual property created in the collaboration [between industry and academic researchers] must be made available for commercial and academic use by every member of the public free of charge for use in open source software, software related industry standards, software interoperability and other publicly available programs as may be agreed to be the collaborating parties" (http://www.kauffman.org/pdf/open_collaboration_principles_12_05.pdf; accessed February 20, 2006). These principles originated in an August 2005 "University and Industry Innovation Summit" in Washington, D.C., organized by the Kauffman Foundation of Kansas City and IBM (http://www.kauffman.org/items.cfm?itemID=662; accessed February 20, 2006).

[24] The critical comments of Dr. Williams of Hewlett-Packard also raise the prospect of competition for industry research collaboration between U.S. and non-U.S. universities, especially for industrial firms with global operations.

11.6. International "Emulation" of the Bayh-Dole Act

The evidence discussed in this chapter suggests that the "catalytic" effects of the Bayh-Dole Act itself on university-industry technology transfer in the United States have been overstated. Nevertheless, a number of other industrial-economy governments are considering or have adopted policies emulating the act's provisions.[25] But many of the discussions by OECD governments on the desirability of "Bayh-Dole type" policies reveal little awareness of the research discussed above that highlights the variety of channels through which universities contribute to innovation and economic growth. The "emulation" of Bayh-Dole in other industrial economies also tends to overlook the importance and effects on university–industry collaboration and technology transfer of the many other institutions that support these interactions and the commercialization of university technologies in the United States.

In Denmark, a 1999 law gave public research organizations, including universities, the rights to all inventions funded by the Ministry for Research and Technology. Under Denmark's previous policy (established in 1957), all such rights had reverted to employees (OECD, 2003). The German Ministry for Science and Education in 2002 altered the "professor's privilege," which gave academic researchers primary responsibility for the decision to file for patent protection on inventions and granted them the rights to any resulting patents. The new policy requires that academic inventors inform their employers of potentially patentable inventions two months before papers disclosing such inventions are submitted for publication, and grants universities four months to determine whether they wish to file for patent protection.[26] In France, a 1999 law authorized the creation of technology transfer offices at universities, and in 2001 the Ministry of Research "recommended" that universities and public research organizations establish policies to assert their rights to employee inventions (OECD, 2003). The Canadian Prime Minister's "Expert Panel on the Commercialization of University Research" recommended in 1999 that universities retain ownership of inventions resulting from publicly funded research and "be held accountable for

---

[25] A recent OECD report (2000) argues that these initiatives "echo the landmark Bayh-Dole Act of 1980" (11).

[26] The new policy aims to ensure that "more inventions are brought to patent offices before they get published" and "is supposed to lead to active licensing transfer from university to industry and to more companies being founded on the basis of intellectual property conceived within the university environment" (Kilger and Bartenbach, 2002).

maximizing returns to Canada," noting that "the proposed IP policy framework will inspire a transformational shift in culture within Canadian universities, as happened in the United States with the passage of the Bayh-Dole Act in 1980" (Public Investments in University Research, p. 28).[27]

In addition to changes in intellectual property policy and employment regulations, a number of related initiatives aim to stimulate the organization and activity of technology licensing offices. Thus the Swedish, German, and Japanese governments (among others) have encouraged the formation of external "technology licensing organizations," which may or may not be affiliated with a given university (see Goldfarb and Henrekson, 2003, for a comparison of Bayh-Dole and Swedish initiatives to enhance university–industry technology transfer).

As this discussion suggests, these initiatives differ from one another and from Bayh-Dole itself. The policy proposals and initiatives represent a selective "borrowing" from another nation's policies for implementation in an institutional context that differs significantly from that of the nation being emulated. Nonetheless, these initiatives are based on the belief that university patenting was an essential vehicle for effective transfer of technology from universities to industry and that Bayh-Dole was essential to the growth of university–industry interaction in science-based industries in the United States during and after the 1980s. They focus narrowly on the "deliverable" outputs of university research, and ignore the effects of patenting and licensing on other channels through which universities contribute to innovation and economic growth.

But if patenting and licensing are indeed of secondary importance as channels for technology transfer and research collaboration in many industries, emulation of the Bayh-Dole Act alone is insufficient and perhaps even unnecessary to stimulate higher levels of university–industry interaction and technology transfer. Instead, reforms to enhance research funding, inter-institutional competition, and autonomy within national university systems appear to be more important. In addition, of course, factors external to the university, such as high levels of labor mobility between industry and academia and venture-capital financing for new firms, have contributed significantly to the role of U.S. universities in spawning new high-technology firms.

---

[27] Although no uniform government policy governs the treatment of university inventions in the United Kingdom, "there is now an increasing trend for Universities to claim ownership" over academic inventions (Christie et al., 2003, p. 71).

Indeed, emulation of Bayh-Dole could be counterproductive in other industrial economies, precisely because of the importance of other channels for technology transfer and exploitation by industry. A narrowminded focus on licensing as the primary or only channel for technology transfer can have a chilling effect on the operation of other important channels, as well as heightening tensions with industry, rather than facilitating collaboration. There are potential risks to the university research enterprise that accompany increased involvement by university administrators and faculty in technology licensing and commercialization, and uncritical emulation of Bayh-Dole in a very different institutional context could intensify these risks.

11.7. Conclusion

Academic entrepreneurship, utilizing the human capital of university faculty and researchers in commercial development of their inventions, has been a unique and significant characteristic of the U.S. higher education system for most of the past 100 years. As noted earlier in this chapter, engagement of U.S. academic personnel in quasi-commercial pursuits reflected a longstanding history of collaborative research between university faculty and industry, as well as the unusual structural characteristics of the U.S. "system" of higher education that created strong incentives for faculty and administrators to seek both financial support and links with industry. Moreover, much of this entrepreneurial activity involved patenting of university inventions and, in some cases, their licensure to industrial firms. This long history of interaction, as well as academic patenting and licensing, contributed to the formation of the political coalitions that led to the passage of the Bayh-Dole Act in 1980.

The entrepreneurial activities of university faculty and the contributions of university research to new-firm formation rely on a much broader array of mechanisms and channels than patenting and licensing alone. Moreover, the growth after 1980 in academic patenting and licensing since 1980 reflects many influences in addition to the Bayh-Dole Act, and much of this growth almost certainly would have occurred in the absence of the act. Indeed, the occasional tendency of university administrators to elevate patenting and licensing to a central position in the processes that mediate the two-way flows of knowledge and technology between universities and industry distorts these relationships and may impede their effectiveness. A substantial body of research suggests that industry and academic researchers interact and exchange knowledge through a diverse array of channels, among which patenting and licensing is but one and in most sectors far from the most important one. As the data discussed earlier in this chapter on academic patenting, licensing, and licensing revenues suggest, however, the biomedical sector is different, and patents appear to be especially important channels for technology transfer. Nevertheless, the case studies summarized in this chapter highlight considerable variation in the importance of patents and licenses even within the biomedical sector.

In spite of the dramatic growth in the literature on this topic, research on "academic entrepreneurship" and technology transfer between universities and industry still lacks an integrated analysis of the various channels through which these processes operate. We know very little, for example, about the interactions among academic patenting, licensing agreements, and flows of personnel between universities and industry. We lack empirical data or analyses on the links between industry-funded research within universities and the operation of different channels of technology transfer between industry and academia.

A richer analysis of the multiple channels of interaction between industry and university research might also support a more balanced approach to managing these interactions by both industrial managers and university researchers. Recent initiatives at the University of California, Berkeley, and Stanford to establish offices of "industrial partnership" that work with campus licensing offices are examples of policies that strengthen an integrated approach by universities to management of multiple channels for university–industry interaction and collaboration that can more effectively balance the competing goals within these programs.[28] Interestingly, however, these efforts to encourage "alliances" or "partnerships" with industrial firms are likely to focus more on established than on start-up firms. This "balancing act" thus has interesting implications for universities' encouragement of linkages with new as well as established firms.

---

[28] The Director of Stanford's Office of Technology Licensing also is in charge of the university's "Industrial Contracts Office," which manages sponsored-research agreements with industry, as well as overseeing materials transfer agreements (MTAs), which govern the transfer among researchers of research tools and materials. Industrial firms supporting campus research can receive licenses (in some cases, royalty-free licenses) to the results of this research. A similar trade-off between maximizing licensing revenues and obtaining industry research funding is apparent in the creation in 2003 of the "Intellectual Property and Industry Research Alliances" office at U.C. Berkeley's licensing office, which absorbed the established Office of Technology Licensing and a new "Industry Alliances Office," charged with overseeing the negotiation of sponsored-research agreements with industry.

References

American Medical Association. 1937. *Principles of Medical Ethics.*

Association of University Technology Managers. 2001. *AUTM Licensing Survey, FY 2001.* Northbrook, Ill.: Association of University Technology Managers.

Association of University Technology Managers. 2002. *AUTM Licensing Survey, FY 2002.* Northbrook, Ill.: Association of University Technology Managers.

Barrett, Paul. 1980. "Harvard Fears Congress May Not Pass Patent Bill." *Harvard Crimson*, October 7.

Broad, William. 1979a. "Patent Bill Returns Bright Idea to Inventor (in News and Comment)."*Science* (August 3), 473–476.

Broad, William. 1979b. "Whistle Blower Reinstated at HEW." *Science*, 476.

Christie, Katerina L. Gaita, Melanie J. Howlett, and Elisabeth M. Webster. 2003. "Analysis of the Legal Framework for Patent Ownership in Publicly Funded Research Institutions." Commonwealth of Australia, Division of Education, Science, and Training.

Cohen, Wesley M., and Daniel A. Levinthal. 1990. "Absorptive Capacity: A New Perspective on Learning and Innovation." *Administrative Science Quarterly*, 35, 128–152.

Cohen, Wesley M., Richard Florida, Lucien Randazzese, and John Walsh. 1998. "Industry and the Academy: Uneasy Partners in the Cause of Technological Advance." In R. Noll (ed.), *Challenges to the Research University.* Washington, D.C.: Brookings Institution.

Cohen, Wesley M., Richard R. Nelson, and John Walsh. 2002. "Links and Impacts: The Influence of Public Research on Industrial R&D." *Management Science*, 48, 1–23.

Columbia University Committee on Patents. August 1974. "Patent Policy." Columbiana Archives, "Patents" Folder, Columbia University in the City of New York.

Colyvas, Jeannette, Michael Crow, Anettine Gelijns, Robert Mazzoleni, Richard R. Nelson, Nathan Rosenberg, and Bhaven N. Sampat. 2002. "How Do University Inventions Get into Practice?" *Management Science*, 48, 61–72.

Cooke, Robert. 2001. *Dr. Folkman's War: Angiogenesis and the Struggle to Defeat Cancer.* New York: Random House.

Cottrell, F. 1932. "Patent Experience of the Research Corporation." Transactions of the American Institute of Chemical Engineers.

Dertouzos, Michael, Richard Lester, and Robert M. Solow. 1989. *Made in America.* Cambridge: MIT Press.

DiGregorio, Dante, and Scott Shane. 2003. "Why Do Some Universities Generate More Start-ups Than Others?" *Research Policy*, 32, 209–227.

Eisenberg, Rebecca S. 1996. "Public Research and Private Development: Patents and Technology Transfer in Government-Sponsored Research." *Virginia Law Review*, 1663–1727.

Eskridge, N. 1978. "Dole Blasts HEW for 'Stonewalling' Patent Applications." *Bioscience*, 605–606.

Etzkowitz, Henry. 1994. "Knowledge as Property: The Massachusetts Institute of Technology and the Debate of Academic Patent Policy." *Minerva*, 32(Winter), 383–421.

Federal Council on Science and Technology (FCST). 1978. Report on Government Patent Policy, 1973–1976. Washington, D.C.: U.S. Government Printing Office.

Geiger, Roger L. 1986. *To Advance Knowledge: The Growth of American Research Universities, 1900–1940.* New York: Oxford University Press.

Geiger, Roger L. 1993. *Research and Relevant Knowledge: American Research Universities since World War II.* New York: Oxford University Press.

Geiger, Roger L. 2004. *Knowledge and Money: Research Universities and the Paradox of the Marketplace.* Stanford: Stanford University Press.

Goldfarb, Brent, and Magnus Henrekson. 2003. "Bottom-Up versus Top-Down Policies Towards the Commercialization of University Intellectual Property." *Research Policy*, 32(4), 639–658.

Government University Industry Research Roundtable (GUIRR). 1991. *Industrial Perspectives on Innovation and Interactions with Universities.* Washington, D.C.: National Academy Press.

Graham, Hugh D., and Nancy Diamond. 1997. *The Rise of American Research Universities.* Baltimore: Johns Hopkins University Press.

Hall, Bronwyn H., and Rosemarie H. Ziedonis. 2001. "The Patent Paradox Revisited: An Empirical Study of Patenting in the U.S. Semiconductor Industry, 1979–1995." *RAND Journal of Economics*, 32, 101–128.

Harbridge House. 1968a. "Effects of Patent Policy on Government R&D Programs." Government Patent Policy Study, Final Report., vol. II. Washington, D.C.: Federal Council for Science and Technology.

Harbridge House. 1968b. "Effects of Government Policy on Commercial Utilization and Business Competition."Government Patent Policy Study, Final Report, vol. IV. Washington, D.C.: Federal Council for Science and Technology.

Henderson, Rebecca, Adam B. Jaffe, and Manuel Trajtenberg. 1998a. "Universities as a Source of Commercial Technology: A Detailed Analysis of University Patenting, 1965–1988." *Review of Economics & Statistics*, 80(1), 119–127.

Henderson, Rebecca, Adam B. Jaffe, and Manuel Trajtenberg. 1998b. "University Patenting Amid Changing Incentives for Commercialization." In *Creation and Transfer of Knowledge*, G. Barba Navaretti, P. Dasgupta, K. G. Mäler, and D. Siniscalco, eds. New York: Springer.

Henig, R. 1979. "New Patent Policy Bill Gathers Congressional Support." *Bioscience*, 29, 281–284.

Hughes, Sally S. 2001. "Making Dollars out of DNA." *Isis*, 92, 541–575.

"Innovation's Golden Goose." 2002. *The Economist,* December 12.

Jensen, Richard, and Marie Thursby. 2001. "Proofs and Prototypes for Sale: The Licensing of University Inventions." *American Economic Review*, 91, 240–258.

Katz, Michael L., and J. A. Ordover. 1990. "R&D Competition and Cooperation." *Brookings Papers on Economic Activity: Microeconomics, 137–192.*

Kenney, Martin. 1986. *Biotechnology: The University-Industry Complex.* New Haven: Yale University Press.

Kevles, Daniel. 1994. "Ananda Chakrabarty Wins a Patent: Biotechnology, Law, and Society, 1973–1980." *Historical Studies in the Physical Sciences*, 25, 111–135.

Kilger, Christian, and Kurt Bartenbach. 2002. "New Rules for German Professors." *Science*, 298, 1173–1175.

Leslie, Stuart. 1993. *The Cold War and American Science.* New York: Columbia University Press.

Levin, Richard C., Alvin K. Klevorick, Richard R. Nelson, and Sidney G. Winter. 1987. "Appropriating the Returns from Industrial Research and Development." *Brookings Papers on Economic Activity*, 3, 783–820.

Lowe, Robert A. 2001. "The Role and Experience of Start-Ups in Commercializing University Inventions: Start-up Licensees at the University of California." In G. Libecap, ed., *Entrepreneurial Inputs and Outcomes*. Amsterdam: JAI Press.

Mansfield, E. 1991. "Academic Research and Industrial Innovations." *Research Policy*, 20, 1–12.

Mowery, David C. 1999. "America's Industrial Resurgence (?): An Overview." In D. C. Mowery, ed., *U.S. Industry in 2000: Studies in Competitive Performance*. Washington, D.C.: National Academies Press.

Mowery, David C., and Nathan Rosenberg. 1998. *Paths of Innovation: Technological Change in 20th-Century America*. Cambridge: Cambridge University Press.

Mowery, David C., and Bhaven N. Sampat. 2001a. "Patenting and Licensing University Inventions: Lessons from the History of the Research Corporation." *Industrial and Corporate Change*, 10, 317–355.

Mowery, David C., and Bhaven N. Sampat. 2001b. "University Patents, Patent Policies, and Patent Policy Debates, 1925–1980."*Industrial and Corporate Change*, 10, 781–814.

Mowery, David C., and Bhaven N. Sampat. 2004. "The Bayh-Dole Act of 1980 and University-Industry Technology Transfer: A Model for Other OECD Governments?" *Journal of Technology Transfer*, 30(1–2), 115–127.

Mowery, David C., and Arvids Ziedonis. 2002. "Academic Patent Quality and Quantity Before and After the Bayh-Dole Act in the United States." *Research Policy*, 31(3), 399–418.

Mowery, David C., Richard R. Nelson, Bhaven N. Sampat, and Arvids Ziedonis. 2004. *Ivory Tower and Industrial Innovation*. Stanford, Calif.: Stanford University Press.

National Science Board. 2002. *Science and Engineering Indicators: 2002*. Washington, D.C.: U.S. Government Printing Office.

OECD. 2000. *A New Economy? The Changing Role of Innovation and Information Technology in Growth*. Paris.

Palmer, Archie M. 1957. *Medical Patents*. Washington, D.C.: National Research Council.

Reimers, Niels. 1998. *Stanford's Office of Technology Licensing and the Cohen/Boyer Cloning Patents, An Oral History Conducted in 1997 by Sally Smith Hughes, Ph.D., Regional Oral History Office*. Berkeley, Calif.: Bancroft Library.

Research Corporation. 1974–1975. *Annual Report*. New York and Tucson, Arizona.

Rosenberg, Nathan, and Richard R. Nelson. 1994. "American Universities and Technical Advance in Industry." *Research Policy*, 23, 323–348.

Shane, Scott. 2002. "Selling University Technology." *Management Science*, 48, 61–72.

Stevens, Ashley J. 2004. "The Enactment of Bayh-Dole." *Journal of Technology Transfer*, 29, 93–99.

Thursby, Jerry, Richard Jensen, and Marie C. Thursby. 2001. "Objectives, Characteristics and Outcomes of University Licensing: A Survey of Major U.S. Universities." *Journal of Technology Transfer*, 26, 59–72.

Trow, M. 1979. "Aspects of Diversity in American Higher Education." In H. Gans (ed.), *On the Making of Americans*. Philadelphia: University of Pennsylvania Press.

Trow, M. 1991. "American Higher Education: 'Exceptional' or Just Different?" In B. E. Shafer (ed.), *Is America Different? A New Look at American Exceptionalism.* New York: Oxford University Press.

University of California Office of the President. 2002. *5 Years of Progress: A Summary Report on the Results of the 1997 President's Retreat on the University of California's Relationships with Industry in Research and Technology Transfer.* Oakland: University of California Office of the President.

U.S. General Accounting Office. 1968. *Problem Areas Affecting Usefulness of Results of Government-Sponsored Research in Medicinal Chemistry: A Report to the Congress.* Washington, D.C.: U.S. Government Printing Office.

U.S. House of Representatives. 1980. "Floor Debate on H.R. 6933."*Congressional Record*, November 21, 1980: 30556–30560.

U.S. Senate, Committee on the Judiciary. 1979. *The University and Small Business Patent Procedures Act: Hearings on S. 414, May 16 and June 6. 96th Congress, 1st Session.* Washington, D.C.: U.S. Government Printing Office.

Weiner, Charles. 1989. "Patenting and Academic Research: Historical Case Studies." In V. Weil and J.W. Snapper (eds.), *Owning Scientific and Technical Information.* New Brunswick, N.J.: Rutgers University Press.

Weissman, Robert. 1989. "Public Finance, Private Gain: The Emerging University-Business-Government Alliance and the New U.S. Technological Order." Harvard University Undergraduate Thesis.

Zucker, Lynn G., and Michael R. Darby. 1998. "Intellectual Human Capital and the Birth of U.S. Biotechnology Enterprises." *American Economic Review*, 88, 290–306.

Zucker, Lynn G., Michael R. Darby, and Maximo Torero. 2002. "Labor Mobility from Academe to Commerce." *Journal of Labor Economics*, 20, 629–660.

12

Academic Entrepreneurship in Europe

A Different Perspective

Mirjam van Praag

12.1. Introduction

In principle, the academic world can foster entrepreneurship in two manners. First, as advocated in Chapter 8, faculty and doctoral candidates working in specific academic disciplines, such as technical, computer, or medical sciences, can commercialize their research results, for instance as entrepreneurs. The second manner is much less studied. It comes down to creating awareness of entrepreneurial opportunities and teaching the needed skills to students, which is the topic of this chapter.

In Section 12.2, I illustrate why entrepreneurship is to be stimulated in schools, in particular in Europe. I then show, based on economic theory (Section 12.3) and recent empirical evidence (Section 12.4) that the returns to education are very high for entrepreneurs, relative to employees. This leads, under some assumptions, to specific policy and research implications (Section 12.5). The bottom line of these implication, is that entrepreneurship can best be stimulated at institutions of higher education, that is, universities. Therefore, entrepreneurship education and awareness programs, in whatever form, should become part of academic curricula. Experiments to determine which sorts of programs are effective should be made possible by university administrators and stimulated by public policymakers. Moreover, novel research is required to determine which types of schools and universities should stimulate entrepreneurship, and which particular entrepreneurial competencies should be taught at what stage of the educational system.

12.2. Why Stimulate Entrepreneurship in Schools, Particularly in Europe?

12.2.1. Entrepreneurship Has Economic Value

Historically, philosophers of science did not hold entrepreneurs in high esteem. It was assumed that they did not enhance society's well-being. Making a profit, the economic definition of the pecuniary return to entrepreneurship, was perceived as robbery ever since Aristotle introduced the persistent idea that economic activity is a zero-sum game where one man's gain is another man's loss.

Today, however, most economists, practitioners of other behavioral sciences, and politicians readily admit the importance of the entrepreneur's role in society. Keeping consistent with Chapter 1's delineation, I define an entrepreneur as an individual who has started up a business, who is self-employed, or who is the owner-manager of an incorporated business, discovering and implementing new opportunities. This prosaic definition deviates from the definitions that theorists provide, especially those who do not base their theories on formal modeling. To them, entrepreneurs are the people who move borders and push boundaries, the ones who are passionate and who swim against the tide of the society in which they are living. However, it is difficult to perform valuable empirical research about entrepreneurship based on such an unquantifiable definition of the entrepreneur.

Entrepreneurs, that is, the business owners and establishers of new firms, are held responsible for economic development, by introducing and implementing innovative ideas or, in Schumpeter's terms *neue Kombinationen* (Schumpeter, 1943). These new combinations include product innovation, process innovation, market innovation, and organizational innovation. Their successful implementation, initiated by entrepreneurs, gives rise to the satisfaction of (new) consumer wants and the creation of firms. The created firms engender economic growth and supply jobs for the working population (see Chapter 6). Hence, by stimulating both a product market and a labor market, entrepreneurs can be given credit for a considerable contribution to the economy. These positive economic consequences justify stimulating successful entrepreneurship by means of public and private policy measures.

12.2.2. Stimulating Entrepreneurship Is Especially Relevant for Europe

In 2005, the European Commission proposed a new start for the Lisbon Strategy focusing the European Union's efforts on two principal tasks: delivering stronger, lasting growth while providing more and better jobs. The new "Partnership for Growth and Jobs" stresses the importance of promoting a more entrepreneurial culture and of creating a supportive environment for SMEs. If Europe wants to maintain or improve its position in the ranking of countries that offer favorable environments for enterprises, it needs more economic growth, more new firms, and more entrepreneurs willing to embark on innovative ventures, thus creating more high-growth SMEs. Therefore, a more favorable societal climate for entrepreneurship needs to be created, not only changing the mindset toward entrepreneurship, but also improving the skills of Europeans and removing obstacles to the start-up, transfer, and growth of businesses.

12.2.3. The European Commission: Create an Entrepreneurial Culture through Education

In 2004, the European Commission adopted a so-called Entrepreneurship Action Plan to create a supportive framework for entrepreneurship policy (Commission of the European Communities, 2006). While various factors influence entrepreneurship, cultural aspects need to be taken into account; in general, Europeans are reluctant to take up opportunities for self-employment and entrepreneurship.

For instance, in the Netherlands, one rarely hears of university students who wish to become entrepreneurs, neither immediately after completing their studies nor later in life. Most students want to work for large companies such as Unilever and Shell. Only 9 percent of students at Dutch institutions of higher education express interest in becoming an entrepreneur (www.jongondernemen.nl/backend/docs/files/129/website/). This percentage ranks low not only in an international comparison, but also when compared with lower level students in the Netherlands.

Therefore cultural support through education and promotional campaigns should stimulate the amount of entrepreneurial activity in the European Union. Traditionally, formal education in Europe has not been conducive to entrepreneurship. However, as attitudes and cultural references take shape at an early age, the education systems can greatly contribute to successfully addressing the entrepreneurial challenge within the EU. Therefore, the European Commission focuses on policy measures to give greater attention to entrepreneurship in education from primary school to university (Commission of the European Communities, 2006).

12.2.4. At What Stage of Education Should Entrepreneurial Mindsets be Encouraged?

Given the desirability of improving the European entrepreneurial climate through the educational system, the question rapidly arises: In what stage of the educational system should the entrepreneurial mindset be stimulated and developed such that the net benefits are greatest?

Devoting resources to encouraging entrepreneurship is most efficient for groups of students or pupils who have relatively high probabilities of being successful as entrepreneurs, for not all entrepreneurs are successful. Many fail: they never hire employees; they never turn a profit; their ventures fail to survive the first period at all; or they go bankrupt. There are the private, psychological and social costs pertaining to unsuccessful entrepreneurship. Thus it is important that entrepreneurial attitudes and skills that mitigate these costs be developed in schools, targeting the greatest possible number of students who have the potential to become successful entrepreneurs. Economic theory and evidence of the returns to education for entrepreneurs indicate that one can locate these groups of students or pupils in terms of the level of the educational system.

12.3. Economic Theory about the Returns to Education for Entrepreneurs

12.3.1. Human Capital Theory

Human capital theory proposes that previous knowledge plays a critical role in intellectual performance. Previous knowledge, embodied in an individual over time, becomes human capital, which assists in the integration and accumulation of new knowledge as well as the integration and adaptation to new situations (Weick, 1996). Knowledge is defined as either tacit or explicit. Tacit knowledge refers to "know how," or the noncodified components of a given activity (Davidsson and Honig, 2003). Explicit knowledge, on the contrary, refers to "know what" and is conveyed in procedures and processes and in institutions such as schools and universities.

According to human capital theory based on the Mincerian specification of the determinants of individual earnings, the main factors that determine earnings are education and experience (Mincer, 1974). Though the empirical validity of human capital theory has mostly been established on the subset of employed labor market participants, there is, a priori, no reason to believe that the same relationship would not hold for the entrepreneurial sector of the labor market. As Davidsson and Honig (2003) indeed assert, solving complex problems and making entrepreneurial decisions utilizes, among others, an interaction of both tacit and explicit knowledge.

12.3.2. "Screening" Theories

The accumulation of human capital, for instance by means of schooling, is not only acknowledged for its productive effect on the quality or quantity of labor supplied, as posited by human capital theory, it also has value as a signal of productive ability in labor markets without complete information (Spence, 1973; Wolpin, 1977; Riley, 2002). In signaling, the party with private information – that is, the employee in the selection and hiring process by employers – takes the lead in adopting behavior that, on appropriate examination, reveals information about his or her own type of productivity. The question is whether the existence of a signaling effect next to a productive effect of education is as likely for entrepreneurs as for employees.

Many of the empirical tests devised to quantify the signaling effect of education for employees (Wolpin, 1977) assume that entrepreneurs do not have a prospective employer and can therefore be treated as an unscreened control group. Such empirical tests would show evidence of the screening theory if the returns to education for employees were at least as high as those for entrepreneurs. However, I question the assumption that such a signal is useless for entrepreneurs, for at least two reasons. First, when acquiring education, the future entrepreneur might invest in it, since he or she intends to be employed first. Second, there might be substantial screening from prospective capital suppliers, customers, and other stakeholders. Education is then used as a signal to these clients and capital suppliers. The economic returns to education could thus very well be of similar levels for employees and entrepreneurs. A comparison of these returns is therefore largely an empirical matter.

12.4. Empirical Evidence of the Returns to Education for Entrepreneurs

12.4.1. Common Opinions

It is commonly thought that higher levels of education are important to be successful as an employee, but not necessarily as an entrepreneur. This is usually justified by examples of successful entrepreneurs who dropped out of school, such as Bill Gates. Most of these entrepreneurs advocate the proposition that successful entrepreneurship does not require any schooling. Thus, if this holds true, schooling would be a waste of time for prospective entrepreneurs. In what follows, I discuss the most important results from quantitative research into the relationship between the performance of entrepreneurs and their education.

12.4.2. "Old Fashioned" Empirical Evidence of the Returns to Education for Entrepreneurs

Two meta-analyses have reviewed hundreds of studies of the relationship between education and entrepreneurship outcomes (Van Der Sluis, Vijverberg, and Van Praag, 2005a, 2005b). A clear pattern seen in the collection of those studies is that education levels and entrepreneurial performance are positively related. On average, entrepreneurs with higher levels of education have higher earnings and their firms are more likely to survive, to grow faster, and to generate higher levels of profits. Moreover, some studies included in the meta-analyses allow a comparison of the rate of return to education for entrepreneurs with the returns to education for employees. These studies indicate that the returns to education are at least as high for employees as they are for entrepreneurs.

Although the studies demonstrated the positive relationship between education and entrepreneurial performance, as well as similar rates of returns to education for entrepreneurs and employees, all results obtained so far are potentially biased, because the estimation and identification strategies used are old-fashioned. In fact, researchers have measured only the relationship between education and entrepreneurs' performance but not the effect of education on entrepreneurs' performance. And the effect of education on performance is not equal to the relationship between education and performance for two reasons. First, the schooling decision is probably endogenous in a performance equation because individuals are likely to base their schooling investment decision, at least in part, on their perceptions of the expected payoffs to their investment. Second, there may be unobserved individual characteristics, such as intelligence and motivation, that affect both the schooling level attained and subsequent business performance: More intelligent individuals pursue higher levels of education and become better entrepreneurs, the latter perhaps even in the absence of any education. Ultimately we are most interested in the causal effect of education on entrepreneurship outcomes: the extra economic gain due to each extra year of education of entrepreneurs. For example, how much more income would Bill Gates have, had he attended another year of college, or what if the neighborhood baker had another year of schooling?

12.4.3. "State of the Art" Methods to Measure Returns to Education

Labor economists have used various advanced methods to measure the causal effect of education on labor market outcomes and thereby account for the potential problems of endogeneity and/or unobserved heterogeneity when estimating the returns to education.

Few of them have organized randomized experiments (Leuven et al., 2003). The evaluation of the causal effect of, for instance, a year of education requires a random assignment of individuals into a treatment group (participating in the education) and a control group (not participating). In this manner, endogeneity does not play any role because the relevant investment decision is forced. Moreover, unobserved heterogeneity can be expected to be absent because assignment into groups is random such that the groups will be similar in terms of all their (observed and unobserved) characteristics. Follow-up measurement should provide insight into individual levels of performance (or income), which is the cross-sectional variation to be explained.

The second strategy uses the variation in schooling and income between identical twins to estimate returns to schooling. This approach has been used to identify employees' returns to education (e.g., Ashenfelter and Krueger, 1994; Behrman and Rosenzweig, 1999; Rouse, 1999; and Bonjour et al., 2003). The basic idea is that monozygotic twins share the same genetic endowment and usually experience even more similar environments than nontwin siblings or dizygotic twins. It seems, then, that comparing monozygotic twins should control thoroughly for otherwise unobserved heterogeneity in intelligence, family background, and the like. However, this estimation strategy does not account for the described endogeneity problem.

The third strategy identifies causal effects using an instrumental variable (IV) approach (e.g., Oreopoulos, 2006). The idea is to imitate a field experiment where economic characteristics are randomly allocated among individuals to estimate their effects on income. This strategy therefore enables the unbiased measurement of the effect of schooling, for instance, assuming a random allocation of schooling levels amongst individuals, independent of their expected payoffs (endogeneity issue) or relevant unobserved background variables (unobserved heterogeneity). Applying IV requires the availability of valid instruments; this condition is rarely met.

The general conclusion of studies using these strategies to identify causal effects is that measuring the mere relationship between education and labor market outcomes renders too low estimates of the "real" returns to education (Ashenfelter et al., 1999). However, this conclusion pertains only to the returns to education for employees, not for entrepreneurs. Labor economists have neglected entrepreneurs when estimating the returns to education. Hence, there is a gap in our knowledge: the returns to education for entrepreneurs in comparison to employees that result from using methods that identify causal effects. Some recent studies have tried to fill this gap (Van Der Sluis et al., 2005c; Parker and Van Praag, 2006; Van Der Sluis and Van Praag, 2006).

12.4.4. "State of the Art" Empirical Evidence of the Returns to Education for Entrepreneurs

A persistent and significant finding from these recent studies, two based on American data and one based on Dutch data, is that the returns for a year of formal education are greater for entrepreneurs than for employees, on average. In other words, people benefit more from their education when they become entrepreneurs later on than when they become employees. For instance, a marginal year of formal education renders a 10 percent higher average hourly income for employees in the United States, whereas the corresponding return for entrepreneurs is 14 percent (Van Der Sluis et al., 2005c). Hence, the difference is not only statistically significant, but also of economic importance. Our study pertaining to the Netherlands also supports that the returns to education are relatively high for entrepreneurs vis-à-vis employees (Parker and Van Praag, 2006).[1]

How can we explain the novel and consistent finding that the returns to education are higher for entrepreneurs than for employees? Based on the "screening" hypothesis, we would actually expect the opposite to be the case: The returns to education for employees would be higher because they are not only caused by their increased productivity due to the knowledge and skills they produce in school; their degree also has value as a signal of motivation and/or intelligence to prospective employers. Prospective entrepreneurs would not benefit from this signaling value because they lack prospective employers.

These research results render two explanations. The first is based on the Dutch study (Parker and Van Praag, 2006): Education has not only productive value, but also signaling value for employers and for entrepreneurs. Entrepreneurs with higher levels of education have better access to start-up capital, which, in turn, generates better business performance. Capital suppliers also value degrees, just as is the case for prospective employers.[2]

The second explanation is based on one of the American studies (Van Der Sluis et al., 2005c): Returns to education are especially high if individuals can control their working environment. Entrepreneurs have, in general, more decision authority and freedom than employees to employ their scarce resources, such as their human capital, to develop activities that increase the returns to their inputs. Thus, it is no wonder that the returns to education are higher for entrepreneurs than for employees, who are limited in their capacities to use their resources productively due to often slowly adapting organizational structures in large and existing firms.

---

[1] Parker and Van Praag (2006) have only measured the returns to education for entrepreneurs such that a direct comparison with employees is impossible. However, the returns they measure are high in comparison to the returns to education that Levin and Plug (1999) find for the Netherlands when using the same methodology. The methods used by labor economists to measure the returns to education can also be criticized. They do not consider the number of years and hours of labor that individuals choose to supply by, for instance, working part-time or retiring at a certain age. The more hours one works over a lifetime, the higher will be the total return to education. This effect of the amount of labor supplied is not revealed by measuring the variance in incomes across individuals at a certain point in time in response to different levels of education, as is the usual manner. Hence, the difference between the returns to education for entrepreneurs and employees would be even higher if the average number of hours of labor supply were higher for entrepreneurs than for employees.

[2] Other stakeholders, such as clients, business relations, and business partners will probably "screen" too.

12.5. Policy and Research Implications for Europe

12.5.1. Assumptions

What does the research finding that the returns to education are higher for entrepreneurs than for employees imply for policymakers? Two assumptions are required to arrive at unambiguous policy implications. The first assumption is that the higher private returns to education for entrepreneurs go together with higher social returns to education for entrepreneurs than for employees: Not only does the entrepreneur benefit more from a higher education than an employee, but also the society as a whole benefits.[3] A second assumption is that only three studies, one pertaining to the Netherlands and the other two pertaining to the United States, can indeed form the basis for policy implications in Europe, where the levels, growth rates, and impact of entrepreneurial activities lag behind those in the United States.

12.5.2. Stimulating Entrepreneurship among University Students

Given these assumptions, the research results indicate that those people with higher levels of education in particular should be stimulated to think about entrepreneurship, and prospective entrepreneurs should be encouraged to pursue higher levels of education.

Based on (1) our results that the returns to education are relatively high for entrepreneurs, (2) the current lack of institutional arrangements in Europe to stimulate entrepreneurship in schools and universities, and (3) the positive effects of a larger pool of more potentially successful entrepreneurs on economic outcomes in Europe, in terms of economic growth and the entrepreneurial climate in general, the educational system should start implementing entrepreneurship programs at universities.

12.5.3. Finding Instruments to Stimulate Entrepreneurship among University Students

The next question is: What are good instruments to stimulate entrepreneurship among university students? Entrepreneurship education is part

---

[3] Currently, Oosterbeek, Ijsselstein, and Van Praag are estimating the social returns to education for entrepreneurs and employees separately.

of the program at various levels of education in many countries. Nevertheless, hardly any research into the effectiveness of entrepreneurship education or its ideal form has been conducted.

Programs are often evaluated based on responses of program participants to questionnaires. Respondents may then indicate to what extent their enthusiasm for entrepreneurship has increased as a result of their program participation. That type of research has little value, and it is unfortunate that public policymakers use it as a source of information. The major disadvantage is that the results only apply to students who have chosen to participate in entrepreneurship education, or to a self-selected group of participants whose enthusiasm for entrepreneurship is already present. A comparison to a control group is absent. Moreover, the indicators used to assess the programs' effectiveness are often not relevant or are highly subjective. For instance, a stated increased enthusiasm for entrepreneurship after having participated in the program is relevant, but learning entrepreneurship competencies and actually starting up a business later on is relevant too, but seldom measured.[4]

12.5.4. Randomized Field Experiments Should Be More Common

Research to evaluate entrepreneurship education programs using pre- and post-measurements of entrepreneurial competencies in a randomly selected treatment and control group is required to effectively evaluate entrepreneurship education. The differences in entrepreneurial competencies and intentions across the treatment and control groups before and after the program are compared, such that the effectiveness of the program is measured in an unbiased manner for a representative group of students. Currently, Oosterbeek, Van Praag, and Ysselstein are conducting such a field experiment studying the effectiveness of one of the Young Achievement programs at a Dutch school of higher vocational education. Young Achievement is a large organization that facilitates a specific type of entrepreneurship education in schools in Europe and the United States. As part of this program, groups of students start up a real enterprise in a legally protected environment. They not only write a business plan but actually develop a product or service, gather start-up capital, and bring their

---

[4] Besides, the relationship between entrepreneurial competencies and the extent of increased motivation to become an entrepreneur is an interesting indicator of program effectiveness. The outcome would be favorable if students who have low levels of entrepreneurial competencies learn so in the program and are discouraged from becoming entrepreneurs.

product or service to the market. This entrepreneurship education program is widely appraised and sponsored by national departments of education and economic affairs, as well as by the European Commission. Nevertheless, we do not know whether, to what extent, or in which respect the program is effective.

12.5.5. Public Policymakers as Well as School Boards Should Develop a Different Attitude

In general, schools and their boards are unwilling to facilitate the type of research required to evaluate entrepreneurship education programs because it limits the freedom of students or pupils to select particular courses as a consequence of the randomized distribution of students across the treatment and the control group. Schools actually consider the freedom of students to select courses as an important driver of the school's quality. However, this view is rather short-sighted: High-quality evaluation of programs is the only manner in which high-quality programs can be guaranteed or even defined.

European governments should encourage and facilitate such randomized experiments. Policymakers should start involving researchers with programs before instead of after their implementation. Economic policymakers could take the medical sciences as an example. In this discipline, experimentation by assigning a medicine to a treatment group and a placebo to a control group is very common to develop useful academic knowledge, even though the possible consequences of assigning people to either group can be severe.

12.5.6. New Research Questions Should be Posed and Answered

The European Commission, among other groups, advocates that entrepreneurship should be not only a course in schools; the entire school curriculum should encourage entrepreneurship. Currently, the European educational system teaches repetition and obeying rules and devotes little attention to leadership, renewal, and creativity. But what would be the result of an innovative educational program that is more widely entrepreneurial? Would the returns to formal education for entrepreneurs, and perhaps also for employees, be yet higher? Research into the effectiveness of a more entrepreneurially oriented educational system is relevant and as yet has not been performed.

Furthermore, research to answer the question regarding at which educational stage entrepreneurship education is most effective for the development of specific competencies is entirely lacking. Some skills would perhaps be better developed in primary school, whereas others can be more effectively taught at later stages, for instance, at universities. We must also determine which types of education are particularly beneficial for developing entrepreneurs. If we have more knowledge about that, entrepreneurship could be particularly stimulated at these schools. In this respect, only Ed Lazear (2005) has found relevant evidence: "jacks-of-all-trades," that is, individuals with broad educational and diverse career backgrounds, have better opportunities to become successful entrepreneurs than do specialists.

12.6. Conclusion

Academia can foster entrepreneurship in two ways. Besides the commercialization of research, there is a second manner that is much less studied: creating awareness of entrepreneurship choices and teaching entrepreneurship skills to students. The European Commission advocates that Europe should develop an entrepreneurial culture within the educational system. It is most efficient to start developing the entrepreneurial mindset for those groups of students or pupils who have the best prospects in terms of entrepreneurial performance. Contrary to common wisdom, economic theory and recent empirical evidence indicates that students with higher levels of education are more likely to become successful entrepreneurs. The returns to formal education are very high for entrepreneurs, higher than for employees. This novel finding resulted from applying modern identification strategies, commonly used to measure the returns to education for employees, to entrepreneurs. This implies that prospective entrepreneurs should be stimulated to pursue higher education and that the choice for entrepreneurship should be stimulated at institutions of higher education. How? That should be indicated based on field experiments that schools and universities should enable and that public policymakers should facilitate and stimulate. Moreover, new research questions should be posed and answered to determine whether and how the entire school system could become more entrepreneurial and at what types and levels of the educational system specific entrepreneurship competencies could best be developed.

A more entrepreneurial climate for students at universities will probably have a positive spillover effect to researchers: Researchers will become more entrepreneurial in terms of the type of questions they pose and the research methods they use to answer the questions related to the role of academia to foster entrepreneurship through the educational system.

References

Ashenfelter, Orley, and Alan Krueger. 1994. "Estimates of the Returns to Schooling from a New Sample of Twins." *American Economic Review*, 84(5), 1157–1173.

Ashenfelter, Orley, Colm Harmon, and Hessel Oosterbeek. 1999. "A Review of the Schooling/Earnings Relationship with Tests for Publication Bias." *Labour Economics*, 6, 453–470.

Behrman, Jere, and Mark Rosenzweig. 1999. "Ability Biases in Schooling Returns and Twins: A Test and New Estimates." *Economics of Education Review*, 18(2), 159–167.

Bonjour, Dorothe, Lynn Cherkas, Jonathan Haskel, Denise D. Hawkes, and Tim Spector. 2003. "Returns to Education: Evidence from U.K. Twins." *American Economic Review*, 93(5), 1799–1812.

Commission of the European Communities. 2006. "Implementing the Community Lisbon Programme: Fostering Entrepreneurial Mindsets through Education and Learning." *COM* (2006), 33.

Davidsson, Per, and Benson Honig. 2003. "The Role of Social and Human Capital among Nascent Entrepreneurs." *Journal of Business Venturing*, 18, 301–331.

Lazear, Edward. 2005. "Entrepreneurship." *Journal of Labor Economics*, 23, 649–680.

Leuven, Edwin, Hessel Oosterbeek, and Bas Van Der Klaauw. 2003. "The Effect of Financial Rewards on Students' Achievement: Evidence from a Randomized Experiment." SCHOLAR Working Paper Series, WP 38/03.

Levin, Jesse, and Erik Plug. 1999. "Instrumenting Education and the Returns to Schooling in the Netherlands." *Labour Economics*, 6, 521–534.

Mincer, Jacob. 1974. *Schooling, Experience and Earnings*. New York: Columbia University Press.

Oreopoulos, Philip. 2006. "Average Treatment Effects of Education when Compulsory School Laws Really Matter." *American Economic Review*, 96(1), 152–175.

Parker, Simon C., and C. Mirjam Van Praag. 2006. "Schooling, Capital Constraints and Entrepreneurial Performance: The Endogenous Triangle." *Journal of Business and Economic Statistics*, 24, 416–431.

Riley, John. 2002. "Weak and Strong Signals." *Scandinavian Journal of Economics*, 104, 213–236.

Rouse, Cecilia. 1999. "Further Estimates of the Economic Return to Schooling from a New Sample of Twins." *Economics of Education Review*, 18(2), 149–157.

Schumpeter, Joseph A. 1943 (1911). *The Theory of Economic Development*. Cambridge: Harvard University Press.

Spence, A. Michael. 1973. *Market Signaling: Information Transfer in Hiring and Related Processes*. Cambridge: Harvard University Press.

Van Der Sluis, Justin, C. Mirjam Van Praag, and Wim Vijverberg. 2005a. "Education and Entrepreneurship in Industrialized Countries: A Meta-Analysis." Tinbergen Institute Working Paper No. TI 03-046/3.

Van Der Sluis, Justin, C. Mirjam Van Praag, and Wim Vijverberg. 2005b. "Entrepreneurship Selection and Performance: A Meta-Analysis of the Impact of Education in Less Developed Countries." *World Bank Economic Review*, 19(2), 225–261.

Van Der Sluis, Justin, C. Mirjam Van Praag, and Arjen Van Witteloostuijn. 2005c. "Comparing the Returns to Education for Entrepreneurs and Employees." Tinbergen Institute Discussion Paper No. TI 04-104/3.

Van Der Sluis, Justin, and C. Mirjam Van Praag. 2006. "Identifying the Difference in Returns to Education for Entrepreneurs and Employees: Identification by Means of Changes in Compulsory Schooling Laws." Unpublished working paper, Tinbergen Institute.

Weick, Karl. 1996. "Drop Your Tools: An Allegory for Organizational Studies." *Administrative Science Quarterly*, 41, 301–314.

Wolpin, Kenneth I. 1977. "Education and Screening." *American Economic Review*, 67, 949–958.

13

Creating an Entrepreneurial Economy

The Role of Public Policy

Heike Grimm

13.1. Introduction

Policy-making for the promotion of regions (e.g., subnational spatial entities) and nations has dramatically changed. Over the last few decades all levels of government, from federal and regional to municipal, have become key players in the promotion of the entrepreneurial economy (Gilbert, Audretsch, and McDougall, 2004; Audretsch, Grimm, and Wessner, 2005). In this context, Audretsch and Thurik (2000) demonstrate that the re-emergence of entrepreneurship and the shift from a market economy to an entrepreneurial economy accelerated due to increased globalization and led to the development of new entrepreneurship policies, which were implemented at all levels of government. As outlined in Chapter 1, and explored in more detail in Chapter 10, the entrepreneurial economy is driven by change and innovation and is characterized by a high degree of turbulence and diversity. This stands in contrast to the managed economy. In this context, Haltiwanger provides fresh data showing that "creative destruction" – meaning a high turnover rate of new but also dying firms which is one characteristic of an entrepreneurial economy – is conducive to economic growth:

The high net growth and high volatility of young firms points towards creative destruction interpretations of U.S. growth dynamics.... [I]t is the process of creative destruction that is contributing to growth. With creative destruction, there is ongoing innovation and market experimentation with a high degree of churning contributing to growth. Of course, this implies that some firms are successful and grow while others are not successful and contract (and perhaps exit). Amongst young firms since both outcomes are likely it is hardly appropriate to target young firms as the sources of growth. Rather again, the high net growth and volatility of young firms is a feature of healthy creative destruction dynamics ongoing amongst U.S. businesses. (Haltiwanger, 2006, p. 20)

Using the tabulations of a few longitudinal datasets, Haltiwanger shows that job creation in the United States is mainly generated by new and young firms. He underlines that, at the same time, these job-creating young firms are very volatile and often tend to fail. In other words, the idea that new and young businesses create many new jobs is valid, but the jobs are not permanent; in other words, job security is not guaranteed. This again shows the differences between the market and the entrepreneurial economy. The idea that everyone can have stability in their lives – which dominated people's thinking and attitudes during the post–World War II period until the 1970s – no longer works because postmodern globalization has accelerated at a high speed.

The acceleration of globalization contributed to the shift from the market to the entrepreneurial economy, which has had a deep impact on policy-making: Policymakers in industrialized countries face the challenge of having to develop new policies and strategies to generate economic growth within their regions and nations.

The purpose of this chapter is to discuss the role of new entrepreneurship policy as one component of a wide range of new policies that were created and implemented in the United States at an early stage of postmodern globalization. This chapter demonstrates that due to the diversification of public policy approaches as well as the openness of the American people and of institutions to adapt to these new policies, the United States has upheld its status as a global economic superpower over the last decades. Special reference is paid to new entrepreneurship policy that has promoted university patenting and the commercialization of university-generated inventions since the early 1980s. During this period, a variety of new policies were created in the United States while a supply-side revolution was taking place.

The chapter draws conclusions and suggestions for policymakers as to how the spillover of knowledge generated by university research can be improved to better generate economic growth and employment creation by reviewing the changes in economic (specifically, innovation and technology) policy-making in the United States and Germany since the 1980s. In this context, the important role of non-content-related key factors of successful policy-making will be emphasized by specifically addressing the crucial role of timing, decentralization of decision-making, and institutional (as well as individual) self-governance. These components are crucial for enabling scientist-entrepreneurs and institutions such as universities to compete successfully at the local and global levels. In other words, it is not only the content and design of a policy that matters but also the timing and implementation strategy that turns such a policy into a successful one. By comparing policies for the promotion of scientist-entrepreneurs in the United States versus Germany, the importance of these side components become apparent.

13.2. Technology and Growth

Patenting has a regional aspect: Certain areas (such as subnational entities or city regions) are specialized in particular technological fields and locations (Audretsch and Feldmann, 1996). Sonn and Storper (2003) showed that the share of U.S. metropolitan areas in specific patent areas has risen steadily since the 1970s, implying the existence of a subnational dimension to the geography of innovation. In this context, UCLA's Zucker and Darby (1996) demonstrated that "star scientists" work physically close to their home universities.

These findings have major implications for policy. Economists have long recognized that technology is unequally distributed across areas. Most firms do their patenting in their home countries: On average, European firms' foreign subsidiaries patent only 7.4 percent of total patents outside their home country; U.S. firms, only 4.2 percent; and Japan, only 1.2 percent (Patel and Pavitt, 1991).[1]

Technological progress together with the patenting and commercialization of innovations is, in other words, a national and, to an even higher degree, local issue. Technological capacities and innovations are localized in specific places. Economists measure this by examining the location of patented innovations.

These findings show that a strong emphasis on technology and innovation policy became one of the cornerstones of successful policy-making in the global economy by putting pressure on existing institutions to shape innovation processes and to become agents of change. I refer primarily to institutions that promote research and development (R&D) and generate different kinds of innovation, to educational systems and career pathways that aim at educating the knowledge-based community and increasing the number of qualified science and technology workers, and to major

[1] Exceptions are small rich countries: Belgium 45.7%, Canada 28.1%, Netherlands 73.4%, etc.

research programs and organizations. On the one hand, all these institutions shape and create new and innovative actors and thus the resulting entrepreneurial capital, or the capacity of a region or economy to generate entrepreneurship. On the other hand, the new actors are dependent on a supportive cultural and entrepreneurial environment in order to cope with global challenges as well as institutions that are aware of the important role of knowledge flow and spillovers.

13.3. The Role of Spillovers from University-Based Research

Spillovers from university-based research have been achieved through the commercialization of university-generated knowledge. Within this context, patents are shifting to the center of public policy discussions. In addition, the role of universities in a future innovation system needs to be realigned with the challenges of a knowledge-based society. The shift toward entrepreneurial universities will intensify in the near future as a result of an acceleration in the speed of creation and diffusion of innovations and new knowledge at a global scale.

Patents are important as a unique and highly visible mechanism for transferring technological knowledge to the private sector for a variety of reasons (Archibugi and Michie, 1995). First, a patent is an internationally acknowledged legal instrument for the protection of technological knowledge. Second, as a result patents confer a series of exclusive monopoly rights that provide effective protection against imitation and misuse as well as incentives to invest money in research if the investor can profit from the economic returns deriving from respective results. Given the fact that the majority of university inventions are embryonic, and additional development is needed to get them ready for commercial exploitation, incentives to encourage the necessary public and private investments are essential for transforming these inventions into economic values (Jensen and Thursby, 2004). The economic literature has shown empirical evidence of the benefits of knowledge spillovers from university patenting (Jaffe, 1989; Acs, Audretsch, and Feldman, 1992). In this context, Audretsch, Taylor, and Oettl (2005) provide fresh and compelling evidence with their research, concluding that "scientist entrepreneurship is the sleeping giant of commercialization." Differing from existing research, Audretsch et al. did not rely on measuring and analyzing the commercialization of university research using solely the intellectual property disclosed to and registered by technology transfer offices, as this may lead to systematic underestimation of commercialization and innovation emanating from university research. Instead, the researchers questioned those factors that inhibit scientist commercialization by measuring the propensity of scientists funded by grants from the National Cancer Institute (NCI). According to their findings, more than one out of four patenting NCI scientists started a new firm selling and exploiting their innovation in the market. In other words, far more scientists become entrepreneurs than otherwise registered by technology transfer offices. Therefore, other research approaches have systematically underestimated the power of scientist entrepreneurship.

With the growing importance of commercializing innovations from scientists' research, universities are challenged to take on a new and more active role in performing these new duties to a satisfying and successful end. They need to take a direct role as actors in regional and national economic development and policy-making in order to support scientist entrepreneurs optimally. The increased focus on commercialization of university research has led to the development of university policies and initiatives that promote such activity. Some initiatives may be induced "top-down" by the government and its agencies, while other initiatives are emerging "bottom-up" from entities or individuals at universities (Goldfarb and Henrekson, 2002). Following changes in government control and management during the last decades, universities have also had to demonstrate their vital economic role and positive societal impact in order to obtain public acceptance, support, and, above all, funding. Many countries have reformed universities with an emphasis on achieving greater autonomy, becoming more competitive, receiving performance-based funding, and increasing commercialization of the results of public research (OECD, 2000a, 2000b). In most industrialized countries, the university support of commercialization and technology transfer increased substantially with the development of new policies and institutional support mechanisms to improve technology transfer. Universities are supposed to contribute to economic development more actively than in the past by interaction with the local industry and with other types of commercialization, such as the establishment of new firms and spinoffs.

13.4. The Emergence of Entrepreneurship Policy

Since the mid-1980s, there has been a rapid increase in the commercialization of public-funded research, especially in the United States, Europe, and Japan. The key channels for commercialization are not only patents and licenses, but also research joint ventures and the formation of spinoffs

(Lockett et al., 2005). One of the key policies to promote commercialization in the United States was the Bayh-Dole Act of 1980. This legislation passed intellectual property rights from the federal government to the universities, giving them the opportunity to profit from locally based research, turning the results into innovative and practical goods; this turned the process upside-down with a bottom-up policy approach (Rasmussen et al., 2006). With the Bayh-Dole Act, universities became responsible for developing entrepreneurial strategies, complete with the autonomy to decide the best approach to profit from their research. This shift challenged universities to design and implement policies for competing not just within their regional setting, but also at the national and global level.

Interestingly, this challenge reached American universities at an early stage of postmodern globalization, which was triggered in the 1970s. It is worth elaborating briefly on economic and innovation policy-making in the United States since the 1980s to better understand how America managed to keep its status as the global economic superpower over multiple decades during the twentieth century. By developing a variety of appropriate policies and strategies at each stage, which helped to maintain economic and political strength, the United States was able to shift gears from the manufacturing economy that dominated the post–World War II era to the fast-changing knowledge-based global economy. At the same time, this brief review provides the opportunity for better understanding why countries such as Germany missed the opportune moments to change and implement new policies at critical junctures.

13.4.1. Early U.S. Response to Globalization: The Diversification of Public Policy

It is worth noting that the United States is characterized as having the capacity to develop and adapt quickly to new public policies that respond to and successfully answer the challenges of globalization. Since the early 1980s, most industrialized countries have carefully evaluated U.S. policy and then copied its best practices. This tendency to copy American policies was widespread. Looking more closely at American policy-making, there are some crucial differences with regard to the overall framework, timing and implementation strategies. Although specific elements such as the Bayh-Dole Act were copied by European countries, including Germany and Sweden, the meta-policy framework never changed.

Reagonomics

Under President Ronald Reagan, the United States shifted to a strongly business-friendly, supply-side economic policy that America had not previously utilized during the twentieth century. This shift was profound and had lasting repercussions. Characterized by significant tax cuts, increasing national debt, and cuts in social spending, combined with deregulation – which spread across all areas of economic and public life – Reagan's policies smoothed the path toward a full-blown service economy. This not only gave rise to the widely disparaged "McJob" but also created highly qualified and superbly paid jobs in the computer industry and other high-tech fields.

The so-called Reagonomics was welcomed with open arms by many Americans who believed it would better cope with global and national challenges. Nonetheless, strong criticism was leveled at, among other things, the severe cuts in social spending and the enormous defense expenditures (a further pillar of Reaganomics). In the 1980s, the Cold War took on new dimensions, and the fear of nuclear escalation felt by people in both East and West gave birth to numerous peace movements. The barely considered downside of a strict supply-side economic policy included an unprecedented gaping hole in public finances. Under Reagan, the national debt increased from one billion to almost three billion U.S. dollars. Yet what really gave cause for concern was not so much the overall level of public debt (a level that was, on average, similar to Europe's or Japan's), but rather its meteoric rise. This was accompanied by the extremely low household savings rates seen in the 1980s. Thus, by the end of Reagan's time in office, the United States was no longer in a position to finance its private sector investments through domestic savings.

One positive effect of Reagan's new economic policy was the significant stimuli of research and development in high-tech industries. With the introduction of new entrepreneurship polices such as the Small Business Patent Act (a 1980 federal law that was initiated by former President Jimmy Carter that permits government grantees and contractors to retain title to federally funded inventions and encourages universities to license inventions to industry), the Bayh-Dole Act (which became effective in 1981), the 1984 passage of U.S. Public Laws 98-620 and 96-517 (the Patent and Trademark Amendments Act), universities were encouraged to license technologies for commercial exploitation. With these acts, the responsibility for the commercialization of innovations developed by scientist entrepreneurs was placed on the universities. With decentralization focusing on universities, an effort objected to by these institutions at that time, Reagan paved the way for increasing institutional self-governance, a requirement for universities that wish to compete globally and profit from their ideas and innovations. The Reagan administration recognized that there was a need for decentralization and institutional self-responsibility for the commercialization of innovation deriving from universities at this early stage: Universities are not only centers for higher education but also engines of innovation and centers for regional economic growth and employment creation.

With the introduction of new entrepreneurship as well as the renewal of innovation and technology policies, new university and education policies were subsequently developed. In other words, a wide range of new policies was developed, part of a supply-side revolution that let the state off the hook and made individuals and institutions responsible for their own well-being and development.

In this context, despite (or perhaps due to) all the negative aspects that Reagan's economic policy entailed, which were heavily criticized all over the world, especially by opponents of the arms trade, Ronald Reagan prepared his country for a globally networked economy characterized by elements of decentralization of policy-making, deregulation, and the transfer of autonomy in decision-making processes to public institutions such as universities. No other country on earth was better positioned than the United States for the challenges of globalization in the 1990s (Bierling, 1992; Anderson, 1997).

America's Response to Recession

Ronald Reagan's successor, George Bush senior, followed the new supply-side approach without putting emphasis on the further development of sophisticated new public policies such as entrepreneurship, innovation and technology policies. The economic policy of George Bush senior came under severe pressure at the beginning of the 1990s as the signs of recession mounted in July 1990. He responded in a panicky and haphazard manner, however, with no clear concept for overcoming the recession evident, and the country was gripped by a sense of paralysis. Negative statistics and figures played their part in casting doubt on Bush's competence in matters of economic policy. During the eight years Reagan was in office, gross domestic product (GDP) had grown by an average of 2.8 percent. By the end of 1992, Bush faced a growth rate of only 1.2 percent. As if that were not enough, unemployment rose to 7.8 percent, even though Bush had inherited the lowest jobless rate since 1973 (5.2%) on entering office. During the phase of the recession that fell between 1990 and 1992, a total of 2.2 million jobs were lost within an astonishingly short period of time (Bierling, 1992, 37–38).

Yet Bush's greatest mistake was violating his campaign promise: "Read my lips, no new taxes" (Germond and Witcover, 1992; Schild, 1998). His failure to uphold this promise, which was of utmost importance to the American people cemented the resentment they felt toward their President. When Ronald Reagan's successor entered his second election battle, he had little chance against an opponent who displayed such an innate mastery of the political sphere.

"It's the Economy, Stupid!"

"It's the economy, stupid!" is something Bush really should have learned from his first election campaign. Yet, of all people, it was his opponent in the 1992 election battle, Bill Clinton, who coined this election slogan. The brainchild of Clinton's adviser, George Stephanopoulos, the slogan perfectly matched the prevailing *Zeitgeist*.

Although Clinton initially had political defeats and disappointments, for example, with health policy and gays in the military, his economic policy was marked by his own individual style: the Democrat was the most conservative President in terms of fiscal policy since Harding's stint in charge of government affairs in the 1920s. With surprisingly little fuss, he executed a radical break with traditional, more democratic principles of social welfare and income security by setting the right to assistance against the obligation to work and to help oneself. He welcomed globalization and technological change with open arms, thereby gaining friends in the private sector. Clinton was one of the few Democrats of the 1990s who succeeded in following the oft-proclaimed but seldom achieved "third way" between the old ideologies of the right and left of center.

13.4.2. U.S. Innovation and Technology Policy-Making since the 1990s

Clinton's economic approach implied a strong focus on the promotion of innovative small- and medium-sized companies as well as entrepreneurship. He further developed and improved innovation and technology policies to better face the global challenges. Innovation became a key word for

success, and the promotion of innovation coming not just from universities but also from small firms that adapt quickly to economic changes was
one of his key concerns. Clinton underlined the crucial role of entrepreneurship for the competitiveness of the country in many public speeches[2]
and through new entrepreneurship policies.

In addition to the existent policies promoting innovative entrepreneurs,
the Commerce Department developed, for example, the Advanced Technology Program (ATP). Established in 1990, the ATP shares the costs of
industry-defined and industry-led projects selected through merit-based
competitions similar to the Small Business Innovation Research Program
(SBIR) (Wessner, 1999, 2005). It expanded significantly under Clinton.

Manufacturing R&D will receive particular attention from ATP, ARPA and other
federal agencies. SEMATECH, an industry consortium created to develop semiconductor manufacturing technology, will receive continued matching funds
from the Department of Defense in FY94. This consortium can serve as a model
for federal consortia funded to advance other critical technologies. Programs
will be encouraged in the development of a new automobile, new construction
technologies, intelligent control and sensor technologies, rapid prototyping, and
environmentally-conscious manufacturing. (Clinton and Gore, 1993, 9)

The Clinton administration's strategy to place stress on public funding
for promoting innovation from scientist entrepreneurs as well as small-
and medium-sized businesses was skeptically received by the public and
the industrial community. Clinton's successful policies were grounded in a
unique confluence of historical events, centering on the conclusion of the
Cold War and the emergence of the New Economy. During his administration, 5.9 million new small- and medium-sized businesses were generated and 22 million new jobs were created. No other country in the
world could keep up with such economic development. I believe that this
was due to an early strengthening, continuous renewal, and diversification
of new entrepreneurship and other public policies.

13.5. The Diffusion of Entrepreneurship Policy to Germany

In Germany, regional actors became involved in innovation and technology policy in the 1990s. Before then, innovation and technology policy-
making was primarily a federal duty and was performed top-down across
Germany. The high emphasis on technology and innovation policy as

---

[2]   Such as in his speech on "Technology for America's Economic Growth; A New Direction
to Build Economic Strength," held on February 22, 1993 (Clinton and Gore, 1993).

pursued in the 1990s, as well as increased intervention from federal, state, and local governments in technological development and diffusion, was (and is) not indisputable (Dreher, 1997, 26–31). With regard to the principle of subsidiarity, the government should mainly fulfill the task of providing a favorable legal and institutional environment and should stimulate, but not govern, the innovation processes (Koschatzky, 2000). As previously noted, technology is unequally distributed at the national (and global) level, resulting in the policy-making conflict that public promotion of innovative places tends to reinforce regional disparities while, at the same time, generating economic growth. With regard to the practical implementation of regionally oriented innovation policy, for many years the German governments tried to find a balance between the promotion of "hot spots" and structurally disadvantaged regions through the so-called *Gießkannenprinzip* (watering can) program. Metaphorically, this describes how the federal government sprinkled funding across all German regions, and it characterizes a strategy that provided all subnational entities with some public funding, rather than picking one winner (Grimm, 2005). Theoretically, the primary purpose of regionally oriented innovation policy was the promotion of clusters and the improvement of the efficiency of regional innovation systems.

The ongoing regionalization of innovation and technology policy-making in the 1990s resulted in the development of new entrepreneurship policies at the end of the 1990s. In December 1997, the Federal Ministry for Education and Research (BMBF) launched the EXIST program to promote university-based start-ups. One of the major objectives was to intensify the regional cooperation between universities, applied universities, the business sectors, and public actors that are part of local innovation systems. The BMBF pursued four major objectives (BMBF, 2000):

1. The permanent establishment of a "culture of entrepreneurship" in teaching, research, and administration;
2. The increasing knowledge transfer and spillover of academic research into an economic added value;
3. The encouragement of the great potential for business ideas and start-up personalities at universities; and
4. A significant increase in the number of innovative start-ups resulting in job creation and generating economic growth.

Only five out of 109 proposals submitted to the BMBF were positively evaluated and funded.

In addition, the so-called InnoRegio (innovative regions) contest was launched mainly to improve the innovative capacities and employment situation in the areas of the former East Germany. The major goal was the development of regional concepts and projects for exploitation of local innovation potentials. Only 25 out of the 440 proposals submitted to the BMBF were given InnoRegio status.

The EXIST and InnoRegio contests were initial endeavors in the implementation of new entrepreneurship policies while pursuing the goal of better exploiting innovative capacities from both private and public innovators through the development of new tools of networking and cooperation. Although the approach to invest in these contests, which turned a selection of German regions into agents of change, was a change of paradigm in the German technology and innovation policy, there was no formal emphasis on encouraging and facilitating knowledge spillovers.

13.5.1. Entrepreneurship Policy as Competitiveness Strategy

The Bayh-Dole Act and the passage of U.S. Public Laws 98-620 and 96-517 served as a best practice model for legal and institutional initiatives in countries such as Germany, Denmark, the Netherlands, Sweden, Spain, and Brazil (Goldfarb and Henrekson, 2002). These laws came as reaction to murky rules and low commercialization rates. The new laws instituted a policy approach that allowed universities to retain property rights to inventions deriving from government-funded academic research and to charge royalties on intellectual property. The purpose of these acts was to keep the government out of the commercialization process and to provide universities with incentives for setting up technology transfer offices or other institutional structures that promoted commercial exploitation of research outputs (Jaffe, Trajtenberg, and Henderson, 1993; Mowery, Nelson, Sampat, and Ziedonis, 2001; Mowery and Ziedonis, 2002). With this U.S. bottom-up policy approach, specific federal rules and provisions disappeared and the universities regained room for developing appropriate policies to become entrepreneurial. At the same time, U.S. universities implemented explicit regulations governing reporting of inventions, assignment of patents, as well as inventor's share and income distribution throughout their commercial exploitation.

The U.S. model is particularly focused on setting a policy framework that allows universities to experiment and implement the policy that is the best practice for their particular university (Goldfarb and Henrekson, 2002). On the contrary, the German top-down approach and institutional setting defines quite strictly how university patents are entitled across all universities within the country. Although the Bayh-Dole Act might not have been as significant for the increase of university–industry spillovers as well as patenting and licensing by university researchers, as often enthusiastically underlined and as rightly assessed by Mowery in this volume (Chapter 11; see also Mowery et al., 2001), I would like to point out that this policy came at the right time and with the right incentive. The timing for such a policy at the beginning of the 1980s was perfect and operated, in my opinion, as a trigger for an impressive increase in university patents as a proportion of all patents within the U.S. and as one major incentive for universities to account for an entrepreneurial environment within their faculties and at their campus. It contributed to a regionalization of university policy-making, which helped universities to find their own best practice policy approach in alignment with the global challenges as well as the specific local setting. This approach helped to pave the way for turning American universities into entrepreneurial universities that explore their own policies to increase their budgets in times of reduced funding coming directly from the state (during the 1980s and 1990s, state support for public universities dropped significantly) and to compete for innovative and academically outstanding faculty members.

In Germany, neither the policy initiatives nor the timing matched with the global challenges ahead. From the 1960s to the 1980s, the world observed a dramatic closing of the economic and technological gaps between the major industrial powers. Along with this, and increasing competition between the economic superpowers, the United States and Great Britain changed their economic approaches and shifted from demand-oriented economic governing to a supply-sided revolution. In addition, new policies were introduced and developed. Entrepreneurship policy (including the Bayh-Dole Act) started to receive a prominent role in the policy toolbox. In Germany, the demand-oriented approach was neither questioned nor reformed in spite of the economic challenges that lay ahead.

The fall of the Berlin Wall in 1989, although a surprise to policymakers, served only to accelerate the pace of globalization. Competitiveness and innovation challenges increased. Overwhelmed and taken by surprise by the quiet revolution in East Germany in 1989, the West German policy framework was transferred to East Germany without much discussion in order to accomplish political and economic unification quickly while ignoring that West Germany already faced significant policy and economic challenges, among them a lack of innovativeness and decreasing global competitiveness (Bellendorf, 1994; Audretsch, 1995). Both inadequacies should have been addressed at the end of the 1980s, but during the emotional high following German reunification the policies were sent east without further analyzing whether they were appropriate, for both continuation in the West and implementation in the East. It was assumed that the policies would automatically work even though academics and policymakers alike did not understand at that time what these policies positively contributed to regional development and entrepreneurship. Although it is clear that the speed of globalization has been underestimated by politicians, policymakers and citizens alike, the traditional public policies have not yet been questioned or redesigned.

In the United States, on the other hand, an astounding openness to redesign and to replace old policies occurred throughout the 1980s and 1990s. Another shift in policy-making took place: while some policies were developed to react quickly to the global economic challenges in the 1980s, responding to the recession of the early 1990s, the Clinton administration developed an amazing policy mix.

Created in 1982 and renewed in 1992, the SBIR program served as another example of new entrepreneurship policy for promotion of the commercialization of innovation from university and small business research (Audretsch 2002). The implementation of the SBIR program at the beginning of the 1980s and its renewal in 1992 showed that the federal government put strong emphasis on the role of new entrepreneurship policy in bridging the gap between universities (and small businesses) and the marketplace, thereby encouraging local and regional growth (Wessner 2005). Interestingly, when the SBIR program was created in the early 1980s, universities strongly objected to the program and skeptically reacted to their new role and to that of being responsible for a successful university-led commercialization process.

In the course of the decade of the 1990s, this perception of the program significantly evolved. In the commercialization-sensitive environment created by Bayh-Dole, SBIR awards were increasingly seen as a source of early-stage financial support for promising ideas. (Wessner 2005, 82)

13.5.2. Bayh-Dole Made in Germany

In 1998, some 42 percent of all patent applications came from ten German so-called planning regions, leaving 58 percent to the remaining eighty-seven German planning regions. Patenting activity was at this point highly concentrated in a few regions, although the distribution of universities and applied universities and other research institutes is fairly even across the country. Koschatzky concluded in 2000,

This patent behaviour in research institutes and especially in universities points to the fact that the innovative and technology transfer potential of many universities and their respective regions is still not fully utilized. (Koschatzky, 2000, 15)

In 2002, more than twenty years after Bayh-Dole was implemented in the United States, the German Ministry for Science and Education took the initiative and altered the so-called Gesetz über Arbeitnehmererfindungen (ArbNErfG). Prior to this revision, all rights on inventions resulting from academic research made by university professors were retained by the latter which was known as "professor's privilege" (*Hochschullehrerprivileg*). They could decide solely about legal protection and commercial exploitation of their findings, but were at the same time responsible to meet all expenses and bear all risks in case of patenting and commercialization. In accordance with the new Section 42 of the ArbNErfG the university professor privilege was abolished, transferring the property rights on inventions deriving from on-campus research to the universities rather than to the academic inventors. Furthermore, these inventions must be reported to the university administration within the two-month period before publication, which permits their commercial evaluation and legal protection. In case of patenting, the inventor's share amounts to 30 percent of gross income generated by the commercial exploitation of the university-owned invention.

In 2002, the Federal Ministry of Education and Research launched an action plan, the so-called Exploitation Offensive (*Verwertungsoffensive*), to create an appropriate professional infrastructure at universities to improve the institutional environment for patenting and the exploitation of patents (BMBF, 2001). In the first three-year period the universities were granted federal funding to create Patent Exploitation Agencies (*Patentverwertungsagenturen*, or PVA), which offer expertise on legal and other questions related to the commercialization of university-based research and innovations. Not only do they support and help them through this process, but they also motivate academic researchers to think of the commercialization of inventions. The goal was to turn these agencies into self-funded ones with future returns from patent commercialization. The intended effects of the PVAs were to give university staff strong incentives to walk the commercialization route and to save them from a complex, expensive as well as time consuming patenting process (Bartenbach and Hellebrand, 2002; Bartenbach and Volz, 2002).

Compared with other highly industrialized countries, such as the United States, Germany was delayed in the development of new entrepreneurship and innovation policies. There are many reasons for this. Legal and cultural aspects strongly influenced the overall hesitation in changing policy-making styles and strategies, as did a number of political aspects, such as the fall of the Berlin Wall in 1989.

The German federal government made the necessary legal adaptations to conform to global standards, such as better promoting the commercialization of patents and improving the degree of commercial exploitation of university research at the beginning of the twenty-first century. Following the basic idea of Bayh-Dole, property rights on innovations were transferred to the universities; technology transfer offices and PVAs were created to encourage scientists to go down "the entrepreneurial route" (Audretsch et al., 2006b). Differing from innovation and university policy in the United States, the German government pursued an institutional and legal top-down approach. The same policy now applies to all public universities in Germany. These universities depend heavily on public funding for the finance of new technology transfer offices and the commercialization process. A benchmarking of university and new entrepreneurship policy together with a decentralization of responsibility and decision-making is still missing. Although education policy is the responsibility of individual states, not the national government, top-down federal policy was developed to promote the commercialization of university-based research and innovations.

13.6. Conclusions

This chapter identified the emergence of a new public policy approach to generate economic growth. In this context, universities play a crucial role in innovation and new business development. There is no doubt that there is an increasing dominance of knowledge-based jobs in highly developed countries. In this context, universities became lynchpins of a highly competitive educational and economic development. Universities are not just educational centers, they are also engines for research and development that should closely cooperate with local businesses and public actors. Universities are the "local heroes" promoting not just educational goals but local economic development needs that help not just communities but countries to compete. This is especially the case for countries such as Germany, which invest substantial sums of public funding in universities and expect them to play a crucial role as engines of change, innovation, and higher education.

From the university perspective, the policy challenges became manifest. The commercialization of research and innovation developed by scientist entrepreneurs working at universities has gained importance since the 1980s. The federal and state investment in public universities is wasted if new knowledge, expertise, and product innovation are not commercialized. This should be of major concern in times of tight budgets.

In the United States, there is significant variation across states and regions, with some universities such as MIT and Stanford now recognized as global centers of innovation, while others are much less active and less successful in commercializing new technologies. The contribution of U.S. universities to innovation and growth is, nevertheless, widespread. In Pittsburgh, for example, the University of Pittsburgh and Carnegie-Mellon have become the largest employers in the region and are spurring the creation of innovative new firms, helping to reduce the reliance of the regional economy on steel production.

Though there are differences, the U.S. universities understand that they play a major role for both the educational and economic well-being of their region and the entire country. Pushed by policies implemented at the beginning of the 1980s that were not perceived as positive at that time (such as the Bayh-Dole Act), the universities began developing their own policies and strategies to better exploit university research and innovation. The national government pursued a decentralization strategy, giving universities full responsibility to develop their own best practice strategies for commercialization of university-based research. The bottom-up policy framework, which is fruitful for the commercialization of scientist entrepreneurs' research, was characterized by two major policy components: decentralization and institutional self-autonomy.

In Germany, on the contrary, the regionalization process was enforced by the federal government but without decentralization of responsibility. Consequently, universities have severely restricted autonomy, depending heavily on not just federal and state funding but also federal and state decision-making processes. Universities still lack competencies and the legal freedom to develop their own policies.

References

Acs, Zoltan J., David B. Audretsch, and Maryann P. Feldman. 1992. "Real Effects of Academic Research: Comment." *American Economic Review*, 82, 363–367.

Anderson, Martin. 1997. *The Ten Causes of the Reagan Boom, 1982–1997*. Stanford: Hoover Institution Press.

Archibugi, Daniele, and Jonathan Michie. 1995. "The Globalization of Technology: A New Taxonomy." *Journal of Economics*, 19(1), 121–140.

Audretsch, David B. 1995. "The Innovation, Unemployment and Competitiveness Challenge in Germany." Discussion Paper FS IV 95–6, Wissenschaftszentrum Berlin.

Audretsch, David B. 2002. "Standing on the Shoulders of Midgets: The U.S. Small Business Innovation Research (SBIR) Program." *Small Business Economics*, 20(2), 129–135.

Audretsch, David B., and Maryann P. Feldman. 1996. "R&D Spillovers and the Geography of Innovation and Production." *American Economic Review*, 86(3), 630–640.

Audretsch, David B., and Roy Thurik. 2000. "Capitalism and Democracy in the 21st Century: From the Managed to the Entrepreneurial Economy." *Journal of Evolutionary Economics*, 10(1), 17–34.

Audretsch, David B., Aldridge Taylor, and Alexander Oettl. 2005a. *"The Knowledge Filter and Economic Growth: The Role of Scientist Entrepreneurship."* Max Planck Institute of Economics, Entrepreneurship, Growth and Public Policy Group, Working Paper, 10 April, 66 pages.

Audretsch, David B., Heike Grimm, and Charles W. Wessner. 2005b. *Local Heroes in the Global Village. Globalization and New Entrepreneurship Policies.* New York: Springer Science + Media Inc.

Audretsch, David B., Max C. Keilbach, and Erik E. Lehmann. 2006. *Entrepreneurship and Economic Growth.* New York: Oxford University Press.

Bartenbach, Kurt, and Ortwin Hellebrand. 2002. "Zur Abschaffung des Hochschullehrerprivilegs (§42 ArBEG) – Auswirkungen auf den Abschluss von Forschungsaufträgen." *Mitteilungen der Deutschen Patentanwälte*, 165–170.

Bartenbach, Kurt, and Franz-Eugen Volz. 2002. "Erfindungen an Hochschulen – Zur Neufassung des §42 ArBEG." *Gewerblicher Rechtsschutz und Urheberrrecht*, 743–758.

Bellendorf, Heinz. 1994. "Die internationale Wettbewerbsfähigkeit der deutschen Wirtschaft im weltweiten Strukturwandel: Konzeptionelle Analyse und empirische Beurteilung." Europäische Hochschulschriften, Reihe 5, Volks- und Betriebswirtschaft, 1502.

Bierling, Stephan. 1992. "Zur Lage der US-Wirtschaft. Bestandsaufnahme und Perspektiven am Ende der ersten Amtszeit von George Bush." *Politik und Zeitgeschichte*, 42(44), 35–42.

BMBF. 2000. *"EXIST – University-based Start-ups, Networks for Innovative Company Start-ups."* Bonn: Bundesministerium für Bildung und Forschung.

BMBF. 2001. *"2. Förderrichtlinie, des Bundesministeriums für Bildung und Forschung zur BMBF-Verwertungsoffensive – Initiative Innovation durch Patentierung und Verwertung (IPV)."* Bonn: Bundesministerium für Bildung und Forschung.

Clinton, Bill, and Albert J. Gore. 1993. *Technology for America's Economic Growth: A New Direction to Build Economic Strength.* DIANE Publishing Company, July.

Dreher, Carsten. 1997. "Technologiepolitik und Technikdiffusion. Auswahl und Einsatz von Förderinstrumenten am Beispiel der Fertigungstechnik." Karlsruher Beiträge zur wirtschaftspolitischen Forschung, Band 5, Baden-Baden.

Etzkowitz, Henry, and Andrew Webster. 1998. "Entrepreneurial Science: the Second Academic Revolution." In Henry Etzkowitz, Andrew Webster, and Peter Healey (eds.), *Capitalizing Knowledge.* Albany: State University of New York Press.

Germond, Jack W., and Jules Witcover. 1992. *Mad as Hell: Revolt at the Ballot Box 1992.* Warner Books.

Gilbert, Brett A., David B. Audretsch, and Patricia P. McDougall. 2004. "The Emergence of Entrepreneurship Policy." *Small Business Economics*, 22(3–4), 313–323.

Goldfarb, Brent, and Magnus Henrekson. 2002. "Bottom-up versus Top–down Policies towards the Commercialization of University Intellectual Property." *Research Policy*, 32(4), 639–658.

Grimm, Heike. 2005. "Assessing Entrepreneurship Policies Across Nations and Regions." In David B. Audretsch, Heike Grimm, and Charles W. Wessner (eds.), *Local Heroes in the Global Village: Globalization and New Entrepreneurship Policies.* New York: Springer Science + Media, 145–172.

Grimm, Heike. 2006. "An Exploratory Transatlantic Study with Local-Global Perspectives." *International Journal of Public Administration*, 39(13), 1167–1193.

Grimm, Heike. 2007. "It's the Economy, Stupid." In Dietmar Herz, *USA Verstehen.* Vienna: Südwind-Buchwelt, 60–64.

Jaffe, Adam B. 1989. "Real Effects of Academic Research." *American Economic Review*, 79, 957–970.

Jaffe, Adam B., Manuel Trajtenberg, and Rebecca Henderson. 1993. "Geographic Localization of Knowledge Spillovers as Evidenced by Patent Citations." *Quarterly Journal of Economics*, 108, 577–598.

Jensen, Richard A., and Marie C. Thursby. 2004. "Patent Licensing and the Research University." September 2004, NBER Working Paper No. W10758. Available at SSRN: http://ssrn.com/abstract=590773.

Koschatzky, Knut. 2000. "The Regionalisation of Innovation Policy in Germany – Theoretical Foundations and Recent Experience." *Arbeitspapiere Unternehmen und Region*, R1/ 2000. Karlsruhe: ISI.

Lockett, Andy, Donald S. Siegel, Mike Wright, and Michael D. Ensley. 2005. "The Creation of Spinoff Firms at Public Research Institutions: Managerial and Policy Implications." *Research Policy*, 34, 981–993.

Martin, Ben R. 2003. "The Changing Social Contract for Science and the Evolution of the University." In Aldo Geuna, Ammon J. Salter, and W. Edward Steinmueller (eds.), *Science and Innovation: Rethinking the Rationales for Funding and Governance.* Cheltenham, U.K.: Edward Elgar.

Mowery, David C., and Arvids A. Ziedonis. 2002. "Academic Patent Quality and Quantity before and after the Bayh-Dole Act in the United States." *Research Policy*, 31, 399–418.

Mowery, David C., Richard R. Nelson, Bhaven N. Sampat, and Arvids A. Ziedonis. 2001. "The Growth of Patenting and Licensing by U.S. Universities: An Assessment of the Effects of the Bayh-Dole Act of 1980." *Research Policy*, 30(1), 99–119.

OECD. 2000a. "Benchmarking Industry–Science Relationships." OECD Paris.

OECD. 2000b. "Highlights." OECD Paris.

Patel, Pari, and Keith Pavitt. 1991. "Large Firms in the Production of the World's Technology: An Important Case of Non-Globalisation." *Journal of International Business Studies*, First Quarter, 1–21.

Rasmussen, Einar, Øystein Moen, and Magnus Gulbrandsen. 2006. "Initiatives to Promote Commercialization of University Knowledge." *Technovation*, 26, 518–533.

Reynolds, Paul. 2005. "The Global Entrepreneurship Monitor: Implications for Europe." In David B. Audretsch, Heike Grimm, and Charles W. Wessner, eds., *Local*

Heroes in the Global Village: Globalization and New Entrepreneurship Policies. New York: Springer Science + Business Media, 174–175.

Schild, Georg. 1998. "Der amerikanische 'Wohlfahrtsstaat' von Roosevelt bis Clinton." *Vierteljahrshefte für Zeitgeschichte,* 4, 579–616.

Sonn, Jung Won, and Michael Storper. 2003. "The Increasing Importance of Geographical Proximity in Technological Innovation: An Analysis of U.S. Patent Citations, 1975–1997." Paper presented at "What Do We Know about Innovation? Conference in Honour of Keith Pavitt," Sussex University, UK, copy available from http://www.sussex.ac.uk/Units/spru/events/KP_Conf_03/.

Wessner, Charles. 1999. *The Small Business Innovation Research Program SBIR, Challenges and Opportunities.* Washington, D.C: National Academy Press.

Wessner, Charles W. 2005. "Entrepreneurship and the Innovation Ecosystem. Policy Lessons from the United States." In David B. Audretsch, Heike Grimm, and Charles W. Wessner (eds.), *Local Heroes in the Global Village: Globalization and New Entrepreneurship Policies.* New York: Springer Science + Media, 67–89.

Zucker, Lynne G., and Michael R. Darby. 1996. "Star Scientists and Institutional Transformation: Patterns of Invention and Innovation in the Formation of the Biotechnology Industry." *Proceedings of the National Academy of Science,* 93, 12709–12716.

"Entrepreneurial Capitalism" in Capitalist Development

Toward a Synthesis of Capitalist Development and the "Economy as a Whole"

Zoltan J. Acs

14.1. Introduction

The concepts that Schumpeter developed have experienced a renaissance in the last few decades of the twentieth century. This was in large part due to the technological revolution, especially in the United States, which rediscovered the importance of innovation and entrepreneurship, the process by which new opportunities are discovered and implemented (*Theory of Economic Development* (1911 [1934], hereafter *TED*). However, despite the renaissance of his thought, Schumpeter has remained hostage to *Capitalism, Socialism and Democracy* (1950 [1942], hereafter *CSD*), with its emphasis on the large corporation and the state. Therefore no acceptable theory of the economy as a whole has emerged.

CSD is in fact a theory of the economy as a whole. The reason that Schumpeter never returned to the "lost" seventh chapter is that at the time he was writing *CSD* in the early 1940s the institutions of economic development were on a track fundamentally different from that of today. This was the world of "managerial capitalism," the transition from capitalism to socialism, where the entrepreneurial function as well as the entrepreneurial class would disappear. The large corporation, by taking over the entrepreneurial function, not only makes the entrepreneur obsolete, but also undermines the sociological and ideological functions of capitalist society.

This is so obvious that I am surprised that scholars even debate this point (Acs, 1984). An interesting question remains, however: How would Schumpeter close the model of capitalist development, given what has happened to the institutional structure of society since his death? With the ascendance of market economies all over the world, which Audretsch and I call the "emergence of the entrepreneurial society" (Acs and Audretsch, 2001), *CSD* offers very little that fits the modern world. We suggest that the starting point of this synthesis should be the "lost" chapter 7, "The Economy as a Whole," from the first edition of the *TED*. The point of chapter 7 is to connect the entrepreneur to the economic development of society as a whole. According to Schumpeter (2002, 130 [1911]):

It is not only an economic, but also a social process of reorganization that takes its origin from him. The social pyramid does not consist in economic building blocks.... His position as entrepreneur is essentially only a temporary one, namely, it cannot also be transmitted by inheritance: a successor will be unable to hold on to that social position, unless he inherits the lion's claw along with the prey.... One cannot speak in the same sense of a class of entrepreneurs and not ascribe to it quite the same social phenomena as one can of those groups, where one finds the same people and their successors remaining in the same position for a long time. Certainly, all those who are entrepreneurs at a certain point of time, will find themselves in situations which have so much in common with entrepreneurial challenges that it suggests alignment of behavior of their self consciously and coherently acting together. But in the case of the entrepreneur this alignment of behavior is much less emphasized and it leads much less to the formation of common dispositions and to a common set of customs and general cultural environment than in the case with other "classes."... Then we can pose the question as to how it can be explained – according to our conception – that the social culture of a nation is at any point in time a unity and that the social development of culture of any nation always shows a uniform tendency?

The current chapter offers a model of economic development of society as a whole that is consistent with the early edition of *TED* by placing the entrepreneur, the one who pursues innovative activity, as noted in Chapter 1, at the center of economic development and by focusing on his or her role as an agent in economic development. In this interpretation we cast the United States as the first new nation, the product of a shift in human character and social role that produced the English Revolution and modern American civilization. This new character type, the agent, possessed unprecedented new powers of discretion and self-reliance yet was bound to collective ends by novel emerging forms of institutional authority and internal restraint (Dewey, 1963).[1] The agent is responsible for the entrepreneurship–philanthropy nexus through which development occurred.

We make two contributions toward this end, one minor and one major. First, we offer an alternative to the sources of incremental versus radical

---

[1] One could argue that the recent antitrust case against Microsoft was as much about anticompetitive behavior as about violating this social contract.

innovative activity in an entrpreneurial economy (Acs and Braunerhjelm, 2005). We propose a Romerian solution to the question of where opportunities come from in an entrepreneurial economy. At the core of the new growth theory is the concept of technological knowledge as a nonrival, partially excludable good, as opposed to the neoclassical view of knowledge as an entirely public good. Knowledge is a nonrival good because it can be used by one agent without limiting its use by others. This distinguishes technology from, say, a piece of capital equipment, which can be used only in one place at a time. Technology in many cases is partially excludable because it is possible to prevent its use by others to a certain extent.

This partial non-excludability of knowledge suggests that industrial R&D may generate technological spillovers (Grossman and Helpman, 1991, 16). There are many ways in which spillovers take place; for example, the mobility of highly skilled personnel between firms represents one such mechanism. Silicon Valley has a regional network-based industrial system that promotes learning and mutual adjustment among specialist producers of complex technologies. The region's dense social networks and open labor markets encourage entrepreneurship and experimentation resulting in knowledge spillovers (Saxenian, 1994). This leads to what can be called a "Knowledge Spillover Theory of Entrepreneurship."

Second, the agent, who started out as an entrepreneur, transcends his or her role, as Schumpeter suggests in the quote above. While it is recognized that much of the success of the American economy is due to its entrepreneurial spirit, what is increasingly recognized is that there is another crucial component of American economic, political and social stability. Writing in 1957, Merle Curti advanced the hypothesis that "philanthropy has been one of the major aspects of and keys to American social and cultural development" (Curti 1957, 353). To this we would add that philanthropy has also been crucial to economic development. Further, when combined with entrepreneurship, the two become a potent force in explaining the long dominance of the American economy. We suggest that by analyzing the entrepreneurship–philanthropy nexus, we can better understand how economic development occurred and what accounts for American economic dominance. Through philanthropy much of the new wealth created historically has been given back to the community to build up the great social institutions that have a positive feedback on future economic growth and stability. For example, John D. Rockefeller gave back 95 percent of his wealth before he died (Acs and Phillips, 2002).

The next section documents the transition from a managerial to an entrepreneurial economy. The third section identifies the Romerian contribution to our understanding of where opportunities come from and what that means relative to the early work of Schumpeter. This is important because Schumpeter in his early work did not pay attention to the origins of opportunities. In the fourth section we develop a mechanism to close the Schumpeterian model by focusing on the role of philanthropy in the reconstitution of wealth, the entrepreneurship-philanthropy nexus. The final section concludes.

14.2. From Managerial to Entrepreneurial Capitalism

In *TED*, Schumpeter unveiled his concept of the entrepreneur against the backdrop of economic development. He looked on economic development not as a mere adjunct to the central body of orthodox economic theory but as the basis for reinterpreting a vital process that had been crowded out of neoclassical economic analysis by the static general equilibrium theory. Schumpeter draws attention to the role of the entrepreneur, who is a key figure and plays a central role in his analysis of capitalist evolution.

Schumpeter uses a blend of economics, sociology, and history to arrive at his unique interpretation of "the circular flow of economic life." He shared Marx's view that economic processes are organic and that change comes from within the economic system. It is the entrepreneurs' social function that is central to his theory. Schumpeter made the entrepreneur into a mechanism of economic change. The system is driven by innovation, and the innovator makes things happen; for Schumpeter this is the role of the entrepreneur (Schumpeter, 2005).

Schumpeter makes a distinction between the innovative function of the entrepreneur and the financial function of the capitalist. For Knight (1921), a member of the Chicago School, the entrepreneurial and capitalist functions are inextricably intertwined. Entrepreneurs must finance themselves and bear the risk of failure, and by definition are recipient income claimants. Thus, for Knight, the superior foresight of the entrepreneur and his willingness to bear financial risk must go hand in hand. However, "[i]f we choose to call the manager or owner of a business an 'entrepreneur' then he would be an entrepreneur of the kind described by Walras, without special function and without income of a special kind," wrote Schumpeter (*TED*, 45–46).

The existence of the entrepreneur, as a member of a social class, is what gives rise to continued self-generated growth through the pursuit of innovative activity. According to Heilbroner (1985, 690), it is

[the] essentially unadventurous bourgeois class that must provide the leadership role, it does so by absorbing within its ranks the free spirits of innovating

entrepreneurs who provide the vital energy that propels the system. In Schumpeter's theory the entrepreneur is the person who innovates. In this system, the underlying "pre-analytic" cognitive vision is thus one of a routinized social hierarchy creatively disrupted by the gifted few.

Three decades after the original publication of *TED*, it was the large corporation and the rise of socialism that drew attention to Schumpeter's gloomy prospects for economic progress. As Schumpeter himself wrote in 1942 in *CSD*, the ideologically plausible capitalism contains no purely economic reason why capitalism would not have another successful run. The socialist future of Schumpeter's drama, therefore, rested wholly on extraordinary factors. When large corporations take over the entrepreneurial function, they not only make the entrepreneur obsolete, but also undermine the sociological and ideological functions of capitalist society. As Schumpeter (1942 [1950], 134) himself wrote in a classic passage:

Since capitalist enterprise, by its very achievements, tends to automatize progress, we conclude that it tends to make itself superfluous – to break to pieces under the pressure of its own success. The perfectly bureaucratized giant industrial unit not only ousts the small or medium-sized firms and expropriates the bourgeoisie as a class, which in the process stands to lose not only its income but also what is infinitely more important, its function. The true pacemakers of socialism were not the intellectuals or agitators who preached it but the Vanderbilts, Carnegies and Rockefellers.

As the large firm replaces the small- and medium-sized enterprise, economic concentration starts to have a negative feedback effect on entrepreneurial values, innovation, and technological change. Technology, the means by which new markets are created and source of that "perennial gale of creative destruction" that fills the sails of the capitalist armada, may die out, leading to a stationary state.[2] This view of the future of capitalist society held by Schumpeter (1942 [1950]) was not universally accepted. Keynes (1963) was much more optimistic about the economic prospects for our grandchildren.

---

[2] This inherent tension between innovation in hierarchical bureaucratic organizations and entrepreneurial activity has been more recently echoed by Williamson (1975, 205–206), who suggested a division of labor between large and small firm innovation: "I am inclined to regard the early stage innovative disabilities of large size as serious and propose the following hypothesis: An efficient procedure by which to introduce new products is for the initial development and market testing to be performed by independent inventors and small firms (perhaps new entrants) in an industry, the successful developments then to be acquired, possibly through licensing or merger, for subsequent marketing by a large multidivisional enterprise. ... Put differently, a division of effort between the new product innovation processes on the one hand, and the management of proven resources on the other may well be efficient."

Nevertheless, in long-run economic progress, prosperity gives way to stagnation when the rate of basic innovation remains at a low level. This of course did not happen, at least not in the United States. However, after surging at a 2.8 percent annual rate from 1948 to 1973, nonfarm business productivity growth dropped in half, to 1.4 percent from 1973 to 1995. Although the 1.4-percentage-point decline may seem trivial, compounded over time, it had enormous consequences. At the former rate, living standards would double every twenty-five years or so; at the latter rate, this doublings would take twice as long, or over fifty years. Without the entrepreneurial transformation of society, this rate of decline in productivity might have easily continued.

Why was Schumpeter wrong about the future of capitalist society? We believe he made this mistaken forecast in part because he was writing when the world was on a socialist trajectory after the Russian Revolution, with communism spreading throughout Eastern Europe and China. He did not err by missing the essential feature of the class struggle – the principal driving force of history – the struggle between "elites and masses, privileged and underprivileged, ruler and ruled." He erred by underestimating the deep-rooted nature of the entrepreneurial spirit buried within American civilization. While for Marx the principal struggle is between privileged and underprivileged, for Schumpeter, as in the transition from feudalism to capitalism, the quintessential struggle is between "elites and elites: merchants and aristocrats, entrepreneurs and bureaucrats, venture capitalists and Wall Street" (Acs, 1984, 172).

Perhaps Schumpeter did not see – partly because of his European background – that the entrepreneurial spirit would emerge from America's past and rise to challenge and ultimately to extinguish the embers of bureaucratic hegemony, bringing to an end the era of managerial capitalism. Kirchhoff (1994), building on Schumpeterian dynamics, demonstrated that entry of new business is a necessary condition for economic development if long-run market concentration and declining innovation rates are to be avoided. The re-emergence of entrepreneurship in the United States during the 1980s and its positive channeling must be seen as triumphs of the capitalist system.[3]

---

[3] Of course other countries also experienced a revival of capitalism during this time period, most notably in the United Kingdom under Thatcher. For a discussion of the different institutional frameworks, see Porter (2000) on Japan, Streech and Yamamura (2002) on Germany, Levy (1999) on France, and Acs and Karlsson (2002) and Henreksen and Jakonsson (2000) on Sweden.

It is now widely recognized that much of the success of the American economy in recent years and, historically, is due to its entrepreneurial spirit as individuals pursued innovative activity. Individual initiative and creativity, small business and wealth creation, are indelible parts of the American spirit. As a result of the recent technological revolution, both the general public and government officials are keenly aware of the role of the entrepreneur in job and wealth creation and economic growth (Hebert and Link, 1989). This view is consistent with Schumpeter's early view of entrepreneurship in *TED* and in his book *Business Cycles*; however, this revival is inconsistent with much of *CSD* (Mathews, 2002, 3).

In *The Changing Structure of the U.S. Economy* (1984), I identified the deep structural change in the United States and predicted a decades-long transition from managerial to entrepreneurial capitalism. Three distinct features of our increasingly entrepreneurial economy are noteworthy:

1. *Firm structure is more dynamic.* Coming out of World War II, the U.S. economy was dominated by large firms, typically oligopolies (industries characterized by only a few firms). Turnover among the largest firms in the economy was limited, and new firms played a minor role. In the last several decades, this has changed dramatically. New firms offering new products and services – in information technologies, biotechnology, and retail – and foreign entrants in the traditional industries (autos and steel, to name a few) have been a main, if not the main, drivers of economic growth (Caves, 1998).

2. *Individuals and markets are replacing bureaucracies.* In the managed economy, there was an implicit compact between "big labor, big business and big government" (Galbraith, 1967). That compact, if it ever existed, clearly is now gone. Labor's share of the workforce has fallen dramatically; big business is in flux (with constant changes in the rankings of America's leading firms). In an entrepreneurial economy it is the individual who plays an important role in identifying opportunities and exploiting them through new venture creation (Acs and Armington, 2006).

3. *Innovation is very different in managerial and entrepreneurial economies.* New firms, led by risk-taking entrepreneurs, are disproportionately responsible for "radical" or "breakthrough" technologies. The innovations that now characterize modern life – the automobile, telephone, airplane, air conditioning, personal computer, and Internet – all were developed and commercialized by entrepreneurs. At the same time, large firms have been essential to mass-produce the innovations of entrepreneurs. However, because radical innovations tend to lead to faster overall

growth than incremental improvements, it is no coincidence that the information technology revolution that statistically has accounted for the significant acceleration in U.S. productivity growth over the last decade was largely sparked by entrepreneurial companies (Acs and Audretsch, 1987).

14.3. Knowledge as a Source of Entrepreneurial Opportunity

How does all this relate to the work of Schumpeter, that is, the early Schumpeter? The answer is provided by Nelson (1993, pp. 90), who wrote:

In his *Theory of Economic Development*, Schumpeter is curiously uninterested in where the basic ideas for innovations, be they technological or organizational, come from. Schumpeter does not view the entrepreneur as having anything to do with their generation: "It is not part of his function to "find" or "create" new possibilities. They are always present, abundantly accumulated by all sorts of people. Often they are generally known and being discussed by scientific or literary writers. In other cases there is nothing to discuss about them, because they are quite obvious.

While Schumpeter did not worry about where opportunities come from, a generation of economists spent the better part of half a century trying to figure out the relationship between technology, economic growth and public policy (Nelson, Peck, and Kalachek, 1967). After the revolutionary work of Romer, however, we now know that the opportunity set is expanded, and economic growth is explained to a large extent by investments in knowledge and human capital (Jones, 1995).

Romer's most original contribution (1990) is the separation of economically useful scientific-technological knowledge into two parts. The total set of knowledge consists of the subsets of nonrival, partially excludable knowledge elements that can practically be considered as public goods and the rival, excludable elements of knowledge. Codified knowledge published in books, scientific papers or patent documentation belongs to the first group. This knowledge is nonrival because it can be used by several actors at the different times. On the other hand, it is only partially excludable, because only the right of applying a technology for the production of a particular good can be guaranteed by patenting, while the same technology can spill over to further potential economic applications as others learn from the patent documentation. Rival, excludable knowledge elements are primarily the personalized (tacit) knowledge of individuals and groups, including particular experiences and insights developed and owned by researchers and business people. According to Romer (1994, 204):

New growth theory started on the technology-as-public good path and worried about where technology came from, but it soon backed up and reconsidered the initial split that economists make in the physical world. New growth theorists now start by dividing the world into two fundamentally different types of productive inputs that can be called "ideas" and "things." Ideas are nonrival goods that could be stored in a bit string. Things are rival goods with mass (or energy). With ideas and things, one can explain how economic growth works. Nonrival ideas can be used to rearrange things, for example, when one follows a recipe that transforms noxious olives into tasty and healthful olive oil. Economic growth arises from the discovery of new recipes and the transformation of things from low to high value configurations.... This slightly differentiated cut leads to insights that do not follow from the neoclassical model. It emphasizes that ideas are goods that are produced and distributed just as other goods are. It removes the dead end in neoclassical theory and links microeconomic observations on routines, machine design, and the like with macroeconomic discussions of technology.

Equation (14-1) summarizes how the two types of knowledge interact in the production of economically useful new technological knowledge (Acs and Varga, 2004):

$$\mathring{A} = \delta H_A^\lambda A^\varphi,　\tag{14-1}$$

where H_A stands for the number of researchers working on technical knowledge production, A is the total stock of technological knowledge available at a certain point in time, $\mathring{A}$ is the change in technological knowledge resulting from private efforts to invest in research and development, and δ, λ, and φ are parameters. Equation (14-1) can explain economic growth by showing that on the steady state growth path the rate of per capita GDP growth equals the rate of technological change ($\mathring{A}/A$). In the long run the rate of productivity growth determines the rate of advances in average living standards.

The particular functional form of knowledge production in Equation (14-1) is explained by the assumption that the efficiency of knowledge production is enhanced by the historically developed stock of scientific-technological knowledge. Even the same number of researchers becomes more productive if A increases over time.

In the words of Grossman and Helpman (1991, 18):

[T]he technological spillovers that result from commercial research may add to a pool of public knowledge, thereby lowering the cost to later generations of achieving a technological break-through of some given magnitude. Such cost reductions can offset any tendency for the private returns to invention to fall as a result of increases in the number of competing technologies.

A is assumed to be perfectly accessible by everyone working in the research sector. However, as follows from the modification of Jones (1995), spillovers from the stock of codified knowledge might not be perfect. Hence the value of the aggregate codified knowledge spillovers parameter φ should be between 0 and 1.

However, this theory does not go far enough. Not only codified but also noncodified, tacit knowledge can spill over. The value of λ in Equation 14-1 reflects the extent to which tacit knowledge spills over within the research sector and the economy at large. The process by which knowledge spills over from the firm producing it for use by another firm is exogenous in the model proposed by Romer (1990). That model focused on the influence of knowledge spillovers on technological change without specifying *why* and *how* new knowledge spills over. Yet the critical issue in modeling knowledge-based growth rests on this spillover of knowledge. The new growth theory offers no insight into what role, if any, entrepreneurial activity and agglomeration effects play in the spillover of tacit knowledge. While the new growth theory is a step forward in our understanding of the growth process, the essence of the Schumpeterian entrepreneur is missed. As pointed out by Schumpeter (1950), "the inventor produces ideas, the entrepreneur 'gets things done' . . . an idea or scientific principle is not, by itself, of any importance for economic practice." Indeed, the Schumpeterian entrepreneur, by and large, remains absent in those models.

Consequently, despite the gains in terms of transparency and technical ease obtained by imposing strong assumptions in the endogenous growth models, these advantages have to be measured in relation to the drawbacks of deviations from real world behavior. In our view, the result has been that the endogenous model fails to incorporate one of the most crucial elements in the growth process: transmission of knowledge through entrepreneurship, entry and exit, and the spatial dimension of growth. The presence of these activities is especially important at the early stages of the life cycle, while technology is still fluid. A second generation of new growth theorists recognized that Schumpeter's entrepreneurship was missing from these models, and incorporated entry through "R&D races" into the model (Aghion and Howitt, 1992).

While this was a step forward, the essence of agency was missing from these models. There is a "missing link" between new growth theory and entrepreneurship theory. In Schumpeterian theory we have no explanation of where opportunity comes from or how it is expanded, and in Romerian theory the Schumpeterian entrepreneur is missing. These models assume that knowledge and economic knowledge are the same and that knowledge spillovers are ubiquitous. Acs, Audretsch, Braunerhjelm, and Carlsson (2004) identify entrepreneurship as the "missing link" in converting knowledge into economically relevant knowledge, and Acs, Audretsch, Braunerhjelm, and Carlsson (2005) develop a "Knowledge Spillover Theory of Entrepreneurship" that links knowledge production to innovation. The knowledge spillover theory provides a focus on the generation of entrepreneurial opportunities emanating from knowledge investments by incumbent firms and public research organizations that are not fully appropriated by those incumbent enterprises. Thus the development of new growth theory reinforces the seminal contributions made by Schumpeter a century ago on the importance of entrepreneurship and innovation for economic development.

14.4. The Entrepreneurship–Philanthropy Nexus

In this section we build on the above idea and develop a theory of philanthropy to close the model in *TED* and develop a theory of the economy of the whole. Linking philanthropy to economic prosperity is not new. In *Corruption and the Decline of Rome*, Ramsay MacMullen (1988) discusses how charitable foundations were partly responsible for the flourishing of Rome, and their decline coincided with the loss of the empire. The roots of American philanthropy can be found in England in the period from 1480 to 1660. By the close of the Elizabethan period, "it was generally agreed that all men must somehow be sustained at the level of subsistence" (Jordan, 1961, 401). Though the charitable organizations at the beginning of this period in England were centered on religion and the role of the Church, by the close of sixteenth century, religious charities comprised only 7 percent of all charities (Jordan, 1961, 402).

How is this philanthropic behavior explained? According to Jordan, there was the partly religious and partly secular sensitivity to human pain and suffering in sixteenth-century England (Jordan, 1961, 406). Doubtless, another important motivating factor was Calvinism, which taught that "the rich man is a trustee for wealth which he disposes for benefit of mankind, as a steward who lies under direct obligation to do Christ's will" (Jordan, 1961, 406-7).

The real founders of American philanthropy were the English men and women who crossed the Atlantic to establish communities that they hoped would be better than the ones they had known at home (Owen, 1964). The Puritan leader John Winthrop forthrightly stated this purpose in the lay sermon, "A Model of Christian Charity," which he preached on the ship *Arabella* on the way to the new world in 1630 (Bremner, 1960, 7). The Puritan principles of industry, frugality, and humility had an enduring impact on America (Tocqueville, 1966 [1935]).

Beginning with the Puritans, who regarded excessive profit making as both a crime and a sin (and punished it accordingly), there is a long history of Americans who have questioned the right of people to become rich. In view of the popular prejudice against ostentatious enjoyment of riches, the luxury of doing good was almost the only extravagance the American rich of the first half of the nineteenth century could indulge in with good conscience (Tocqueville, 1966 [1835]). To whatever extent it is true that donating was the only luxury allowed the rich in the first half of the nineteenth century, things had certainly changed by the second half of the century when Andrew Carnegie, Andrew Mellon, James Buchanan Duke, et al. were making their fortunes.

One of the greatest nineteenth-century philanthropists was George Peabody, a man of modest beginnings who through canny investment gained a fortune and through impeccable honesty gained a reputation for integrity. Two considerations seem to have been most influential in his philosophy of philanthropy. One was a deep devotion to the communities in which Peabody was reared or in which he made his money. The other was a secular vision of the Puritan doctrine of the stewardship of riches: his desire, in the simplest terms, to be useful to mankind. In his lifetime, Peabody donated over $8 million to libraries, science, housing, education, exploration, historical societies, hospitals, churches, and other charities (Parker, 1971, 209).

Peabody's most enduring influence, however, lies in the precedents and policies formulated by the Peabody Education Fund Trustees. This fund not only paved the way for subsequent foundation aid to the South after the Civil War but also influenced the operational patterns of subsequent major foundations, including John D. Rockefeller's Education Board, the Russell Sage Foundation, and the Carnegie Foundation. The thesis that George Peabody was the founder of modern educational foundations was best expressed in the *Christian Science Monitor* (as cited in Parker, 1971, 208):

George Peabody was in fact the originator of that system of endowed foundations for public purposes which has reached its highest development in the United

States. . . . It is interesting to consider the many ways in which the example set by him has been followed by visioned men of means in the United States. . . . In a sense the Peabody Fund was not the only monument to George Peabody, for the example he set has been followed by a host of other Americans.

Andrew Carnegie exemplified the ideal Calvinist. Carnegie put philanthropy at the heart of his "gospel of wealth" (Hamer, 1998). For Carnegie, the question was not only how to gain wealth but, more important, what one should do with it. *The Gospel of Wealth* suggested that millionaires, instead of bequeathing vast fortunes to heirs or making benevolent grants by will, should administer their wealth as public trusts during life (Carnegie, 1889). Both Carnegie (at the time) and Jordan (as a historian) suggest that a key motive for philanthropy is social order and harmony. It is plausible that philanthropists such as Carnegie took a longer term approach and realized that their interests necessitated assisting the worthy poor and disadvantaged: That is, they exhibited enlightened self-interest as opposed to altruism.

In the United States, much of the new wealth created historically has been given back to the community, to build up the great social institutions that have a positive feedback on future economic growth (Myers, 1907). For example, it was precisely the great private research universities of Stanford, MIT, Johns Hopkins, Carnegie-Mellon, Duke, and Chicago, among others created over a century ago by American philanthropy, that played such a critical role in the recent American successes ("The Knowledge Factory," 1997).

We suggest that American philanthropists – especially those who have made their own fortunes – create foundations that, in turn, contribute to greater and more widespread economic development through opportunity, knowledge creation, and entrepreneurship. This was Andrew Carnegie's hope when he wrote about the "responsibility of wealth" over a century ago, and it still inspires entrepreneurs today, though they usually express it in terms of a duty to "give something back" to the society that helped to make their own success possible. The founders of modern American philanthropy tried to provide answers to problems that were national in scope at a time when national governments were weak.

The American model of entrepreneurship and philanthropy in the nineteenth century was followed by a period of progressivism (increasing role of government) in the early twentieth century and then World War I. Though the period of the 1920s was one of technological change and prosperity, underlying economic problems resulted in the collapse of the world economy into the Great Depression of the 1930s. This period, together with that of World War II, changed the role of the government and the philanthropic activities of the entrepreneur. It is not our point here to argue that the role of philanthropy is to provide social welfare, that is, health insurance, social security, unemployment insurance. Indeed, the rise of the state in the twentieth century was in some ways a rise of social welfare provided by government.

This function, however, is distinct from the pure function of philanthropy that arises from issues of wealth. The welfare state, with its high marginal taxes, high inheritance taxes, anti-trust laws, and abolition of private property in some cases, tried to eliminate the role of private wealth altogether. In fact, in a socialist state the only role for philanthropy might be religious giving. What is interesting is that in the United States the rise of the welfare state did not coincide with a decline in philanthropy. In fact, according to a study by the National Bureau of Economic Research (Dickinson, 1970), total private domestic philanthropy as a percentage of GNP between 1929 and 1959 increased from 1.7 percent to 2.3 percent, respectively. It averaged 2.1 percent during the period. This figure is not significantly different from the 2.5 percent that Americans contributed to philanthropic causes in 2003. According to the Johns Hopkins nonprofit sector project, this figure is the highest in the world, followed by Spain, Britain, and Hungary.[4] In the United States, almost 80 percent of donations are by individuals. Why did Americans continue to fund philanthropy at least at a constant level, even as the federal government stepped into the business of social security? According to *Newsweek* ("The Land of the Handout," 1997, 34):

> There's no escaping the brutal truth: the nation famous for capitalism red in tooth and claw, the epicenter of the heartless marketplace, is also the land of the handout. It's not really such a paradox. Both our entrepreneurial economic system and our philanthropic tradition spring from the same root: American individualism. Other countries may be content to let the government run most of their schools and universities, pay for their hospitals, subsidize their museums and orchestras, even in some cases support religious sects. Americans tend to think most of these institutions are best kept in private hands, and they have been willing to cough up the money to pay for them.

We had suggested that American philanthropists created foundations that in turn contributed to greater and more widespread economic prosperity by investing in the future of America. Therefore, the thing that differentiates American capitalism from all other forms of capitalism

---

[4] See Salamon and Anheier (1999).

(Japanese, French, German, and Scandinavian) is its historical focus on both the creation of wealth (entrepreneurship) and the reconstitution of wealth (philanthropy).[5] Philanthropy remains part of an implicit social contract stipulating that wealth beyond a certain point should revert to society (Chernow, 1999). Individuals are free to accumulate wealth; however, it must be invested back into society to expand opportunity (Acs and Dana, 2001).

Though it has been recognized that the philanthropists of the nineteenth century made possible the basis for wealth creation and social stability, this has not been quantified and placed within the framework of private and social costs and benefits (America, 1995). Take as an example the difficulty in calculating the *ex post* benefits of the creation of the University of Chicago by the Rockefeller family. The number of Nobel Prize winners at the University of Chicago is one measure of the social benefits that have been reaped by the Rockefeller family investment. Certainly, there was no immediate private benefit to the Rockefeller family, since the contributions occurred several generations later.

Therefore, the entrepreneurship–philanthropy nexus has not been fully understood by either economists or social scientists, in part due to a narrow view of self-interest as a fundamental institution of capitalism. Recently Jeffrey Sachs has articulated a position by which to judge our philanthropic activities based on past accomplishments. According to Sachs, writing in *The Economist*, creating opportunity for future generations is about creating knowledge today, and the model to study is the Rockefeller Foundation ("Sachs on Globalization," 2000, 83):[6]

The model to emulate is the Rockefeller Foundation, the pre-eminent development institution of the 20th century, which showed what grant aid targeted on knowledge could accomplish. Rockefeller funds supported the eradication of hookworm in the American South; the discovery of the Yellow Fever vaccine; the development of penicillin; the establishment of public-health schools (today's undisputed leaders in their fields) all over the world; the establishment of medical facilities in all parts of the world; the creation and funding of great research centers such as the University of Chicago, the Brookings Institution, Rockefeller University, and the National Bureau of Economic Research; the control of malaria in Brazil; the founding of the research centers that accomplished the green revolution in Asia; and more.

---

[5] For a statement on the nature and logic of capitalism, see Heilbroner (1985). Of course it is the institutional framework that differs from country to country and not necessarily the logic of the system.

[6] For a theory of knowledge in economic growth, see Arrow (1962) and Romer (1990). For an application to the regional and global economy, see Acs (2000).

In "managerial capitalism" wealth creation, wealth ownership, and wealth distribution was in part left up to the state. However, in an entrepreneurial society it is individual initiative that plays a vital role in propelling the system forward. Entrepreneurial leadership is the mechanism by which new combinations are created, new markets are opened up, and new technologies are commercialized that are the basis for prosperity. In an entrepreneurial society, entrepreneurship plays a vital role in the process of wealth creation and philanthropy plays a crucial role in the reconstitution of wealth. The execution of this, as we have argued above, was based on the development of a new character type possessing unprecedented new powers of discretion and yet bound to collective ends. This interpretation is also consistent with Schumpeter's chapter 7.

This model of entrepreneurial capitalism, despite the unequal distribution of wealth, with its sharp focus on entrepreneurship and philanthropy, should be encouraged. Rather than constraining the rich through taxes, we should allow the rich to campaign for social change through the creation of opportunity. In the past the fight against slavery had some very wealthy backers. If we shut off the opportunities for wealthy individuals to give back their wealth, we will also shut off the creation of wealth, which has far greater consequences for an entrepreneurial society.

However, these views of giving back are not universally shared even in the United States. The rich have retreated from facing the challenge of how to reconstitute their wealth ("Most Generous Americans," 1998, 88). Such views are not really fashionable among scholars of philanthropy and more than a few of the professionals who staff foundations. For example, a book recently published by MIT Press on American foundations argues that philanthropic foundations mostly serve as vehicles for advancing the economic and social interests of their benefactors (Dowie, 2001). At an American Assembly meeting a few years ago, the participants (most of whom were professionals who worked for foundations and other non-profit groups) produced a statement calling on philanthropists to do more to redistribute their wealth from the "haves" to the "have nots." Carnegie would have been appalled since he thought that philanthropists should prevent such redistributive schemes by fostering greater economic opportunities.

14.5. Conclusion

In this chapter we have suggested that a theory of economic development based on the early edition of *TED* that includes the "lost" chapter 7 represents a viable option to bridge the gap between economic development and the economy as a whole. Once the sources of opportunity are reconstituted, we suggest that the relationship between opportunity, entrepreneurship, and philanthropy may provide the institutional foundation for building a Schumpeterian theory of society as a whole. This entrepreneurship–philanthropy nexus that has not been fully explored by either economists or social scientists may provide the bridge between Schumpeter's *Theory of Economic Development* and the famous chapter 7, "The Economy as a Whole." American philanthropists – especially those who have made their own fortunes – create foundations that, in turn, contribute to greater and more widespread economic development and social stability.

References

Acs, Zoltan J. 1984. *The Changing Structure of the U.S. Economy: Lessons from the Steel Industry.* New York: Praeger.

Acs, Zoltan J., and Catherine Armington. 2006. *Entrepreneurship, Geography and American Economic Growth.* Cambridge: Cambridge University Press.

Acs, Zoltan J., and David B. Audretsch. 1987. "Innovation, Market Structure and Firm Size." *Review of Economics and Statistics,* 69, 567–575.

Acs, Zoltan J., and David B. Audretsch. 2001. "The Emergence of the Entrepreneurial Society." Swedish Foundation for Small Business. Stockholm, Sweden, May 2001.

Acs, Zoltan J., and Pontus Braunerhjelm. 2005. "The Entrepreneurship-Philanthropy Nexus: Implications for Internationalization." *Management International Review,* 45, 111–144.

Acs, Zoltan J., and Leo P. Dana. 2001. "Contrasting Two Models of Wealth Redistribution." *Small Business Economics,* 16(2), 63–74.

Acs, Zoltan J., and Ronnie J. Phillips. 2002. "Entrepreneurship and Philanthropy in American Capitalism." *Small Business Economics,* 19(3), 189–204.

Acs, Zoltan J., and Charlie Karlsson. 2002. "Institutions, Entrepreneurship and Firm Growth: The Case of Sweden." Special issue of *Small Business Economics.*

Acs, Zoltan J., and Attila Varga. 2004. "Entrepreneurship, Geography and Technological Change." ERSA Conference paper, European Regional Science Association.

Acs, Zoltan J., David B. Audretsch, Pontus Braunerhjelm, and Bo Carlsson. 2004. "The Missing Link: The Knowledge Filter and Entrepreneurship in Economic Growth." CERP Working Paper 4783.

Acs, Zoltan J., David B. Audretsch, Pontus Braunerhjelm, and Bo Carlsson. 2005. "The Knowledge Spillover Theory of Entrepreneurship." CEPR Discussion Paper 5326.

Aghion, P., and P. Howitt. 1992. "A Model of Growth through Creative Destruction." *Econometrica,* March, 323–351.

America, Richard F. 1995. *Philanthropy and Economic Development.* Westport, Conn.: Greenwood Press.

Arrow, Kenneth J. 1962. "Economic Welfare and the Allocation of Resources for Invention." In Richard Nelson (ed.), *The Rate and Direction of Inventive Activity.* Princeton: Princeton University Press, 609–626.

Bremner, Robert. 1960. *American Philanthropy*. Chicago: University of Chicago Press.

Carnegie, Andrew. 1889. "Wealth." *North American Review*, June.

Caves, Richard. 1998. "Industrial Organization and New Findings on the Turnover and Mobility of Firms." *Journal of Economic Literature*, 36, 1947–1982.

Chernow, Ron. 1999. *Titan: The Life of John D. Rockefeller Sr*. New York: Vintage.

Curti, Merle. 1957. "The History of American Philanthropy as a Field of Research." *American Historical Review*, 62(2), 352–363.

Dewey, J. 1963. *Philosophy and Civilization*. New York: Capricorn Books.

Dickinson, Frank. 1970. *The Changing Position of Philanthropy in the American Economy*. National Bureau of Economic Research, Distributed by Columbia University Press, New York.

Dowie, Mark. 2001. *American Foundations: An Investigative History*. Cambridge, Mass.: MIT Press.

Galbraith, John K. 1967. *The New Industrial State*. Boston: Houghton Mifflin.

Grossman, Gene, and Elhanan Helpman. 1991. *Innovation and Growth in a Global Economy*. Cambridge, Mass.: MIT Press.

Hamer, J. H. 1998. "Money and the Moral Order in Late Nineteenth and Early Twentieth-Century American Capitalism." *Anthropological Quarterly*, 71, 138–150.

Hebert, Robert F., and Albert N. Link. 1989. *The Entrepreneur: Mainstream Views and Radical Critiques*. New York: Praeger.

Heilbroner, Robert. 1985. *The Nature and Logic of Capitalism*. New York: Harper and Row.

Henreksen, Magnus, and Ulf Jakonsson. 2000. "Where Schumpeter Was Nearly Right: The Swedish Model and Capitalism, Socialism and Democracy." Working Paper no. 370, Stockholm School of Economics.

Jones, Kenneth. 1995. "R&D Based Models of Economic Growth." *Journal of Political Economy*, 103, 759–784.

Jordan, W. K. 1961."The English Background of Modern Philanthropy." *American Historical Review*, 66(2), 401–408.

Keynes, John M. 1963. *Essays in Persuasion*. New York: Norton.

Kirchhoff, Bruce A. 1994. *Entrepreneurship and Dynamic Capitalism: The Economics of Business Firm Formation and Growth*. Praeger Studies in American Industry. Westport, Conn., and London: Greenwood.

Knight, Frank Praeger. 1921. *Risk, Uncertainty and Profit*. New York: Houghton Mifflin.

"The Knowledge Factory."1997. *The Economist*, October 4, pp. 1–22.

"The Land of the Handout." 1997. *Newsweek*, September 29, pp. 34–36.

Levy, Johah D. 1999. *Tocqueville's Revenge: State, Society and Economics in Contemporary France*. Boston: Harvard University Press.

MacMullen, Ramsay. 1988. *Corruption and the Decline of Rome*. New Haven: Yale University Press.

Mathews, John A. 2002. "Introduction: Schumpeter's 'Lost' Seventh Chapter." *Industry and Innovation*, 9(1–2), 1–6.

"Most Generous Americans." 1998. *Fortune*, February 2, p. 88.

Myers, Gustavus. 1907. *History of Great American Fortunes*. New York: Modern Library.

Nelson, Richard. 1993. *National Innovation Systems: A Comparative Analysis*. New York: Oxford University Press.

Nelson, Richard, M. J. Peck, and E. D. Kalachek. 1967. *Technology, Economic Growth and Public Policy*. Washington: Brookings Institution.

Owen, David. 1964. *English Philanthropy 1660–1960*. Cambridge: Belknap Press of Harvard University.

Parker, Franklin. 1971. *George Peabody: A Biography*. Nashville: Vanderbilt University Press.

Porter, E. Michael. 2000. *Can Japan Compete?* London: Macmillan Press.

Romer, Paul. 1986. "Increasing Returns and Long Run Growth." *Journal of Political Economy*, 94, 1002–1037.

Romer, Paul M. 1990. "Are Nonconvexities Important for Understanding Growth?" *American Economic Review*, 80(2), 97–103.

Romer, Paul M. 1994. "The Origins of Endogenous Growth." *Journal of Economic Perspectives*, 8(1), 3–22.

"Sachs on Globalization." 2000. *The Economist*, June 24, pp. 81–83.

Salamon, Lester M., Helmut K. Anheier, et al. 1999. "The Emerging Sector Revisited." Johns Hopkins University Institute for Policy Studies Center for Civil Society Studies.

Saxenian, AnnaLee. 1994. "Lessons from Silicon Valley." *Technology Review*, 97(5).

Schumpeter, Joseph A. 1934 (1911). *The Theory of Economic Development*. Cambridge: Harvard University Press.

Schumpeter, Joseph A. 1950 (1942). *Capitalism, Socialism and Democracy*. New York: Harper and Row.

Schumpeter, Joseph A. 2002 (1911). "The Economy as a Whole: The Seventh Chapter of Schumpeter's The Theory of Economic Development." Translated by Ursula Backhaus. *Industry and Innovation*, 9, 93–145.

Schumpeter, Joseph A. 2005. "Development." *Journal of Economic Literature*, 43(1), 108–120.

Streech, Wolfgang, and Kozo Yamamura. 2002. *The Origins of Nonliberal Capitalism: Germany and Japan in Comparison*. New York: Cornell University Press.

Tocqueville, Alexis de. 1966 (1835). *Democracy in America*. New York: Harper and Row.

Williamson, Oliver E. 1975. *Markets and Hierarchies: Analysis and Antitrust Implications*. New York: Free Press.

Index